Leibniz:
A Contribution to
the Archaeology of Power

ENCOUNTERS IN LAW AND PHILOSOPHY
SERIES EDITORS: Thanos Zartaloudis and Anton Schütz

This series interrogates, historically and theoretically, the encounters between philosophy and law. Each volume published takes a unique approach and challenges traditional systemic approaches to law and philosophy. The series is designed to expand the environment for law and thought.

Titles available in the series

STASIS: Civil War as a Political Paradigm
Giorgio Agamben

On the Idea of Potency: Juridical and Theological Roots of the Western Cultural Tradition
Emanuele Castrucci

Political Theology: Demystifying the Universal
Anton Schütz and Marinos Diamantides

The Birth of Nomos
Thanos Zartaloudis

Leibniz: A Contribution to the Archaeology of Power
Stephen Connelly

General Advisor
Giorgio Agamben

Advisory Board
Clemens Pornschlegel, Institut für Germanistik, Universität München, Germany
Emmanuele Coccia, Ecole des Hautes Etudes en Sciences Sociales, France
Jessica Whyte, University of Western Sydney, School of Humanities and Communication Arts, Australia
Peter Goodrich, Cardozo Law School, Yeshiva University, New York, USA
Alain Pottage, Kent Law School, University of Kent, UK and Sciences Po, Paris
Justin Clemens, University of Melbourne, Faculty of Arts, Australia
Robert Young, NYU, English, USA
Nathan Moore, Birkbeck College, Law School, University of London, UK
Alexander Murray, English, Queen's University Belfast, UK
Piyel Haldar, Birkbeck College, Law School, University of London, UK
Anne Bottomley, Law School, University of Kent, UK
Oren Ben-Dor, Law School, University of Southampton, UK

edinburghuniversitypress.com/series/enlp

LEIBNIZ:
A CONTRIBUTION
TO THE
ARCHAEOLOGY
OF POWER

Stephen Connelly

EDINBURGH
University Press

For Rose

Edinburgh University Press is one of the leading university presses in the UK. We publish academic books and journals in our selected subject areas across the humanities and social sciences, combining cutting-edge scholarship with high editorial and production values to produce academic works of lasting importance. For more information visit our website: edinburghuniversitypress.com

© Stephen Connelly, 2021, 2022

Edinburgh University Press Ltd
The Tun – Holyrood Road
12(2f) Jackson's Entry
Edinburgh EH8 8PJ

First published in hardback by Edinburgh University Press 2021

Typeset in 11/13 Palatino by
Servis Filmsetting Ltd, Stockport, Cheshire

A CIP record for this book is available from the British Library

ISBN 978 1 4744 1806 5 (hardback)
ISBN 978 1 4744 1807 2 (paperback)
ISBN 978 1 4744 1808 9 (webready PDF)
ISBN 978 1 4744 1809 6 (epub)

The right of Stephen Connelly to be identified as the author of this work has been asserted in accordance with the Copyright, Designs and Patents Act 1988, and the Copyright and Related Rights Regulations 2003 (SI No. 2498).

Contents

Illustrations

Figures

Tables

Acknowledgements

I would like to thank Tara Mulqueen for our long chats on the nature of association and community. Early versions of Chapters 4 and 5 were presented at the Critical Legal Conferences at the University of Sussex in 2014 and University of Kent in 2016, and the comments and questions of Anton Schütz and Donatella Alessandrini, among many others, at the latter event were particularly appreciated. Groundwork on the relationship between Leibniz and Neoplatonism was presented at the University of Wrocław (at the kind invitation of Mirosław Sadowski) in 2016. Developed versions of Chapters 5 and 6 were presented at the Warwick Continental Philosophy Conference and the EUTOPIA History of Ideas Conference with Cergy-Pontoise, both in 2019. I would like to thank Céline Roynier, Stuart Elden, Filip Niklas and Alex Underwood for their questions and suggestions. Finally, the findings of Chapters 7 and 8 were to be presented, at the kind invitation of Maria Drakopoulou and Connal Parsley, at Kent Law School in 2020. Events, however, delayed this research seminar.

In preparing this text I had the assistance of several people, including Fabienne Allegret-Maret, the extremely kind and patient Thanos Zartaloudis, Iulia Nicolescu, Helen Riley, Peter Hallward, Gil Leung, Illan Wall, Laura Williamson, Raza Saeed, Marinos Diamantides, Ania Zbyszewska and John Snape. I am particularly indebted to Anton Schütz for his careful and patient review of the manuscript. I learnt much from the process.

This book was partly written on study leave granted by the University of Warwick School of Law. I must also thank the Deutsche Nationalbibliothek and the Universitätsbibliothek at the Goethe Universität, both in Frankfurt am Main for hosting me.

Abbreviations

As readers of Leibniz are aware a critical edition of Leibniz's complete works has been in preparation for almost a century, and so at present it continues to prove necessary to rely on several partial editions of Leibniz's works, some of which are quite venerable and lack modern critical apparatus. In this book I use the following abbreviations for commonly cited editions. Other works used are cited in full, and can be found referenced in the bibliography.

A: German Academy of Sciences (ed.) *G.W. Leibniz: Sämtliche Schriften and Briefe* (Berlin: Akademie Verlag, 1923–). Reference are to series (*Reihe*) and volume (*Band*).

AG: Roger Ariew and Daniel Garber, *G.W. Leibniz: Philosophical Essays* (Indianapolis: Hackett, 1989)

C: Louis Couterat (ed.) *Opuscules et fragments inédits de Leibniz* (Paris: Alcan, 1903)

DM: *Discourse on Metaphysics*, in L: 303, by reference to paragraph number.

Du: L.L. Dutens (ed.) *G.G. Leibnitii Opera Omnia* (Geneva: 1768)

Ger: Carl Gerhardt (ed.) *Die Philosophischen Schriften von Leibniz* 7 vols (Berlin: Wedimann, 1875–90) reprinted (Hildesheim: Olms, 1965)

GM: Carl Gerhardt (ed.) *Leibnizens Mathemathische Schriften* 7 vols (Berlin: A. Asher 1848–63) reprinted (Hildesheim: Olms, 1962)

Gr: Gaston Grua (ed.) *G.W. Leibniz: Textes inédits d'après des manuscrits de la Bibliothèque provincial d'Hanovre* 2 vols (Paris: Vrin, 1948)

L: Leroy E. Loemker (ed.) *G.W. Leibniz: Philosophical Papers and Letters* (Dordrecht: Reidel, 1969)

Acknowledgements

M: André Robinet (ed.), *Leibniz Monadology* (Paris: PUF, 1954) references are to the paragraph number.

NE: Peter Remnant and Jonathan Bennett (eds), *New Essays on the Human Understanding* (Cambridge: Cambridge University Press, 1996)

Ri: Patrick Riley (ed.) *The Political Writings of Leibniz* (Cambridge: Cambridge University Press, 1972)

Introduction

Activity and power

In his book, *Creation and Anarchy*, Georgio Agamben writes that 'it is ... worth reflecting on the fundamental function that modal verbs develop in our culture and in philosophy in particular'.[1] Agamben has in mind the modal verb 'to be able to' which he links to Aristotelean conception of potential (*dunamis*), and its supersession, at the hands of medieval theologians, by the modal 'to will to' (*velle*). This change of emphasis can be situated within the broader transformation, examined by the inspiring Gwenaëlle Aubry,[2] of the senses of activity (*energeia*) and particularly in-potency (*dunamei*) from Aristotle, through Plotinus, to Aquinas and Duns Scotus. It is a change which sees power evolve from being merely what an active substance could possibly do (and might fail to do), to a dominating force of creation or coercion which begins to approach the modern, disciplinary sense of political power. In this movement, Agamben argues,[3] the modalities of possibility, contingency, impossibility and necessity are constantly rearticulated, and greater or lesser emphasis is given to one term or other. Power and activity, the central terms of the science of being, are inflected by modalities, just as the verb 'to walk' gains new meaning when we attach 'to ought to'. 'I have the power to' morphs into the modern 'I must will the power to'.[4]

The contribution of this work is to locate Leibniz within that wider archaeology of power, and to show how the universal jurisprudence which Leibniz developed from the 1660s into the 1690s can be considered as a transformative encounter with the concepts of activity, power *and* modality. Yet Leibniz does not necessarily orient himself by reference to the

1

polestar of power; rather, his rearticulation of activity, power and modality is motivated at least in part by the conflictual relationships between Reformed and Scholastic theology, between natural law and natural right, and between mechanistic natural philosophy and human freedom. Any account of Leibniz's views on power must situate him in his context.

To guide this investigation: I pose the following overarching questions:

(a) How does Leibniz reconfigure the classical divide between activity and power, in the context of natural law?
(b) How does Leibniz deal with the problems for divine justice posed by a materialist account of power (*potentia*) proposed variously by Hobbes and Spinoza?
(c) How does Leibniz use modality to formulate his theory of justice, and what consequences does this have for the activity–power relationship?

The challenge Leibniz sets for any archaeology of power is that ostensibly he swims against the tide: he appears to reinstate the Aristotelean priority of activity over power, and to demote power (*potentia*) to that cause which cannot be reduced to a substantial form's own volitional act. That is, *potentia* becomes once again a mark of finitude. Yet it will be seen that it is through modality that Leibniz affirms the primacy of power, even if he eschews the nomenclature of *potentia*. To do this Leibniz develops the notion of an internalised 'state space' which determines what is morally necessary and impossible, and this state space will structurally occupy the position previously filled by *potentia* and *dunamei* in the metaphysical systems of his predecessors. Leibniz will then use this configuration to define obligation and right, and thereby link his technical conception of power to the modality of the ought to do. In this he opens the way to Kant's notion of universal imperative which, as Agamben notes, binds together modality and potency. What is necessary becomes what ought to be willed, and what is right ranges across what is possible; a possible whose conditions are determined by power.

In order to extract this complex movement from Leibniz's work it is necessary to explore the particular contexts and problems with which the German thinker engages. This is methodologically justified not least because Leibniz's movement of the chess pieces of activity and power are subtle, and can only be clarified, and in the case of potency, identified, when thrown into archaeological relief. Given the sheer volume and richness of Leibniz's work, it has proved necessary to impose certain boundary conditions to achieve this. Temporally, I have limited myself to Leibniz's early and middle periods (roughly 1663–79 and 1680–1700). The subject matter is focused on, if necessarily not limited to, Leibniz's legal theory, and this determines also a focus within our time period. Leibniz's key jurisprudential works are developed in the early period, and our recourse to the middle years is largely due to Leibniz's continued work and emendation of those texts and the ideas they contain. When we come to the key jurisprudential texts in this work, I will discuss their various drafts and subsequent amendments or affirmations as appropriate. I would also emphasise that I have chosen not to focus too greatly on Leibniz's definition of justice as the charity of the wise. It plays its part in Chapters 7 and 8, but Leibniz's theory of justice has been the subject of several important works, notably by Gaston Grua, Nicholas Riley, Christopher Johns and René Sève, and on whose work I rely. My research object is not justice itself, but the 'how' of how we think about law. One might anachronistically say that I am interested in Leibniz's theory of how lawyers (should) make sense of their moral world, though one could also argue that it is about how Leibniz's moralised world *makes* sense for legal subjects. With the outer scope of this study determined, this work proceeds as follows.

The first four chapters review some of the metaphysical assumptions underpinning Leibniz's legal theory, particularly those pertaining to activity and power. Indeed, the respective analyses of activity and power might be said to provide two threads through this work. Chapter 1 introduces Leibniz's notion of the *suppositum* which I trace back through Scholasticism to certain interpretations of the Aristotelean metaphysics of activity (*energeia*). Chapter 2 provides a broader discussion of activity and its relation to the metaphysics of power in Aristotle (*dunamei*) and the Schoolmen (*potentia*). I introduce a hermeneutic tool – the square of power – which then provides a framework for what follows. Chapters 3 and 4 now take up the thread of power and its relation to the will: Chapter 3 provides Scholastic context for the theory of the will, while Chapter 4 exposes possible reasons why Leibniz seeks to bring will and power together as subalterns of action and endeavour; a move which appears to demote power from its primary function in Scholastic thought.

Chapters 5 through 8 are the legal theoretic core of this work, and here the methodology shifts from a contextualisation of Leibniz's early and middle period thinking to a specific focus on legal texts. Chapters 5 and to a degree 6 might be said naturally to follow Chapters 1 and 2 in that their main concern is how the Leibnizian supposit or activity helps us to understand the central thrusts of both the *De Casibus Perplexis* and the *Nova Methodus Discendae Docendaeque Jurisprudentiae*. I seek to establish that it is the rational structure of suppositive activity as such which motivates Leibniz's claims as to a commonality in juridical reasoning and a need for a teaching of law through reflecting the innate structures of this activity. These legal texts, however, also indicate developments in Leibniz's thought whereby he begins to elaborate the complementary function of the world, or state space, in which this jurisprudential activity takes place. Chapters 7 and 8 engage in a detailed reading of the various versions of Leibniz's *Elementa Iuris*, seeking to show in particular how Leibniz's theory of will and *potentia* (Chapter 4) presupposes such a concept of primary matter, or primary passive force, which in the juridical context may called a 'state space'. This state space replaces the concept of *potentia* inherited from the Schoolmen. Against the background of modal theory, I argue in particular that appreciation of the role of the state space allows us to understand the function of universal obligation and prohibition in Leibniz's thinking, and their difference from the particular rights of legal actors.

My overall argument will amount to describing the following arc. With the doctrine of the *actus purus essendi*, Aquinas establishes that a self-actualising activity, such as the being of God, amounts to a power (*potentia*) in this sense: it stands as an exemplary principle and so cause for all other substantial activities. This reconceptualisation of power runs against the Aristotelean division between activity and in-potency, in which in-potency has the character of a deficiency. The Thomist theory of power goes through several mutations at the hands of thinkers such as Duns Scotus and Suárez, and is put in particular issue through the philosophies of Hobbes and Spinoza, who transform power from a divine principle to something possessed by all humans in different, physically (and natural legally) determined ways. Faced with these transformations, Leibniz appears to reaffirm Aristotle's metaphysics: he advances a theory of the supposit or subject as self-actualising activity shared in some way by God and rational creature. At the same time he relegates *potentia* to a specific expression of endeavouring (*conari*), and further-more contrasts it with acting and its expression in will. Here he meets the material philosophers of power, Hobbes and Spinoza, halfway by understanding power as a determina-tion of substantial activity but also as a potency that can be appropriated for the purposes of the actualisation of the individual. The effect of this relegation, however, appears to produce an imbalance in Leibniz's metaphysics. Like his Scholastic and natural legal predecessors (such as Grotius) he looks to external determination as the source of *potentia*, for it must come from without if it is to be appropriated. But if particular actions derive from substantial activity, where do particular powers derive from, if not some primary potency? The pre-Leibnizian history of power seems to have at least this unity: that there is a primary potency at work which is suffered by finite creatures as their God and/or their World. As I follow Leibniz's thinking on the supposit and *potentia* into their applications in the legal texts, we will find that Leibniz reconceptualises what may once have been under-stood as power under a new name: the state space. It amounts to Leibniz internalising the externality of *potentia* within each substance as its moral world, and placing on each practical agent a universal set of obligations and prohibitions defined by that world. It is this internalised universal moral world which, I claim, is Leibniz's most novel contribution to the concept of power and which sets the stage for Kantian practi-cal philosophy.

A technical comment

The central drive of the first four chapters will be to establish the framework which underpins Leibniz's legal theory, principally by situating it within the history of the concepts of activity, potency, formality and reality. All these terms and their Scholastic and Leibnizian cognates will be introduced as I proceed, but there are four key logical terms which I employ that are modern, and while they have cognates in Leibniz's thought, I believe the best course of action is to lay bare my interpretation of these terms from the outset, at least so that the reader be notified of their significance for the author, but hopefully also to avoid any confusion for those of a legal background who may encounter them for the first time. The terms are these:

(a) extension;
(b) intension;
(c) pretension; and
(d) contension.

Each term draws on the radical 'tension' from the Italian *tendo* and Greek *teino*, suggesting as it does a directed movement of stretching out.[5] The easiest way to understand these terms is to examine how they explain a fifth key notion which is absolutely essential, in my opinion, for comprehending Leibniz's very strange metaphysics: *equivalence*. Let us take them in turn to see how equivalence operates in each case. *Extensionality* concerns the interior elements of things, and the clearest modern example of an extensional object is a set – a collection of discrete objects which can also be sets. For example, {4, 4, 4} is a set, with the contents of the set being all the objects between the brackets, separated for convenience by commas. To say two sets are extensionally equivalent, we ask 'Do the two sets contain exactly the same objects?' Thus {4, 4, 4} and {4, 4, 5} are not equivalent because they contain different things, while {4, 4, 4} and {4, 4, 4} are equivalent. Indeed, strictly speaking, the object '4' is itself extensionally equivalent to the object '4' so that the following are all equivalent: {4, 4, 4} and {4, 4} and {4}. This last point indicates just what extensionality is interested in: the *inside* of objects; and the sort of thing it is blind to: relationships *between* objects.

Historically, extensionality proved popular from the late nineteenth century onwards following the set-theoretical innovations of Cantor, particularly among the logical positivists in the Anglosphere. The weight and admitted brilliance of this heritage can therefore skew our appreciation of the import and priority of extensionality as a logico-philosophical basis, and may indeed render one blind to the possibility of the existence of other logical bases for philosophy prior to Cantor (or at all). Alain Badiou admits as much in *Logics of Worlds*. His astonishing *Being and Event* provided a set-theoretical account of ontology which lost nothing of the vitality of Cantor's original discoveries, but, as noted above, set theory is blind to relationships between objects and as an ontological tool in the hands of the unwitting it can have all the power of a kitchen blender: it makes great soup but at the expense of texture. To Badiou's credit *Logics of Worlds* attempts among other things to supplement a set-theoretic ontology with a logic of relations based on the powerful mathematical toolkit known as category theory. The logical aspect of this theory – categori(c)al logic – could be defined in contradistinction to set theory as that logic which is concerned not with the contents of objects, but only with the relationships between them.

Consider the following object: (4, 4, 4), which we will call a *list*. The important point about a list as we define it here is that there is an order and a length. Speaking purely in terms of relationships there are three objects related together here, and they are in the order shown. (4, 4, 4) is not equivalent to (4) or any other list of 4s save (4, 4, 4) because no other list relates exactly three objects in that way.

When we assess equivalence by reference to relationships alone, this can be named *intensional equivalence*.[6] Intensional equivalence is critical to understanding Leibniz's thinking, though this may not yet be apparent from that first example. An intuitive way of thinking about *intensionality* is to think of intensions as arrows indicating relationships. Take a lecture theatre with 100 seats. At 10am there is a lecture on property law for 90 students. We can assign each student to the seat they decide to sit in using arrows, one from each student to their respective seat. At 11am, by some cruel administrative fate, the same students are to attend a lecture in the same theatre on company law. The students may stay in the same seats or move around in the break between lectures. We can compare the two seating arrangements *student → seat* by comparing the arrows or relationships at 10am with those at 11am. If they are the same in the case of each arrow – if each student chooses the same seat each time – then the two collections of relationships are said to be intensionally equivalent. Now you might naturally think of these arrows as simply placing student and seat side by side in a list, but it is far better to think of the *movement* of each student to a seat to grasp the active sense of intensionality.

Another example from physics: a heavenly body in the cosmos as understood by Descartes and Leibniz. We are not interested in the content of the planet; just where it is now and where it is going to. Over time the planet moves from its initial position p_0 through space to some final reference position p_t, and we could describe that motion with an arrow, like this: $p_0 \rightarrow p_t$. This motion discloses two important things. First, that the planet arrives at point t depends entirely on its motion beginning at point o *and is conditioned by it.* However, second, this conditioning tells us that the motion or arrow itself is translatable to anywhere in space. The relationship symbolised by the arrow has a generalisable aspect also. This generalisable motion or arrow is the relationship between the two states of the planets (or whatever bodies), and it is this arrow or movement which intensionality concerns itself with. How then can we ensure that our arrow $p_0 \rightarrow p_t$ specifies just this heavenly body and not another? Remember, we have refused to look at the object itself to do this; only its relationships. Well, one way to identify just this heavenly body is to do just what Descartes did: ask not only where the heavenly body is going, but also how it arrived at its starting point in the first place. So now we have two arrows: $p_0 \rightarrow p_t$ proceeding from our object, and also $o \rightarrow p_0$ which is an arrow from some arbitrary reference point for all objects called the 'origin'. In this way all objects are identified by reference to the origin and their next movement. So, another naïve way of thinking about intensional equivalence is to say: two objects are equivalent if they have the same arrows pointing at them (if any) and the same arrows pointing from them (if any).

In our primary area of focus – matters of jurisprudence – we find Leibniz interested in conditional relationships which are structurally similar to physical motions. Leibniz defines a conditional proposition as having the following 'content': that if the prior is true, the posterior is true.[7] In modern language this amounts to saying: if condition p_0 then consequence p_1, or again $p_0 \rightarrow p_1$. In like manner the consequential relation is generalisable, and indeed we may well ask: we are assuming condition p_0, but what is the origin of that condition p_0, or in more natural language, if condition p_0 caused the effect, what caused condition p_0 (and so on)?

For the purposes of interpreting Leibniz, it is enough to grasp this naïve notion that Leibniz is interested not in the extensional content of objects, but the relationships or arrows between them, and that these arrows represent verbs – movements of being, of thought and of (physical) action. We shall see that if one strictly ignores extensional difference one can posit a metaphysics in which substances are not contained in a single 'world'; that each substance can constitute its own world without windows on the others, provided that all the intensional information defining each substance's relationships in that world is equivalent.

Pretensionality plays almost as great a role in this work as intensionality. The neologism is suggested by Leibniz's consistently stated thesis that the possible pretends or claims (*prétend*) to exist. As we shall see in detail in Chapter 4, it is not so much the possible that actively pretends to existence; rather, the possible only pretends to existence under the action of some entelechy (the End). For Leibniz that entelechy is mediately the more or less perfect rational mind, and ultimately the wholly perfect actuality of God. This duality is essential, for merely formal possibility is nothing unless a self-actualising substantial form determines a global purpose for this possibility: the actualisation of the substantial form. In this way every compossible logical possibility is subject to a *valuation* with respect to its dominant substantial form, a valuation apprehended as 'its' pretension to exist. What is best is referred to the perfection of a substantial form, though it may appear to be claimed by and move from the possibility.

9

Pretensionality concerns the relationship between an object and a principle, or innate idea. The most concise and powerful example of this notion can already be found in the first Proposition of Proclus' *Elements of Theology*: 'there can be no multiplicity which does not participate in unity'. According to one perspective, and here Cantor and Badiou spring to mind again, this proposition includes the claim that a multiplicity cannot be unless it is submitted to the action of unification. In other words, as subsequent propositions reveal, it is the action of the One to evaluate the multiplicity of primary matter and make of it an intelligible being as a collection of discrete units or simplest forms. Yet this action is not operative or causal, but participative. Matter moves towards unity in the exemplary presence of the One. In this example we see that each discrete unit is defined only by its having become a discrete unit, and that as such its claim to existence is as good as any other such unit – they are exchangeable with respect to value. We thus have a notion of particular *pretensional equivalence*, though if we are strict, we should compare the universal pretensional valuations of two entelechies to determine whether these entelechies are equivalent. Let us imagine, for example, some discrete units of wood and metal nails. Then we may also posit a unity which combines these, which we call a table. In one sense the table has just as much unity as each piece of wood and each nail, but in another crucial sense, the unity of the table composes more subordinate unities within itself. The table simply acts to be a table, but its composing unities are brought under that activity and function to support its actualisation. Observe that each nail could have done a great many things (been used in a door or a fence), and that we might describe these possible uses as 'degrees of freedom'. Well, now this nail functions as part of a table, and in this restriction on what a nail can do by its subordination to the table's actuality, we can begin to grasp just what pretension is all about: a certain kind of functional explanation closely linked to relationships of order of respective components *for* some actuality. The restriction has a positive side for the nail, however. For Leibniz there is no reason why a nail should choose one possible state (in a door/ in a table etc.). These are simply formal possibilities. By being related to a table's actuality – by being subject to a pretension – one of the nail's possible states now claims a right to existence as part of that table. Under pretension the formal becomes the real.

For its part, the table's actuality is referred to its capacity to order and bring unity to these disparate and subordinate unities, and the more such unities that 'pretend' towards tabularity, the more 'reality' we say the table possesses. We might further observe both that each nail itself composes ferrous molecules, and that the table composes part of human habitation. In this way, each level of combinations may indeed be combinations of other combinations, and so on to an infinity in which only the One is capable of providing for unity for all. By observing the respective structure of these combinations – how they are respectively ordered in terms of combination and level – we may draw equivalences between them and thereby make valuations as to their relative complexity, that is, the number of composing combinations, which Leibniz terms their 'degree of reality'.

Chapter 4 proceeds to account for pretension according to the way the term is deployed by Leibniz in his philosophy, and not by means of a logical apparatus that we would need to impute. The core intuition, though, can be stored for future use: entelechies as final principles invest matter with pretensions to exist, and Leibniz will regard God as the pre-eminent such entelechy.

What I call *contensionality* plays less of a role in this work, although I do not wish completely to exclude its relevance for understanding Leibniz's thinking. Briefly, using intensionality, and regarding extensionality as a special minimum case of intensionality in which intensions are reduced to zero, one can begin to construct theoretical 'worlds' constituted of objects and such relationships as are desired (subject to strict criteria which I shall pass over). One such world could consist of an object '1' and a movement or operation that says, 'given object x let there by an object x'' known as its successor'. Such a world would consist of a central 1 and an expanding series of branches to successors of 1 in all directions. We might take the same world and add additional operations which require that there can be only one, unique successor of 1 at every step. This world would look like the system of natural numbers.

Now, both these worlds have objects and relationships, so are they equivalent? Clearly not given that the latter world is subject to additional intensional information. *Contensional equivalence* is this comparison of the objects *and* relationships of a whole world. Remarkably, as Badiou investigates in the *Logics of Worlds*, the system of (non-)equivalence relations between worlds can also be studied, and is in my opinion one of the most important areas of investigation in logical foundations. I have chosen the term contensionality to describe this system of global relationships partly thanks to a suggestion by the combinatorial logicians Curry, Feys and Craig[8] who suggest 'contention' for the logical analysis of the significance of an object or relationship within one world *by reference to* the objects and relations of another world. Contensionality then is a theory of how meaning and signification operate, for it deals with the interpretation of one world by reference to its contextualisation by another. Academics deploy contensionality all the time: a methodology is a contension because it interprets, say, the observed facts of punishment by reference, say, to the discursive world of Foucault or the discursive world of positive penal law. For the purposes of this work contensionality will play only a negative role, for we will examine how Leibniz seeks to establish that all moral matters are reducible to the same juridical activity of God and the same, common world that he creates.

By way of summary then, the reader should be alive to the difference between extensional and intensional thinking, and to the centrality of intensionality – and as the reader will see, the word 'intensionality' can here almost be replaced with the word 'activity' – to Leibniz's metaphysics. In Chapter 4 the notion of pretensionality will stand forth as the theoretical mechanism Leibniz deploys to convert the logically possible into the real by reference to the entelechies of finite and divine substantial forms. At the very least, they become a hermeneutical device for understanding Aristotle's entelechies. Yet this technical discussion should be taken as underpinning the rest of this work, for the principal methodology will comprise a contextualisation (indeed, a contension!) of Leibniz's natural legal doctrine within the history of ideas by reference to primary and secondary literature. This

Introduction

discussion amounts to a technical abstraction of key notions from the contexts in which they emerge in what follows.

Notes

1. Georgio Agamben, *Creation and Anarchy: The Work of Art and the Religion of Capitalism* (Adam Kotsko trans.) (Stanford: Stanford University Press, 2019), p.62.
2. Gwenaëlle Aubry, *Genèse du Dieu souverain* (Paris: Vrin, 2018); see also her *Dieu sans la puissance: dunamis et energeia chez Aristote et chez Plotin* (Paris: Vrin, 2006).
3. Agamben, *Creation and Anarchy*, p.63.
4. Ibid. p.63.
5. See Plato's *Crito* 47c, cf. *Thaetetus* 163a, and the antonym in *Gorgias* 458b.
6. Not to be confused with intentionality, which is a term of art both in phenomenology and in the work of Aquinas. I discuss Aquinas' use of intentionality in Chapter 1, 'The distinctions and unity of *Trinity. Mind*'.
7. *De Conditionibus*, A:VI, i, 102, Def.1.
8. Haskell Curry, Robert Feys and William Craig, *Combinatorial Logic* Vol. 1 (Dordrecht: N. Holland, 1958).

One

From Trinity to Mind:
The Intensional Basis of the Law

1. Introduction

It is strange thing that a philosopher so determined to elaborate a juridical theory justifying the City of God should settle
upon a metaphysics in which individuals are absolutely dis-
joint and separated. How can Leibniz speak of community,
of a kingdom of grace, when a philosophy of perception and
reflection encloses every substantial form within itself and
denies it even windows on the 'world'? Leibniz's solution to
this self-imposed restriction is to look not to subject or object
of lived experience, but to look to the very activities of being,
thinking and acting themselves. I propose to examine what I
regard as a critical fragment on the structural equivalence of
Mind and Trinity to establish Leibniz's reliance on the equivalence of these activities as the basis for community both in
formal and practical spheres. The inner structure expressed
by this fragment will appear at several points in this chapter
as I draw out its significance, and this initial treatment will
pave the way for a complete analysis of the structure itself in
Chapter 2.

My examination is organised according to two interpretative themes. In the first half of this chapter I investigate
the Scholastic doctrine of the supposit, taken up by Leibniz,
and indicate its origin in the doctrine of activity and power
which Aquinas derives from Aristotle via Plotinus. I argue
that Leibniz understands the supposit as a perfected activity
of being, knowing or acting, which is expressed in persons
and phenomena. In the second half of this chapter, I show
how Scholastic debates on being-in-common provide interpretative context for Leibniz's own account of the community of substantial forms. I seek to link the supposit to the

primary or innate ideas that Leibniz discusses in his middle period to argue that it is the supposit which affords community between substantial forms. The supposit enables community, I claim, by means of intensional equivalence: that kind of equivalence in which we concern ourselves not with the similarity of various entities that think, nor that of diverse objects of thought, but rather with the equivalence of the movement of thinking itself. I also highlight a problem community raises: if substances are the same in some essential respect, what continues to differentiate them? The initial answer of this chapter – that differentiation is due to reality, and so power – will lead naturally to the investigation of power and the real in the three chapters that follow.

This work will ultimately permit us, in Chapters 5 and 6, an interpretation of Leibniz's jurisprudential theory which emphasises his claim as to fundamental commonality of juridical thinking as such. To do this, however, we must spend some time drawing together the influences which allowed Leibniz to advance such a doctrine.

2. The divine activity

Let us turn to then to the context from which emerges Leibniz's intensional theory of *supposita* or substantial forms, as he calls them up to the end of his middle period (1699). Our methodological concern is that Leibniz's accounts both of *supposita* and of activity not only draw on Scholastic philosophy, but find their most expansive expression within Leibniz's natural theological works. If contextualisation is to occur, this chapter must provide a degree of framing of those works if only to aid the reader. I would therefore like to begin by providing a broad outline of the metaphysics of activity and power from Aristotle through to Aquinas.

A particular difficulty for the reader is that the Schoolmen bind the natural philosophy of activity and power to their own theological concerns. A central such concern is providing for a coherent explanation of the Trinitarian structure of God, understood as the three moments: *esse, nosse* and *velle*, or being, knowing and willing. As is well known, in the thirteenth century this broad Trinitarian model, inherited from Augustine, is reinterpreted and clarified by Thomas

Aquinas amongst others thanks to the reception of that part of Aristotle's surviving works that passed via the Arab world. As Étienne Gilson notes, there results a tension between theological orthodoxy concerning a Trinity heavily influenced by Neoplatonism, and the logical power of the works of Aristotle, a thinker owing no allegiance to an Abrahamic god.

This tension is most acute in the way Aquinas takes the Stagirite's discussion of being (*einai*) and, as Gilson suggests, 'extracts the latent order' in the *Metaphysics* in order to explain *esse*. This, Gilson argues,[1] is achieved in three stages. *First*, a primary philosophy must take as its object that which is supremely intelligible, and this object is that which is common to all other things: being (*ens commune*). Now having grasped this common object, our philosophy must interrogate it, and the route to understanding is via its causes. Thus the *second* stage investigates the intelligible causes of all being. It is a move which abstracts from the sensible given in favour of the abstract intellectual, and in so doing constitutes the intellect as replete with formal essences of things. In this search for the causes of all things the mind comes to rest on universal causes and, ultimately, the Prime Mover as the maximally intelligible cause. *Third*, then, metaphysics seeks to understand the Prime Mover. We now are dealing not with a formal idea, but with an actually existing substance, indeed a substance whose essence is existence and which is cause of self. This third perspective engages in a description of the properties of such a Being – notably its activity and power – and the nature of its causal relations with itself and others. This Being is the object of metaphysics proper.

One can discern in this analysis the involution that occurs already in Greek thought, and particularly in the hands of Plotinus, as Gwenaëlle Aubry has shown. Aristotle's analytical discovery of the Prime Mover as an *ousia energeia* or perfected activity is inverted such that the perfected activity of the Prime Mover becomes a *dunamis pantôn* or power-to-all that is the principle of a system measured according to perfection. We have been led to the One and we are invited now to review the three stages of metaphysical analysis from an inverse perspective. It is this One, accessible to all rational souls through metaphysics, which is the *ens commune* – the being apprehended in any intellectual act. It is in and for this

One that the intellectual act of delineating the principles of created things is united with the causal prowess of that very act, for given that this One is established as cause of every cause, it possesses immediate access to every such formal essence. It is this One which is capable even of bringing about its own actualisation, is capable of rendering concrete and real that which was merely formal.

Yet the Neoplatonist inversion of the Aristotelean analysis of being into a cosmological procession from the One remains problematic for the Abrahamic theologians. Plotinus and Proclus continue to regard unity as cause of being, and thus being, its properties, and so divinity, as lower in the order of reasons; a doctrine wholly untenable for the Christians. There is need for a further inversion, as we shall see, whereby being is raised to first principle and takes on the functions of unity, which is to say the function of unification itself. Being becomes the means by which all the other metaphysical properties and attributes are knotted together in God.

We can imagine permutations of three key terms within this metaphysics: being, activity and power. Gwenaëlle Aubry has succinctly shown how the permutation of these three terms is varied at key moments in the history of philosophy prior to Early Modern period:[2]

(a) For Aristotle activity (*energeia*) stands at the head of the system and being is analysed by reference to it. Power is understood as in-potency (*dunamei*), which is to say that power is the incompleteness of an ordered activity in achieving its end, that is, what activity aims to actualise but has not yet achieved. To be in-potency is to lack actuality (*entelecheia*).

(b) With Plotinus we see a reappraisal of potency at the expense of activity. The *dunamis pantôn* (omnipotence) can be understood as perfect organising principle which is the final cause of the being and activity of created things. Named the One, it stands in priority to being and activity, both as cause and End.

(c) The third permutation of activity–power–being, in which being is raised to the apex of our triad is heralded by Aquinas. Activity and absolute power (*potentia*) are now regarded as flowing from a necessary and perfect being as the power (*virtus*) of its being: God constitutes Himself as One and Good by a pure act of being, and it is this *actus purus essendi* which as organising principle is the foundation of his absolute power.

The argument of this work rests on the centrality of *energeia*, understood as activity, for Leibniz's notion of legal thought. Insofar as *energeia* is understood as an activity we will see that Leibniz is more faithful to Aristotle than Aquinas, and in this way: for Aquinas there is a need to regard the activity of God, instantiated in the relations of the Trinity, as both eternal and simple. Combine that with the methodology of natural theology – the continuous abstraction from sensible nature – and the resulting tendency is to do that which Aristotle appears to reject, namely to find at the root of all things fixed and immovable forms rather than a principle of self-movement. Leibniz characteristically will maintain the orthodoxy of being's primacy while reallocating activity within this prevailing Trinitarian structure and reducing by a certain measure the role of power. In short, activity will resume its primacy and power will be an effect, in the last analysis, of the encounter between the finite acts of creatures. A central result for the history of legal philosophy is that it is activity – particularly intellectual activity epitomised by juridical thinking – and not power which will come to play being's role of a 'common activity' if you will, and so a means by which persons are bound together by law.

The nexus between Leibniz's doctrine of activity and theological concerns is perhaps most succinctly expressed in a phrase that Leibniz repeats throughout our period of study; a phrase that introduces us to a very technical Scholastic term: actions are of supposits (*actiones sunt suppositorum*). In what follows I shall endeavour to situate Leibniz's thinking on activity within his theological context; to discuss key theological debates which will clarify why Leibniz should appear to regard activity, and not power, as the means of unifying a world.

3. *Trinity. Mind*

Sometime during the middle of 1671 Leibniz sketches out a ... matrix in which he relates the triune nature of God to the structure of the mind in act. The Akademie Edition has named the fragment '*Trinitas. Mens*', and I follow this nomenclature:[3]

BODY. WORLD	TRINITY. MIND	
Space	Intellect	Being (*esse*)
Figure	Imagination	Knowing (*scire*)
Motion	Will. Power	Act (*agere*) or
		endeavouring (*conari*)

As Maria Rosa Antognazza has noted,[4] this sketch for the *Elementa de Mente* exhibits a most interesting combination of Scholastic Trinitarian thinking (the *esse–nosse–velle* triad) and the mechanism Leibniz had encountered in his recent reading of Hobbes (the linkage of will and power through conation). The matrix contains a great deal of information which it will be necessary to unpack, even if we limit ourselves to a consideration of activity and disregard for now the question of power. A preliminary reading of the matrix draws our attention to the following apparent equivalences: (i) between the structure of corporeal nature (BODY. WORLD) and the incorporeal (TRINITY. MIND); (ii) within the incorporeal realm, between Trinity and Mind, thus implying also finite minds; and (iii) between each of the terms of a triad (the columns), for it seems indeed that they are to be united as one. Two differences are also worthy of remark: (a) between the headed columns and the third column, where it is quite apparent that the third column deploys verbs that range across the nouns in the first two columns; and (b) the duality of will/power and the verbs to act/endeavour, in the bottom row. As this latter point pertains to power, I reserve discussion of it to subsequent chapters.

  As this book's principle focus is the law I will not engage directly with debates concerning the relationship between body and mind; my emphasis is rather on legal thought and so the activity of jurisprudential thinking. I wish therefore to concentrate our attention on two equivalences and one distinction from the above, each of which I argue help us to understand Leibniz's thinking about law and to contextualise them in theologico-political debates. These questions are:

(a) How is it possible that the three aspects of Leibnizian mind and Trinity (intellect, imagination, will) are deemed equivalent such that they can subsist in the same individual?
(b) How is it possible that different individuals – the Trinity and a given mind – can be treated by Leibniz as equivalent in structure but not the same individual substance (the Spinozan problem)?
(c) What is the theoretical purpose of the distinction between the nominal *Trinity. Mind* column and the verbal column in the above matrix?

The answers to these questions will clarify the central role activity plays in Leibniz's thought. In what remains of this chapter I tackle questions (a) and (b). These answers will provide a basis for engaging with question (c). in Chapter 2.

3.1 The distinctions and unity of *Trinity. Mind*

The role of the supposit
Leibniz's matrix immediately imports into the Mind the theological problems inherent in the Trinity, and not least how it is that if God is simple, he can unite the three persons and the divine attributes in one. For surely to do so would impute multiplicity to God. The potential solutions proposed by the Schoolmen are several and subtle, and because Leibniz appears reticent to disclose his Scholastic inspirations, though he seeks to conform 'with the principles of the noblest Scholastic[s]',[5] it can be difficult to isolate which proposed solutions help us understand Leibniz's own position. I follow the indication of Leroy Loemker[6] that our route to understanding Leibniz's thinking on Trinity and Mind is through the concept of the supposit. With the phrase '*actiones sunt suppositorum* [actions pertain to supposits]', which Leibniz deploys in his 1668 notes *On Transsubstantiation*, in the *Discourse on Metaphysics* (1686), and in the published *On Nature Itself* (1698) – thus throughout our period of study

– we have a term of art which points us to both a theological problem and a subset of possible solutions. To establish this, my argument proceeds in four stages which require a contextualisation of the notion of 'supposit'. First, following closely the work of Gwenaëlle Aubry, I describe how Aristotle develops the notion of *ousia energeia* to describe the perfected action of the Prime Mover, and how Aquinas takes up this metaphysical structure and modifies it by ascribing power to God in a new way as active potency (*potentia activa*). Second, I show how that debate concerning power provides the framework for interpreting Aquinas' account of the supposit. I claim not only that for Aquinas a supposit is one of the markers of a substantial individual, and that it is equivalent to a perfected action productive of power, but also that Aquinas argues that more than one supposit is active in the mind of God viz. being, knowing and willing. Third, I use the foregoing framework to critique Brandon Look's reading of Leibniz on the supposit, showing that Look's account remains wedded to a form–matter interpretation of Aristotle which is, given what we have established concerning activity and power, not appropriate when dealing with *ousia energeia*. Finally, I present Leibniz's own account of the supposit, particularly in the context of its deployment as part of an argument concerning transubstantiation.

The metaphysical structure of the problem

Drawing closely on Gwenaëlle Aubry's inspiring work on power from Aristotle to Aquinas,[7] we can set out a metaphysical structure which will assist our understanding of the supposit. Now, during the argumentation of his *Metaphysics*,[8] Aristotle leaves behind the well-known division of form and matter and develops a deeper division between two terms: *energeia* and *dunamis*. The former derives from *en-ergon*, and thus has the sense of 'being-at-work', whereas the latter can already be found in Plato's *Theaetetus* and has a sense of power to do. *Energeia* and *dunamis* are said to be contraries in the sense that *energeia* describes what is actual about a substance, whereas *dunamis* is that which the substance has the capacity to do but which it is not presently doing. Both terms have a universal sense in that they range across numerous individual actions and passions respectively. Thus, the activity (*energeia*) of walking implies a sequence of steps; the respective potentiality of not walking or standing still, implies individual impediments to progress in a direction. The latter understanding of what is implied by or subaltern to 'not walking' is designed to indicate the contrary nature of the implied terms: step and impediment. If the step is an action, the impediment is a passion with respect to the action. For this reason, we can speak of these subalterns as active potency and passive potency. Finally, observe that the passive potency of the individual impediment is both qualitatively different from the particular action (the step) and qualitatively and quantitatively different from the universal activity (walking as such). Hence it is also said that the activity and the passive potency are in contradiction, and the same can be said for any two terms which are both quantitatively and qualitatively opposed.

The interplay between *energeia* and *dunamis* helps Aristotle to measure the perfection of things. If the activity is walking, then the steps are attempts at achieving the end or *telos* of having walked (Meta IX [1047a20–30]). The perfected manifestation of the activity is its actuality (*entelecheia*). To the extent that the activity is not achieved due to impediments to individual actions, we say that each individual action has suffered a passion – a passive potency – and that generally the activity is not perfected but still incomplete and potential in some way. We can thus envisage a movement from activity to active potency, and a movement from active potency, determined by passive potency, back to activity and seeking to actualise it as *entelecheia*. A circular process.

From this basic structure Aristotle develops a new usage that plays on the sense of *dunamis*: *dunamei* or in-potency (Aubry, 'Ousia energeia', p.828, see further p. 63). Aristotle appears to define it as the principle of the motion ordered by the act that is also that being's end and its own proper good.[9] From the foregoing we see that Aristotle is describing just that process from activity to action to *entelecheia*, to the extent incomplete by virtue of some determination by *dunamis*.

From these insights, Aristotle has occasion to consider a substance which is not subject to impediment and so potentiality. Such a substance is an activity which implies a series of acts and each such act is not determined in any way, such that all acts are perfected and the activity is fully actualised. Here there is a complete lack of in-potency (*dunamei*) such that the activity of substance is perfected. Aristotle calls this special limit case *ousia energeia*[10] – essential activity – and calls the substance which achieves this perfected circular process the Prime Mover. It is to be observed that while these considerations do use the language of movement, Aristotle is explicit that his findings extend beyond movement to ontological matters.[11]

For Aquinas the activity par excellence is being (*esse*), and starting not with finite things but with God, his first philosophy arrives directly at that individual who achieves essential activity with respect to *esse*. Thus, we are invited to consider the activity of being and the acts it implies, the elaboration of a thing's nature as its essence. Following Aristotle, we could argue that there is a limit case of an entity which is no way impeded from elaborating its essence, and in this case the essence is fully developed and the entity's being is fully actualised. This said, for Aquinas it is more important that such a case be not just a possible special case, but that it be necessary. This is achieved, in Aquinas' view, by observing that any other entity may well endeavour to elaborate its nature, but while it may well order its actions to actualise an activity *formaliter* – it may produce all the determinations that define 'going for a walk' – the one thing a finite entity cannot do is give being to going for a walk. And this for the simple reason that to suppose otherwise would be to suppose that if the entity can grant being to 'going for a walk', it can grant being to itself in any respect and so cause itself to be. This, Aquinas holds, is not the case for finite entities, but it is the very definition of God. Whereas all other creatures must obtain being from another source, and so are marked by potentiality (*potentialitas*) and lack, God's activity is being, and to elaborate himself is to actualise that being. The result: his essence does not differ from his being, needing only his being and nothing else: his essence is his being (*sua essentia est suum esse*).[12]

Now one might question whether Aquinas has advanced that far from Aristotle's *ousia energeia* with this argument. There are innovations, particularly in the way that essence shifts from being the aggregate of actions (a static, elaborated nature) to describing the activity of being in its self actualisation (the whole process), but perhaps even this is implicit in *ousia energeia*, and only appears novel when set against an interpretation of Aquinas which regards essences as fixed and definitional. Aubry establishes,[13] however, that it is Aquinas' next move which achieves the rupture.

We have our circular process – essence as being – but whereas for Aristotle this defines both a completedness or lack of potentiality and a certain immobility, Aquinas now reintroduces power. The circular process becomes itself a node with respect to which power can be spoken of in a new sense. Here, in the *Summa contra Gentiles* in particular,[14] terminological distinctions are identified between *potentialitas* and words such as *posse*, *potestas* and *virtus* which imply power in the sense, I would say, of capacity to bring about an action in another. The central point here is that Aquinas identifies an ethical character to the perfection of God's being, in the Aristotelean sense that others apprehend this perfection as an excellence and seek to move towards it. It is this procurement of movement which marks the divine *virtus essendi* (power or force of being), but also indicates that the movement does not flow from God; rather it flows from that second entity which apprehends this power. On this basis Aquinas and his followers can speak of an order of eminence graded according to degrees of perfection, each creature being measured by their *virtus* and being moved to others of greater perfection according to their measure.

To illustrate his point, we may, as Aquinas does on occasion (and indeed the Neoplatonists on whom he draws), use the analogy of fire (the sun is the best example) and heat.[15] The sun itself, Aquinas will argue, is essentially hot and could not be itself without this heating activity. In other words, its power-of-heating is fully actualised for itself. Wood is not essentially hot but becomes so in the presence of the sun's irradiation. It thus receives heat from the flame and becomes like it according to its *potentiality* to receive the heat: its power-for-heating. The sun, however, according to Aquinas' understanding of physics, loses nothing of its heating capacity in this. It remains immobile and eternally irradiating without any diminution to this perfected activity.

Thanks to Aubry's endeavours, we hopefully have been able to set out a basic metaphysical framework of an activity which acts and through this perfectly actualises itself. Furthermore, we understand that *esse* is the primary activity to be analysed according to this framework, and that the perfection of the activity gives rise to a new understanding of power. My argument will be that the notion of supposit which Leibniz inherits from Aquinas and the Schoolmen is built upon this framework of perfected activity implying act, and act moving to actuality.

The supposit in Aquinas

It seems that the term 'supposit' first appears in Aquinas' *Summa Theologiae* ('ST') during his treatment of the question of the plurality divine persons. Aquinas wishes to deal with the following problem: to an individual substance should belong a single essential definition which allows us to pick it out, but if three persons are said of God, are there not three essences, three persons, three substances even? But if we deny this by claiming that our distinction of persons is entirely verbal, not real, then the doctrine of the Trinity seems to be a mere analogy by humans and not really in God. It is just a 'manner of our speaking' and no basis from which to draw theological conclusions. How then to find the three persons in one substance with one divine essence without imputing plurality? Aquinas identifies one route to a solution in Aristotle's *Metaphysics V* [1017b10–25], where the Philosopher argues that substance is twofold. On Aquinas' reading, substance:

> In one way ... means the quiddity of a thing, signified by its definition, and thus we say that the definition means the substance of a thing; in which sense substance is called by the Greeks *ousia*, what we may call 'essence'. In another way substance means a subject or 'suppositum,' which subsists in the genus of substance. To this, taken in a general sense, can be applied a name signifying an intention [*intentionem*]; and thus it is called 'suppositum.'(ST I, q.29, a.2)

In saying that one sense of substance is as an individual's thisness and determination (the *tode ti kai khoriston*), Aquinas follows Aristotle directly, but in saying substance can also mean a subject or supposit, he appears to introduce a very strong interpretation of the relevant source. After all, Aristotle says substance can mean 'the ultimate substratum' (*hupokeimenon eskhaton*) and in the preceding discussion he gives the traditional Greek examples of earth, fire and water 'and everything of the sort'. Aristotle adds that he is speaking of the ultimate substratum 'which is no longer predicated of anything else' (rather everything else is predicated of it). This is perhaps suggestive of a certain materiality, given that Aristotle exemplifies the definitional meaning of substance by reference to shape and form.[16] It certainly seems a little surprising that Aquinas should adopt this distinction of senses of 'substance' – as definition and as substrate – and then so wholly depart from the materialistic sense of substrate in favour of expressive 'intentions'. Has Aquinas cited the Stagirite as authority even as he has substituted 'intentions' for materiality?

The confusion is avoided on further examination of Aristotle's *Metaphysics*, in light of the readings by Aubry[17] and Focillon.[18] In *Metaphysics* VIII Aristotle returns to a consideration of the substrate, seeking to apply the logic of the categories to his explanatory candidates: matter and form. His analysis will lead to a proposal for better explanatory tools, but at this stage Aristotle's focus is on matter alone and the argument that matter itself may be investigated for its behaviour as if it had form beneath that imposed by, say, the craftsman. The Stagirite's illustrations are helpful: the matter of the sea is water, but the smoothness of the sea is also an aspect of this water.[19] Aubry argues[20] that it is Aristotle's claim that matter is *ousia in-potency* which sets up the possibility of also considering matter as *ousia in act* (*hos energeian*). In the given example the water is the *ousia* in-potency; the smoothness of the water is its actuality which expresses a kind of form through the matter. In a second example, air is the *ousia* in-potency of weather; stillness is the *ousia in act* of the air.[21] Accordingly substance is said in three senses of matter as substrate: as *ousia* in-potency, *ousia* in act, and the substance which is the combination of these.[22]

We have then in the material substrate two possible senses of substance also, and their combination. Yet Aquinas for his part is not speaking of matter but of individuals, and

Aristotle is clear that matter lacks the relevant thisness (*tode ti*) to constitute an individual. Aquinas is nevertheless drawing on an argument concerning matter for support. Why? Well it would seem that Aquinas is following Aristotle in constantly abstracting from the given as he moves towards a science of being. Aquinas extracts what is still active from the twofold distinction within material *ousia* and combines this with the formal essence provided by definition. The motivation appears to be that we are dealing with incorporeal beings, namely God and minds, and accordingly:

> ... in things not composed of matter and form, in which individualization is not due to individual matter—that is to say, to 'this' matter—the very forms being individual-ised of themselves—it is necessary the forms themselves should be subsisting 'supposita'. Therefore 'suppositum' and nature in them are identified. (ST I, q.3, a.3)

I would suggest that Aquinas has sought to resolve his theological problem of the divine persons by use of this *form of argument* of Aristotle now transposed to the incorporeal realm. Specifically, having identified a sense of substance as a substrate, and this substrate as material, Aquinas observes that the material substrate can be either *ousia* in act or in-potency. Now, here in-potency signifies the passive potency proper to matter, and improper to individuals as such, and so he discards this candidate for the supposit leaving *ousia* in act. But then has not Aquinas recovered the *ousia energeia* of Aristotle – the self-perfecting activity of substance – which Aquinas makes the basis and measure of a substance's per-fection and power? I claim that this is just what Aquinas has done: *that a supposit is the self-perfecting activity of an individual.*

To achieve this abstraction, Aquinas proceeds in stages to replace matter with rational nature, and then replaces rational nature with essence, and so ultimately with the pure act of being. It is a move which is perhaps most clearly seen in Aquinas' second 'Quodlibetal Question':

> What the nature signifies includes only what belongs to the reason of the *species*; however the supposit possesses not only what pertains to the reason of the species, but also

other things which belong to it *accidentally*; and thus the supposit is signified according to the whole, whereas the nature, or quiddity, [is] the formal part. However, in God alone there is found no accident beyond his essence, for his existence is his essence, as has been said; and therefore in God the supposit is *wholly identical* with the nature. In an angel, however, it is *not wholly identical*: for there is something that belongs to it accidentally beyond what belongs to the reason of its species, since the existence as such of the angel is beyond its essence or nature . . . (Emphasis in original)[23]

This move sets up the following hierarchy. Our basic structure is an activity–action couplet, where the action of interest is the development of a rational nature. By way of analogy we may thing of a program as a series of intensional instructions to do this and that (*if* input = 'name?' *then* output = 'my name is Stephen') and the results of that program doing those things – what the program actually writes – as the actualised rational nature which follows. At the bottom of the hierarchy we have the human, whose activity endeavours to write its rational nature. But what makes a human a human – its rational nature – is not a complete individuating state of this particular human. Humans need other things to actually exist; they lack a certain actuality, or, in Aristotelean language, they are by definition in a state of potentiality. On the one hand the human needs non-human nature (matter), such as food to exist. On the other hand, Aquinas argues, the human cannot exist unless its existence as such is granted by God, so likewise the human rational nature is lacking in this way. On the middle rung of the hierarchy, Aquinas posits angels which do not have need of matter to actualise their rational natures, but they still require existence to be granted by God. Thus angels are fully actual as regards their rational natures *but for* the definitional limitation that they lack existence unless granted to them by another.

This leads us to the limit case of God at the top of the ladder. Gwenaëlle Aubry[24] underscores just what Aquinas does: he grants to activity an essentialising causality, the effect of which is the divine essence, but also this divine essence is not a 'structure' or 'nature' separate from the act, the divine essence *is* the structure of essentialising causality: the *actus purus essendi*.[25] Aubry highlights the following from the ST: 'And since in God there is nothing potential [*potentiale*] . . ., it follows that in Him essence does not differ from his being. Therefore his essence is his being [*Sua igitur essentia est suum esse*]' (ST I, q.3, a.4). This all suggests a shift of focus away from the result of activity. We are no longer particularly concerned with a static nature which is the product of activity, but rather with an activity which produces itself. But then the product is the activity (of being), and accordingly we focus on an essence which is the activity of being. Returning to our maritime example, we now look to the propagating 'waviness' of waves, or to use Aquinas' own analogy already discussed in the preceding subsection, to the thermic activity of what is hot:

> Now the maximum in any genus is the cause of all in that genus; as fire, which is the maximum heat, is the cause of all hot things. Therefore there must also be something which is to all beings the cause of their being, goodness, and every other perfection; and this we call God. (ST I, q.2, a.3)

As we saw earlier, if wood is hot, its heat has been transferred to it by another thing that is hot, and indeed the hotness of the wood consists in this transfer and not in something intrinsically in the wood. Yet there is a thing which is by its nature hot, and this is fire (and more particularly for Aquinas' predecessors, the sun), which both produces heat to make it what it is and to affect others. By analogy then, some things *be* because they are caused to be by something that *is*, but there is a thing which is which causes itself to be – again the pure act of being.

We see that the relevant activity is the structure of being (*esse*), but we should remain mindful that Aquinas faces a theological difficulty: unlike the Prime Mover, the God of Christian dogma is three persons. For Aristotle, as Aubry has brilliantly shown,[26] the Prime Mover, while immobile, is the *simple* principle of motion, wish and so forth.[27] The Trinity, however, is of three persons or *supposita*. This is the structure Aquinas elaborates and which it seems Leibniz will adopt. The texts suggest that only if some non-real distinction is maintained between supposit and divine essence, and then between the three *supposita*, can Aquinas maintain orthodoxy. We make the following comments on Aquinas' considerations concerning these three *supposita*.

Taking his cue from Aristotle,[28] Aquinas argues that knowledge can only come from the actual, not the potential, and that proof that an intellect knows a thing is measured by whether it has actualised (we might say 'demonstrated') the thing. But God demonstrates Himself perfectly, thus he knows Himself completely. Likewise, proof of capacity to will a thing is measured by actualisation (we might say 'production') of the thing. God produces Himself perfectly, and so wills absolutely.[29]

Aquinas therefore reprises a version of his *sua essentia suum esse* argument. The formal distinction between knowing and willing breaks down in the self-actualisation of God. The activity of thinking posits what is *potentially* God, and being unlimited, this idea is perfectly conceived. The activity of willing perfectly *actualises* that idea of God. There is thus no part of the thought that is not realised in the volition. Formal potentiality collapses into real actuality, and this movement is the suppositive activity of being.

However, the internal structure of each supposit is still to be distinguished. Unlike *esse*, *nosse* gives rise to a procession in God named the Word (or the Son). Aquinas defines procession as 'intelligible emanation' which is not the object of what is thought but the 'intelligible word that proceeds from the speaker but remains in him'.[30] While Aquinas is keen to deny that this emanation is anything like Aristotelean motion or Neoplatonic irradiation, the negative reference to these notions is still instructive. In my view Aquinas regards the Word as a structured, organising activity according to what is intended by the 'speaker'.[31] Like heat or motion, but at the level of mind, the Word sets ideational entities in motion in a determinate fashion. Aquinas speaks of a substance as both a 'subject' and as 'expressive of an intention' that proceeds from the activity of God.[32] By 'expressive of intention', Aquinas means: '. . . by way of an intelligible emanation, for example, of the intelligible word which proceeds from the speaker, yet remains in him. In that sense the Catholic Faith understands procession as existing in God' (ST I, q.27, a.1). Aquinas clarifies his conception of procession according to a doctrine of similarity:

> For whenever we understand, by the very fact of under-standing there proceeds something within us, which is a conception of the object understood, a conception issuing from our intellectual power and proceeding from our knowledge of that object. This conception is signified by the spoken word; and it is called the word of the heart signified by the word of the voice. (ST I, q.27, a.1)

The difference from *esse* is that *esse*'s own activity is what is set in motion once more (if we can speak of cycles of self-action), whereas with procession the divine mind emanates an infi-nite number of likenesses (unities) of its activity by means of determinations of the first *Idea Dei* (the eternal ideas).[33]

Likewise, *velle* is structurally distinguished from *esse* and *nosse*. Unlike *esse* and like *nosse* it is a procession, but unlike *nosse*, *velle* is not generative.[34] This latter distinction com-prises a number of factors:[35] First, to think is necessarily to think being, and so the divine intellect has perfect knowledge of God whose essence is being. Likewise, all things that think, think being and so at least have a perfected knowledge of being.

Volition is a different matter. One may posit a distinct moment in which God's action to actualise himself has not yet terminated, and then argue that in its potentiality this action wills perfection by achieving God, but such a hypothe-sis Aquinas deems false.[36] God perfects himself immediately, and it is precisely in this *virtus essendi* that his perfection and Goodness consists. Furthermore, we have seen that the power of this perfection is not a power of the perfect to do something it has not done, for then it would be imperfect; rather it is a power which procures a different entity to act and so move towards it. God's will, as it were, is this perfected action which draws others towards itself. Hence Aquinas says:

> ... although God wills things apart from Himself only for the sake of the end, which is His own goodness, it does not follow that anything else moves His will, except

His goodness. So, as He understands things apart from Himself by understanding His own essence, so He wills things apart from Himself by willing His own goodness.[37]

If the action of the divine will is transitive at all, it is because the Good of the divine perfection is communicated to others, but even this is brought about by God willing His own goodness, and thus by doing so in the presence of all things having access to being.

Correspondingly, whereas the intellect proceeds by similitude, generating that which is like the cause. The will proceeds by a kind of difference, in that it 'inclines to the thing willed . . . toward an object'. More specifically, the thought proceeds by likeness because it moves to generate itself in its objects. Will (and particularly Love), on the other hand, moves towards that in an object which it recognises already in itself.[38] Accordingly, *velle* is a principle of selection from the generations of *nosse*.

By working back from these structural differences between the three *supposita*, and by taking the limit case in which each activity is both subject and its own object, these distinctions disappear in this reflexive result. The result, though, is not the object of first philosophy; the theologian's interest is the suppositive activity that produces it: 'Since God then is not composed of matter and form, He must be His own Godhead, His own Life, and whatever else is thus predicated of Him' (ST I, q.3, a.3).

I understand supposit then as an activity proceeding from and expressive of an intension, that is, expressive of one of the three designated activities of being, knowing or willing.

A final comment on the use of the term 'supposit'. The reason for the nomenclature is given in the already cited quotation: it is an expressive name of an intention, where intention means a stretching (*teino*) of will towards some end.[39] When this intention is rational, it is called a 'person'.[40] This suggests a directed incorporeal activity. We will obtain a further understanding though from the supposit's use by Aquinas in solving the problem of the divine persons. Aquinas considers this objection: when I ask you what are the three things in God, you respond 'three persons', which, the objection continues, can only be understood as three essences. In his reply,

Aquinas argues that the 'What?' question confuses two possible responses corresponding to the meanings of substance. 'What?' could mean 'What is in God that defines God?' to which the answer is 'the divine essence'. But 'What?' could also mean 'What acts or occurs in God?', and the response to this is 'three persons'. Aquinas actually phrases this latter point as 'What swims in the sea? A fish' but this is expressly used to exemplify a *suppositum* and thus an intentional act.[41] The sense of the example seems to be that we are not signifying any particular fish, or even genus of fish, but indicating the act of swimming in the sea and asking 'What is it that would act in the sea in this way, if not the sea-substance?' It follows that when we speak of the divine persons, we are asking 'What acts in God?' and not 'What defines God?' In the latter case the unity of essential definition is assured, in the former we can appreciate that there are three different intensions or activities at work in God.

An alternative reading of Aquinas in the Leibniz literature?

In the foregoing I have departed from the interpretation given by Brandon Look in his 'Leibniz and the "vinculum substantiale"'.[42] For this purpose I am only interested in Look's account of Leibniz's early and middle period views. While an incredibly important topic, the doctrine of the *vinculum substantiale* or substantial bond is explicitly developed in the late period and thus falls outside the scope of this work. I would agree with Look, however, that the earlier work to be discussed below is highly instructive regarding Leibniz's direction of travel.

Now, Look argues that supposit means the individual substance that combines matter and form, and that as God is without matter, his supposit is equivalent to his form or nature. In support Look cites a number of the articles of the *Summa* discussed above and I let my reading speak for itself: that (i) *per* Aubry, Aquinas starts from Aristotle's own abandonment of form and matter in favour of *energeia* and *dunamei*; and (ii) that he regards the pure or perfect activity of God as a ground of his power, a power which is expressed as the *supposita* or divine persons. Look's analysis – that supposit is equivalent to nature – is apparently best represented by Aquinas' questions on the incarnation in *ST Tertia Pars*.

Here we find:

> But if there is a thing in which there is nothing outside the
> species or its nature (as in God), the suppositum and the
> nature are not really distinct in it [*ibi non est aliud secundum*
> *rem suppositum et natura*], but only according to the reason-
> ing of intellect, inasmuch it is called 'nature' as it is an
> essence, and a 'suppositum' as it is subsisting. (ST III, q.2)

Yet this text requires great care: as we have seen, Aquinas
does not wish to impute into God a real distinction that
would support a severability and so a notion that two individuals are in God. Hence the statement that in God, nature
and supposit are not *really* distinct but only rationally so. It
is only in finite things which are considered as compositions
of form and matter that nature and supposit are really distinct, for while the nature rests specific, it is the supposit or
actuality which also includes determination by accidents and
individuating principles, that is, that which could not have
been included. This point is critical for Leibniz's account of
the supposit, as we shall see.

We can first note that in the *Pars Prima*, Aquinas may also
appear to assert that the supposit is a composite of matter of
form. This, however, is not normally the case, for he notes
that for 'things composed of matter and form, the nature or
essence must differ from the "suppositum" '.[43] As we have
seen, it is only God, who 'is his own essence', and that in
this case essence and supposit are identical. In humans, by
contrast, the supposit is expressed through formed matter.
Essence is described as that whereby a thing is what it is, an
equivalent of the *to ti en einai* of Aristotle (*Meta.* VII, 7). The
essence is thus activity from which the various properties of
a thing emanate and to which they are necessarily referred.
Essence is the answer to the question 'What?' or 'Quid?' and
thus it is named the quiddity of any given thing. Aquinas
provides us with an important indication of his thinking on
this: 'the essence of a thing is that which is expressed by
its definition'.[44] The essence of a thing is not equivalent to
its definition; the definition *expresses* the essence, and the
essence stands as ground for the definition. I claim that this
ground, in rational entities at least, is the self-actualising

34

activity of the supposit. In God this supposit is his essence; in finite creatures this supposit endeavours to express itself in its form, this form seeking to engage matter in constituting the individual as concrete *ens actu* or *ens potentiâ*. Supposit is not form and matter; it is the active ground for them.

By way of example of Aquinas' thinking on this point, we can usefully consider the divine persons. That the divine nature and the three persons rest rationally separate is then the basis for Aquinas' reply to art.2 objection 1. Aquinas has already argued that in the incarnation the divine nature is not in Christ the man; rather human nature. But, the objection runs, if nature and supposit (person) are not distinct, then the divine person is not in Christ either. On both a weak and strong reading, Look's interpretation must support the objection. If supposit and nature are identical in God, then denial of one necessarily denies the other. If supposit includes nature (and nothing else in God), then denying the premise (God's nature is in Christ) excludes the consequent (the person is in Christ). But this is false, objects Aquinas: it is the Word (that is, the Son[45]) which is united with human nature and not the divine nature. As technical as this is, Aquinas is noting that the substantial existence that is the Word as supposit expresses itself through incarnation. The human nature is activated by the supposit; it receives the supposit's perfected activity and so behaves otherwise than might be expected of a finite human nature left to its own devices. Furthermore, this unification of the Son and human nature in no way produces addition to or change of the divine nature. Accordingly, the act of union is *'in persona, non in natura'*.[46]

Yet, following objection 3 to the same article, union 'in the person' suggests that the individual human nature with which the Word united already has its one personality, which is to say it is already a substantial individual because otherwise it would be human nature in general. Does this imply that by supposit (person) we mean the union and not an element of what is united? In response, first we must remember that we are dealing with a theological special case: what is being united is the Word and an essence; matter is not relevant to Aquinas' discussion. Second, Aquinas replies[47] that taken alone human nature is a substance, but a substance in the same sense that Socrates' hand is a substance and incapable of subsisting separate from Socrates. When Aquinas states that Word and human nature unite in the person, he means that the divine person – the Son – is the perfection or whole which makes the human nature complete. This underlines that the union is not an aggregation of two parts of equal rank, but an inclusion of human nature in the activity of a divine person, which inclusion perfects that nature. Accordingly, while we speak of the person as the unity of Word and human nature, this is because the Word is the unifying activity for the human nature, and not an element of a third person or supposit. Surely to suggest otherwise, that a divine person on unification with human nature constitutes a further person, would suggest the possibility of two Christs, indeed a potentially infinite number of divine persons.

Étienne Gilson tells us[48] that faced with the problem of accounting for a plurality of supposits and indeed attributes in God, Duns Scotus proposes to speak of a difference between formal and essential distinction. The logic of formal truth (*alia formaliter vera*) distinguishes by means of definition within a formal order, and is proper to finite intellects. The logic of identity (*et alia per identitatem*), which is proper to the infinite intellect, looks to the identity of two terms in a third in which they disappear at infinity.[49] The logic of formal truth cannot identify the metaphysical relation which binds the two, and in the last analysis of abstraction what it is that makes 'man' is at best named 'quiddity'. It would be for Nicolas Cusanus to develop in *De Docta Ignorantia* an analogous proof of the viability of such a logic of identity from geometry.

Whatever we may feel about the niceties of these points, it must be admitted that *supposita* may, even in God, be considered distinct from natures if incarnation is to be possible.

The net result is an important division between nominal individuality (definition of substance) and active personhood (determination of subjectivity by intension). But has Aquinas not simply shifted the problematic into the distinction of incorporeal acts? He cannot escape the Philosopher's authority that this second sense of substance, on which the Angelic Doctor relies, is still substance. Any distinction of supposits is still, in a manner of speaking, a distinction of substance that threatens God's simplicity and gives rise the very objections and contortions discussed above. The confusing appeal to a rational rather than real distinction of supposit and nature is hardly satisfactory. If Leibniz is to make use of the supposit, does he inherit these same issues? We return to this problem once we examine how Leibniz uses the supposit.

Leibniz's use of the supposit

How then does Leibniz deploy the supposit? The earliest text (*c.*1668) treats of transubstantiation and immediately indicates that activity is central to this notion. It is worth underlining that what Leibniz seeks to demonstrate is that: 'Bread and wine, losing their own substance, acquire the substance of Christ's body; . . . only their appearance or accidents remaining; the substance of Christ's body being present' (A:VI, i, 508; L:115). With the Scholastic apparatus at our disposal, we are sensitive to the proposed change of substance within the bread and wine, and we suspect that intensional activity will have some role to play.

Leibniz proceeds by clarifying the terms of art, and he begins with substance, which he defines as 'being which subsists in itself', that is:

> . . . that which has a principle of action within itself. Taken as an individual, being which subsists in itself, or substance (either one), is a *suppositum*. In fact, the Scholastics customarily define a *suppositum* as a substantial individual. Now, actions belong to supposita [*actiones sunt suppositorum*]. Thus a *suppositum* has within itself a principle of action, or it acts. Therefore a being which subsists in itself has a principle of action within it. (A:VI, i, 508; L:115)

Though this is the first link in Leibniz's chain of reasoning, it very much assumes a specific theological direction, which, however, Leibniz will modify. As discussed previously, the *suppositum* could be identified with the act producing an essence (or potency). However, Leibniz is stressing that the act is also reflexive. I claim that Leibniz is here inspired by the *actus purus essendi* to argue that the substance of which Leibniz speaks is that whose act produces its own active essence, and that, *pace* Brandon Look, is why *suppositum* appears to refer to a composite.

Now it is precisely the distinction between activity and essence which will play a recurring role in the remaining *Demonstration*. Indeed, at the heart of the argument is a very definite decision to make activity the means by which (i) essences can be reordered within a hierarchy; and (ii) in its perfection, a transcendental principle of that reordering. That is, activity becomes a means of selection, division or judgement.

Leibniz asks us to note well that 'bread and wine are not transessentiated but transsubstantiated'. This indicates that bread and wine are composites of essence and supposit, and that what will change is the supposit. Before transubstantiation, Leibniz argues that the body of the bread and wine would be mere accidents or appearance without a *suppositum* of some sort. It is this *suppositum*, he has argued in Part I of the *Catholic Demonstrations* (L:110–11), which is the principle of motion in all bodies, which is to say the principle of variation of its essence. But what is this pre-subsisting supposit? Here there appears to be a slight regress in the argumentation, but what Leibniz envisages is a change of level. The pre-subsisting *suppositum* will be that which is appropriate to universal physical nature; the new *suppositum* will be that part of physical nature appropriated to Christ.

Leibniz's argument, appears to be this: the divine mind thinks a great many ideas, but each idea is defined as only having the potentiality to receive being from God. Once created, these substances may act, but what causes their action, or at least their endeavour to action? Leibniz would reject any sense in which God is the motive cause of action. Rather, he places *supposita* in bodies and defines a substance as that which has a principle of action within itself (the supposit) (L:117). But then is Leibniz claiming that bodies are capable of spontaneous motion, against both physical evidence and theological orthodoxy? Not at all. He claims that: the substance of 'bodies which lack reason is union with the universal mind' which acts as their 'concurring mind' (L:116). These *supposita* are the principle of action in bodies, but they are so in the presence of the concurring divine mind. If we think back to the way in which divine power is exercised in Aquinas, whereby it is the perfection of the divine will which is communicated to things and which procures movement from them, then perhaps we have a thesis for Leibniz's concurrent mind theory. It is because the *supposita* in bodies are in the presence of the divine concurring mind that they themselves initiate action. And so a principle of action in a body produces a variation of essence that is at least an infinitesimal motion from itself. Without the supposit a body does not possess this minimal principle of self-movement and then is merely accident or appearance. This motive *suppositum* corresponds to the verbs *agere* and *conari* (striving) in Leibniz's *Trinity*. *Mind*, though he does not use the term *conatus* in the *Demonstration*.

What happens on transubstantiation is that the supposit *agere/conari* identified with God is changed for a new supposit. The supposit in question is Christ:

> That whose substance is in its union with a concurring mind is transubstantiated when its union with the concurring mind is changed. . . . Hence bread and wine as bodies, when the concurrent mind is changed, are substantiated into the body of Christ, or taken up by Christ. (L:116)

Again, the 'species' of bread and wine has not changed;[50] rather the active principle has changed. But in what sense exactly? If the concurring mind thesis is indeed analogous to the presence of a perfected will in Aquinas, then the subsidiary bodies which compose to constitute the bread and wine, and so are 'normally' governed by a supposit which is appropriate to such bodies, are with transubstantiation placed in the presence of Christ. The effect seems to be somewhat like iron filings in the presence of a magnet: the individual bodies are all activated to switch round to this new metaphysical pole. The magnet does not move the filings; the filings move in the presence of power which would subsist whether the filings were present or not. Likewise, the perfection of Christ does not move the bodies composing the bread; the bodies move in the perfected presence of the concurring mind of Christ, according to the perfection of its own *activity* (supposit) and not *virtus, potestas* or any synonym of power Aquinas employs. Crucially, it is the individual *supposita* in these bodies which are activated, not the bodies themselves. At all levels, activity engages with activity.

Having said this, Leibniz is at pains to argue that not all the composing bodies are so activated. This is presumably because he fears that a complete transubstantiation would surely just produce a duplicate Christ. The bread and wine do remain ostensibly breadlike and winelike. He argues then that the transubstantiation is not so thoroughgoing as to constitute the bread and wine a new Nature within a Nature. Leibniz tells us that those essences which are not incompatible with the supposit can remain. Only essences which are incompatible with activity are lost. It therefore seems that the new supposit takes up the bread and wine, activates them, only insofar as is necessary to become identical with the body of Christ.

Hence my argument that for Leibniz activity, not power, becomes the positive means of selecting and organising essences, and that for essences to be individualised – exist – they require the gracious gift of activity by a concurring mind.

There is also one considerable difficulty in Leibniz's *Demonstration. Trinity. Mind* of 1671 proposes a distinction of *supposita* between *esse, scire* and *agere/conari*. The *Catholic Demonstrations*, however, appear only to speak of the intervention of mind, though 'mind' is to be understood in a new way as a principle of activity (L:118). In later works, we encounter a division between perception and appetite, but again the present text speaks only of perceptions (L:113). Does will in fact play no role?

To this I respond that the reference to mind signifies *esse–scire–agere* as a whole. There is no duality between a thinking Christ and a bread–matter which endeavours to act. Being, thinking and acting are all activities in Christ. Furthermore, in the *Catholic Demonstrations* we are dealing with limit cases. As we have seen, in God knowing and willing are coterminous in their perfection and God's ideas are indeed the active principle of every single body that lacks reason, for He is unrestrained by another. In similar vein the transubstantiation does not fail at least on the side of Christ; again the intellection of the concurring mind is not disappointed by the will. Finally, when Leibniz seeks to demonstrate the immortality of the human mind he has no occasion to consider acts of will of finite creatures over bodies. But this line of investigation, where the finitude of rational creatures leads to an operative difference between intellect and volition, is on the horizon of the text. The Supplement to the *Demonstrations* begins to consider action and passion in the context of explaining the difference between God's organisation of exterior bodies by means of *supposita*, and Christ's organisation of his body. The difference here is that God's idea is in every body as *suppositum* in fact, but the relationship between these bodies are different; 'they are, moreover, as action and passion'.[51] Christ on the other hand organises the relations of his body as are required for compatibility. Does this note suggest that volition would play a role at least when we consider the relative action and passions of creatures, whereby will does not achieve what is understood? I would venture that here, as the Supplement breaks off, we have a situation of a writer reappraising as he writes. Leibniz asks himself whether it is possible for Christ's mind to concur in more than one body at once. He might have fallen back on infinite power, but a theological difficulty with this (Leibniz has spent the *Demonstrations* remonstrating with his imagined opponents) is that Christ has already completed his generation in his body, and constitution of further bodies would suggest the incarnation is an incomplete act of God. Leibniz decides to give God the responsibility of allowing Christ to be in two bodies at once: 'For whatever God can think, that he can also do – at least if he wishes and holds it for the best . . . [ends]'. Thinking and doing – volition remains present just beneath the text.

For the purposes of this work it suffices to establish that the supposit is not an ad hoc device deployed in the *Demonstrations*, nor a synonym for form combined with matter. The supposit is rather a synonym for a perfected activity capable of expressing itself in particular actions, and it continues to be used through the early and middle periods we are studying. Proving the latter statement is uncontroversial, for in the 1686 *Discourse on Metaphysics* Leibniz writes: 'In the first place since activity and passivity pertain properly to individual substances (*actiones sunt suppositorum*) it will be necessary to explain what such substance is' (DM §8). We can find the same usage in 'On Nature itself, or on the Inherent Force of Created Things' which Leibniz published in the *Acta eruditorum* in September 1698.[52]

Our main focus will be Leibniz's legal texts which are prepared prior to these texts (in the early period), and so it is
enough to see that our thinker still adopts the supposit as at
least explicative of his own thinking on substance well into the
middle period. In holding that the supposit is a useful entry
point into understanding Leibniz's thinking on substantial
activity, I do not believe that I stray from Leroy Loemker's
own indication, or indeed the suspicions of Look. We have a
Scholastic notion of the supposit as a self-actualising activity
which constitutes a subject and person and which stands as a
principle in relation to its productions. Leibniz's explicit and
repeated referencing of the notion should, I believe, be taken
on board subject to Leibniz's own refinements, such as a refo-
cusing on activity at the apparent expense of *potentia*. Indeed,
equipped with the supposit as activity we can unpack several
other aspects of Leibniz's thought, not least the problem of
intensional equivalence.

3.2 The community of Trinity and Mind

Our second question concerning *Trinitas. Mens* pertains to a
key debate within Scholastic philosophy: how is it possible
that different individuals – the Trinity and a given mind –
can be treated as equivalent in structure but not the same
individual substance? Both Trinity and mind share the same
activities, the same *supposita*: *esse–scire–conari*, yet if God and
creature share the same act of being, for example, is it the case
either that they are the same being (risking Spinozism) or
that being adds nothing to our discussion (undercutting the
ontological proof)?

Being in common – Scholastic antecedents
Drawing closely on the analyses of Gaston Grua and Étienne
Gilson,[53] we might summarise the Scholastic positions as
follows. According to Aquinas the being of God transcends
the ordered genus of finite beings and cannot be known
through analysis of the latter. However, it is not the case that
Aquinas resorts to negative theology or simplistic analogy
either; he combines the orders of causal power and the essence
of being to provide for a middle way for being, between univocity and equivocity.[54] Aquinas argues[55] that being might be

understood a bit like the causality of heating and the essence
of hotness, such that a hotter thing heats the cooler (cause),
but what is hot by itself is essentially so. In like manner God's
being is necessarily part of his essence and in the highest
degree, such that this being is communicated by the act of
being (part of God's power) to that which is not, constituting
a causal order of being. The result is that Aquinas ties essence
to causality, using the transcendent priority of cause over
effect to distinguish what appears otherwise to be essentially
the same: the being of God and creature. Likewise, insofar as
a creature is good, this good is only said in a way analogous
to the goodness of God, but the *degree* of goodness is com-
parable to the eminent goodness of God. In this way it is possible to draw out a hierarchy of creatures according to their
degrees of perfection.[56]

To expand on this point, God, being simple and perfect,[57]
is said to have goodness and wisdom, but these are only
separable in finite thought; they are one in God. Further,
they are pre-eminent in God, and this by dint not of lack in
finite creatures but by excess in God. This pre-eminence is
said to be communicable[58] to creatures thus permitting a due
hierarchisation of nature according to the degree to which
each creature is graced with this pre-eminence.[59] By knotting
together the formal aspect of being in God's essence, with
the causal order of the world, Aquinas grants the power of
being and of creation a certain well-ordered, inbuilt hierarchy anchored in perfection.

We have a fine line here. Unlike Maimonides who regards
these properties or names of God (the Good etc.) in an entirely
negative fashion, such that they will never tell us anything
about the unknowable God, Aquinas does believe that names
such as goodness and wisdom are correctly attributable and
that it is only in their eminence and simplicity that they move
'beyond' the capacities of finite intellects. In this way Aquinas
seeks to maintain a degree of rationality on the side of the
divine against those who would advance negative theologies.
In short, the essences of all things remain accessible to finite
intellects in principle.[60]

John Duns Scotus seeks to allow each creature to have
immediate access to God's being while upholding the orthodoxy of God's transcendence of the genera of finite beings.

Scotus's univocity is commonly summarised as the proposition that being is said of God and creatures in the same way. It is worth noting though that the bridge the Subtle Doctor constructs requires univocal being to be understood as an activity situated in the being of God. The being in question is cause, but also principle (or perfection).[61] It is not that we know God directly, but that by finding being in things we may abstract the deficiencies of finitude in order to discover a perfect being. The same applies for all attributes, and so perfection of God. God and creature are of the same order of reasons, subject to the same rational attributes. But different as to perfection.

The structural core of this concept of being is the principle of non-contradiction, shared by God and creatures alike. This point should alert us though to the difference of metaphysical registers on which Scotus operates. Scotus has God construct a virtual world of possible entities, or quiddities, which do not exist unless created by act of God's will. These quiddities are real beings though – they have the being that must be predicated of this possible world constituted by God, and given that that being is entirely due to God's cause directly and in each case in the same way (they are all *virtualiter*) they share this same being in common: the *communitas entis in quid*.[62] This being subtends any quiddity which may be caused to exist, but it is neutral for finite beings in the sense that it does not distinguish between quiddities that are chosen to exist or otherwise.[63]

By placing the causal activity of being as the initial position for any 'grounded' knowledge of God, Duns Scotus sets the intellectual act as prior to the volitional act such that essence precedes existence. The focus of natural theology shifts slightly from an abstraction from what exists that leads us to analogise strongly with God, to an abstraction from the formal reasons for things, from essences in God. A virtually possible world ruled by non-contradiction is tractable for the purposes of passing to the perfections of a simple God. Given that quiddity is privileged, the corollary is a lessened role for effective causality and so the passage to existence, which passage adds nothing to our knowledge of God. Indeed, why God should choose to actualise this or that remains beyond our knowledge and thus appears utterly arbitrary – whence the subsequent attribution to Scotism of the epithet: voluntarism.

The equality of powers of intellect and will in Aquinas becomes a radical difference in Duns Scotus. In an extremely rich discussion, Aubry shows[64] how this difference is founded in the contingency of the divine will. It appears that Duns Scotus takes as his starting point Aristotle's observation that an individual may, for example, choose to sit or choose not to sit. Now it is impossible that the individual be sitting and not sitting simultaneously, but at least for Aristotle,[65] if an individual has chosen to sit and he could be standing, that state of standing accompanies the sitting as a logical possibility. These two states – sitting and not sitting – are contraries, and in a certain sense we see the finitude of the individual in their having perfected the act of sitting (they are sitting) but having not actualised the corresponding act of standing, which remains a potentiality.[66]

Observe how both sitting and not-sitting (the logical contraries) are united by a third term, which Aristotle identifies as the activity of the individual who chooses to (not) sit. This insight permits a new investigation with respect to 'science' and 'craft'.[67] Aristotle gives the example of medicine, which combines the knowledge of health and unhealth, but more importantly disease which is more than simply a logical negation of health, but is something against the nature of the healthy human. Here the rational activity of medicine stands over both health as its act, and over *against* disease which is the contrary of health and not implicated by the rational activity. In other words, disease stands in contradiction to medicine as rational activity, and it is in this sense that I comprehend Aubry's own account of 'contrary and contradictory active *potentiae*' in Duns Scotus.[68] Aubry argues that Duns Scotus takes what is apparently a purely logical doctrine in Aristotle and rearticulates it as an explicitly 'metaphysical' doctrine of real causation. The focus now is on the relationship between the opposed real states of affairs and the individual that unites both possible actualities. Yet it is not the individual as such which grounds possible states of affairs, nor that individual's intellect which enumerates those states of affairs (I can stand/I can sit). Rather it is the individual's will which forms the basis of the choice to stand or sit, and thus contains within itself 'potentially' contrary and as appropriate contradictory states of affairs. Furthermore,

Duns Scotus is at pains to point out that what is in issue here is the will as *cause* of these contradictory outcomes, and so it is for this reason that Duns Scotus stresses precision in his phrasing: '. . . I say "something is caused in a contingent manner" and not "something is contingent" '.[69]

In Chapters 3 and 4 I will expand on this account of science and craft as the basis of contingency and so becoming, but it is perhaps enough to observe that the choices artisans make in composing the real are situated in a will that 'contains' contradictory potencies and is thereby contingent and free. By analogy from the artisan, so the Creator, and so the choices made in composing not simple things such as tables and houses, but individuals such as humans: *quiddities*. In this way we are led to consider what chooses between contingent states of affairs in the world, and are thus drawn to consider the will, and ultimately to consider the divine will as that which is by definition capable of the infinite choices necessary to realise quiddities. At the same time though the community of quiddities, being in God's will, remains due to the simplicity of God – Scotus denies any community of being between actually existing entities.[70]

As Gaston Grua explains,[71] Duns Scotus never makes God and creature coincide in anything real, and he only concedes to them a common univocal attribute in a weakened sense in order to explain how we can know without our own simple concept. For him the divine unity or simplicity excludes the formal distinctions between divine attributes, and even the distinction of Thomist reason such that are thus not several perfections in God. Rather there is one alone and indistinct which coincides absolutely with his essence, or rather attributive concepts or names which only express the diversity of his effects. This minimises the community of being in its greatest degree, making common being only the least starting point for any attempt at theology.

In the times that followed, Grua tells us,[72] the discussions between the Thomists and the Scotists continued. Suárez, the first author of a metaphysics that had split from Aristotelean commentary, favoured Duns Scotus, despite his more empiricist epistemology, by calling being *real* since it is possible and not contradictory, and an abstraction made from actual existence. Although known from existence and distinct from experience by reason alone, essence is thus conceivable alone and first as with Duns Scotus, and metaphysics is the science of essence, not of existing beings. On the other hand, in abstracting from the differences between created and uncreated in its first analytic movement to essence, metaphysics conceives of being as common to all beings, univocal in one sense, although the infinite and finite, God and creatures, are distinguished in its second movement returning to existence, and are but analogues by analogy of attribution. This said, however, all the analogies of Suárez's 'special part' to his *Disputations* rest on and lead back to the univocity of the general part, and it would not be uncommon, Grua claims, for his followers to slip back into univocity. Indeed, Leibniz will say of Suárez's writings that 'there is gold in that dross', picking out several theses including 'God's communion with created things'.[73] Leibniz does not, as Grua notes, make any reference to analogy.[74]

Leibniz and the community of thought

Whether inspired by Suárez and his school or otherwise, Leibniz adopts the position that the being of God and of all creatures is in common, and Gaston Grua has argued as much.[75] But in what does commonality consist? Grua argues that the commonality arises because of 'the laws of being common', but our investigation of the supposit as an ordered activity leads us to claim that it is the equivalence of this ordered activity which ensures equivalence across substances, not the 'dead' laws decreed for each substance. Leibniz appears not to have engaged directly with the question of being in common in a dedicated text, but Grua shows that references to the doctrine are littered across his theological, mathematical and metaphysical work, with a particular concentration through the middle period and in his responses to Arnauld and Locke. A survey of these treatments will, I claim, admit of the active *suppositum* interpretation of *esse–scire–agere*.

The thread of this analysis traces the *esse*–intellect relation in the first row of the column and the way in which this intellective supposit sits at the heart of both God and all creatures, differentiated only by their degrees of perfection – their powers of acting and understanding insofar as rationally ordered in intellect. The core this discussion can be found in Book II of the *Nouveaux Essais* (written up from notes in 1698). Here the question of being is framed according to the language of substance and attribute, and though obviously addressing Locke, given Leibniz's 'difference on principles' from Locke, this text offers much when considered opposite Descartes and Spinoza.[76] Taking for example the Spinozan structure, we have substance as that which conceives itself and so is self-caused, and attribute as the means by which the intellect grasps the essence of substance.[77] The attributes, however, are not static, but verbs of substance which define it eternally, and take two forms known to humans: thinking and extending.[78] Spinoza then uses the attributes, being the sole defining characteristics of infinitely different substances, to establish that any two substances with the same attributes must in fact be the same.[79] To my mind this is nothing but an argument as to intensional equivalence: it is not comparison of content (substance) which determines equivalence, but rather comparison of act. Commonly this action will be a relationship between things, but in the Spinozist case the 'thing' is only self-related. Finally, we note Spinoza's assertion that the more attributes a substance has, the more reality or being it expresses; God or Nature being the one substance which expresses itself through infinitely many attributes thus having the most reality or being.

With this background in mind, Leibniz, playing the role of *Theophilus*, admonishes his interlocutor *Philalethes* for attempting to distinguish two substances by a complete abstraction of all differentiating characteristics:

> If you distinguish two things in a substance – the attributes and the predicates, and their common subject – it is no wonder that you cannot conceive anything special in this subject. That is inevitable, because you have already set aside all the attributes through which details could be conceived. ... The same alleged difficulty could be brought against the notion of *being*, and against all that is plainest and most primary. (NE:218)

The argument denies substantial difference; all difference is due to the differing attributes of a substance. Furthermore, this insight applies *mutatis mutandis* to all primary notions, including *being*. The difference from Spinoza is that Leibniz will distinguish substances by their attributes (which for him include being), and will argue that being also is capable of distinction. Does that render Leibniz a thinker of plurivocity? Not so, for Leibniz permits distinctions according to two registers which nevertheless allow him to retain a community of beings: (i) he will regard being, along with knowing and endeavouring, as *primary* or *innate ideas* that express the rational activity of God, thus permitting intensional equivalence at the core of creaturely existence; (ii) he too will link being and reality, but will use reality to distinguish what attribute cannot. In this last section I deal with the first issue.

The core of Leibniz's argument is that the self-actualising activity of being and knowing are both the essence of God and creatures, and as such place in the human a more intimate reflective knowledge of God's being and knowing than the knowledge humans have of the physical world. Furthermore, the self-actualising production of these activities, the enaction of being and of necessary or eternal truths, are Leibniz's primary notions. These notions are shared by God and rational creature, not because they think the same object nor because they are the same thing which thinks, but because their activity of being and of knowing is intensionally equivalent. Acting or endeavouring are a different matter (one which engages Leibniz's use of *potentia*) and will be examined in the chapters that follow.

Perhaps the clearest statement of this view, beyond the parallels sketched in the *Trinitas. Mens* of the early period, is found in an unsent letter dated 14 July 1686 and intended for Arnauld. Here Leibniz debates the following problem: if each substantial form of an individual contains a complete account of its actions, and it is through this that the individual is differentiated from others, then how can one individual be morally compared to another? They all have different paths which they endeavour to follow; one cannot say that because Peter did do something, that Paul should have done it in his place. Furthermore, how can an individual even make comparisons with his prior actions, for a substantial form (or entelechy) is a 'source' of particular actions but 'doesn't have memory or consciousness'. The substantial form:

... won't have what makes someone the same person in morals, making him capable of punishment and reward. That is reserved for rational and intelligent souls, who have very great privileges. It could be said that intelligent substances or persons express God more immediately than they express the universe, whereas bodies express the universe more immediately [*plustost*] than they express God. For God is himself a thinking substance who is more intimately in touch with persons than with other [purely corporeal] substances, and joins with persons to form a society, the republic of the universe, of which he is monarch. (To Arnauld (unsent) 14 July 1686, Ger:II, 75–6.)

Echoing Aquinas, I say that Leibniz proposes a philosophy of expression in which particular phenomena, like signs, express an anterior activity. The model, as far as I read it, makes a distinction between the series of derivative actions that in aggregate make up a substantial form's course during its life, and the activity which this series expresses. This primary activity is not God's activity in the sense that a human's actions are derivable from God's activity directly. That would be Spinozism. Rather, the primary activity expressed does pertain to each intelligent substance; Leibniz's point is that the primary activity of a finite intelligent substance itself expresses the being and knowing (and to a degree the acting) of God. There is a certain structural rapport between divine and finite activities, which Leibniz seeks to describe in a subsequent letter through a series of analogies:

One thing expresses another (in my language) when there is a constant and settled relation [*rapport*] between what can be said of the one and the other. It is thus that a perspectival projection expresses its pure geometric form [*géométral*]. This expression is common to all forms, and it is a genus of which ... intellectual knowledge is a species. Yet this expression occurs above all because all substances sympathise. (To Arnauld, 9 October 1687, Ger:II, 112.)

While it is not altogether clear what Leibniz means by 'sympathise' in the context substance, especially because substantial or monadic relations will remain in issue into the late period, this passage is instructive because it confirms a certain degree of structure. We have a hierarchy of genus and species between the expression at the substantial level and the individual actions of a substance. This might be understood as the relationship between the topological constants of a square (it has four vertices) and the infinite variety of its possible appearances under deformation through projection. At the higher level of genus we have the expressive relation between all substances (including God, by the previous paragraph). This confirms the suggestions of *Trinitas. Mens* that verb and noun columns are deliberately distinguished, and that Trinity and Mind are placed by Leibniz on the same structural plane.

Yet is substantial 'sympathy', according to an expressive structure, all that Leibniz can offer us during our period of study? Well it seems that Leibniz is prepared to flesh out his doctrine by isolating also the particular genera of activity, notably being and knowing, as part of his theory of primary or innate notions, developed in his middle period notes on Locke which would become the first two books of the *Nouveaux Essais*.

As to primary notions, Leibniz appears to argue that though a substantial form describes an operation of organising matter as the definition of an individual, we may always find in that substantial form root organising principles, of which being is the first. This does not mean, however, that an individual's substantial form is identical to God's. Leibniz's *Theophilus* is provoked into the following response when *Philalethes* advances the Spinozist doctrine that all finite things are modifications of the same substance: 'If that inference were valid, it would also follow that since God, finite spirits and bodies "participate in the same common nature" of being, they will differ only in the "different modification" of the being.'[80]

Leibniz goes on to refer back to an earlier definition of substance redolent of his substantial form or complete concept theory of substance, using this to underline that properly substances and concrete things must be considered before accidents and abstractions. A number of things are going on here. Descartes and Spinoza held that substances were replete with Scholastic 'occult qualities' that clouded thought, and to combat this Descartes made the attributes of thought and extension – attributes of substance – the logically and mathematically well-ordered bases of all philosophy. Substance remained, but only acted as a bearer of attributes and their modifications. Spinoza could be said to have taken the next step of simply reducing the number of substances to one. Leibniz is diverting readers away from the Cartesian conclusion of a common nature which could erroneously be drawn from his use of the categories of substance, attribute and mode, an intention confirmed in a late period letter to De Volder ('two individual substances should be distinguished more than modally').[81] He emphasises the substantial form as being that about which we can determine those primary aspects which must 'necessarily be the case' and those derivative ones which are found to be the case through other things.[82]

Now to be fair to Spinoza, we might adopt a Leibnizian lens of activity and say that he too differentiates finite creatures and he does so by reference to substantial activity (for Spinoza *potentia*). The thinking individual already expresses the divine activity when she thinks the clear and distinct truth of her own thought. The object for the practical Spinozist is to locate and think all such self-actualising thoughts, of which the most powerful is the *idea Dei*. Observe then that humans are indeed distinguished by the possession of power understood as deriving from just these especial thoughts self-actualising within the divine substance. It remains the case that all substances are the same, but we do have a suggestion for our understanding the community of substances in Leibniz: these special ideas that express substantial activity.

What are these primary aspects of any substance? Later in the *Nouveaux Essais* Grua shows[83] how Leibniz again encounters these questions, and *Theophilus* reiterates both that knowledge of the doctrine of substances 'in common'[84] and of the membership of angels and minds of common ideas depends on our understanding of thought and of God,[85] but in these later discussions Leibniz does not wish to reopen the investigation of 'innate ideas'.[86] We are instead referred then to Book I of the *Nouveaux Essais*:

The ideas of *being, possible* and *same* are so thoroughly innate that they enter into all our thoughts and reasoning, and I regard them as essential to our minds. . . . I have said too that we are so to speak innate to ourselves; and since we are beings, being is innate in us – the knowledge of being is comprised in the very knowledge that we have of our selves.[87]

As before 'essence' is not a definition but what is expressed by a definition: self-actualising activity. Here 'being' is identified as innate not because the word 'being' or even its signifying capacity are shared, but because being as activity is essential to being a substance. Likewise, possibility and similarity – picked out because of the Lockean subtext – flow from what it is to be a rational substance, or a substance whose act of being is inherently rational and constitutes intellect. For Leibniz, it would seem, it is a contradiction to claim that an intelligent substance does not innately know being and knowing – a doctrine after all common to Descartes and Spinoza.

Is this being the same being as that of God? I underline again that the relationship is expressive of an exemplar: that this being is a principle (or final cause) of the being of finite creatures and that as such the complete concept of the finite creature must express the concept of being elaborating intellect as part of itself. The substantial form of a creature differs formally from God in that the former's concept, while containing being, also contains some unspecified conceptual differentia other than those which are properties of God (such as necessary existence). These differentia, about which Leibniz is remarkably coy in the *Nouveaux Essais*,[88] are subordinate to the core activity of being that substance expresses. Hence 'God belongs to me more intimately than my body'.[89]

Finally, in the *Discourse on Metaphysics* Leibniz will go as far as to identify this being that resides in creatures so completely with that of God that it even expresses that most divine of properties in us – infinitude: 'That could be called an essence which includes all that we express, and as it expresses our union with God himself, it has no limits and nothing goes beyond it' (DM §116). I read Leibniz as arguing that in this sense being is common to both God or creatures, but being is not completely determinative of the substantial activity of any two substances. This hierarchy appears to follow both a Scholastic and Neoplatonic division between a primary substance, created substances, their life in the world as souls, and their bodies. Leibniz has sketched out a relationship of expression between God and Mind considered as active substances, and a derivative relation between finite Minds and particular actions (and passions). Hence he writes in the 1686 *De Deo Trino*: 'Now, what happens to a certain extent in a created Mind occurs in God in the most perfect manner' (A:VI, iv, 2292). This is not a statement of analogy, as Antognazza claims,[90] but a stronger claim, supported by our foregoing discussion, of structural equivalence of activities otherwise distinguished by perfection. From what we have seen, the general structure of *Trinitas. Mens* appears to have been preserved at least up until the 1690s.

This leads us naturally to this question: if primary notions are the raw material of any substantial form that guarantee a communal relation with God, then what differentiates God from rational creatures? If being is innately known to every thinking thing, and this being is guaranteed to be rational by God, then why are the activities of finite substances not only equivalent to the divine activity, but identical with it as Spinoza suggests? The short answer, I claim, is that Leibniz will use degree of *reality* to distinguish substances, and so apparently follow the Schoolmen as much as the natural rights theorists in grounding human lack in its subjection to power, of God, nature or other humans. If being and knowing permit communion with God, it is between act and endeavour that Leibniz appears to locate a fundamental differentiator. This in turn engages questions of will and of *potentia* which we must examine in some detail in the chapters that follow.

4. Conclusion

The doctrine stated in *Trinitas. Mens* is that Trinity and Mind express the same activities of *esse–scire–agere seu conari*. These intensional activities are identified with the Scholastic *supposita*, which are understood as self-actualising organisational principles that are, at least miraculously, transferable between bodies such as the Host. Leibniz sets up a hierarchy between the primary *supposita* (being, knowing, acting) in God, and their expression in finite rational substances.

At a lower level each generic activity is itself expressed in specific actions (and passions). At the level of thought, intelligible being is expressed in intellect; knowing is expressed in images or phenomena; acting or endeavouring is expressed in will or *potentia*.

In this way Leibniz appears to make two key movements in the history of power. He reinstates Aristotelean activity (*energeia*) and its perfected correlate entelechy as his supreme concept that unites God and human in a regime of expression. *Potentia* appears to be relegated to a specific moment of endeavour, and is thus subordinated to the volitional supposit. But is this appearance deceptive? We saw that the Thomist notion of power flows from the self-actualising activity of God: the *purus actus essendi*. Does not the Leibnizian notion of expression of activity amount to a theory of *potentia* under a different name?

This question is complicated. On the one hand Leibniz seems motivated by the challenges of Hobbism and Spinozism to reduce *potentia*'s metaphysical role, while at the same time affirming the positive explanatory aspects of *potentia* within any nascent physics. Leibniz will do this by linking *potentia* to degree of reality, that is, to the number of other substances which an individual is able to express. On the other hand, Leibniz's relegation of *potentia* poses its own metaphysical difficulties. First, does he mean to say that the Aristotelean counterpart of *energeia* – *dunamei* as in-potency – has no place in his philosophy, and that all is activity? Second, and perhaps more forcefully, if Leibniz is to adopt a theory of finitude in which primary activity is expressed in particular acts determined by passions, from where do the particular passions derive if not from a primary potency?

This leads us to the question of differentiation of substances. If all rational substances express the same activities, one wonders how we might distinguish God and rational creature, and we have shown that Leibniz too appears to advance a strong sense of univocity, not least because the Leibnizian *esse* is bound up with intellect (and space) and is not a pure homogeneity. Yet what, in terms of *esse* as such distinguishes God and creature? As with Duns Scotus the answer is power, but Leibniz will reaffirm a notion of rationalised eminence using his definition of power as graded by perfection or degree of reality. In the next chapter I propose to situate this move in the wider context of the theory of power, and show how Leibniz's rationalisation of power helps us to understand the relationship between *esse–scire–agere seu conari*. This discussion will take us into the 1690s and Leibniz's physical innovations, and will prepare the ground for a more detailed investigation of the will, power and their interrelation.

Notes

1. Étienne Gilson, *L'Être et l'essence*, 3rd edn (Paris: Vrin, 2008) pp.82–3.
2. Gwenaëlle Aubry, *Dieu sans la puissance: dunamis et energeia chez Aristote et chez Plotin* (Paris: Vrin, 2006) pp.13–14.
3. Gr:559: A:VI, ii, 287–8. The translation is taken (and modified following suggestions by Lloyd Strickland) from Maria Rosa Antognazza, *Leibniz on the Trinity and the Incarnation* (Gerald Parks trans.) (New Haven: Yale, 2007) p.43.
4. Antognazza, *Leibniz on the Trinity*, p.44.
5. L:117.
6. L:119 n.11.
7. Aubry, *Dieu sans la Puissance*, pp.89ff., in conjunction with Aubry, *Genèse du Dieu souverain* (Paris: Vrin, 2018) pp.175ff. In writing this book I had initially thought to direct readers to Aubry's work and thus assume a certain amount of knowledge, but given both the quality of that work and legal readership of this, the editors and I ultimately concluded that this summary would be beneficial. All mistakes in it are my own. The references that follow are drawn from Aubry's work unless otherwise stated.
8. *Meta.* VIII [1026a33–b2]; XII [1070b17–1072a20].
9. *Meta.* IX, 6–7, particularly [1049a1–16], and Aubry, *Genèse*, p.22.
10. *Meta.* XII [1071b20].
11. *Meta.* IX [1046a1–3], as indicated to me by Anton Schütz.
12. Thomas Aquinas, *Summa Theologiae* (hereafter the 'ST'), in the *Opera Omnia. Leonine Edition*, vols 4–12 (Vatican City: Typis Polyglottis Vaticanis, 1882–) I, q.3 a.4, r.
13. Aubry, *Genèse*, pp.206–7.
14. Critical edition of P. Marc, C. Pera and P. Caramello (eds), *Liber de veritate catholicae Fidei contra errores infidelium deu Summa contra Gentiles* (hereafter 'Contra Gentiles'), vols 1–4

(Turin and Rome: Marietti, 1961), I, 28, 2, where the roman numeral refers to the Book number within *Contra Gentiles*.

15. See e.g. ST I, q.36, a.3, r.1.
16. *Meta.*V [1017b25].
17. Aubry, *Dieu sans la Puissance*, pp.82, 85.
18. Henri Focillon, *La Vie des formes* (Paris: PUF, 1964) p.51.
19. [1043a25].
20. Aubry, *Dieu sans la puissance*, p.84.
21. [1043a23].
22. [1043a26–7].
23. 'Nam in significatione naturae includitur solum id quod est de ratione *speciei*; suppositum autem non solum habet haec quae ad rationem speciei pertinent, sed etiam alia quae ei *accidunt*; et ideo suppositum signatur per totum, natura autem, sive quidditas, ut pars formalis. In solo autem Deo non invenitur aliquod accidens praeter eius essentiam, quia suum esse est sua essentia, ut dictum est; et ideo in Deo est *omnino idem* suppositum et natura. In angelo autem *non* est *omnino idem*: quia aliquid accidit ei praeter id quod est de ratione suae speciei: quia et ipsum esse angeli est praeter eius essentiam seu naturam; et alia quaedam ei accidunt quae omnino pertinent ad suppositum, non autem ad naturam' (my emphasis). *Quaestiones de quodlibet*, q. 2, art. 2, col., in Aquinas, *Opera Omnia. Leonine Edition*.
24. Gwenaëlle Aubry, '*Ousia Energeia* and *actus purus essendi* – from Aristotle to Aquinas: Some Groundwork for an Archeology of Power' (2015) *Tijdschrift voor Philosophie* 827–54.
25. ST I, q.25 a.1.
26. Aubry, *Dieu sans la puissance*, pp.89ff, but also pp.168ff., *Meta.* [1046a1] and *Meta.* XII [1073a13ff].
27. E.g. *Contra Gentiles* I, 20, 9: 'Nulla potentia infinita est potentia in magnitudine. Potentia primi motoris est potentia infinita. Ergo non est in aliqua magnitudine. Et sic Deus, qui est primus motor, neque est corpus neque est virtus in corpore.'
28. *Meta.* IX.
29. ST I, q.14, a.3, and I, q.1, a.2.
30. ST I, q.27, a.1.
31. Ibid.
32. ST I, q.29, a.2.
33. '. . . He has knowledge even of things that are not.' ST I, q.14, a.9.
34. After a certain manner mirroring Proclus, who holds in his

Elements of Theology that substances are differentiated hierarchically by their generative productivity (e.g. props.8, 9). Proclus, *Elements of Theology* (E.R. Dodds trans.), 2nd edn (Oxford: Clarendon Press, 1963).

35. ST I, q.27, a.4.
36. *Contra Gentiles* I, 28, 6: 'Unumquodque perfectum est inquantum est actu; imperfectum autem secundum quod est potentia cum privatione actus. Id igitur quod nullo modo est potentia sed est actus purus, oportet perfectissimum esse. Tale autem Deus est. Est igitur perfectissimus.'
37. ST I, q.19, a.2, r.2.
38. ST I, q.27, a.4, r.2.
39. ST I, q.47, a.1.
40. Ibid.
41. ST I, q.29, a.4, r.2.
42. Brandon Look, 'Leibniz and the *"vinculum substantiale"'* (1991) 30 *Studia Leibnitiana: Sonderheft*, p.61. David Grumett follows Look in this: *Teilhard de Chardin: Theology, Humanity and Cosmos* (Leuven: Peeters, 2006) p.110.
43. ST I, q.3, a.3.
44. Ibid.
45. Aquinas follows and expands on Augustine: 'eo Filius quo Verbum, et eo Verbum quo Filius' (ST I, q.27, a.2, *Contra Gentiles*, IV, 11.
46. ST III, q.2, a.2, r.1
47. ST III, q.2, a.2, r.3.
48. Étienne Gilson, *Jean Duns Scot: Introduction à ses Positions Fondamentales* (Paris: Vrin, 1952) p.244.
49. Gilson, *Jean Duns Scot*, p.251.
50. L:117.
51. A:VI, i, 512; L:119.
52. L:502; Ger:IV, 506: 'actiones sunt suppositorum'.
53. Étienne Gilson, *L'Être et l'essence*, 3rd edn (Paris: Vrin, 2008) ch.3.
54. Étienne Gilson, *Le Thomisme – Introduction à la philosophie de saint Thomas d'Aquin* (Paris: Vrin, 1989) pp.123–5.
55. *Contra Gentiles* II, 15.
56. Henry of Ghent follows Aquinas this far: *Summa* q.2, a.21, *Summa (Quaestiones Ordinariae), arts I–V* (2001). G.A. Wilson (ed.), *Summa (Quaestiones Ordinariae), arts I–V* (2001), in *Henrici de Gandavo Opera Omnia* (Leuven: Leuven University Press, 1979 et seq.) (initially also Leiden: E.J. Brill).
57. ST I, q.1, a.3 and a.7.
58. ST I, q.13, a.8, ad.3.

59. ST I, q.13, a.12; I, q.14, a.8.
60. Henry of Ghent differs from Aquinas here, claiming rather that the rightly reasoning finite intellect discovers that the being of God and of creatures are distinct (see *Summa* above).
61. Gaston Grua, *Jurisprudence universelle et théodicée selon Leibniz* (Paris: PUF, 1953) pp.32–3.
62. Gilson, *Jean Duns Scot*, p.99.
63. Ibid. p.105.
64. Aubry, *Genèse*, pp.244ff.
65. *Meta.* IX, 2–3 [1046a36–1047b1].
66. As Aubry notes, Aristotle is less than strict in his use of in-potency (*dunamei*) and possibility (*dunaton*) in these passages of *Meta.* IX.
67. *Meta.* IX, 2 [1046b6] and expanding the point, 5 [1047b31–1048a10].
68. Aubry, *Genèse*, p.245.
69. Duns Scotus, *Treatise on the First Principle*, quoted by Aubry, *Genèse*, p.245.
70. Gilson, *Jean Duns Scot*, p.368.
71. Grua, *Jurisprudence*, pp.34–8. And here I am much indebted to Grua (with interpretative assistance from Gilson) for the discussions of Nominalism, Cusanus and Suárez, to which I add certain comments and clarifications to emphasise the bearing on the doctrine of community of being.
72. Ibid.
73. NE:IV, viii, §9; NE:431.
74. Antognazza reads Leibniz otherwise: Maria Rosa Antognazza, 'Leibniz de Deo Trino: Philosophical Aspects of Leibniz's Conception of the Trinity' (2001) 37 *Religious Studies* 1–13 at p.9.
75. Grua, *Jurisprudence universelle*, pp.34–8.
76. Spinoza's concept of substance becomes an explicit target in the correspondence with De Volder (letter of 10 November 1703, L:532).
77. *Ethics* Part I, Definitions.
78. See Stephen Connelly, *Spinoza, Right and Absolute Freedom* (Abingdon: Routledge, Birkbeck Law Press, 2015) ch.1.
79. *Ethics*, Part 1, prop.5.
80. NE:II, xiii, §18; NE:150.
81. Letter of 20 June 1703, AG:174.
82. NE:II, xii, §6; NE:145.
83. Grua, *Jurisprudence universelle* p.71.
84. NE:IV, viii, §9; NE:432.
85. NE:III, i, §5; NE:276.

86. NE:IV, x, §1; NE:434–5.
87. NE:I, iii, §3; NE:101–2.
88. NE:II, xxiii, §§2–3; NE:118.
89. Ibid. This appears to echo the Neoplatonic doctrine that each effect participates its cause; that the cause can be found in and expressed by the effect. See e.g. Proclus, *Elements* props.7ff.
90. Antognazza, 'Leibniz de Deo Trino', p.9.

Two

Potency and Supposita

1. Introduction

If I am correct that *esse, scire* and *agere* play the role of *supposita* in Leibniz's philosophy during our period of analysis, what is the precise difference between them? Why three different rows in *Trinitas. Mens*? The difference, I claim, results from Leibniz's engagement with the concept of power (in-potency; *dunamei*). Our focus now shifts from activity and supposit, to a closely implicated debate concerning the relationship between activity and potency. The original actuality/in-potency distinction is inherited from Aristotle, who argued that the presence of *dunamei* marks a negative determination of activity and so of perfection (*energeia*; entelechy) and consequently there is no *dunamei* in the Prime Mover. But Leibniz writes in the shadow of the Schoolmen, and as Gwenaëlle Aubry has expertly shown it is Aquinas who returns power to God and has him wield it as sovereign over his creation. Importantly power is used to explain the productions of *nosse* and *velle* by *esse*; Son and Spirit by Father; creatures by the One.

Building respectfully on that research programme, I ask whether Leibniz advances a similar doctrine of power; whether *esse, scire, agere* are to be understood not as activities in themselves but as powers of creation with respect to each other according to the hierarchy of the *Trinitas. Mens* matrix. I will proceed by outlining Aquinas' understanding of act and power and use this to interpret *Trinitas. Mens*. This will lead us to question in detail whether Leibniz has in fact relegated power in his system – removed it from the divine being – reversing a move made by Aquinas with respect to Aristotle. I will seek to establish that:

(a) Leibniz effects a terminological demotion of power (*potentia*) to a notion defined relative to action and passion. The effect appears to be to deny a predication of power to God, restoring the Aristotelean characterisation of the Prime Mover as pure activity.
(b) Yet, power continues to play a key role for Leibniz, though he prefers not to use the term as his contemporaries might and deploys several names for this notion.
(c) In particular, I claim that Leibniz will seek to replace what Aquinas calls the *potentia* of a supposit or person with his notions of suppositive activity and expression.
(d) In this chapter we shall isolate Leibniz's own signification of his term *potentia* as pertaining to particular acts and passions that are derivative of primary active and passive forces.

To do this, in the first two sections I am going to revisit our discussions of the Aristotelean and Scholastic theory of power, from its negative notion of in-potency, to its status as a positive effect of a substance on another. If in Chapter 1 I provided a general account of what is at stake, I now want to re-present this debate in terms of its innate conceptual structure, so to speak. This approach will set up a 'square of power', which is an interpretative device that I will use to demonstrate the alterations Leibniz is making to the traditional theory. It also will provide a useful device for comparisons with Grotius and Hobbes in due course. In the third section I follow the advice of the Stagirite and indeed the Schoolmen, and work back from Leibniz's physical account of power and his innovations concerning active and passive forces in his middle period, to abstract his theory of activity and potency. Using this abstract structure, which I find is congruent with what I call the Aristotelean square of power, I examine in the fourth section how power is accounted for in Leibniz's theory of substantial forms (or 'immaterial entities'), and here mark Leibniz's metaphysical innovations whereby *potentia* is demoted to activity.

A word of caution though: there is another sense of 'power' more akin to dominion (let us accept a naïve understanding of this word for now), which is at play in Leibniz's thought. Now Aquinas appears to suture power in the sense of dominion to power in the sense of *dunamis*; *potentia* then occludes the significance of this innovation. As just noted, Leibniz will reverse the terminological fusion whereby dominion+*dunamis* becomes *potentia*, but this does not mean, I claim, that a notion of power as dominion is not present. Rather, as we will see in this chapter and the following, the notion of power as dominion can be found in the relationship between *supposita*. The reader should bear this decoupling of the two senses in mind in what follows.

2. Rationalising power

2.1 The Scholastic framework: Aquinas and power

Giorgio Agamben, in his essay 'On Potentiality',[1] argues that Aristotle's *Physics* and *Metaphysics* see a shift in analysis of being from the form/matter opposition of his earlier work to one between *energeia* and *dunamis*.[2] This is not a mere replacement of terms within an accepted framework; rather *energeia* and *dunamis* seem to operate along a different line of attack, and to confuse form and *energeia* for example is to commit a serious error.[3] I would agree that form and matter should not be confused with *energeia* and *dunamis*, but nor do I think that form and matter should be jettisoned insofar as they are considered causally.

The structural relationship of the core terms of art is neatly encapsulated by Aubry:

> The term '*energeia*' ('act', 'actuality') was itself invented by Aristotle. *Dunamis*, on the other hand, was already found in classical Greek, where it means 'force', 'strength', or 'potency' in the sense of active power. In correlating *dunamis* with *energeia* and coining the phrases *dunamei/ energeia* ('in-potency/in-act'), Aristotle invented a new concept, namely that of in-potency. In-potency is no more reducible to active power than it is to passive potency.[4]

I propose to focus on the Scholastic, particularly Thomist, understanding of the Philosopher's thinking on *energeia* and *dunamei*. I take for granted the problematic[5] rendering of the two terms by Aquinas as *actus* and *potentia*, though in English

I follow Aubry in rendering these in act and in-potency. The value in adopting the Thomist perspective for interpretative purposes will shortly become apparent.

We might understand the Thomist take on the Aristotelean schema as follows: at a higher level of generality we have the opposition – the qualitative contraries – of *actus* and *potentia*; directly beneath these at the level of particularity we have form and matter also as contraries. Form stands as the subaltern of *actus*; matter as the subaltern of *potentia*. This can be represented in the familiar Apulean square:[6]

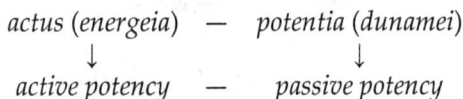

$$actus\ (energeia) \quad - \quad potentia\ (dunamei)$$
$$\downarrow \qquad\qquad\qquad\qquad \downarrow$$
$$active\ potency \quad - \quad passive\ potency$$

Having constructed this 'square of power' (as I shall call it for convenience), we can understand why Aquinas, in his perceptive reading of the Philosopher, would argue in the *Summa Theologiae* that 'active potency is not contrary to act, but is rather founded upon it'.[7] He argues this because:

(a) By definition, the relationship between the general *actus* and particular active potency is a subaltern one, and not one of contrariness.
(b) Active potency is understood to be formal in the sense that a substance is in active potency if it works in accordance with its nature and not the nature of another (whereby it would be passive).
(c) Save in the case of God, *actus* is considered as only contingently in the entity whose nature is set into action, but this *actus* is a condition of that entity's being in action as an individual.

Aquinas then doubles this square of power so that we may speak of the form/matter relation across two registers: the immaterial and the material:

Thus, matter and form divide natural substance, while potency and act divide being in common [*ens commune*]. Accordingly, whatever follows upon potency and act as such is common to both material substances and immaterial created substances: to receive and be received; to perfect and be perfected. (*Contra Gentiles* II, 54, 10)

If we apply this doctrine to the first row of *Trinitas. Mens* much is revealed. As you will remember, this row runs: Space (Body. World) – Intellect (Trinity. Mind) – *esse*. The suggested reading would then be:

(a) *Esse* stands as being in common to both the intellective and spatial substances.
(b) *Esse* at least *should* comprise potency and act, though as we shall see, it is a special case of pure act.
(c) Intellect and space stand as active potencies which receive and are perfected by *esse*.
(d) Insofar as finite intellect and space are not pure form but rather mixtures of form and matter, we are referred not to world and Trinity, but to body and finite mind.

While I speak of form (which as we will see becomes essence and nature in Leibniz's middle period), it is important to appreciate that the 'form' columns are to be taken in the sense of active potencies of *esse–scire–agere seu conari* – something clearest in their physical deployment in the *Specimen Dynamicum* to which we turn later in the chapter. For now let us take as our working hypothesis that *Trinitas. Mens* is nothing but a triple product of the *energeia*–active potency relationship on the left hand side of the square of power which may be represented for the 'Mind' column as follows:

esse	*scire*	*agere seu conari}*	*general, energeia*
↓	↓	↓	
intellect	*imagination*	*will.power}*	*particular, active potencies*

The same can be done with the Body. World column.

What immediately strikes us is that Leibniz has not explicitly included in-potency (*dunamei/potentia*) in the *esse* column at any point; apparently he relegates potency (*potentia*) to the lowest row of the *Trinitas. Mens* column alongside 'will'. Is it therefore the case that Leibniz removes in-potency from being entirely, or is it the case that this *potentia* bears a different sense of in-potency, and in-potency remains implicit in *esse*? This is not an idle question, for as Aubry has shown, the fate of in-potency marks a critical division between Aristotle and Aquinas. Indeed, given the role *potentia* and its primary cause play in Leibniz's theory of jurisprudence, we must approach this apparent relegation and its normative import with extreme caution. Having drawn up the square of power as a reference comparator for *Trinitas. Mens* we must now approach the Leibnizian matrix again from the Thomist background and ask two related questions: (i) why is the treatment of in-potency so important for Aquinas and Leibniz; and (ii) how can our understanding of in-potency thus obtained help us to understand the further divisions of *Trinitas. Mens*, namely between material and immaterial entities, and between the rows of the matrix?

2.2 The power of God – a return to Aristotle?

The 'square of power' helps us consider mixtures: for example, form and matter are mixed to constitute a material nature which then receives *actus* as a condition of its individuation. The square also prompts us to analyse extremal cases; entities which are unmixed or pure. We can already see this process in action in Aristotle's deduction of the Prime Mover:

> And it will still not be enough even if [this something] does function, if its *ousia* is *dunamis*; for there will not be eternal motion, since that which exists in-potency [*dunamei*] may not exist. Therefore there must be a principle of this kind whose *ousia* is *energeia*. Furthermore these substances must be immaterial; for they must be eternal if anything is. Therefore they are *energeia*. (*Meta*. XII, 1071b18–22)

Putting to one side the argument against infinite regress of causes which Aquinas will deploy, we can examine the logical moves as a double purification and then a kind of equivocation. First, it is observed at the level of being that because *dunamei* is a potentiality to become a perfected substance, any substance which is a mixture of *energeia* and *dunamei* could possibly not exist,[8] whereas what is sought is a necessary being. We are thus looking for a nature of a thing which is pure act and without potentiality. But a nature can be a mixture of form and matter, and matter is implied by in-potency, so any such mixed nature would assume at least in principle in-potency. The desired nature then is pure form (*ousia*), a conclusion bound up with the finding that the desired substance is immaterial; that it is without matter in a positive sense. The two nodes on the right of the square are reduced into the left-hand side. Reduced because now *ousia* plays a modified role, being as it is 'caused' by *energeia* or set to work for some end. There is thus reintroduced an 'auxiliary' potentiality in this sense: *ousia* is set to work by *energeia* to produce some effect, but either that produces change (and so implies potentiality) or it does not such that *ousia* is set to work in a manner which is unchanging, absolutely perfect and without potentiality. But is this not the definition of pure *energeia*? In which case, we are to believe, *ousia* immediately completes its work in 'bringing about' *energeia* and the 'auxiliary' potentiality we deployed for investigating this process is radically excluded.[9] We have thus the unusual case of *energeia* working through *ousia* to cause *energeia*, which is the circular motion Aristotle seeks to establish.[10]

A side effect of this collapsing of the square into a circular motion is that the relationship of efficient causality between active and passive potencies, and the relationship of final causation between *dunamei* and *energeia*, is collapsed into the two nodes of the *energeia–ousia* relationship. *Energeia* efficiently causes the object of its act, which is the *ousia* of itself, but this *ousia* fully takes hold (*metalepsis*) of its self-cause which is also its end, and accordingly *ousia* reproduces its cause perfectly.[11] The Philosopher concludes: 'For the actuality of thought is life, and god is that actuality; and the essential actuality of god is life most good and eternal.'[12]

As we already saw briefly in Chapter 1, Gwenaëlle Aubry's striking intervention is to demonstrate how Aquinas is able to reintroduce *potency* into the Prime Mover. One thread of her detailed argument is this: that whereas for Aristotle the formal *ousia* of God is set to work by receiving his *energeia* (and this produces God's necessary existence), for Aquinas, who ostensibly accepts that there is nothing '*potentiale*' in God, (i) the infinite *actus* of God is *esse*, and (ii) the essence of

God is his *esse*, whence in him essence does not differ from being. The result:

> Pure act – that is, being in its fullness and perfection – is that which exercises the very power of being without limit (i.e., that in which the power of being is not limited by the power-for-being, that is by the mere ability to be).[13]

In effect, the *ousia* of the Prime Mover provided for a formal structure of the Prime Mover, whereas the Thomist God is not so restrained or determined, but is rather actually infinite being even as to form. This *ousia* or essence is now the activity of a self-actualising substance, a self-essentialis*ing* actualisation or *actus purus essendi*. In short, the essence worthy of *esse* is as unlimited as *esse* and so is itself 'pure'.

This move would seem to go even further than the Philosopher in excluding potentiality from God, but Aubry further shows that the opposite occurs: the unlimited nature of God's actuality produces an excessive being, that is, a being which goes beyond what might be required for God's self-subsistence. To put this another way, being unlimited, God is not simply necessarily capable of his being, which would see himself as the end of his capacity to be, but actualises more being even than that. This, Aubry argues, allows Aquinas to grant God a new kind of power, the whole power (*potestas* or *virtus*) of his being, which can be received fully by himself but only as a mode by any other entity.

I do wonder if Aquinas' break with Aristotle may be described as so radical. On the one hand it is critically important that the Thomist God's essence is identified with *esse*, for this delimitation of the structure of God permits an excessive or infinite creative actuality. On the other hand, power is not so much reintroduced *into* God as a direct product of his construction. I claim in particular that the '*tota virtute esse*' is misplaced if regarded as bound together in God with *esse* itself. Rather we already have our Thomist construction of God in which *essentia* and *esse* are identified and whereby *esse* is unrestrained in its reproduction. I claim with respect that the whole *potestas* or *virtus* of being is what that entity – God as *causa sui* – exemplifies with respect to all other entities that it creates. Such a power stands as principle (cause) of all things.

Take for example the text from the *Summa contra Gentiles* on which Aubry relies:

> Therefore, if there is something to which the whole power of being belongs, it can lack no excellence that is proper to any thing whatsoever. But for a thing that is its own being it is proper to be according to the whole power (*potestas*) of being. For example, if there were a separately existing whiteness, it could not lack any of the power (*virtus*) of whiteness. For a given white thing can lack something of the power (*virtus*) of whiteness through a defect in that which receives the whiteness, for it receives the whiteness according to its mode and perhaps not according to its whole power (*posse*) of whiteness. God, therefore, Who is His being, as we have proved above, has being according to the whole power (*virtus*) of being itself. (*Contra Gentiles* I, 28, 2)

I would offer the following interpretation: we hypothesise a separately existing whiteness, but then by hypothesis it must set its white essence to work by 'whitening' itself, and being an essence which is purely white, the actuality of its whiteness perfects itself as a separately existing whiteness (assuming this be possible). It is only as this construct that this whiteness-substance has the *virtus* of whiteness, and it lacks nothing in this power because of the appropriateness of its essence. But insofar as we consider anything else which could be affected by this whiteness-entity, that affected thing's essence is not whiteness-as-such and so can only receive whiteness to the degree that essence is capable of so doing. Thus the *virtus* (and not *potentia*) of whiteness, and the correlate power (*potestas*) of being, are intelligible primarily in the sense Aquinas describes: as that which is suffered by some second thing. Now this is the conclusion Aubry herself tends to; my slight disagreement is that *posse* and *esse* are not bound together in God (*esse* and *active potency* are), but rather *posse* is the product of the *esse–act* twofold operation. Aquinas states as much in *De potentia Dei*, where he argues that:

(a) we speak of power in relation to act. Now act is twofold [the *causa sui*]; the first act which is a form, and the second act which is operation. Seemingly the word 'act' was first universally employed in the sense of operation, and then, secondly, transferred to indicate the form, inasmuch as the form is the principle and end of operation. And so, Aquinas tells us, in like manner power is twofold: active power corresponding to that act which is operation: and seemingly it was in this sense that the word 'power' was first employed; and passive power, corresponding to the first act or the form: to which seemingly the name of power was subsequently given.[14]

(b) When we say that God acts from his essence it is a manner of speaking; he is the principle of himself and other things. So, we can say this God's essence is his power *qua* cause. But essence is a reason for some effect, not its cause and so the attribution of power to essence is a manner of speaking derived from the way finite creatures are subject to external causality.[15]

I claim therefore that it is more appropriate to say that *posse* derives from the twofold and reciprocal action between *esse* and operation (efficient), and operation and God as entity (operative and final). On this understanding we can recover the Trinity understood as a relationship of actuality and power. The first moment sees *esse* efficiently cause the form of its essence, but its essence is identical with *esse* so nothing determinate is constituted. This essence is then finally caused by the same *esse*, which sees the essence perfected, and being perfected as existing. The reciprocal action of twofold *esse* then is the principle of a power: the power of thinking which has as its essence the whole movement from *esse* via operation to the actualisation of God. Likewise, this act of thought efficiently produces the intellect, and the intellect is perfected by the final causality of the divine thought. The power of this twofold relation then is volition, and we see willing efficiently bringing into existence such things as together constitute the world. This cyclical process is mapped onto the Trinity and it is telling that Aquinas should feel the need to develop a term for such a power – *spiration*:

In every action two things are to be considered, the 'suppositum' acting, and the power whereby it acts; as, for instance, fire heats through heat. So if we consider in the Father and the Son the power whereby they spirate the Holy Ghost, there is no mean, for this is one and the same power. (ST I, q.36, a.3, r.1)

Spiration would become a significant term for his Neoplatonising successor Henry of Ghent,[16] but already with Aquinas it aims to encapsulate even at the level of the Trinity itself the twofold motion whereby Father 'directs' or commands the Son, as a mason directs the hammer, to produce the Spirit, but that this production is result of 'the same spirative power belong[ing] to the Father and to the Son' and not due to the Father alone.[17]

So, how can spiration assist in our understanding of Leibniz's *Trinitas. Mens*? If spiration is bound up with *posse*, what is the effect of his apparent relegation of *potentia* to a cognate of will alone? I respond that this shift of the name *potentia* is indicative of a certain restoration of Aristotle's thought, but it is not primarily driven by a concern for expelling potency from God. Indeed, in a theological text from sometime between 1683 and 1686, entitled *De Deo Trino*, Leibniz appears happy to deploy '*potentia*' in the Thomist sense of a product of activity passing down the persons of the Trinity:

> For the Father multiplies the person of the Godhead, while he thinks himself, and while he loves himself. Therefore the Son is generated from the Father, the Holy Spirit proceeds from the father and son, since the intellect presupposes the power of acting [*potentia agendi*], and the will presupposes both the power of acting and the power of understanding . . . (Gr:179, A:VI, iv, 2292)

Has Leibniz reverted to the Thomist doctrine of power? This seems not to be the case, for he deletes an immediately subsequent statement in his first draft that all this conforms to catholic doctrine and sacred scripture,[18] and continues:

> . . . although, on the other hand, understanding and being understood, loving and being loved, are common to all three persons; however only the Son is generated by the primary essential intellect, only the Spirit proceeds from

71

the primary essential love, whereby it is said that God reflects in himself several persons in one. (Ibid.)

In the first quotation Leibniz appears to be adopting Thomist language as an affectation, for the second quotation appears to re-explain the Trinity in a new manner. As Antognazza puts it, Leibniz now claims that the distinction of persons now arises from the activity of self-reflection itself.[19] Gaston Grua appears to agree that the usage of 'potentia' in this text is rhetorical, for he explicitly excises it from his own transcription of *De Deo Trino*.[20]

It would seem that Leibniz actively seeks to explain what the Schoolmen do through the mechanism of power by means of suppositive activity and reflection. I would venture that by continuing to found generation on an essential activity, Leibniz has in one sense moved not so far from the pure essentialising act of Aquinas. Nevertheless, he refuses the language of *potentia* that Aquinas predicates of this essentialising movement. As part of this decision, he eschews the 'purity' of the divine act in favour of a rational essentialising activity which we have already established flows from *esse* itself, and so is prior even to individual acts of thought. This restores after its own fashion a certain limitation or determinateness to *esse* which is lost when *ousia* became a pure essence equivalent to *esse*, for now *esse* sets to work a rational order which is perfected by the infinite intellect in the act of thinking.

What we have done is to indicate in certain theological texts further evidence, precisely where the Schoolmen use *potentia*, of Leibniz's ostensible decision to relegate *potentia* in favour of a rational and reflective activity. But on what basis does Leibniz do this? What are his metaphysical premises? In the next section we review the square of power to see how Leibniz rearranges the metaphysical chess pieces in favour of activity. The route to understanding, in mimicry of first philosophy, moves from the concrete and physical to the theoretical.

2.3 Power 'between' entities

I have found what I call the 'square of power' to be a useful hermeneutic tool for analysing the role of activity and power in the work of Aristotle and Aquinas, and it proves no less useful when we engage with Leibniz's physics, on which so much has been written[21] even if this internal logical structure is not explicitly identified. Daniel Garber for example, is clear that by the time[22] of the *Specimen Dynamicum* of 1695[23] Leibniz has in place the fourfold distinction we would expect given the treatment of actuality/in-potency by Leibniz's forerunners. The relevant passage highlighted by Garber is worth quoting at length:

> *Active force* (which might not inappropriately be called *power* [*virtus*], as some do) is twofold, that is, either primitive which is inherent in every corporeal substance *per se* . . . or *derivative*, which, resulting from a limitation of primitive force through collision of bodies with one another, for example, is found in different degrees. Indeed, primitive force (which is nothing but the first entelechy) corresponds to the *soul* or *substantial form* . . . Similarly, passive force is twofold, either primitive or derivative. And indeed, the *primitive force of being acted upon* [*vis primitiva patiendi*] or of *resisting* constitutes that which is called *materia prima* by the Schoolmen, if correctly interpreted. This force is that by virtue of which one body cannot be penetrated by another body, but presents an obstacle to it, and at the same time is endowed with a certain laziness, so to speak, that is an opposition to motion, nor, further, does it allow itself to be put into motion without somewhat diminishing the force of the body acting on it. As a result, the *derivative force of being acted upon* later shows itself to different degrees in *secondary matter*.[24]

The foregoing suggests the following, familiar logical structure:

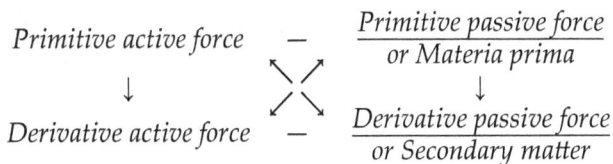

Primitive active force — *Primitive passive force or Materia prima*

↓ ✕ ↓

Derivative active force — *Derivative passive force or Secondary matter*

I do not wish to engage in the physical consequences of this model, for example in understanding mass or velocity; rather the logical and metaphysical relevance of it for our understanding of power in *Trinitas. Mens.* Here the logical structure plays the stronger interpretative role, for we find the following information presented:

(a) At the lower level of physical events, the Scholastic notions of active and passive potencies are now named as formally opposed derivative forces of action and passion.

(b) At the higher level, the Scholastic notions of activity (in act, from *energeia*) and potentiality (in-potency from *dunamei*) are reflected in the formally opposed primary forces (*virtutes*)[25] named primary active force, and primary passive force or primary matter.

(c) The relationship *primary–derivative* is one of implication or conditionality, reflecting that found between activity/potency and active/passive potencies in the Thomist doctrine.

(d) Leibniz expressly identifies primary active force with the first entelechy, intimately linked in Aristotle's work to *energeia* suggesting that its relation to derivative active force is formal in the sense of determining the form of this force. Leibniz states that he calls entelechy 'primitive force to distinguish it from the secondary, what one calls moving force, which is a limitation or accidental variation of the primitive force'.[26]

(e) This variation of entelechy by means of an accident suggests thereby the influence of the material forces on the right-hand side of square. The square suggests two possible such interactions:

    a. One of opposition with the mass (derivative passive force) of a second body, leading to change in particular motion which, however, is conserved in the collision as a whole (conservation of momentum).[27]

    b. One of contradiction with the 'dead force' (*materia prima*) whereby this primary passive force 'solicits' a variation in the motion under consideration.[28]

It is to be observed that both these interactions provide further kinds of causal interaction according to a Thomist interpretation: (i) direct impact can be read as a material cause, or

Leibniz's accident; (ii) solicitation as a (mediate) final causality insofar as the derivative motion is drawn under the influence of the immaterial primitive forces.

Support for the role of both efficient and final causes in the *Specimen Dynamicum*'s exposition is given in that text itself, where Leibniz argues that the two kingdoms of efficient and final causes 'permeate each other, yet their laws are never disturbed, so that the maximum in the kingdom of power and the best in the kingdom of wisdom take place together' (L:442), but the precise relationship, though suggested only at this stage by a Thomist interpretation, is difficult to ascertain and requires a more thorough examination when we consider the will. I just wish to underline the influence on Leibniz of a doctrine in which *energeia/dunamei* permeate with respect to derivative forces, not least because this division becomes stark when we move to consider Leibniz's doctrine of the juridical state space.

2.4 *Potentia* and the complete concept of an individual: internalising power

I claim that as Leibniz develops his understanding of his 'immaterial entities' (the *supposita*) he is led to differentiate created substances from God by means of their degree of power. However, power is no longer referred to as an external principle which stands in contradiction to the acts of a finite substance, as with the Schoolmen (and even Hobbes and Grotius). Rather, power becomes internalised within the finite substance as that which must be added to finite will to make up the deficiencies that derive from created substance's inherent finitude. As such, Leibniz holds that whereas *esse* and *scire* 'truly' express the equivalent activities in God, finite *agere seu conari* are predefined to require both acts expressing what an individual is (volitions) *and* endeavours that express what it is not (*potentiae*). Judgement, the practical assessment of the usefulness of *potentia* to volition, is grounded on a necessary ignorance of *potentia*.

The route to Leibniz's 'immaterial entities' passes via physical phenomena, just as their discovery in Aristotle amounts to an abstraction of certain features of the 'square of power'. As we saw in our discussion of Peripatetic and Thomist

in-potency, it is a question of considering and then excluding the modifications of an essence in act, modifications due
to *dunamei* and to passive potency. However, the idealistic
nature of Leibniz's system in which physical phenomena are
not direct interactions between substances but harmonious
variations in perception and appetition within each substance means that our discussion of physical interaction is
already a discussion of the internal power relations of an
entity. Accordingly, I begin by briefly considering the modified essence in act in the physical context as already internal
to an entity, before moving to consider immaterial forms.

   With the 'square of power' interpretation we have the raw
elements with which to construct any given corporeal entity
in Leibniz's system and so understand in logical outline how
power (*posse*) operates within these entities. Daniel Garber
draws our attention to a definition of corporeal substance
from the *Contra philosophiam Cartesianam* of May 1702 which,
though doubtfully[29] later than our period of examination,
well expresses the continuing Scholastic and Peripatetic
influences:

> Primitive active force, which Aristotle calls first entelechy
> and one calls the form of a substance, is another natural
> principle [i.e. cause] which, together with [primitive][30]
> matter or passive force, completes a corporeal substance.[31]

Similarly, in *De Ipsa Natura* (1698) we find:

> ... primary matter is merely passive, but it is not a com-
> plete substance. And so, we must add a soul or a form
> analogous to a soul, or a first entelechy, that is a certain
> urge [*nisus*] or primitive force of acting, which is itself an
> inherent law, impressed by divine decree.[32]

In considering a single entity or substance of Leibniz's
middle period we are not considering the oppositions of the
'square of power' we have deployed as between entities but
are now moving to consider that situation, already identified in Aquinas, where the entity is self-subsistent and so
brings many of our formal logical oppositions within itself.
The Scholastic influence prompts us to consider our square

of power as collapsed into a corporeal substance whereby we find that the primary active force (entelechy) elaborates a nature (*natura*) which requires a more or less subtle organisation in time of primary matter as extension, that is, matter understood not as mass but as impenetrability or repugnance to co-situation.[33] Observe immediately a certain circularity of the structure under consideration: we do not have a mere opposition: actuality–*materia prima,* but rather the entelechy acting through a nature with a view to organising *materia prima.* Once *materia prima* is understood in effect as that which is organised into a resisting extension,[34] an extension which is organised by a given entelechy according to its nature, Leibniz's move of collapsing this cognate of in-potency into a substance seems plausible: why not regard this extension as impregnable precisely due to its continuous organisation by the *esse* in a given entity?[35] This is not quite a monadology yet. However, in the 1690s it is arguable that Leibnizian primary matter remains a construct of the divine mind as space for us, as is suggested again when we review the first row of *Trinitas. Mens*: space–intellect–*esse.*

Yet the definition of corporeal substance as a nature enacted in primary matter remains redolent of the process of *energeia–ousia–dunamei* which we have reviewed above. The difficulty is that Leibniz makes nature a thing that is set to work in each created substance, but surely by virtue of divine omniscience this nature is part of the general intellect? Are we to understand that the divine power fully elaborates each nature, only for creatures to suffer material modifications to their own productions of particular nature? How does Leibniz account for and remain faithful to the surgical intervention he has made whereby *esse* instantiates itself not as a 'pure' being but as intellect or rational being? It seems that Leibniz is aware of this difficulty and he deals with it by making a distinction between essence and nature. The distinction is made in the critically important §16 of the *Discourse on Metaphysics*:

> That could be called our essence which includes all that we express . . . But that which is limited in us can be called our nature or our power [*puissance*], and in this regard that which goes beyond the natures of all created substances is supernatural.

In making this essence/nature distinction we return to the issue of power, for Leibniz is inscribing a division whereby the relationship between *supposita* is explained by reference to essential activity, while power (*puissance*) is referred to an infra-substantial aspect of the finite individual – that which marks it as part of its world. Each substance is nothing but this same continuous actualisation by God of a whole world 'according to the diverse views he has of [it]' (DM §14). This is the active decree which amounts to the essence that includes all we express. In this way 'all our phenomena, that is to say, all the things that can ever happen to us, are only the results of *our own being*'.[36] Leibniz does not use *potentia* to describe this relationship of expression save rhetorically in *De Deo Trino*, only then to rearticulate it.

It is not, however, simply God's differing perspectives which constitute the particular substance in this middle period discourse. At this point it is traditional to focus on the positive 'complete concept' theory of created substance which Leibniz advances in DM §12, but given our focus on power we might also benefit from considering particularisation as a function of this raising of intellect to the level of being. For Leibniz, having made intellect and space both generalised and necessary conditions of all created substances, decrees a rationalist hierarchy by which all created substances are measured. Hence our thinker writes:

> ... a substance ... expresses the universe *in conformity* to that perspective, if God sees fit to render his thought effective and to produce that substance. And since God's perspective is always true, our perceptions are also always true; it is our judgements, *which come from ourselves*, which deceive us. (DM §14, my emphasis)

Due to the priority of *esse*–intellect each substance created by God immediately expresses being as rationally ordered being. Leibniz is even prepared to hold that finite perceptions cause by *scire* are true because they express God's perceptions from that substance's perspective. Hence again we find a rational *ens commune* for all thinking substances.

Leibniz differentiates created rational substances by what they do with the true perceptions shared with divine

thought. We are told that finite minds make poor judgements because these judgements derive not from God but
from finite substances. Being and knowing having been
accounted for, this leaves acting as the candidate for the deficiency of judgement. As we shall discover in the following
chapters, judgement is an appreciation of the best among
the various claims of matter to existence. Importantly for
present purposes that movement to existence is caused by
the end, and this end is one of two principles: the individual entelechy and the variety of the World. We therefore
recur to that which the Schoolmen called *potentia*. But now
a question: if Leibniz wishes to oppose activity and particular will to *potentia*, and also wishes for the very potency of
potentia to derive from the 'external' World of a finite individual, does he not have a fundamental contradiction with
his claims that deficient judgements originate in us (and so
are not due to external determination), and ultimately that
substances do not interact directly (and so cannot determine
each other)? Having moved *potentia* to be the subaltern of
the acting or endeavouring activity, he begins, obliquely, to
consider how to deal with the purportedly external cause of
that *potentia*.

Purely from the perspective of the supposit (i.e. excluding
'complete concepts' at this point) it is a question of the difference of activities emanated by the divine intellect – a thesis
which Leibniz already holds in his *Catholic Demonstrations* as
we have seen. It is an analytic question here of considering
primary powers (*virtutes*) abstracted from their derivatives,
and thereby getting at the heart of the differences of powers
of substances. In a 1690s revision note to his *Nova Methodus*,
Leibniz writes that:

> *Activity* or *force* is perceivable in the mind alone; that
> is, the state of a thing from which change follows. ...
> There is a double force – that of acting and that of resist-
> ing. The former is immaterial, the latter material, which
> resists action though it does not act unless impelled from
> without. Immaterial forces are separate intelligences, as
> well as primary souls or entelechies in bodies. The simple
> maximum exercise of force is conatus towards action. (L:92
> n.17)

Leibniz is thus happy to consider separate intelligences and to make the Scholastic[37] distinction between material and immaterial forces that allows purely immaterial substances to be posited, such as angels (L:368). Already Aquinas furnishes us with an understanding of how power distinguishes separate intelligences untrammelled by corporeality. As we would expect, the distinction turns on the impurity of created act; the act of the angel (for the Thomists: understanding) also involves in-potency with the effect that the power of the angel always remains to be exercised or perfected. Only God can perfect his complete understanding; angels must become understanding in time. This incorporeal model is then further explicated with an important but terse addition to Aquinas' *question* on angels considered absolutely: 'God produces the creature by His intellect and will',[38] the appreciation of which is enhanced by consideration of the Scotist position as explicated by Étienne Gilson:[39]

(a) Insofar as infinite intellect, God knows an infinity of quiddative beings which are named Ideas and which are quidditatively distinct, but which do not possess a distinct existence. They only exist as part of the existing divine intellect.

(b) Insofar as infinite volition, God elects those Ideas which he wishes to exist together from all the possible relations between all the quiddities.

(c) Each existing substance possesses a double unity:
   a. The unity of its quiddity: in a composite quiddity this means the unity of all the subsidiary quiddities that go to make up that composite.
   b. The unity of its existence: in a composite quiddity this means that each of the composing quiddities also exist.

(d) Such a composite is nothing other than a substantial form.

(e) A *haecceity* (thisness) is that supreme or fullest substantial form which actualises all the necessary substantial forms and quiddities required to constitute itself as an *individual*.

(f) *Haecceity* escapes knowledge insofar as it escapes definition.

The point is not so much that both intellect and will are involved in creation of finite substances (though this is terribly important for Leibniz also), but that the difference of power is measured by reference to composition of other quiddities and substantial forms of quiddities, and this measure is, as one would expect with the Schoolmen, definitional or essentialist. Thus, even at the level of immaterial substances, unaffected by corporeal percussion, we have a suggestion of how a substantial form or *haecceity* is limited in its power. It is limited according to that substantial form's definitional power. By way of discussion: a *haecceity* as the fullest, individualising substantial form may be defined by the substantial forms that it actualises into itself, and perhaps even by the subsidiary substantial forms that they themselves actualise, but in principle a *haecceity* need not know every quiddity that it needs to actualise to be itself if a substantial form that it does know undertakes that organising task for it. Hence a horizon can be drawn between a substantial form A and the subsidiary forms $B_1, B_2 \ldots$ which it organises according to its will, and those subsidiary forms $C_1, C_2 \ldots$ at lower levels, so to speak, which the A does not know but which are organised by the intermediate forms $B_1, B_2 \ldots$ These unknown forms $C_1, C_2 \ldots$ on which the first substantial form relies are its *potentiae* (or its nature in a possessive sense). And in this way a definitional line is drawn which distinguishes even a purely immaterial substance such as an angel from a God who is nothing but pure act.

What for Scotus seems to be a somewhat formal exercise becomes for Leibniz a key and active feature of his theory of power (and ultimately of law). Already in the *Catholic Demonstrations* we have seen how substances are differentiated *realiter* in just this way:

> The substance of each thing is not so much mind as it is the Idea of a concurrent mind. In God there are infinite, really diverse substances, yet God is indivisible. The ideas of God are substances, but not the essences, of things. (L:118)

A finite substance is a real, not formal, Idea of God. This substance is, and insofar as its activity is *esse*, this *esse* (i) is its own activity and not God's, but (ii) it expresses God's *esse* which is its essence. I respectfully disagree with Adams's argument[40] that substantial form can be identified with the essence, because (i) the essence is a part of the whole divine intellect whereas the substantial form is distinguished from that essence by its very actuality; (ii) each substantial form only contains everything that could happen to it, however contingent, because it contains *esse*–intellect as its very condition of being in the world, not because the substantial form itself includes everything it expresses (something Leibniz expressly denies in DM §16); and (iii) the horizon between conceptual necessity and contingency is to be defined both by the substantial form's depth of activity in composing substances and the variable power to undertake this at any given time, that is, *scire*–imagination mirrors *esse*–intellect.

The real distinction is thus operative and essential for Leibniz. It allows him to claim, he believes, that rational substances can express the being and knowing of God 'truly' from a certain perspective, and still differentiate substances. This is because the domain of being and knowing is the rational or *formal*, whereas the realm of action or endeavouring, of will, is the *real* composition of substances.

As we saw in Chapter 1, in the context of Leibniz's discussion of transubstantiation, the parallels with the Scotist doctrine are apparent. What here Leibniz terms 'Ideas' are not static definitions but the principles of organisation themselves – activities which organise without yet knowing all that it is that they organise. With the Eucharist the substance of Christ organises the bread, but (and we must presume this to be a choice) does not actualise itself in all the parts of the bread so that the bread remains sufficiently 'bread-like' for the purposes of communion. The Scotist language of composition of quiddities is taken up in the notion of concurrent mind, but likewise Leibniz strictly observes the distinction between God's intellection of quiddities in the whole intellect (essences) and the individuation of substances as minds in the act of 'naturing' themselves. And the power differential between ideas is measured by the cognitive penetration of the active principle into the world it organises:

> In idea there is contained ideally both passive and active potentiality, both active and passive intellect. Insofar as the

passive intellect concurs, there is matter in the idea; insofar as the active intellect, there is form. NB. Bread and wine are not transessentiated but transubstantiated. (L:118)

The usage of active and passive potentiality clearly evokes Thomism, but it appears that even as early as the *Catholic Demonstrations* Leibniz is taking what he will call act (and ultimately will) and *potentia* and integrating them both within the very idea of a substance. Each possible mind is now defined by its specific activity which is, as it were, 'hungry' for other substantial forms to organise. Each organising or concurrent mind really only makes sense when it is spontaneously organising other substantial forms, but it is only contingent, not necessary, that a mind know all the substantial forms that it must organise. It may rely on intermediate substantial forms for this task. Of course, a mind could know its world down to all its simplest elements – this is guaranteed by the divine decree of *esse*–intellect – but this infinite act of *scire* defines God alone; all else must only partially illumine their world. With this reading we may aid R.M. Adams in his interpretation[41] of *Discourse on Metaphysics* §16, already quoted:

That could be called an essence which includes all that we express, and as it expresses our union with God himself, it has no limits and nothing goes beyond it. But that which is limited in us can be called our nature or our power [*puissance*], and in this regard that which goes beyond the natures of all created substances is supernatural.

Here essence and nature are distinguished, but also nature is linked to *potentia*. Leibniz, lacking recourse to pre-planned essences striving for perfection, makes a nature the inbuilt product of our finitude. This is surely another key moment in what Agamben describes as a shift to efficiency and operativity, for whereas under the Thomist regime the focus was on the perfection of a form expressing an immutable essence, with Leibniz the precise point of moral pressure is activity as such and its ability to conform with God's acts or decrees.

In this way primary passive force (*materia prima*) appears under the name *potentia* to be relegated to a subaltern position where its stands as a relative term marking the inefficacy of finite substance and its need of many other substances to actualise itself. The Leibnizian innovation with respect to power, then, is that *potentia* is internalised as a derivative of the *agere/conari* activity, this activity including already within itself what it lacks as substantial form and thus needs to realise for itself if it is to achieve perfection. We will see however, that Leibniz does not abandon *materia prima* or primary passive force entirely, for he still requires a cause for particular *potentiae*. He will reconfigure *materia prima* under a new guise.

3. Conclusion

For Aristotle *dunamei* (in-potency) was a negative determination of *energeia* (activity) of equal metaphysical rank: *dunamei* was the formal contrary of *energeia*, not its subaltern. A substance in-potency was less perfect than one which was pure activity. With Aquinas, via Plotinus, *potentia* is not a formal contrary but is now generated by the pure act of being. If anything, *potentia* exceeds the act of being, even if being remains principle and *potentia* product. For his part, Leibniz appears to revert in some measure to the Stagirite's teachings. Activity stands once more as primary positive principle; *potentia* becomes once again a negative determination. Yet *potentia* is also demoted: rather than determining primary activity, *potentia* is regarded as a determination of derivative actions such that *potentia* is both contrary to action and subaltern – the very definition of being in contradiction. These innovations raise several questions which go to the heart of the jurisprudential relationship between obligation and power on the one hand, and justice on the other. Our dogged focus up to this point has been on activity, and specifically the eternal and spontaneous activities of being and knowing respectively. These questions of power and obligation include:

(a) Leibniz places primary passive force inside substances as a concept relative to the finite activity of the substantial form. What though is the precise relationship between the substantial form and this matter, and what bearing does it have on questions of natural law?

(b) On a related note, the matter of election of what is to be created has been implicit in our discussion (and explicit at times with respect to being and intellect). From our discussion of substantial forms as ideational acts it is already apparent that a choice has been made as to which ideas move from the general intellect to actual existence, and we can expect that a similar choice be made with respect to the possible. In what does this choice consist?

(c) The power of a substantial form is measured according to its organisational continuity. But given that a substantial form need not know about the organisation of every part of matter to exist, why should we care and what does this mean for justice?

These questions are pertinent because Leibniz's doctrine of power refuses to be reduced to one of simple efficiency. Efficiency plays a part in the exercise of power from actuality through essence and nature, but at all times Leibniz maintains that final causes play their part in the end for which that efficient causality is exercised. As we shall see, the relationship between substantial form and passive forces is exactly the point of departure for Leibniz's arguments for a kingdom of ends, and the just exercise of power.

Notes

1. In Giorgio Agamben, *Potentialities: Collected Essays in Philosophy* (Stanford: Stanford University Press, 1999), p.177.
2. Cf. e.g. Jonathan Beere, *Doing and Being: An Interpretation of Aristotle's Metaphysics Theta* (Oxford: Oxford University Press, 2009), p.173; Franz Brentano, *On the Several Senses of Being in Aristotle* (Rolf George trans.) (Berkeley: University of California Press, 1975); Michael Frede, 'Aristotle's Notion of Potentiality in Metaphysics Θ', in T. Scaltsas, D. Charles and M.L. Gill (eds), *Unity, Identity, and Explanation in Aristotle's Metaphysics* (Oxford: Oxford University Press, 1994), particularly pp.173–93.
3. H.F. Cherniss, *Aristotle's Criticism of Plato and the Academy* (Baltimore: Johns Hopkins University Press 1944) ch.III referenced by Gwenaëlle Aubry, '*Ousia energeia* and *actus purus essendi* – from Aristotle to Aquinas: Some Groundwork for an Archeology of Power' (2015) 77 *Tijdschrift voor Filosofie* 827–54, p.828.

4. Aubry, '*Ousia energeia*', p.828.
5. Stephen Menn, 'The Origins of Aristotle's Concept of Ἐνέργεια: Ἐνέργεια and Δύναμις' (1994) 14 *Ancient Philosophy* 73–114. See also Daniel Graham, 'The Etymology of Entelecheia' (1989) 110 *American Journal of Philology* 73–80 and cf. G.A. Blair, 'Aristotle on Ἐντέλεχεια: A Reply to Daniel Graham' (1993) 114 *American Journal of Philology* 91–7. See also Blair's, 'Unfortunately, It Is a Bit More Complex: Reflections on Ἐνέργεια' (1995) 15 *Ancient Philosophy* 565–80.
6. The various mechanics and difficulties of the logical square cannot possibly be entertained here. The essential characteristics are these: (i) the upper row is distinguished from the lower by quantity: the upper is total, the lower particular, and the arrows indicate that the particular is implied by or a subset of the totality; (ii) the left column is distinguished from the right by quality: the right column is the negation of the left. The lines between the columns indicate contrariety. Each corner is qualitatively and quantitatively in contradiction to the corner transversally opposite. Kant argued that the arrows of implication are extremely weak, especially when we consider the relation necessity $\supseteq$ existence.
7. ST I, q.25, a. s.1.
8. The possibly not is indeed the modality of passive potency: see *Posterior Analytics*.
9. Aubry, '*Ousia energeia*', p.831.
10. *Meta.* XII. 1072b1–15.
11. *Meta.* XII. 1072b16–20.
12. *Meta.* XII. 1072b25.
13. Aubry, '*Ousia energeia*', p.831.
14. *De Pot.* q.1 a.1, r.
15. *De Pot.* q.1 a.1, ad.1.
16. See e.g. Juan Carlos Flores, *Henry of Ghent: Metaphysics of the Trinity* (Leuven: Leuven University Press, 2006).
17. ST I, q.36, a.3, r.2.
18. A:VI, iv, *varianta* to 2292.
19. Maria Rosa Antognazza, 'Leibniz de Deo Trino: Philosophical Aspects of Leibniz's Conception of the Trinity' (2001) 37 *Religious Studies* 1–13 at p.8.
20. Gr:179.
21. E.g. Daniel Garber, *Leibniz: Body, Substance, Monad* (Oxford: Oxford University Press, 2009) and the bibliography there; Martial Gueroult, *Leibniz: Dynamique et Métaphysique* (Paris: Aubier Montagne, 1967); Paul Lodge, 'Force and the Nature of Body in Discourse on Metaphysics §§17–18' (1997) 7

Leibniz Review 116–24; Michel Fichant 'Les concepts fondamentaux de la mécanique selon Leibniz en 1676' in CNRS
(eds), *Leibniz à Paris: 1672–1676: Symposion* (Wiesbaden:
Steiner Verlag, 1978) pp.219–32.

22. For Leibniz's post-1700 view, which is beyond the scope
of this work, see R.M. Adams, 'Primitive and Derivative
Forces' in his *Leibniz: Determinist, Theist, Idealist* (Oxford:
Oxford University Press, 1994) ch.13.

23. GM:236–7; L:436–7. We also find the core of this tetrapartite
division in explicative revisions to the *Nova Methodus* (1667)
which Leibniz undertook in the 1690s, L:97 n.17.

24. Garber, *Body, Substance, Monad,* p.133.

25. Cf. L:73.

26. Ger:IV 473, quoted in Garber, *Body, Substance, Monad,* p.138.

27. L:448.

28. L:438.

29. Garber rightly questions the dating of the piece, given that
by 1702 Leibniz was entertaining a monadological metaphysics (Garber, *Body, Substance, Monad,* p.137 n.24).

30. Garber's addition makes sense – of the two senses of matter,
the next quotation indicates that primary matter is that completed by an entelechy.

31. AG:252; GM: VI 98–106.

32. Quoted in trans. by Garber, *Body, Substance, Monad,* p.142.

33. AG:252, Leibniz discusses a sponge as opposed to a dense
object.

34. E.g. AG:252.

35. The Neoplatonic reference point for this understanding of
extension would be props.1 and 7 of Proclus' *Elements of
Philosophy.*

36. DM §14 (my emphasis); see also DM §9. Cf. also 'Within our
self-being there lies an infinity . . . God belongs to me more
intimately than my body' (L:368).

37. E.g. ST I, q.50 and q.54.

38. ST II-I, q.50. a.1.

39. Étienne Gilson, *Jean Duns Scot: Introduction à ses Positions
Fondamentales* (Paris: Vrin, 1952) p.678–9.

40. Adams, *Leibniz,* p.86.

41. Ibid. p.89.

Three

Will: The Scholastic Heritage

1. Introduction

In this chapter and the next I investigate Leibniz's doctrine
of the will, once more contextualising it within the Scholastic
doctrines of will and power. To do this I provide, in this
chapter, a broad account of volition and power, reading
Aristotle and Aquinas with the aid of Gwenaëlle Aubry and
others. This will set up a more detailed discussion of what
may be considered the pinnacle of this line of thought in the
doctrines of the real and creatable advanced by John Duns
Scotus. Yet another theory of power is also influential, and
we engage with Leibniz's thought on will and power in the
light also of Hobbes and Spinoza, for whom *potentia* takes
on a positive role justified by the new science. Our examination thus sees Leibniz weave a theory between the kingdom
of Nature, governed by physical laws of power, and the
kingdom of Grace in which the ends of the Schoolmen retain
their juridical role. Finding reconciliation for these competing
visions leads Leibniz to the theory of pretensions, in which
the contingent power of the material is ultimately referred
both to subjective will and the actuality of a God who stands
as guarantor of the juridical coherence of the world – all pretensions or claims of matter refer ultimately to the perfection
of the One.

2. Power and domination

Aquinas' reintroduction of power into God does seem to be
a striking move, but it may not be as innovative as Aquinas'
terminological twist makes out. Our suspicions have deep-
ened as we saw a certain proximity between Aquinas' spi-

rating and generative *potentia* and a renewed Leibnizian rational activity capable of reflection and expression. Indeed, the conceptual space for a new kind of power is to be found in Aristotle's *Eudemian Ethics,* even if the Stagirite does not apply it to the Prime Mover. In this section I outline this concept which I claim is a partial origin for the Thomist sense of power, before showing that it is just this concept which is so important for Leibniz's own response to Spinoza. As the title to this section suggests, I distinguish this concept of power by the term 'domination', for reasons dictated by the source language.

Our context is an abrupt turn in the *Eudemian Ethics* at Book II, Chapter 6 in which the Stagirite sets the scene for a subsequent treatment of virtue by seeking to determine the bounds of practical action. The chapter is difficult, but at its heart is an analysis of causes (or principles) in order to determine which causes are within the human's capacity, for surely only they fall to be considered as part of an ethical treatise. Part of the difficulty derives from Aristotle's introduction of several terms of art to describe the different species of the principles, that is, causes which are the origin of some effect and are not themselves caused. Anthony Kenny has done us the service of laying out the divisions Aristotle intends as follows:[1]

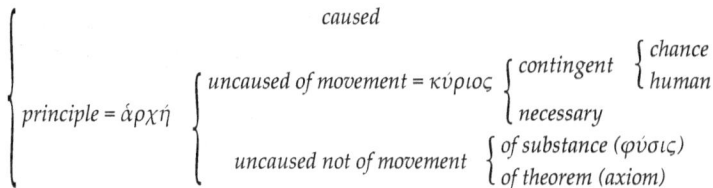

$$
\text{principle} = \dot{\alpha}\rho\chi\acute{\eta}
\begin{cases}
\text{caused} \\
\text{uncaused of movement} = \kappa\acute{\upsilon}\rho\iota o\varsigma
\begin{cases}
\text{contingent}
\begin{cases}
\text{chance} \\
\text{human}
\end{cases} \\
\text{necessary}
\end{cases} \\
\text{uncaused not of movement}
\begin{cases}
\text{of substance } (\varphi\acute{\upsilon}\sigma\iota\varsigma) \\
\text{of theorem (axiom)}
\end{cases}
\end{cases}
$$

Our interest is in the uncaused of movement (*kýrios*), and particularly those human and chance principles of movement. The key passage explaining the domain of action of the human is translated by Kenny:

(1) So if there are some things that are that admit of being otherwise, it is necessary that their principles be likewise. For what results from necessary things is itself necessary, but things from thence admit of becoming the opposite.

(2) What depends on men themselves [*eph autois* – from themselves] is, a great deal, of this kind of thing, and they themselves are the principles of things of this kind. (3) So, of the actions of which man is principle and master [*arché kai kýrios*] – of those at least of which he is in control of whether they occur or not – it is clear that they admit of existing or not, are under his dominion [*kýrios*]. (4) But of what depends on him to do or not to do, he is himself the cause; and that of which he is the cause depends on him. [1222b41–1223a9, translation modified from '*kýrios* = controller' as will be explained.][2]

Kenny and indeed J. Solomon[3] translate the relevant passage such that 'control' and 'controller' stand for '*kýrios*' as appropriate, but the sense of the term generally given in Greek is as 'having power', 'a lord, master' and 'authority'. It is of course the New Testament term for Christ (*ó Kýrios*) and in its genitive form *to kyriakós* (= the [house] of the Lord) is the root of the word *kirk* and so *church*.[4] I propose to follow this more legalistic translation – master/*dominus* – given the light it sheds on Thomist theory and on Leibniz.

On Aristotle's analysis *kýrios* is a specific capacity to initiate movement, and in humans it pertains to the contingent insofar as some possible's existence or otherwise does indeed fall within the dominion of the human in question. More precisely, the human is a contingent principle of practical action, which is to say that (i) practical actions are movements; (ii) movements depend on principles; (iii) but the principle of that movement which is practical action is called dominion; (iv) so insofar as the human is the principle of a practical action, he is also master (*kýrios*) of that act. Aristotle will go on to divide contingent acts into actions and passions in a sense not unfamiliar to us from later treatments of the seventeenth century. Of greater import is the emphasis on that which is within the dominion of man insofar as it is capable of coming to exist or otherwise. Aristotle gives us the example of aging, which is a human action in the sense that it flows from the *arché* of the human to age, but is only within the dominion of the human in the broadest sense for while it is a movement (to age), the human could not act otherwise. Only those actions which are the principles of the existence or otherwise of some thing are within the dominion of a master in the technical sense (*kýrios tou einai*).

Superficially this all suggests the following intuitive model: humans have a domain of possible action, and they select a determinate course of action from this domain by causing it to exist – a simple agency account of ethics. The problem with this account is that it ignores that we are dealing with (i) the uncaused, so we should not be speaking about humans causing anything; (ii) principles (*archai*), and not causes in the strictly physical sense; (iii) an architectonic premised on the principle, such that we cannot introduce human agency as a source of some new, unbidden motion in the world. Point (iii) is really at the heart of what I will loosely call the human agency account: the claim that (the power of) desire moves from the human agent down to produce practical effects, in parallel with a model of the intellect which moves from the thinking mind to particular thoughts. Furthermore, I shall claim that a simple agency account offers little insight in comprehending the Scholastic comprehension of power and dominion. We are looking for an account which is consistent with the terminology of principle and the uncaused.

Drawing together the work of Lloyd Gerson and Aubry[5] on Plotinus and Aquinas we may sketch just such an account. We start with a contrast: activity as cause. We have the One (our Neoplatonised Prime Mover), which may first be understood as the cause of movement and, more fundamentally by the time of Aquinas, as the cause of being (*causa essendi*) as such. We have seen that this One acts without limitation, this pure act is its activity, and that at least with Aristotle this derives from the claim that there is no potency (deficiency) in the Prime Mover. Plotinus and ultimately Aquinas will regard the activity of *esse* as that which causes finite things to exist. To say that the One caused some *A* to be, they speak of the presence of the One not in the sense that *A* existing implies the One existing *with A*; rather, using Aquinas' terminology, the One's activity of being causes *virtualiter* through the essence of *A* and renders it active. Given that the One is self-caused it could be said to be virtual to itself also, whereby we have the idea of the One as activity as such.

We might say that the Neoplatonists and Aquinas reintroduce power into the One at just this juncture, because they see in the One's nature as *actus purus essendi* not just a logical maximum derived from Aristotle's metaphysical premises, but also something exemplary in the ethical sense. Considered from this perspective the terminology changes from a discourse of causes and activities to one of principles and potentialities. The One, by virtue of the purity of its act of being, is now considered a principle towards which all finite things, comprising activity and potency, are said to move. A new name is accorded to the One as principle: it is the Good just insofar as it manifests that towards which every finite thing is construed to tend, the complete actualisation of its nature. They tend, but they do not ultimately achieve this actualisation. Their potency remains manifest in that very striving for the Good.

This interpretation allows a precision of the status of power for the Neoplatonists and Aquinas. Strictly speaking one might say that the One continues to be devoid of potentiality because it is the pure actuality of the One-Good which elicits the potential in all finite things towards that One-Good. Aquinas again institutes a useful terminology: a given principle brings about this tendency *eminently*, and the world of actuality is ordered according to the eminence of principles. To say then that a principle dominates another entity and so has power over it might more accurately stated as: the principle elicits the potency of the finite thing to motion.

Returning then to Aristotle's structure of domination, we can see that an agency model is far too simple. It is the principle on the far left which procures the potencies of things to the right, and that it is the role of mediate things to elect between all those things which express a tendency to exist. The long quotation from Aristotle earlier in the section makes this distinction between cause and principle clear in clauses (2) and (3) but is rendered a little less approachable because it treats directly of the ethical domain of humans, which stand mediately between the Good and simplest things. The essential idea can be drawn out by observing that the nature of each actual substance stands as principle for those substances which are functionally subordinated to it. To take a common example, the knife's many potencies tend towards the principle of a human insofar as the knife serves, say, to cut food or clothing for the human. Thence the manner of speaking of dominion, whereby potency or power is ascribed to the human with respect to those functionally subordinate substances whose potencies tend towards inter alia the principle that is this or that human.

Observe what has happened here: the potentiality, properly speaking, is to be situated in the knife given that it is the knife which is passive with respect to the human action of its use. Yet by a certain sleight of hand the potentiality of the knife is understood as a power *for* its principle – the human – and not for the knife itself, and then this power is referred to the principle. It is a short step from here to saying that the power of the knife for the human is the power *of* the human for itself, the knife being regarded as some kind of composing element or disposition of the human in question. This distinction in the movement of power, from below up in the order of actuality, is marked by the language of domination (*kýrios*) in the *Eudemian Ethics*. It is a distinction which, if borne in mind, assists comprehension of certain theological problematics that follow and which are highlighted by Olivier Boulnois and Gwenaëlle Aubry.[6] If one speaks of the infinite power of the One, as first the Stoa and the early church fathers were wont to do, one can see how a certain lapse in thinking might creep in whereby power is identified with *dunamis* in the One. Either then you contradict the definition of the one as pure activity, or you may speak of a power of the One which is excessive but which still flows as cause from the One. This latter route then presents a problem of theodicy: the excessive power is infinite by definition, but either the One does everything in its power, denying choice, or the One chooses, implying some limitation and so unactualised potentiality in the One.

Yet Olivier Boulnois has brilliantly argued[7] that the difficulties of this question concerning divine choice result from this malformation of the question. If power is understood as domination, and *dunamis* is referred to the tendency of subordinated substances to their principle, then a more nuanced theological account is possible. The One-Good can be understood as pure act and fully actual, and just by virtue of this perfection every finite substance tends towards the Good. We have not so much a question of choice as of bounty. As Gwenaëlle Aubry frames it,[8] we have a movement from the in-potency of entities in the world (from which God is excepted) to the potency of entities in the world insofar as they tend towards the more perfect, to the potency of the One-Good which is the most perfect and therefore is said to procure just this tendency. We have a shift from *dunamis panton* – capable of all – to *pantokrator* – generator of all.

In what follows I use this theoretical basis to engage with the Scholastic doctrine of the will and so set the scene for a treatment of Leibniz's account of volition. The key lesson we have learned already helps us provide a critique of Kenny's own attribution to Aristotle of a theory of will. A good summary of this debate has been provided by Christof Rapp; for our purposes the arguments are these: that Kenny sees in the Aristotelean *boulesis* the first statement of a will-concept, while Ingram goes further, following Aquinas, by explicitly equating the Stagirite's *boulesis* (wish) with *voluntas*. Richard Sorabji remains unconvinced, for in a detailed exegesis[9] he finds at least two 'clusters' of actions, namely (i) actions of freedom and responsibility, and (ii) actions of wish and desire, but finds no attempt to combine these in a will-concept that amounts to a Thomist rational appetite. These criticisms seem largely merited: Aristotle nowhere defines the will explicitly in a manner equivalent to Aquinas. Indeed, there is argument about whether the term *boulesis* should be translated as will, and not as Rapp suggests, 'wish'. Yet if we can find the roots of a theory of volition in the Stagirite's ethics, we must look to the motion of potency from the less to the more perfect, and so situate volition, however understood by subsequent thinkers, as located within an interlocked order of eminence and domination. If a separate will can be attributed to the Aristotelean mind at all, it moves not of its own accord, but is a tendency of a substance's potentiality towards and elicited by an exemplar. Hence I must quibble with Rapp's account of Aristotelean rational wish:

> The concession I want to make is this. Having introduced notions of wish and choice, Aristotle describes men as the *arché* of their actions. One could try to boil that down to the claims we already heard of, that certain desires are the origin of movement in us etc. I think there are several reasons for going for the stronger claim. This time it is not

one or the other desire which is said to be the *arché*, but man (*anthropos*), and he does not speak of the *arché* of a motion but an action . . .[10]

Rapp goes on to discuss how Aristotle envisages the action being referred back to the *arché* of man as its ruling part, so that it is responsible for the beginning and end of the action, but Rapp is 'not exactly clear what to make of this'. The whole discussion continues to be inflected by notions of agency. Once one conceives of desire as moving towards a principle, and that desire is a multi-layered reality of functional dependence, much of the interpretative difficulties fall away and one can see how Aquinas would translate *boulesis* as *voluntas*. We are not speaking of causes to motion but principles of ends, and it is the end in question, the *anthropos*, which is the principle to be examined. On the one hand the elicited action is on the side of the subordinate entities, for desire comes from their potency, but on the other the desire must by elicited by an end, and this end goes to the perfection of the *arché*. It is by virtue of this perfection that the *arché* is said to rule or have dominion over the competing desires, suggesting that choice for Aristotle is choice between the actions of all the desires seeking actualisation for the end.

So does Aristotle provide us with a theory of the will? My aim has not been to answer this question, but rather provide a context for the Scholastic doctrine which informs Leibniz's thought. As such I rest on a modified version of Sorabji's thesis: that several of the ingredients of a theory of will combining choice and desire are to be found in Aristotle, though no explicit coupling of these clusters is made. What I tentatively add to the analysis is the role played by power, and the understanding that *boulesis* moves from below in the order of ends towards a principle or *arché* measured by its perfection. This interpretation puts us on guard against an agency reading which has humans exercising an innate 'power of will'. This reading not only aids interpreting Aristotle's *Eudemian Ethics*, it also seems naturally to precede the Neoplatonist and Scholastic doctrines.

Before we examine the views of the Schoolmen though, we should underline a question of attribution which no doubt has occurred to the reader. What is the source of power? The *boulesis–arché* model, and the Neoplatonist relation of principle and power, suggest on the one hand that the least things are characterised by their very potentiality – matter is purest potentiality in this regard. So in one sense of *dunamis* this matter is the source of power. But Aubry establishes that this sense of *dunamis* subsequently changes, and the Neoplatonist notion of *dunamis panton*, attributed to the One, seems to invert the whole logic. Now, having considered the Aristotelean *kurios* from several angles, I would underline that we already have the apparatus for a dual reading of power: to say that a principle has power or dominion is to say that the perfection of the principle elicits the will (*boulesis*) of some other thing to action. In other words, any practical action is a combination of principle and potency, of above and below, with a definite vector from the below to the end above.

At the heart of this section then is this discarding of a simple agency-reading of practical action, whereby a human has some pool of raw power which it can somehow inject into the world, in favour of an understanding of the material as acting towards principles, and that this model implies an embedding of principles and potencies into a hierarchy of perfections. In short, the world of essences proceeding from the cause is mirrored by an inverted world of desire for principles. In the thought of Duns Scotus we find a particularly powerful account of this world of principles and power – the world not of formal essences but of the *real* and the creatable. Our basic framework understood, I propose to focus a significant amount of work on the Scotist doctrine of the real, for its account of possibility and contingency appears highly influential for Leibniz's own thinking of the will and power.

3. Will and the power of the creatable

We owe much to Simo Knuuttila in his work[11] tracing the history of modality, and the parallels he allows us to draw between the Scotist theory of the possible and Leibniz's own work on conditions and contingency. Olivier Boulnois[12] and lately Gwenaëlle Aubry[13] also have done much work to make the subtlety of Scotism visible, and, in Aubry's case, to bring out much of what is most radical in Duns Scotus's treatment of power. Combining this remarkable research with the foundational work of Étienne Gilson[14] my aim in this section will be to provide Scotist context for Leibniz's own innovations in the fields of will and power, with power now being taken in a new sense which will become clear. In the next section I follow these ideas into the jurisprudential thinking of Francisco Suárez. What we will see as certain metaphysical tenets of Scotism, on which we focus in the first section, lead to difficulties for a theory of will on which we focus more directly in the following section.

3.1 Will and potency in Scotus: the creatable

Let us reprise our understanding of Duns Scotus, led primarily by the work of Gilson. Already we have had cause to understand a formal distinction between the merely rationally thinkable and the real, and to make a distinction within the real between quiddities and beings of existence. The quiddities themselves compose according to a hierarchy of being, determined by a causality which is readily linked to the manner in which higher quiddities are constituted from lower quiddities (the heart is an organ of the body). All individuals comprise such a quidditative structure united within what is named a substantial form.

Now, referring back to our square of power, normally speaking each actuality must work through a passive potency to perfect itself as existing. But in the case of the *actus purus essendi Dei* there is no in-potency in God, who has no need of matter to achieve perfection. In Scotist language: *primum effectivum est actu existens*, which is to argue that that whose essence needs no other to exist effects its existence without determination and so absolutely and perfectly – if it is possible, it exists. In this special case then we might analogously speak of the quiddity of God as existing by its own power.

Finite things, however, are limited both essentially and by virtue of being caused. As such, while the divine intellect can posit an infinity of quiddities as that which could possibly exist, something more is required such that some of them come to exist. Duns Scotus then makes a division of being between quiddative being which is founded in God's intellect, and existential being, or creatable being, which derives from God's will. Parallel to the intellect then, one can propose, stands a field of volition (a world) which is constructed from the set of all quiddities and contains as members all those creatables which God elects to come into existence. The set of quiddities stands merely as a source for the construction of a created world, for God elects from among the quiddities only those which combine to produce a world which satisfies the exercise of his absolutely powerful and free will. Indeed, for Scotus creation is the sole preserve of the Creator.

What though, is a *creatable*? Étienne Gilson provides[15] the following example: consider stone which could be carved into a statue. Following the Aristotelean divisions of being, the stone is in-potency a statue precisely because it is capable of receiving the form of statue, whereas once in the stone we can say that the form of statue is in act in that stone. Scotus, however, deploys more Scholastic terminology still: insofar as the stone is in-potency its *potential* is divided into two kinds: subjective and objective. A *subjective power* is the subject of the term of statue in the stone, which means, it appears, that insofar as the statue has been carved the form of statute remains in act but the matter thus perfected as statue continues to provide its in-potency as that statue – its continuing power is called subjective. The would seem to make sense if one remembers the corrupting nature of matter such that the form is never absolutely perfected in any stone, and indeed any finite thing must be a combination of form and matter, and thus always partly in-potency. *Objective power* is that same in-potency of the stone whether carved or not. The stone could always become this statue, or another, and even after being carved it remains open to change (even to cease to be and then become again this statue). Now, clearly the stone only expresses subjective power when it is carved as this statue, whereas even and particularly when uncarved the stone always expresses objective power. To the extent that it does express the objective power of becoming statue, that objective potentiality is called a creatable in the stone.

We may observe two orders at play: the order of intellect and the order of volition. In finite rational creatures their every mode combines the two, for the intellect moves to enumerate the possible, and the will chooses which to actualise according to the twofold Thomist order of practical thought: (i) the end, which is the general good, is moved towards; and

(ii) the will elects the means to that end from the objects it identifies in surrounding matter, for the finite creature exists in a world of other finite things and must produce through them by subjectifying their objective power. In this way the creatable has its order of composition of the finite, its hierarchy, which constitutes a community of existence.

Perhaps the most interesting aspect of this whole structure is its account of finite objective power. Given that none but God can actually create *ex nihilo*, the volitional act of production must engage the creatable in exactly the sense that this particular stone, for example, already has been chosen to express the objective power of becoming statue. Duns Scotus is not least remarkable for having taken brute matter as mere receptacle and endeavoured to grant it some structure, such that a stone (but not water) can be this statue. Yet this makes sense when one considers that finite creatures exist together as combinations of form and matter, and that to a certain extent the object-potency of a stone is partly due to its own nature. The justification for this view is all the more apparent when it is understood that creatables interlock as components of higher creatables. Much of the objective power of a creatable derives from its potentiality to serve as the component of a substantial form: it is all a matter of organisation. And here, in this difficulty over to what is due the power that builds our substantial form as individual, lies one of the most important occlusions in economic prehistory. To what extent is the activity of the substantial form due to its own being-in-work through the matter, and how much does the nature of the matter contribute even as it is treated as nothing but mute receptacle?

Aubry brilliantly exposes Duns Scotus's response to this problematic of assigning credit for power, picking up on the divine monopoly over creation. Even the simplest thing is created, and everything that stands above in the hierarchy of existence must compose the creatables below it, for each finite thing is matter and form. Yet these infinitely many creatables owe their very creatability to the divine will, which is now shown not just as infinite in itself but infinite in the perfection of its volition to create an infinity of real things.

In this way, one might say, even the simplest corpuscle of a world exists not simply because it is logically possible,

though possibility by virtue of non-contradiction completely
determines its nature, but because this possibility becomes
created by act of divine will *for the purpose of the general Good.*
The modal logic must be combined with a deontic logic: 'the
end causes nothing save what is produced through the efficient which loves the end'.[16] The whole centre of gravity of
final causality shifts from those associations and compositions which are closest to God, and is resituated in the lowest
rungs of the system. In this move Aubry finds the origins of
a new and absolute power, but I would like to underscore
an equally subtle innovation: because each possible becomes
creatable by virtue of a divine volition towards the End, it
is endowed with a certain striving to become – an objective
power which it is deemed to offer to the substantial forms
above it.

On this model, grounded in the square of opposition
between subjective action and objective potency, we are left
with a fine question as to where to posit the faculty of will,
which until now we have assumed we understand. If what is
to be created is commanded by the truth of the ideas of God,
then the creature's will to create is surely reducible to its
intellective action, and if we should speak of intellecting the
possible and willing the creation of that possible, then really
this is just a manner of speaking – the determining act is intellectual and the practical result is a passive consequence of my
bodily movements. Yet, if what is to be created is demanded
by the objective power of the creatable in matter, then that
objective potency is ordained by God not the individual, and
so any willing grounded in creatability is a kind of passion.
Where should we site volition: on the side of subjectivity or
objectivity? This question generates significant problems for
Late Scholasticism, as ably exposed by Spinoza, and telling
this story will lay the ground for the subtlety of Leibniz's
treatment.

3.2 The natural legal significance of the Scotist problematic

By locating a certain creatability in matter as its potency
we have seen how Duns Scotus lays bare a dilemma about
where to locate the will – in the subject's action or the object's

potency, or indeed in a hybrid of the two. It should be noted[17] that Duns Scotus is very much aware of this issue: the will is related to its object in such a fashion, he says, that in one sense the object must come first, because the will must have something to will, but in another sense the will is prior because the object cannot initiate the act of volition – just as the intellect thinks, so the will wills, but what it could will is apprehended by the intellect and then given to the will as object. If one is unconvinced by this distinction, to the will Duns Scotus adds a feature not applied to the intellect, namely the capacity not to will. The account runs something like this. The intellect can posit that which thinks as an idea and recognise it as that which thinks, but it is the essence of the intellect to think all it can, formally, and there is no sense in un-thinking thought – if I think I must know that there is thinking. The will is also reflexive, but in the other direction so to speak, for the will does not produce its objects but requires them to be presented to it. Now given an object, the will wills that object, but this willing of the object is also itself an object – the will therefore can will its own willing. And here the key difference intervenes: the will is capable of willing (*velle*) or not willing (*nolle*) what it wills.[18] Thus there is a doubling of elicitation, in which also the willing of an object elicits the will to choose between various possible willed objects. The difficulty remains though: what freedom is there if elicitation is the link between object and will?

Thomas Pink provides an analytic account of the consequences of this problematic for Late Scholasticism, and particular Gabriel Vázquez and Francisco Suárez:[19]

> So one effect of faculty dualism is to make unavoidable for this tradition a hybrid account of voluntary agency. ... Whenever human action occurs, there must be some intrinsically intentional or intrinsically voluntary action, the status of which as agency arises out of its constituting an exercise of immaterial rational motivational capacity – a capacity to be moved by some rational cognition. But the status of first order actions which are exercises of corporeal faculties [is explained] by virtue of there being objects and effects of the intrinsically intentional actions of the will.

While I would agree with Pink that a hybrid explanation is inevitable for this tradition, I would locate it not in
the dualism of intellect and will but in the deeper metaphysical distinction between subjective action and objective
potency discussed in the previous section. By applying the
Aristotelean square, we should expect that any finite event
in the world will be a composite of action and potency, and
this distinction predates the explicit denomination of a will
faculty. Furthermore, the faculty of will is bound to remain
slightly mysterious if it is posited as a dual of intellect. Once
one appreciates that the very practicality of a volition is to
be considered a composition of intellectual action and the
potency of matter, the problematic for the Schoolmen shifts
from where we locate the will to how to avoid reducing it to
either intellect, or potency, or this hybrid of the two which
is then simply an effect of right reasoning and/or chance
encounter with no space for specifically moral agency.

The importance of this Aristotelean-inspired interpretation, refracted through Scotus's theory of the creatable, is
illustrated by reading two key passages from Suárez identified by Pink:

> Voluntariness in the way of an imperated act [*actus imperati*]
> is nothing other than a certain character or denomination
> of the imperated act received from an elicited act, of which
> the imperated act is object and effect. For an imperated act
> is termed voluntary simply because it proceeds from an
> elicited act of the will and is in a measure informed by it
> and with it constitutes one morally significant act.[20]
>
> . . .
>
> Voluntariness in an elicited act of the will comes to nothing
> other than being an act which, in coming immediately
> from the will, is inherently self-willed through a virtual
> and inherent self-reflexion.[21]

The distinct roles played by imperated (commanded) act
and elicited act map readily onto our interpretative structure. Imperated act, as Pink confirms, causes little interpretative trouble for us because in the case of the natural law the
command flows from God via the intellect. This intellectual-
ist theory of command is a common feature of natural law

theories. The imperated act appears, in Pink's terminology, as a first order act, for example, the intention to give alms to the poor. Holding will as a faculty parallel to intellect raises issues for the explanation of elicited act, however. Pink appears to argue that it is the intellect which first elicits volition, and it is this elicited volition which has as its object the actual act of alms giving. This actual act is the imperated or commanded act of the will.[22] I struggle with such a reading. Suárez, by using the very term *elicit* (*actus elicitus*) and subsequently linking this to self-reflection, surely opposes the elicitation of the will to intellect. The will is explicitly 'drawn forth' and is received by the imperated act of the intellect. This makes sense when, as Pink points out, Suárez is at pains to distinguish the immateriality of intellection and the corporeality of volition. Once the role of matter in-potency is accounted for, the corporeality of volition can be explained according to the following order of practical action for a human. The human intellect enumerates possibilities; the human body, being in-potency, is drawn towards a given possibility; this eliciting possibility is then the object (or end) of the will as it moves from the body and not some abstract faculty; accordingly there is a kind of self-reflexion between the action of intellect and the power of the elicited will; the resulting composite is the imperated will – a rational appetite.

With this order of practical action Suárez is able to circumscribe voluntariness as a subset of practical action. Within all the possible motions of matter of a human's environment, Suárez carves out the rational appetite as the human body insofar as it is moved towards its intellectively determined end, namely the human individual as its labour (*ergon*). This division of the practical world into a zone of 'my body expressing my nature' within an environment of contrary determinations, then permits the classical division of action and passion used to discuss the rectitude and success of any action. It also opens up another avenue of attack. If a voluntary action is that action which results from the movement(s) of the body towards an idea delineated by the intellect, and is thus inherently reflexive, then we may look not only to the intellect for defects in its presentation of correct ideas to the will; we may also look to the appropriate constitution of the body in its potency to be elicited by such an object. Given that will is moving from the material and corporeal, and given the contingency of the body compared to the eternal character of reason in the Scholastic world view, an emphasis on corporeal defects is hardly surprising.

Suárez's integration of imperated and elicited will thus resolves the apparent Scotist dualism of faculties in favour of a constituted will. As Pink notes,[23] this is not without problems because one could argue that elicitation adds nothing truly voluntary to the intention to do x. For example, and here Pink quotes Hobbes's response to Bishop Bramhall, there is no difference between imperating that I shut my eyes and them shutting, and my willing that my eyes shut. For Hobbes, and indeed as Pink shows, for Gabriel Vázquez within the tradition, if will is to have any meaning at all it must be considered as a separate action or faculty. Yet whereas Vázquez will simply posit will as this separate faculty and thus source of 'active' voluntariness over against the material world, Hobbes will integrate potency into his account of will by developing an idea of a fundamentally free and physical conatus which is the source of all volitional power, even if that power is subsequently determined.

Terminological equivocation is not the chief danger for Suárez; *that* is provided by Spinoza who in this regard provides a more consistent application of the Aristotelean heritage. Spinoza[24] both accepts the charge of equivocation by collapsing the will into intellect, and enlarges the role of material power as basis for the motive force of physical effects. For Spinoza, all ideas have an affective quality towards which our minds and bodies are determined to move. This movement, insofar as it is conscious, is called desire. There is no need of will, first because it is enough that the idea be posited that we move towards it, and second because there is no question that we do otherwise save where we are prevented by some intervening determination. But most interestingly of all, our capacity to move towards the idea – to construct it as a knowledge tool or a practical tool – is largely determined by our power. Our power derives from our bodies, and our bodies are just particularly intimate tools that we also construct for ourselves with a view to further increasing our power. We grow, and as we grow, we integrate our environment as body, as tools, as city, and in this way our body in this wider sense produces greater power and ensures a more effective pursuit of the ideas we desire. Will, and so moralising about its exercise, becomes vestigial; the raw potency of matter holds centre stage for any ethics. In light of this potential conclusion one can see why Vázquez would prefer to avoid a hybrid theory of will: both components of voluntariness can be so attacked that morality and obedience lose a foothold in the self.

4. Conclusion

The Scholastic heritage bequeathed to Leibniz – the Suárecian integrating key aspects of Scotism – is thus under vital challenge from Hobbes and Spinoza. Leibniz will seek to maintain a certain orthodoxy in that he will uphold a hybrid theory of voluntariness, not least because he wishes to integrate the strength of the new physics into the existing theoretical framework. Yet rather than becoming bogged down in a debate over the priority of the imperating intellect or the elicited or desiring body, Leibniz will seek a third term, a principle of spontaneous action, which will regulate both reason and power.

Notes

1. Anthony Kenny, *Aristotle's Theory of Will* (London: Duckworth, 1979) p.8.
2. Kenny, *Aristotle's Theory of Will*, p.9.
3. As translator of the *Eudemian Ethics* in Aristotle, J. Barnes (ed.), *Complete Works of Aristotle: Revised Oxford Translation*, 2 vols (Princeton: Princeton University Press, 1984).
4. Liddell and Scott's *Greek-English Lexicon*, 21st edn (Oxford: Clarendon Press, 1884).
5. Lloyd Gerson, 'On the Greek Origins of the Actus Essendi' (draft paper not embargoed) <https://www.academia.edu/37305791/DRAFT_On_the_Greek_Origins_of_Actus_Essendi> (last accessed 31 December 2019). Gwenaëlle Aubry, *Dieu sans la puissance: dunamis et energeia chez Aristote et chez Plotin* (Paris: Vrin, 2006) pp.211–13.
6. Gwenaëlle Aubry, *Genèse du Dieu souverain* (Paris: Vrin, 2018) pp.29–31.

7. Olivier Boulnois, 'Un autre concept de Dieu est possible, ou la fin de la Théodicée' (2010) 761 *Critique* 803–14, referenced in Aubry, *Genèse*, p.30 n.2.
8. Aubry, *Dieu sans la puissance: dunamis et energeia chez Aristote et chez Plotin*, pp.212–13.
9. Richard Sorabji, *Necessity, Cause, and Blame: Perspectives on Aristotle's Theory* (Chicago: University of Chicago Press, 1980).
10. Christof Rapp, 'Tackling Aristotle's Notion of the Will' (2017) 41(2–3) *International Philosofical Inquiry* 67–79 at p.77.
11. *Modalities in Medieval Philosophy* (Abingdon: Routledge, 1995); 'Duns Scotus on the Foundations of Logical Modalities' in L. Honnefelder, R. Wood and M. Dreyer (eds) *John Duns Scotus: Metaphysics and Ethics* (Leiden: E.J. Brill, 1996) pp.127–45; with Lilli Alanen 'The Foundations of Modality and Conceivability in Descartes and his Predecessors' in S. Knuutila (ed.), *Modern Modalities: Studies in the History of Modal Theories from Medieval Nominalism to Logical Positivism* (Dordrecht: Kluwer, 1988) pp.1–76.
12. E.g. 'Contingence et alternatives' in O. Boulnois (ed.) *La Puissance et son ombre. De Pierre Lombard à Luther* (Paris: Aubier, 1994) pp.263–85.
13. See 'Duns Scot ou l'infini de la puissance' in her *Genèse du Dieu Souverain* (Paris: Vrin, 2018) ch.5.
14. *Jean Duns Scot: Introduction à ses Positions Fondamentales* (Paris: Vrin, 1952).
15. Gilson, *Jean Duns Scot*, p.434.
16. 'Nihil ergo causat finis nisi quod efficitur ab efficiente quia amante finem.' Duns Scotus, *Tractatus de primo principio*, ch.II, 5, in Ruedi Imbach (ed.), *Traité du Premier Principe* (Paris: Vrin, 2001).
17. See Gilson, *Jean Duns Scot*, pp.574–5.
18. Hannes Möhle, 'Scotus's Theory of Natural Law' in Thomas Williams (ed.), *The Cambridge Companion to Duns Scotus* (Cambridge: Cambridge University Press, 2003) pp.312–31, particularly pp.322ff.
19. Thomas Pink, 'Action, Will and Law in Late Scholasticism' in J. Kraye and R. Saarinen (eds), *Moral Philosophy on the Threshold of Modernity* (Netherlands: Springer, 2005) pp.31–50 at p.37.
20. Suárez, *De voluntario et involuntario*, in Francisco Suárez, *Opera Omnia*, 28 vols (Paris, L. Vivès, 1856–78) vol.4 p.160.
21. Ibid.
22. Pink, 'Action, Will and Law', p.36.

23. Ibid. p.39.
24. For more on Spinoza's theory, see chs.3–5 of Stephen Connelly, *Spinoza, Right and Absolute Freedom* (Abingdon: Routledge, Birkbeck Law Press, 2015).

Four

Will, Power and Pretensionality

1. Introduction

Having provided context through the previous chapter's investigation of Scholastic doctrines of will and power, I now turn to Leibniz's treatment of these matters. As we have noted, a key motivation for Leibniz's reconceptualisation of power is the challenge posed by the natural right theorists, particularly Hobbes and Spinoza, that makes material *potentia* the determining quantum of practical action. The move is not easily dismissed for it is grounded in the new physics of bodies. My argument is that on the one hand Leibniz overturns the discourse of power by reverting to an Aristotelean privileging of pure act and entelechy and demoting power (*potentia*) to a term relative to will in finite things. On the other hand, I claim that Leibniz maintains key features of the doctrine of power, such as domination and subordination, through a theory I name pretensional equivalence. This theory holds that entelechies exert a final cause on matter which converts the formally possible into the real invested with a claim or pretension to exist. The equivalence of pretensions arises, as with intensions, from the anchoring role of God, common to every finite mind, who is the sole entelechy capable of imbuing infinite degrees of matter with such pretensions, according to a hierarchy of interlocking realities. In other words, to understand *potentia* we must situate physical bodies within a primary passive order of the real, or World, created by God. The whole architectonic characterises power as moving from matter to the ultimate End within the context of a world, constituting a flow of pretensions reversionary with respect to the intensions of thought. The siting of particular *potentia* within a world marks a key movement in Leibniz's thought, for while it appears that he has demoted *potentia* to a subaltern of act that signifies finitude, we now come to appreciate that what makes matter potent – pretensions – is constituted by the real structure of a world, by a spatially ordered primary passive force. This pretensional relation between *potentia* and world or space will be a central plank of my reading of the various drafts of *Elements of Law*.

2. The yoking of power to will

Leibniz's response to the threat of both Spinoza and Hobbes predictably mirrors his shift from a doctrine of power to one of activity (or force) in order simultaneously to account for physical discoveries while granting grace a continued role through its characterisation as action. This would suggest that Leibniz will be sympathetic to the Suárecian move of denominating a composite of action and potency 'volition'. Leibniz though does not do this; perhaps he sees how mere composition leads to equivalence of authority between idea and bodily affect, and thus Spinozism. Rather, Leibniz once again seeks the general principle for particular acts and passions. Thinking back to our square of power, a distinction is made between form (active potency) and *energeia*/entelechy, and to these terms Leibniz will ascribe distinct volitional acts:

(a) entelechy = spontaneous action or liberty; and
(b) active potency = free will.

Observe first that Leibniz assigns to will a subaltern role with respect to a more general principle of actuality. In short, he responds to Gabriel Vásquez that there is no faculty of will as a separate principle of action parallel to intellect, but nor does he accept Suárez's view that voluntariness is a composite of particulars where action and potency vie for authority; rather both remain under the authority of a principle: entelechy. Observe second that the division corresponds to that in *Trinitas. Mens* where action and conation are identified as activities, whereas will together with *potentia* are treated as subalterns. Yet in this division Leibniz is at pains to claim that he is not breaking new ground here:

Our will is not only exempt from restraint, but what is more from necessity. Aristotle already remarked that there are two things in liberty, namely spontaneity and choice ... It is not necessary to imagine however that our liberty consists in an indeterminacy or an indifferent equilibrium [which is] impossible.[1]

It would be unfair, however, to claim that the distinction is not also in Hobbes and Spinoza because evidently both deploy substance as performing precisely the conceptual role of *energeia* – substance is a self-caused conation to motion or resistance which is a metaphysical *sine qua non* if any causal interaction between bodies is to be accounted for. If we consider again Suárez's structuring of volition, we can see where Leibniz innovates. If Hobbes can say that any motive action (including willing) begins in conative endeavour, and Spinoza can claim that it is conative resistance which is the requisite potency for any individual act in accordance with its nature, then at that point where Suárez would speak of elicitation of potency towards an object presented by intellect, Leibniz will posit a third principle of action: entelechy as object the creation of which is claimed by constituent possibilities.

In what follows I explore how Leibniz synthesises this theory, established broadly by the time of the drafts of the *Nouveaux Essais* in the 1690s, from his earlier engagements with mechanism. This analysis will provide the tools we need to engage with Leibniz's practical thought which subtends his treatment of law.

2.1 Saving the will?

Not wishing to spring surprises I will argue that Leibniz applies his subalternating distinction between primitive and derivative forces (between *energeia*/entelechy and motion, for example) to the question of volition, making a similar distinction now between spontaneous entelechy (acting or endeavouring) and volition. As to entelechies, these amount to active real principles which, as with Scotist substantial forms, have need of subordinate quiddities for the purposes of composing themselves. Where Duns Scotus sees creatables, Leibniz initially sees possibilities which claim to exist, but their claim to exist does not come from themselves but is adjudged of them by a substantial form which can compose them. Later, existence will be regarded as a spectrum of power, that is, reality, but I argue that even so Leibniz will continue to grant substantial forms the power to confer a pretension to exist on possibles. Now because a number of possibles could satisfy a need of a substantial form, their necessity for that form is only hypothetical, which permits choice. Yet save in the case of God, every finite substantial form does not extend its knowledge of its requirements to the deepest realms of the world; substantial forms dominate many others through a veil of ignorance. The spontaneous action of the entelechy extends across diverse choices, and each derivative moment is called a volition. Save in God this volition is always determined by another – determined by what is in-potency, such that every finite act of willing is always a combination of the derivative nature or form of a supposit and matter. This material determination, to the extent we are ignorant of its reasons, is experienced as an affect, and the resulting combination of potency and rational force produces the affect itself: the mode. Modes can be considered positively or negatively, and when considered positively we are speaking of the yoking of the material potency for the benefit and perfection of the entelechy. Whatever subordinate substantial form is engaged, unwittingly or otherwise, its activity is now demanded of it as its possible relations are actualised within the greater whole. This demand for the perfection of the substantial form is experienced as the valuation of the thing as good. But each substantial form, insofar as possessing mind (and so intellect and will) is double: it pursues the good ordained by its own entelechy, but has within itself also the being and so entelechy it shares with God, and from this it receives a second mediate end: the creation of Good, whereby each finite mind also encounters objects in the world which serve and are demanded to exist by that Sovereign power.

In this way, maintaining the clear distinction between actuality and active potency, Leibniz will attempt to navigate between a Spinozist determinism which renders the will obsolete, and a theory of free will which resorts to a mysterious faculty or defers this resort by having reason mediate between human and divine free will (and so command). In what follows I draw out three key interpretative arguments supportive of this reading: (a) that the possible's demand to exist is linked to force, but the force is on the side of a superior substantial form; (b) that the will is a derivative force which yokes objective potency; and (c) that by the time of the *Nouveaux Essais* the double notion of freedom of will, between the primary, spontaneous force and derivative volition, is a central tenet of Leibniz's doctrine.

Objective power: is force relevant?

Our first question is whether reference to Leibniz's physics can in any way assist our interpretation of matters of the will. Given that Leibniz argues for the use of final causes as explanatory principles in physical investigations, it would seem strange that he would keep the areas of nature and grace completely separate, yet by engaging with a scholarly claim that force has no immediate part to play in contingency we may underline the utility of Scotism for interpreting Leibniz's theory of the will.

Our present issue turns on the status of possibles and their pretension or claim to exist. Remember, for Duns Scotus there is a distinction between possible and creatable, and it is the exercise of sovereign will which selects the latter, imbuing the possible with an objective power that is regarded as valuable by the mind (the creatable becomes an objective good for the will).

In seems quite clear that Leibniz also regards the 'possible' as possessing a certain power, which he variously describes as an endeavour or pretension to exist. Indeed, using the work of Paul Rateau[2] we can trace the terminological evolution of the 1680s whereby what begins as each essence's pretension (or right) to exist becomes a propensity, then a demand to exist (*exigentia existentiae*), a force of existing, and finally a conative endeavour. For example:

> Every essence or reality demands existence just as every effort demands motion or its effect, provided of course nothing prevents it. And every possible includes not only possibility but also the *effort* actually to exist, not that things that do not exist possess an effort, but because this is

demanded [*postulant*] by the ideas of essences that actually exist in God.[3]

Rateau correctly identifies the need on Leibniz's part not to collapse this propensity into mechanism, for Spinozism follows. Where I depart from Rateau is in explaining just what Leibniz is doing, for Rateau – in order ingeniously to preserve the jurisdiction of grace – argues that this demand to exist is neither a force nor a species of it; rather, the right of each essence is a claim to the exercise of force by a sovereign power.[4] There is great merit in this interpretation, yet I am inclined to argue that force continues to play its part, but that the locus of the demand is slightly more differentiated than an appeal to God: the force of the demand is seated in the substance which perceives the possibility under consideration and the claim arises from the activity (and so idea) that the mind has of the possibility and not from the possibility itself. While Rateau makes the bold claim that Leibniz actively excises the term 'force' from any relation to pretension to exist,[5] I would argue that the metaphysical structure Leibniz erects, which links demand to affect, affect to will, will to power and power to reality as perfection, strongly favours a continued interpretation of force as 'in play', provided we maintain the necessary distinction between primary and derivative force. In support of this reading I argue as follows:

(a) *Argument for a distinction between the formal and the real*: that just as in Duns Scotus and Suárez,[6] Leibniz too deploys two orders of 'possibility', the modal necessary and the contingent. For example, when in DM Leibniz advances his complete concept theory of the substantial form, he appears to speak directly to Spinoza when he says that a complete definition of a circle is a poor example because it will 'destroy the distinction between contingent and necessary truths'. Leibniz proposes to contrast the necessary with the 'assured' (hypothetical):

> The other [sequence] is necessary only *ex hypothesi*, and by accident, so to speak, and this connection is contingent in itself when its contradictory implies no contradiction. A connection of this kind [is based also]

> on God['s] free decrees and on the sequence of events
> in the universe. (DM §13)

Leibniz goes on to show that these decrees result 'assuredly' from the choice of the best, that is, the rejection or non-choice of 'imperfection'.

That Leibniz deploys just this distinction is well known in the literature, particularly due to the centrality of the logical/possible versus physical/hypothetical distinction in Christian Wolff's work, and the powerful critique of Leibniz–Wolff modality by Hegel in his chapter on 'Actuality' in the *Science of Logic*.[7] It is highly relevant to Leibniz's legal theory and he will return to it in later chapters. I thus regard the presence in Leibniz of the division between logical possibilities flowing from the intellect, and the contingency of the choices amongst those possibles that derive from 'free decrees', to be uncontroversial.

(b) *Argument that pretension is a mediate state between possibility and actual existence*: that the intellect is produced by being and is absolutely known to God, but that God then acts (*agit*) to select from what is merely possible those things which are compossible in a world and in so doing invests them with a pretension to exist. Hence Leibniz writes: 'Thus the essences of things clearly depend on the divine nature, and existences on the divine will. For it is not by their own force [*propria vi*], but by God's decree that they can obtain existence.'[8] We note first that Leibniz is speaking of essences, not natures (save God's own), orienting us to the divine activity. This also suggests that existence should be considered at this level and not at the level of finite natures. The Scotist notions of creator and creatability, which Aubry highlights in the form '*efficans-effectabile*', seem to come to Leibniz, who coins '*existentificans*' to describe the efficacious act of producing existence-seeking in things. Such a distinction would then explain why Leibniz does not say that essences 'need God's decree to exist' but that by that decree 'they can obtain existence' and in notes from the 1690s, that they are '*existiturire*' (existence-seeking).[9] Leibniz appears to be describing a permission to exist, not an effective production of existence, which accords with a doctrine of creation. God creates the essences that could exist in this world; the creation *ex nihilo* is his privilege. Were God to effect all existence, then everything compossible would have to exist at once and finite minds would not exercise free will over what may exist.

In short then, the conation to exist in no way derives from mere possibility, but is an objective potency impressed upon a possible by the will of some primary force (principally God).

(c) *Argument for a distinction between eternal forms and universal realities*: that there is a kind of objective reality beyond what exists, constituted by innate ideas. The term 'reality' evokes the realities of Duns Scotus, which operate as alternatives to the formal ideas of the essentialists. The pinnacle of realism is the *haecceitas* – the real individual, but Leibniz attacks this notion in his early *Dissertation on the Principle of Individuation* (1663),[10] preferring rather a total concept theory of the individual entity. Yet the Scotist *haecceity* receives much attention in the *Dissertation*,[11] and it seems to me that middle period Leibniz has fully integrated the real within his complete concept model, where it now distinguishes contingent existence from possible essence. Leibniz's most detailed engagements with existence as such unsurprisingly take place in various drafts of the ontological argument. In 1678 he presents the following:

> As in the region of eternal truths, or in the field of ideas that exists objectively [*a parte rei*], there subsist Unity, the Circle, Potency, equality, heat, rose, and other realities or forms or perfections, even if no individual beings were to exist, and these universals were not to be thought about; so also there among the other forms or objective realities is found *actual existence*, not as it is found in the World and in examples, but as a universal form.[12]

It seems to me that these ideas *ex parte rei* will become the innate ideas of the *Nouveaux Essais*, but that suggestion is secondary for our purpose. I wish to draw out four points: (i) The field of ideas that exists *a parte rei* is highly suggestive of the Scotist and Suárecian distinction between formal and real, indicating that this field is one not of the merely possible, but the (quidditatively) real. (ii) That this objective reality is not individual but can be individuated in the World and in examples. (iii) To underline the latter point, there is one universal form which cannot be actualised in the World, but nevertheless exists. (iv) Existence is actualised as the derivative of some force. Here we recover a version of the Aristotelean proof of the Prime Mover's existence: in the finite case the derivative action is determined by some passion; in the divine case the derivative is unlimited and manifests itself absolutely.

(d) *Argument from the interlocking nature of substantial forms*: that were existence solely due to God's decree, finite substantial forms would only have a servile will; rather actual existence is decreed by substantial forms. From the foregoing, God creates the objective realities, which is to say that the compossibles of a world express a tendency to exist before they are actualised, and it is that tendency which derives from the divine will. Insofar as we speak of objective realities other than the universal form, their actual existence is found in the World and in examples. But what decrees the actual existence of finite things? The *General Inquiries about the Analysis of Concepts and Truths* from 1686 is highly suggestive:

> I say therefore that an Existent is an Entity that is compatible with the most; that is, an entity which is maximally possible, and so all coexistents are equally possible. Or, what comes to the same thing, an existent is what pleases an intelligent and powerful [mind?]; but thus Existence itself is presupposed. However, it can at least be defined that an Existent is what would please some Mind, and would not displease some other more powerful [mind], if any minds at all were assumed to exist. Therefore the matter comes to this, that that is said to exist which would not displease the most powerful [Mind], if a most powerful mind were assumed to exist. ... [It] can thus be defined: That

exists which pleases some <(existing)> mind ('existing' not needing to be added if it's a question of non-simple propositions), and does not displease a more (absolutely) powerful mind.[13]

Delaying briefly a treatment of the idea of possibility as subject to degree, we also see Leibniz defining existence by reference to the pleasure of minds of differing degrees of potency *inter se*, further supporting the view that pretensions do not originate in possibles (at least in this middle period). Furthermore, it is quite apparent from the concluding definition that the reference point for pleasure is an absolutely powerful mind, such that in any case, should the actualisation of a compossible please a finite mind, it is a necessary condition of that finite pleasure in every case that the absolute mind is pleased by that compossibility. Inversely, the compossibles only claim existence because they please God, and it is only because they claim existence at all that less powerful minds are capable of finding pleasure in bringing about their actualisation within a finite substantial form.

From this the Scotist model of interlocking substantial forms and quiddities seems but a little step, and it would be unusual that such a model of composition and complexity did not inform Leibniz's thinking about actualisation of existence. Even if he was not aware of the Scotist model (which seems unlikely), he was aware that a similar composite structure of existence (likewise relying on modes and so affects) had been advanced by Spinoza in his 'Physical Interlude' to the *Ethics* Part II.

(e) *Argument from physical categories*: that the distinction between primary and derivative forces discussed in Chapter 2 supports an interpretation of physical events as derivatives of activity and in-potency. On this model, however, the primary force which is the substrate of formal possibility is the activity of the supposit. We are now speaking of some additional factor which is super-added to the formally possible to make it really contingent, that is, to express a pretension to exist. By inspection of our square, the candidate presented is primary passive force. This makes sense as a candidate because (i) the orders of matter, from extension up, are first constituted by the power of God as *in-potency*; (ii) this *in-potency* is a force, such as repugnance; (iii) the model of interlocking substantial forms focuses not on the consideration of formal possibility but the organisation of real possibilities, for example, marble serves statue-ness.

Let us take a dynamic example. If we imagine for the sake of argument a Spinozan-style mind coupled to a simple mass with velocity (thereby having impetus), then one could imagine that the body's continuing pretension to exist in the future, faced with external percussion, is a claim coming from that simple body. But Leibniz is not arguing that such a body lacks a pretension, but that the possible lacks pretension of itself. The pretension derives from a primary passive force, which he, following Spinoza and Hobbes at least terminologically, calls *conatus*. It is the conatus which imbues the merely possible continued motion of a body with exigency.

In this again we see similarities with the Suárecian hybrid theory of will, in which formal idea elicits corporeal volition. In the previous argument we say how finite substantial forms 'assume' component realities to come to exist. The formal possibility of a table could compose both wood and metal as contingent components, and these components are in-potency with respect to table-ness. An actually existing table, as with the motion of a simple mass, composes both formal possibility and the contingency afforded by subordinate realities. The subordinate realities stand, relative to finite creatures, as in-potency to their composition in those finite creatures.

(f) *Argument from degrees of reality or perfection*: that to be precise, existence is not a binary opposition of existing or otherwise, but rather a degree measured by reality or perfection. Tying together our work on the varying senses of power Leibniz deploys, and particularly the manner in which Leibniz redefines power by reference to reality or perfection, we can understand that pretensions form an ordered hierarchy not among what is possible in terms of states (every single possible circle) but in terms of supposits or substantial forms (the real). What is most powerful is that substantial form which actualises the

maximal number of contingent sub-states, but if we speak
of any composite supposit, then what it will actualise
involves very many other subordinate supposits. In an
undated note identified by R.M. Adams[14] as originating
from the 1678–89 period, and entitled 'Existence', much
of the middle period thinking tying reality to existence
is encapsulated, even if ultimately we have no definitive
Leibnizian view on its status as a metaphysical notion:[15]

> ... [I]t seems to be true that existence is a certain
> degree of reality; or certainly that it has some rela-
> tion to degrees of reality. Existence is not a degree
> of reality, however; for of every degree of reality it
> is possible to understand the existence as well as
> the possibility. Existence will therefore be the supe-
> riority of the degrees of reality of one thing over the
> degrees of reality of an opposed thing. That is, that
> which is more perfect than all things mutually incom-
> patible *exists*, and conversely what exists is more
> perfect than the rest. Therefore it is true indeed that
> what exists is more perfect than the non-existent, but
> it is not true that existence itself is a perfection, since
> it is only a certain comparative relation of perfections
> among themselves.

The context is the ontological proof, and we should be
alive to the implication of causality in what appears to
be only a logical argument. Degree of perfection is not
existence but the principle or source (i.e. cause) of existence (L:487). If we account for this then we are seeking
an entity which can cause the most things, and in this
context we immediately return to one of the key Thomist
proofs for God – the regression to a Prime Mover derived
from the Aristotelean corpus: a Prime Mover who is both
efficient and final cause of all things. Insofar as it is final
cause, God is the end because his entelechy is perfected
and all finite things seek that perfection: the argument
from eminence.

In Leibniz we encounter a familiar refrain: for an individual to be perfected it requires contributions from
matter, but there is posited one entity which has no need

of matter and is capable of efficiently causing itself: pure act. Yet this is not the end of the story, for the very nature of perfection with Leibniz comes to mean the ability to maximise compossibility, which I read as maximising the reality of substantial forms. The question of perfection (and so the actuality of entelechy) becomes one of constructing a creator-God: God is not perfected until he has proved capable of creating the most possible things (at least more than any other entity). Thus God's pure act also constitutes himself not merely as thinking an infinite world *formaliter* but as creating the creatables: the substantial forms *realiter*. The shift from formality to reality is marked by the free gift of the pretension to exist. Consequently, the hierarchy of power in the world is determined in the image of the Creator: each thing is the more perfect the more reality it expresses, which is to say that that substantial form is more perfect than another the more it composes other substantial forms into, so to speak, sub-worlds of compossibility bound by this exigence to exist.

Again the pretension to exist of any possible is 'something other', 'something superadded';[16] it derives from the perfection of its source: the *ens perfectissimum* which Leibniz invests at the heart of every substantial form so that it always has immediate access to an unattainable standard.[17]

(g) *Argument from physics*: that in the *Discourse on Metaphysics* in particular Leibniz regards his theory of conservation of *vis viva* as an important justification for the utility of final causes in physics, and thus the linkage between force, reality, perfection and so choice. Leibniz famously shows *contra* Descartes that if I wish to change the velocity of bodies of different mass, it is not simply a case of adding a directly proportionate quantum of velocity to each mass. Rather, I must add more than double the velocity to the heavier mass to achieve the same effect. The Cartesian adherence to quantity of motion, which relies on summing speed, thus falls down as soon as forces are properly accounted for. This argument, drawn from previous notes on the subject, is rehearsed in the DM so that the following metaphysical conclusions may be drawn:

We must see from this that *force* must be estimated by the quantity of effect which it can produce . . . (DM §17)

For considering only what it means narrowly and formally, that is as change of place, motion is *not entirely something real*. . . . The force or the immediate cause of these changes is something more real . . . (DM §18, my emphasis)

Leibniz then proceeds in §§19–22 to discuss the uses of final causes in explaining these matters, and attempts to reconcile efficient and final causes. Let us though focus on the entwining of terms that occurs in these key passages: (i) the formal and real are distinguished. In particular the Cartesian idea of motion as a formal essence 'in' an attribute of distinction is distinguished from 'something more real'. (ii) The real is linked to the notion of force. This in one sense is not new, for Spinoza links reality and power also. (iii) Formal motion is 'not entirely something real', suggesting that the distinction is not absolute but one of degree. (iv) The degree of force, or reality, is manifested by the effect it produces, not by the sum of its efficient causes.

Mechanical events are known by determining the efficient *causes* of formal essences (activity); dynamic events are also known by estimating the *effects* of final causes by reference to realities, that is, as we have seen earlier, the capacity to express many other contingencies (in a physical system). In this way Leibniz elaborates on his key thesis that when a finite substance acts on another, even if that first substance has infinite extension, it may still be deemed limited with respect to the other by assessing the degree to which it expresses the greatest reality, or is perfect (DM §16). It is thus wrong to say that Leibniz excises force from his discussion of perfection. Force is integral to the notion because it is linked to reality, provided that in this way force is understood as expression of many contingent components. With respect to Rateau, his thesis that force ceases to play a part may be suggested by a deep problem for Spinozism – a treatment of force as a homogeneous quantum – when Leibniz's theory measures the degree of informational content (realities) of a world expressed by a substantial form. Thus as two substances interact and the force between them appears to be transferred, what we see rather is that one substance increases its expression of its world, the other decreases its expression, and so the former becomes more perfect; the latter imperfect.

(h) *Argument from finitude*: that it is only because human minds operate *in media res* that it appears that things themselves demand to exist. I refer in particular to the arguments of *On the Radical Origination of Things* (1697) which at once cements many of the foregoing theses but seems also to posit the exigency to exist in the least bodies in a manner verging on materialism: for example: all possible things, or things expressing an essence or possible reality, pretend to existence.[18] What place then human volition?

In fact as the text proceeds, Leibniz will reintroduce morality, but there is no contradiction being crudely covered over. Rather, much of the text's focus on physical matters operates on the basis of the same division between mind and body we find in *Trinitas. Mens*, and the argument makes sense from that perspective. For if we imagine a finite human mind in a corporeal world, it is as much the doctrine of the Neoplatonists and Schoolmen as it is of Leibniz that only an infinitely powerful entity has the wherewithal to create the infinitude of the simplest possibles which make up real extension. Now if our interpretation is correct and everything expressing a pretension to exist derives that exigency from some substantial form, Leibniz's prime candidate for imputing exigency into the components of the continuum is God. Thus, from the relative perspective of a finite mind there are perceived very many such possibles as claiming existence but that claim is not immediate act of will of the finite mind; rather a mediate act of will of God. It is if the finite mind is a watermill standing halfway down a river: it cannot claim that it draws the force of the water to itself; rather it plugs itself into a flow of water exacted by the potential of gravity and gradient. In terms of *Trinitas*.

Mens we find the distribution between Trinity and Mind, between body and World. Hence there is no inconsistency in Leibniz marking this distinction by declaring that 'there is a certain *exigentia* toward existence in possible things or in possibility or essence itself ... that essence in itself tends to exist'.[19] Relative to a finite mind, that tendency is not the will of the individual, and so appears to come from without. Nevertheless, we need to rehearse the doctrine whereby there is no 'without' properly speaking.

For this reason the final paragraphs of the *Origination* text move to consider the moral world, noting that choice consists in the candidates for composition ('the disorder of a part does not destroy the harmony of the whole'), before stating that:

> the law of justice dictates that each [mind] shall participate in the perfection of the universe and his own happiness according to the measure of his own virtue and the degree to which his will is set to work [*erga*] toward the common good.[20]

In such a world the mind must face the demands of very many things, but it is set to work to pursue its own end and that decreed by its master, but this does not lessen the contingency of the choice of parts within the whole. It is within this space that Leibniz will have us little workers demand the existence of the possible within a form which itself composes us and our world.

From the foregoing we see that force remains relevant to an understanding of perfection, and that whereas efficient causes are the province of formal essences (such as motion), dynamics is to be explained by reference to final causes which operate by means of the varying expressions of realities that compose a finite substantial form. This province of the real is governed by divine decree, but we have rather assumed an understanding of the relationship between divine decree (as entelechy) and the volitions which appear in the province of the real. We know that the distinction between formality and reality is at work in Leibniz's thought, and that it is linked to activity, potency and actuality, but what precisely is this actuality (entelechy) and how does it relate to the will? We have seen glimpses of this already, but our discussion would benefit from a change of focus – to the divine principle – to understand by what means formal possibles become realities bearing a pretension to exist. Answering this question will aid us in then considering the finite case: how do creatures effect existence amongst the possibles claiming existence?

By what means does God imbue the possible with a pretension? Actuality

Another way of stating this question is to ask, if not by volition, how does God choose among the possibles. The broad answer is well known: Leibniz's God chooses the best, namely that world constituted of the most compossible realities – unity of differences. Our interest though is not directly what God chooses, but by what act is this choice made. The foregoing discussion tells us that entelechy plays the requisite role of spontaneous choice, but in what does this consist? For Aristotle, entelechy is the actuality of a substance's perfection, by which is meant not that a substance's activity has achieved its end point as a status, but that we can consider this substance's end as its function, and so ask to what degree the substance is now actively and continuously fulfilling this function. There is an aspect of growth to this notion too, for with finite things they must acquire potency to develop their substance so that the resultant developed individual best expresses its continuing *energeia* in the present. Hence *Metaphysics IX*:[21]

> . . . everything which is becoming moves towards its principle, its *telos*. For the for-the-sake-of-which of a thing is its end, and becoming has as its for-the-sake-of-which the end. And *entelecheia* is the end, and it is for the sake of this that the potentiality is acquired. [1050a7–10]

Critically, because this framework suggests complete subordination within an intelligible unity, the primary end of substance is its real unity. Thus, in a manner which Hegel would pick up, actuality of a substance is the manifestation of that substance's own activity for itself.

Aquinas' account links actuality to perfection in its discussion of God:

> Now God is the first principle, not material, but in the order of efficient cause, which must be most perfect. For just as matter, as such, is merely potential, an agent, as such, is in the state of actuality. Hence, the first active principle must needs be most actual, and therefore most perfect; for a thing is perfect in proportion to its state of actuality, because we call that perfect which lacks nothing of the mode of its perfection. (ST I, 4)

The role of agency here is crucial: it is not that God is complete (status) that he is most perfect, but rather that his labour is fully present in himself as his actuality. As if to underline this point, Aquinas states in his third reply that existence is the most perfect of all things, not because existence itself exists, but because it is that which actuates forms so that they exist. Thus, for God and for creature: to exist is to be actual, which is to manifest, if nothing else, the continuous agency of the Principle.

It is this idea of continuous actuality as entelechy which helps us to understand the fulgurations of Leibniz's God. It is not because Leibniz's God has produced himself that he is perfect, but that he also continuously actualises as *supposita*. It is for this reason that Leibniz, perhaps dissatisfied with the metaphorical Thomism characterising his approach to perfection in the opening of the *Discourse on Metaphysics*, sketches out a much tighter treatment of the issue of entelechy and perfection in his so-called *Metaphysical Theses* of the 1690s.[22] It is in this text that we encounter the neologism: *existificans*. Leibniz's argument contains the following relevant claims which work from final causes or principles:[23]

(a) (Implicitly) being is first intelligibility. If anything exists it is *for* a reason. Being is that first reason and is actual in this thing according to its perfection.
(b) The confirmation that formal being is supplemented by real being, and real being results from 'existification' *for* a necessary being and principle, that is, God.
(c) That existence is by degree: all formal possibles exist

because they all receive existification. As such there is no idea which does not pretend to exist in some way (*omne possibile existiturire*[24]).

(d) The choice as to existence therefore is not between the formal and the real, but is (apparently) devolved to Nature in which each thing is in 'conflict' for degrees of reality according to a law of compossibility.

(e) Perfection is just quantity of reality (*quantitas realitatis*), and the whole that exists at any moment is perfect.

(f) Pleasure is the perception of variety *but also* minds are given the greatest consideration because through them one obtains the greatest variety in the smallest space (*in minimo spatio*).[25]

It is this last point which is central also to understanding the divine actuality: finding pleasure in variety is one thing, but it is the agency of all minds in obtaining variety according to a principle of minimisation which is the actuality that is the end of the whole process. This is the linkage between the activity of our minds and that of God: 'Now it is . . . very evident that the created substances depend on God, who conserves them and even produces them continually by a kind of emanation, as we produce our thoughts' (DM §14).

First, we find confirmed that the devolution of the determination of the best to the conflict of finite beings (their wills) is only an apparent ceding of authority. It is not because finite beings are the best that they please God and manifest him; it is because they manifest God's actuality and pleasure that they are the best. Put another way in the physical realm, the doctrine of conservation of *vis viva* ensures a fixed quantum of reality in a given physical system, such as a billiard table. When one billiard ball strikes another and sets it to relative motion, it manifests a greater reality or perfection, but its reality is not its change of motion – rather, its reality is the expression of the constraints (the respective conflicts) of the whole physical system, and it is this system's conflictual actuality which is manifested at this time in that billiard ball most powerfully. The point here is that the physical event is derivative of and manifests its principle, and I claim that by analogy a similar relationship pertains between various particular instances of the best (existence) and God as entelechy manifested by these instances. The world is not simply formal possibility combined with real contingency, but expresses a certain reality which derives from its divine agent. Authority remains with the One; all demands to exist have their principle in this authority.

Second, if we are to conceive of God as thinking Himself and being pleased by this idea then this God is static and lacks entelechy. This God is compelled by the doctrine to fulgurate:[26] He thinks Himself (1) but given that the 'only self-knowledge is to distinguish well between our self-being' (*Selbstbestand*) and our non-being, he also thinks Nothing (0).[27] It is a metaphysical structure which appears to deny spontaneous choice: God produces variety, and conflict between creatures effects the best result. This, however, is to miss the 'necessity of choice' within this conceptual structure that derives from Leibniz's combinatorial work in Leipzig and which subtends his legal work, particularly the *Nova Methodus*. This point appears only to be implicit in Leibniz's work on spontaneity, but its presence seems clear after a fashion: the *ars combinatoria* requires choice to set it in motion and in this is opposed to mechanics. I am not saying that God must choose (the choice is hypothetical); I am saying that it is a prerequisite of a hypothetical choice that there be a choice at all. Choice goes to the concept's heart: there is no intension (function) which proceeds from God to the idea of God and then from God to the idea of Nothing (or vice versa). If God is determined to intend the *idea Dei* then this can be provided for, but then he cannot intend Nothing; if he is given an equilibrium choice then he chooses neither. God must choose in an active sense: choose 1; choose 0; choose 01; and so forth.

Gaston Grua has demonstrated[28] how Leibniz will describe this process as one of self-determination, and it is useful to compare the combinatorial and rational theological understandings of this concept. Already in 1677 Leibniz will claim that to act spontaneously is to determine oneself, and 'we know that the concept *to be determined by itself* does not imply contradiction'.[29] Grua establishes that the doctrine holds through to the *Theodicy*. Here Leibniz writes that the specificity of this determination is that it is reflexive, and by that very means it is not a constraint,[30] at least according to the classical binary of action and passion. Leibniz also describes spontaneity as a form of contingence,[31] but what does this mean? Contingence points us to volition, and to the ability of an idea, plus any requisite potency, to reflect its end. In God though, self-determination is the very exclusion of the Nothing which will constitute potency, for 'pure actuality is simpler than an actuality mixed with potency'.[32] We are left with the ability of an idea of unity which is the limit case of all contingency: 'contingency without constraint'.[33] This seems close to what Hegel will call necessity.

It is this spontaneous choosing that is the actuality or entelechy which is the reason and force behind the reality and perfection of things.

This takes us back to our considerations of Suárez and Vásquez. Like Suárez, Leibniz will regard the will as a particular combination of idea and corporeal potency, but to this he adds not an imperating will which commands whatever, but a spontaneous choosing that decrees by means of the very actuality expressed in volitions. It is a concept which unites determinate possibilities in reason with contingencies in nature to derive will. Unlike Vásquez, lack of restraint bearing on the volitional principle denotes neither a liberty without reason nor an abstract and parallel faculty to the intellect. Entelechy is a manifestation of the activity of the supposit, and is thus 'rational contingency'.[34] A gradation is instituted according to actuality; according to the degree to which this entelechy is manifested by all things, immediately or mediately through subjects, for this is the divine pleasure.[35]

In this way Leibniz reiterates the rationalising move he makes in the *Trinitas. Mens.* There he makes intellect the immediate production of the activity of *esse* – he intellectualises being fully, making it accessible to all rational creatures. Now, in the case of God, he holds that the divine volitions manifest the rationality of the divine being as entelechy. Whereas for knowing activity is rational, for willing the rational is the actual.[36]

2.2 Volition in the *Nouveaux Essais*

Leibniz's thinking on spontaneity and volition whereby he seeks to maintain determinism but not at the cost of liberty, crystallises in Book II of the *Nouveaux Essais* (initially drafted in the 1690s). The core statement may be found in Chapter xxi:

> Volition is the effort or endeavour [*conatus*] to move towards what one finds good and away from what one finds bad, the endeavour arising immediately out of one's awareness of those things. This definition has as a corollary in the famous axiom that from will and power together, action follows; since any endeavour results in action unless it is prevented. (NE:II, xxi, §5; A:VI, 6, 72)

This quotation brings together several key moments in the operation of the will, which operates across two levels: (i) the level of this human's own entelechy or perfection; and (ii) the level of the divine decree, that is, in the relation between subjective and objective pretensions marked by the conjunction: 'will and power'. Here we have the nexus of Leibniz's theory of practical action and a conceptual structure which will inform so much that will follow. What is this power which the finite will requires in order to achieve any action? In this practical sphere power has come to be linked to the pretensions of forms, in their demand to exist. Leibniz's whole practical economy is founded on the interaction of these demands divided by point of view: on the one hand a subjective demand which derives from the body a mind has constructed, which demand is informed by the spontaneity of the mind itself; on the other, demand impressed in the world by the divine decree. The very nature of entelechy is such that will, if it is to attain further action (perfection), must appropriate to itself not only the existing body's power or subjective demand, but in addition some quantum of the objective demand 'God has placed into the world'. Additionally, by virtue of the presence of the divine activity in us (which is the condition of our apprehension of the material world), we have a second entelechy or desire to perfect all things and so organise the world so that a maximal objective demand be satisfied: what Leibniz will call the principle of harmony.

In what follows I consider the *Nouveaux Essais'* account of the operation of the will, and underline how phenomenal realities, or images, are central to this story.

The spontaneous act of the finite mind is the perfection of its substantial form. Once the substantial form has a body, its conatus is expressed derivatively as momentary will. Unlike the mechanical case, however, the mind integrates certain additional factors of its self-production, one moving from the spontaneous entelechy of its substantial form, through the intellect to volition; the other from the roots of all possible things. As to the first movement which was discussed earlier in this chapter, what distinguishes willing minds from physical bodies is their degree of perfection, manifested in this context in their access to the *esse*–intellect that discloses the possible, and *agere*–power of God which grants objective potency or compossibility to substantial forms subsisting as creatable in the divine volition. And as we know, a hierarchy of composition of these forms is constituted, such that a given mind will first grasp those possibilities which can compose with its existing body. All this is, however, a somewhat formal exercise under which will and intellect could be regarded as equivalent. The will's difference is grounded in its being itself a combination of perception and inclination: 'Various perceptions and inclinations combine to produce a complete volition: it is the result of a conflict among them' (NE:II, xxi, §39; NE:192).

From the late 1670s Leibniz has proceeded along both combinatorial and affective lines of argument to explain the conatus 'that arises out of the awareness of things'.

(a) *The combinatorial argument:* that God creates an infinite series of compossible reals which pretend to exist (see the previous section), and faced with the incommensurability of this creation, the finite mind's imagination only extends to some expressive 'horizon' beyond which what is compossible is as yet unknown. God is the root of all possibility, the *radix possibilitatis*.[37] The finite will extends further into the field of the possible than the imagination can perceive. But why should this be?

(b) *The affective argument:* that any finite mind, if it exists, expresses a degree of reality which must compose subordinate substances, and that while the mind's imagination cannot extend into the very depths of the compositions of its bodily organs, nevertheless the contributions of the organs are determined by physical interaction – expression varies and the experience of this variation 'from below' is called an affect.

Much of the work of *De Affectibus* feeds into the *Nouveaux Essais*, but now with an explicit distinction between the kinds of bodily desires which would be all-determining for a Spinozan mind, which desires Leibniz names 'velleity' in a striking hybridisation of Latin into French,[38] and volition which is also determined by the intellect. In other paragraphs Leibniz will describe this upswelling by the more well-known Scholastic term: appetitions.[39] If we think back to our mechanical example, simple bodies express their divinely decreed exigency, but are determined to action and passion. To the extent that each form is composed in a greater, these exigencies appear likewise to be composed resulting in a surging up of countless demands indistinguishable to the imagination. Rather: 'These minute impulses consist in our continually overcoming small obstacles – our nature labours at this without our thinking about it. This is the true character of the disquiet which we sense without cognisance of it.'[40] After a certain fashion the mind faces its own body as matter, as a passion, but because the existing mind composes a subset of substantial forms to its own ends, it has a certain intimacy with these passions, before the mind's reality increases and decreases just as it is aided and caused to suffer.[41]

Here we have the central moment for what would become Leibniz's theory of (monadic) domination. Strictly speaking, Leibniz claims, no actions arise from composing bodies because they are mere aggregates 'like a herd'; actions arise from true substances with entelechy, and what is experienced are merely phenomenal realities. Any change whereby it moves closer to or further from its perfection – the expression of its substantial form – can be named action and passion. To the claim by Philalethes that our bodies possess a passive power to receive impressions from without, Leibniz's *Theophilus* will deny that this is anything other than a way of speaking. The power of our bodies, even if but passive, is simply *une image*.

Has Leibniz expropriated bodies of any real claim to existence? I do not think this is quite correct. Intensional equivalence ensures the community of being; pretensional demand, the community of the *Civitas Dei*. It is quite open to Leibniz to close off substances from each other and claim that other simpler substances are images of substances, because in a strict sense they are. Leibniz's statement may simply be taken as confirming his view of affects generally: that they arise as the inestimable pretensions of an infinity of substances created by God in a hierarchy of composition. To say that they are mere semblances of substances is to make a claim about our inherent ignorance of the sufficient reasons for things, not that corporeal substances are mere fictions. Leibniz speaks not of phenomena, but of 'phenomenal reality', and that 'reality' is surely no idle inclusion of this term of art. If we remember the distinction Duns Scotus makes between fictions (beings of reason) and the quidditatively real, it would not be novel for Leibniz to posit a class of symbols which is expressive of compossibility. And if, as Book III of the *Nouveaux Essais* states, words can be expressive, the more so bodies whose affects require a natural philosophical account. Bodies are real, in the strict Scholastic sense that they express concrete relations and are creatable.

Now we understand the critical role of the incommensurability of the divine creations with our own substantial form: (i) I express my entelechy in the derivative tendencies to motion of various bodies, and these compossible moments are named my will, my demand to exist; but (ii) the world is constituted by an infinity of reals subject to a divine decree that imputes in them demands to exist, but which demand is beyond my perception; and (iii) my knowledge does not extend into the depths even of my own body; thus (iv) my body is the site of an encounter between my subjective demand, determined by my body's acting derivatively to my substantial form, and the objective demand of the world swelling up inside me in layer upon layer of composing forms. My affections – these phenomenal realities or images – are my mind's attempt to imagine the complexity of those countless demands.

What we have though is no chance clash of opposing desires after the Hobbesian fashion; but a much more constructivist programme concerning the affects that builds on and deepens the Spinozist doctrine of the *Treatise on the Emendation of the Understanding* and *Ethics*. My body, to even be a body, must always combine both the form deriving from a primary force, and the materiality of the objective world. Even in the mechanical case, percussions may aid my power of acting without it being necessary that I perceive all that an encounter entails; it is enough that my reality increases and that consequently some portion of what was objective demand to exist becomes now appropriated as a component of my body, and thus also partially expresses my subjective demand to exist.

Observe with Leibniz that this transition to a more perfect state has not changed the nature of the demand: there is only one demand – to exist. Leibniz has set up an infinite dilemma of volitions and pretensions arising from the depths of my body and its world. Leibniz's solution, to use the square of power again, is to move from the derivative to the primary level of activity in-potency, or now primary active and passive force. Primary activity takes on the role of adjudicating between the conflicting claims of matter and spontaneously moves to what it judges to be the best. What has changed is that the mind has been 'presented with perceptions that stand out more', 'opportunities for observation and self-development, so to speak'.[42] I interpret this as claiming that transition to perfection proceeds to illuminating some darker structural component of a substantial form and thereby in a sense reallocating a demand to exist from the world to the individual by means of a sort of appropriation. Every transition to the better is accompanied by the revelation of more possibility, more pretensions. This revelation though arises not in a direct increase in my primary force but rather relies on pretensional equivalence: my will prevails only because there is a pretension in the world which agrees with my substantial form and so carries out its activity through itself. It may seem absurdly occasionalist to regard that Leibniz on a horse need only will the horse to move and if the horse does their pretensions are in agreement, but Leibniz's reliance on the community of being afforded by the intensional nature of *supposita* is the key to the whole operation, provided that we understand that causality is not efficient but participative: the component pretension participates in the superior substantial form by virtue of composition. Thus efficiency remains in the horse's own activity: 'volition can hardly exist without *desire* and without *avoidance*'[43] which arise from all the bodies that compose an actually existing substantial form.

Yet because the mind does not extend into the depths of the component, what is composed is not completely clear, and is imagined as a phenomenal real open to further investigation as our perfection increases. In this way the mind comes to recognise images as expressive of an objective demand, a demand that may or may not aid my power of acting, and accordingly senses this as pleasurable or painful.

Hence these images are not without use, and Leibniz speaks approvingly of the Scholastic description of these surging bodily appetitions as the *motus primo primi*,[44] because we need these first movements to our natural end if not to achieve happiness at least to put us in the way of opportunities for development. The doctrine echoes the proper function theory of the Stoics, who situate the beginning of all practical action in the nature of the least thing.

In conclusion then, when Leibniz describes finite action as requiring will and power he makes his final move in the reconfiguration of power: just as we may speak of physical events as derivative combinations of active motion expressed in passive mass, so we can speak, in the realm of the compossible known to thinking things, of volitional events, or actions, which are combinations of active will and passive pretensions – of subjective action and objective demand. This combination occurs at the subaltern level of derivative act and passion. Each subaltern assumes its universal. The passions or affects are the image of a world, structured according to a hierarchy of the real. The world is the creation of God, and the *potentia* found in this world are pretensions to exist. On the one hand my activity, my supposit, adjudicates between these claims as I reflect on what is best for my self-actualisation. But am I not also located within a global hierarchy of the real, of substantial forms? Am I not also defined by what I am not? For this reason I can recognise the World in affective images, for I take pleasure in choosing, according to a global calculation, the greatest variety, or reality, in order to perfect that world.

2.3 Natural legal consequences of the yoking of power to will

As we saw earlier in this chapter, the Leibnizian model of volition bears certain structural similarities with that advanced by Suárez. Like the Jesuit thinker, Leibniz conceives of the will as a combination of intellectual ideas and bodily potency, and situates the distinct voluntariness of volition in a kind of force or movement from this potency. For Suárez (and here we consider an autonomous mind) the corporeal is elicited to volition by the idea presented by the intellect; for Leibniz this force is a demand or pretension to exist which has a primary cause: entelechy, which stands as the intelligible principle for which the demand is made.

The roles of God and of simplest matter enhance this picture by introducing the classical structure of superior–inferior. We have seen that even the simplest bodies express a pretension to existence, and that all the pretensions that act through the simplest bodies derive first from an arbitrary physical system in which it is located, but ultimately,[45] at the infinitesimal level, from God's creation of *materia prima* (resistance to motion) and its innumerable derivatives (masses). Thus, even the smallest mass point, so to speak, demands to exist or, to put it another way, pretends to express its divine principle. Human action is situated between these poles and is in this way a meeting point of two orders: the formal order of the possible and the real order of the contingent or hypothetical. With respect to its relationship to bodies, every human volition is thus a formal possibility (imagined with a variable degree of clarity) actualised so far as possible by engaging the divinely imputed inclinations of composing bodies (real contingencies). How these bodies are constituted is a secondary question, often beyond the ability of finite minds to know. That these bodies serve their purpose in manifesting the possible is the first concern of volition.

Given these structural differences in the notion of volition from those advanced by Vásquez and Suárez, we would expect that the consequences for natural law would differ quite markedly as between the late Schoolmen and the Hanoverian courtier. Interestingly, Leibniz's decision to use the terminology of demand and of the engaging of potency to achieve an end, provides for a stark contrast which fully underscores Leibniz's faith in rational being.

To see this, I again draw on the research of Thomas Pink[46] into the natural law theory of obligation in Vásquez, Suárez and the Scholastic tradition behind them. In particular I focus on Suárez's positing of a force (*vis*) of owing or 'demand' (*debitus*) which will be used to combat the powerful argument of Vásquez that there subsists natural law even before the decrees of God.[47] I would note here that I do not entirely own Pink's characterisation of *debitus* as a demanding force, and do not suggest terminological link with Leibniz's *exigentia* (*pretension*). Indeed, Leibniz was aware of the *debitus* theory of practical action, as demonstrated by his notes on Bisterfeld from 1663 to 1666: 'Whence theory through IT IS [*EST*], practice through IT IS OWED [*DEBET*], poetics through IT CAN [*POTEST*]'.[48] In his own legal texts Leibniz reserves 'what is owed' (*debitus*) to one way of speaking about obligation, but owing does not serve a definitional purpose with respect to obligation.

Pink shows how Vásquez argues for right reasoning as a ground of natural law, such that a practical action which flows from disordered human reasoning is per se guilty (*culpa*), and this guilt holds even before God and judged and made law. Part of the force of this position comes from the canonical priority of intellect over volition in the order of action – the will can only be moved to action by what is presented by the intellect, and if this preliminary stage fails (phantasy) then what follows can hardly be act at all. The troubling consequence, as Pink notes, is that such a notion of natural law renders the command of a superior inessential for the doctrine. Even if divine law continues to play a part, it appears as both arbitrary and secondary in the order of reasons. Vásquez's free-floating will thus leads to absolutism of command.

Suárez seeks to combat this conclusion by accepting that right reasoning should play a role in assessing the praiseworthiness of practical acts, but by adding an additional feature, namely force:

> In respect of rational nature I distinguish two things: one is that nature itself, insofar as it is the basis of the compat-

ibility or incompatibility with itself of human actions; the other is a certain force [*vis*] of that nature, which we call natural reason. Taken the first way this nature is said to be the basis of natural moral goodness; taken the second way it is called natural law itself, which prescribes or forbids to the human will what is to be done by natural right.[49] (translation modified)

Pink correctly identifies that Suárez has added an ingredient to the equation, and he will go on to argue that this force is characterised as a demand on a person's conscience. Why though does Suárez take this route? I think we need to understand why Suárez feels he is permitted to posit force as a feature that inflects right reasoning. One might think that the Aristotelean model of the intelligible principle as entelechy, transposed to Scholastic theology, would provide such a basis. In the quotation above Suárez clearly distinguishes between a human reason the end of which is *convenientia*, which is to say the appropriateness of an act *for* the human itself, and a nature which exerts force on the human will with respect to natural reason in general, as end. The obvious candidate for the principle of this force is the ultimate End – the Good as actuality of intelligible being – which permits Suárez to assess the appropriateness of an act for that End.

This is not, however, the route that Suárez takes. Rather, as Terence Irwin shows,[50] he makes a distinction between the context of an obligation and the force of that obligation, and is then put in a position to claim that for natural law this pure force posits a demand or ought (*debita*) on our conscience,[51] where our intellect provides the obligatory content produced by right reasoning. This demand, as Pink confirms, continues to derive its force from the will of a superior. Though phrased as a demand, or possibly even a duty, the command theory which looks to the superior–inferior relation appears to hold fast.

With this debate in mind, the Leibnizian innovations are striking. Over and above the matters already discussed in this chapter, two texts are particularly relevant. The earlier *Elements of Natural Law* of 1670–1 might be read in part as a direct response to the Suárecian construction of conscience as bearing a demanding force of internal punishment mechanism. The later, article 30 of the 1686 *Discourse on Metaphysics*, contains in its latter stages a more metaphysically framed treatment of volition, revealing of the dual action of human and divine free will. Given that the 1686 text provides detail only implicit in the *Elements* (even after the latter's middle period revisions), I begin with this. I should add that at this point I will not delve just yet into the precise senses of justice, obligatoriness and right which Leibniz provides in the *Elements*; the focus of this chapter is volition and power as such.

In DM §30 Leibniz proposes to 'give rough indications' regarding the difficult problems inherent in any treatment of the 'action of God upon the human will'. We are well equipped to interpret the sketch though. As we would expect, Leibniz first makes a division between possibility and contingency. God continuously produces thoughts according to established law, and by concurrence (*sc.* intensional equivalence) we too experience this spontaneous production of thoughts. Furthermore:

> . . . by virtue of the decree which he has made that the will shall always strive toward the apparent good, by expressing or imitating God's will under certain particular conditions (with respect to which the apparent good is to some extent a true good), God determines our will to choose what seems to be the best, but without constraining it.

First, the decree in question is that which imputes pretension to exist into all real things or compossibles. Second, therefore, the equivalence Leibniz draws between particular striving towards the apparent good and expressing or imitating God's will is the structural equivalence of the divine and the finite process (*supposit* → *possible* :: *compossible* → *entelechy*) discussed earlier. Third, the use of 'expressing and imitating' indicates that this volitional equivalence, moving from compossibles to the end, has a certain degree, and we would expect that this degree is determined by the power that a finite creature can engage to manifest its ideas. Fourth, while all the affective inclinations of this power help form a volition, the self-determination characteristic of Mind superadds a volitional spontaneity which can nevertheless choose not what the sum of potencies or inclinations want, but what 'I' want, which is first 'I', and second the (apparent) Good. In this way the supposit judges: from amongst the compossibles it makes a division between what is the best to realise and thus what must remain unrealised. Unlike the billiard ball model of forces, therefore, Leibniz will be able to speak of inclination without constraint, grounded in a kind of 'indifference',[52] by virtue of the pretensional equivalence (dare I say, homology) of divine and finite minds, both of which are characterised by two stages of operation: self-determination as will to actualise personal end; practical action as actualisation towards the End.

The resulting construct is fruitfully compared to the doctrines of Suárez and Vásquez. Command, understood as an imposition of obligation with content (do this), does not play an immediate role. Demand does provide requisite force, because it drives the affects, but it is not (always) determinative of minds. Is there though a content-free command of a superior? It would seem not, either. Leibniz appears to put great weight on lack of constraint, and uses no language that would suggest command, but rather has finite human volition expressing or imitating God's will. I claim that the requisite obligatoriness is therefore derived from the role played by entelechy – an entelechy which acts not directly but through the equivalent conceptual structures of human and divine mind. It is because all minds are equivalently constructed as a series of intensions and self-determining pretensions that they concur, save as to power. In this way Leibniz achieves by conceptual homology what Suárez achieves by command without content, and is all the more subtle for it. For moral deficiency is referred to the necessary presence of Nothing in creatures[53] ('original sin') and thus creatures have a built-in requirement to seek power to maximise reality. Our gaze is turned to this lack and away from the conceptual structure which caused all things to be constructed by a division of being and nothing, a structure which is implanted in every mind.

With this structure to hand, we can understand how, in the *Elements*, Leibniz already holds the Schoolmen (and presumably Suárez specifically) to be wrong to look to conscience as the location of moral choice. Rather, he will speak using the language of actuality: of reflection, reality, and thus of perfection. Leibniz criticises the use of conscience to motivate practical action because, he says, it is merely memory of one's own deeds and thus, he implies, entirely contingent. Then he considers those who would place in the conscience certain innate ideas – 'a witness to the just and unjust who tortures the wicked by the mere consciousness of the crime'. Leibniz's pithy response: 'let those consult the oracle who will'.[54] Justice is driven, rather, by delight in maximal reality, and particularly the actuality of intelligent creatures capable of reflecting this reality most fully. 'The gathered splendour constitutes glory.'[55] As stated earlier, at this stage I do not wish to engage with the discussion here of just, obligatory and so forth. I simply wish to demonstrate that by understanding the role actuality (entelechy) plays in Leibniz's practical action, we can observe how he responds to natural law theories of command and demand by means of conceptual equivalence. God wills himself as a spontaneously generative artisan; thus his actuality is manifested as his single presence in maximal reality, or difference. Each mind is conceptually structured in like manner, and thereby is ensured, in principle, ultimately to desire this actuality also, though its means to that end must be through the yoking of potency. This suggests that if one seeks justice manifested in the world, then injustice will derive from the deficient imitation of this guiding concept and/or deficient comprehension of reality. The practical solution which immediately suggests itself is this: the maximisation of conceptual imitation up to the limit of conceptual expression. This will form the guiding principle of Leibniz's theory of legal education.

3. Conclusion: does Leibniz eschew the metaphysics of power?

In the opening section of this chapter we briefly surveyed the Aristotelean account of desire for the end, which is taken by some as the origin of the theory of will. Already in Aristotle we located both duality between desire (*boulesis*) and its principle (*arché*), and a motion inverse to that of intellect, from the desiring matter (potency) to its end. Aristotle sets up a language of domination (*kýrios*) and of the contingent to describe this practical realm. We have further seen how this basic model accounts for a Neoplatonic and Scholastic thinking of power which appears to predicate the potency of desiring matter to the principle that elicits it, and how this metaphysics of the real reaches exceptional refinement in Scotus. Yet Scotus also sows seeds of destruction, for the absolute or excessive power of God procures an unquenchable elicitation of the real, for no number of perfections of creatables can match the divine perfection. The arbitrariness of God is thus mirrored in a superabundant reality; the excess of rationality of God also discloses a certain excess of the formal order in the real (*haecceitas* as excessive individuating principle). An absolute God can thus be taken to choose arbitrarily, or, and this is the line of the new materialists philosophers, the true conclusion is that divine infinity chooses an excess in the real, and our focus must turn to a reality in which conflicting power and desire are the foci of any practical philosophy. Hobbes makes desire the principle of action, collapsing the *arché* into diverse matter. Spinoza equates will with intellect, confirming that God wills as much as He can think, and backs this formal conclusion with a Nature equated to God's infinitude, productive of infinite desire. Both thinkers motivate their philosophies with an excessive *potentia*.

Is it surprising then that Leibniz should use the broadly sketched Aristotelean dualism of principle and desire to synergise the new philosophy of *potentia* with the theology of moral choice (entelechy and so spontaneity)? From Scotus, Leibniz obtains a hierarchy of the real – of the creatables – invested not with the intensions of the formal real of essences, but the pretensions of matter to their entelechies. On the one hand the finite Mind is an entelechy, and this Mind therefore procures movements of self-actualisation in the Mind's 'body' which are named volitions. On the other hand, to explain the world at large, Leibniz must assume the continued presence of God in each mind – an infinite entelechy which moves all matter to *potentia*. It would seem that these pretensions of the real, like the intensions of the formal, are alike in each finite Mind, thus suggesting a parallel doctrine of *pretensional equivalence* of primary matter (its power). The thesis boils down to the claim that, given a two 'perspectives' v and w of finite individuals, and possibilities p_v and p_w in each, then the pretension to existence of p_v is equivalent to that of p_w. This is possible because the pretensions are not for Leibniz the exigencies of subjective imagination but the choices of a God whose being is common to every mind. Three striking results follow immediately:

(a) God's infinite activity and dominion accounts for the pretensions of even infinitesimally small units of matter, something not possible for a finite mind.

(b) Each finite mind may exert a certain exigence on matter according to its entelechy, but worldly experience is marked by the excessive pretensions of a nature set in motion by the excessive demand of an infinite God. Hence the experience of the continuum (space) and the concrete (the quality of 'real' bodies).

(c) Each pretension in the world being guaranteed by the same, common *dominus* or hegemon, Leibniz can argue that every pretension occupies the same single normative order guaranteed by God and, if two finite minds disagree about the rectitude of a pretension, the error 'must' lie with the finite minds and their respective deviation from the common domain of right.

The resulting structure situates the finite individual alone in a world with its God, though it may be useful to proceed as if three tiers are in play, as in *Trinitas. Mens*. In the middle we have the individual whose practical actions – *agere seu conari* – are marked by the foundational dualism of matter's potency insofar as it moves towards its principle or entelechy. Considering only the middle tier, the movement of compossibles towards the finite entelechy is named affect, and insofar as the individual spontaneously acts to actualise possibility for itself, this is called will. This middle tier though is embedded in a world which tends towards the divine principle, not all at once but according to a hierarchy of reality; of interlocking forms serving mediate ends. As we have just seen, the finite individual thus experiences a lower tier, the world, the claims to existence of which are exacted by the higher tier occupied by God. The finite individual, being defined by its presence in a world which is material with respect to it, is from the beginning designed to lack the activity necessary alone to perfect itself. Thereby the action of the finite individual is bound to engage these worldly pretensions as power, and so yoke power to its action as will to reflect its principle – the entelechy of the finite individual. Finally, the co-presence of individual mind and world is doubled also in this manner: the individual is not the ultimate end of the real; the price of a world united in its pretensions is an end which dominates it all – God. Thus also the individual mind is always subject to at least two principles – the perfection of itself and the perfection itself and the world for God.

Understanding the Leibnizian model of will as one which combines entelechy and the surging pretensional potency of matter – an Aristotelean logic invested with force – not only orients us correctly with respect to the flow of practical action in Leibniz's thought. It also situates Leibniz with respect to the history of power, a history which up to Spinoza appears to have shown a uniform tendency in favour of the diminution of activity in favour of power. In one stroke has Leibniz completely reversed this trend, positing cognates of *energeia–entelecheia* as the prime metaphysical agents? This would be to go too far. Although *potentia* is terminologically relativised to will, and subordinated to an effect on matter by a principle of entelechy, several features of the power-discourse remain in situ. Chief among these is the problematic attribution of power, which tends to lead us to a notion of power-wielding. While power moves from primary and derivative matter, these pretensions are due to and ordered by the perfection of the principle, a principle which transcends matter through its infinitude. Spinoza, an explicit advocate of power, offers a greater step forward by placing a self-caused God as immanent to its own potency, making what is thought also what is willed, and so imbuing every aspect of substance with an immediately creative power, the mutual claims of which mediated not by rational decree but by a horizontal struggle of existence pursued according to determinate natural laws. Leibniz's kingdom of ends upholds what is in my opinion juridically central to the metaphysics of power: the end determines a hierarchy and a relationship of master and subordinate. Leibniz may well have eschewed defining right by reference to the accumulation of power under one's dominion, but he does so in favour of a finer scale of domination defined by reflection, in which the virtue or reality of a thing is measured according to the realities or subordinated forms that it composes within itself. If the natural law and natural right theorists of the seventeenth century free nature from God by asking what is naturally justified *even if* God did not exist, Leibniz in effect argues that there can be no claims in the state of nature unless a substance of sufficient actuality is virtually present to it.

Perfection as end may well be understood as seeing in the world the reflection of oneself *and* of God, but the overall tendencies, the means, are the reorganisation of the world so that it reflects self *and* God. And all this is grounded in perhaps the most striking innovation – the pretension itself. Leibniz's God, and derivatively the human Mind, is the cause of power just insofar as the entelechies invest matter with pretensions to exist. Yet something else is also happening here. Leibniz's focus in *Trinitas. Mens* and the related texts has been on suppositive activity and entelechy, and so *God and Mind*'s relationship in a world. But the whole structure is reliant on a third term: God and Mind's relationship *in a world* – the left-most column of *Trinitas. Mens*. Leibniz's move has been to completely define each substantial form not only by what it is (a Thomist account) but just as critically by what it is not. This intervention is most visible in the ostensibly strange demotion of *potentia* to the status of second subaltern of the supposit *'agere seu conari'*. On its own this move would seem to contradict Leibniz's requirement that particular acts and passions have primary causes, and so in this chapter we have investigated the origins of the passions and their power in their pretensions to exist within a hierarchy of the real. This has led us to observe that indeed he not only integrated what he calls *potentia* within the finite creature, but in order to do this he has integrated primary passive force – the World – in the individual also. A passive force however, which is not itself lacking, or passive in the sense of being ineffective. A passive force rather which is the ground of pretensions, and so the striving of matter to exist. We now understand why Leibniz names two *supposita* in the third row of *Trinitas. Mens*: action (*agere*) *and* conari or endeavour.

The first four chapters have sought to explicate the significance of the fragment *Trinitas. Mens*, examining the interrelationship between activity and intensions, and entelechy and pretensions. Our broad structure of interpretation of Leibniz's thinking from his early to middle period, at least, is in place. It is now appropriate to move to consider how the conceptual structure of *Trinitas. Mens* can aid our understanding of the various jurisprudential works that Leibniz developed principally during the 1660s–80s. This approach permits us to test the hermeneutic efficacy of the reading advanced above, but will add much depth to our understanding of Leibniz's thinking of will and power.

Notes

1. *Theodicy* §§34–5, quoted by Gaston Grua, *Jurisprudence universelle et théodicée selon Leibniz* (Paris: PUF, 1953) p.132.
2. Paul Rateau, *Leibniz and the Problem of Evil* (Oxford: Oxford University Press, 2019) pp.97–105.
3. *Notationes Generales* (1683–5) A:VI, iv(A) 557. Quoted by Rateau, *Problem of Evil*, p.98.
4. Rateau, *Problem of Evil*, p.101.
5. Ibid. pp.99–100, although given that he agrees that the demand is an appeal to force he does seem implicitly to qualify this argument.
6. Spinoza deploys the distinction, but while essences in attributes are distinguished *formaliter*, whole attributes are distinguished *realiter*: see *Ethics* I P10 Sch.
7. Hegel's critique of Leibniz–Wolff, I cannot recommend highly enough: M. Kusch and J. Manninen, 'Hegel on Modalities and Monadology' in S. Knuuttila (ed.) *Modern Modalities: Studies in the History of Modal Theories from Medieval Nominalism to Logical Positivism* (Dordrecht: Kluwer, 1988) pp.109–77.
8. *Notationes Generales* A:VI, iv(A), 557.
9. Ger:VII, 289; C:533. Here, as Christophe Bouton notes, Leibniz has attempted to construct a neologism from the future tense of *existere* (*existiturus*). They are 'like the "*existituturientia*" of essences, or the "*existuriens*", terms which designate the tendency towards the existence of possibilities'. Christophe Bouton, *Time and Freedom* (Christopher Macann trans.) (Evanston, IL: Northwestern University Press, 2014) p.37.
10. A:VI, i, 9–19.
11. A:VI, i, 15ff.

12. A:II, i, 392.
13. C:376. See also the strangely foreshortened translation: R.M. Adams, *Leibniz: Determinist, Theist, Idealist* (Oxford: Oxford University Press, 1994) pp.167–8.
14. Adams, *Leibniz*, p.165.
15. Ibid. pp.175–6: at times Leibniz almost appears to collapse existence into essence.
16. Quoted from the *General Inquiries* by Adams, *Leibniz*, p.167.
17. Cf. ST I, q.4, a.4.
18. L:487.
19. Ibid.
20. Ibid.
21. I draw in part on Angus Brook, 'Substance and the Primary Sense of Being in Aristotle' 68(3) *The Review of Metaphysics* (March 2015) 521–44 at p.542. See also Michael V. Wedin, *Aristotle's Theory of Substance* (Oxford: Oxford University Press, 2000); Aryeh Kosman, *The Activity of Being* (Cambridge, MA: Harvard University Press, 2013).
22. C:533.
23. C:534.
24. *24 Metaphysical Theses*, Thesis 6 (1690s?, Ger:VII, 289; C:533). 'Haec ratio est in praevalentia rationum ad existendum, prae rationibus ad non existendum seu ut verbo dicam in Existiturientia Essentiarum, ita ut existitura sint quae non impediantur. Neque enim si nihil existituriret ratio esset existendi.'
25. C:535.
26. M:47.
27. L:368.
28. Grua, *Jurisprudence universelle*, p.139. The extremely concise discussion here inspires what follows.
29. L:178, letter to Eckhard, Summer 1677.
30. Gr:475–8.
31. Gr:354.
32. L:178.
33. Ger:VII, 108, 110.
34. Grua, *Jurisprudence universelle*, p.139.
35. L:489.
36. A complete account of Leibniz's theory of will and *potentia* would engage deeply with his physics of forces and reality, the core of which holds that if one body determines another to greater action, then that second body undergoes an increase in reality, i.e. it expresses more clearly the system it is in. There is simply no space to do this theory justice in this

work, and so readers are referred to the DM (particularly §§15–16) and the *Specimen Dynamicum*. These can usefully be read in conjunction with Daniel Garber, *Leibniz: Body, Substance, Monad* (Oxford: Oxford University Press, 2009).

37. Grua, *Jurisprudence universelle*, p.138.
38. NE:II, xxi, §30; NE:183.
39. NE:II, xxi, §5; NE:173.
40. NE:II, xxi, §36; NE:188.
41. NE:II, xxi, §73; NE:210–11.
42. NE:II, xxi, §72; NE:211.
43. NE:II, xxi, §39; NE:192.
44. NE:II, xxi, §36; NE:189.
45. See the previous chapter.
46. Thomas Pink, 'Action, Will and Law in Late Scholasticism' in J. Kraye and R. Saarinen (eds), *Moral Philosophy on the Threshold of Modernity* (Netherlands: Springer, 2005) pp.31–50.
47. In this Vásquez pre-empts the *etiamsi* of Grotius by half a century.
48. A:VI, i, 152.
49. Suárez, *De Legibus*, V, p.102, quoted by Pink, 'Action, Will and Law', p.42.
50. Terence H. Irwin, 'Obligation, Rightness, and Natural Law: Suárez and Some Critics' in Daniel Schwartz (ed.), *Interpreting Suárez: Critical Essays* (Cambridge: Cambridge University Press, 2012) pp.142–62.
51. Pink footnotes the following in support of his reading of a demand: 'Ratio autem est, quia legislator potest simul sua lege obligare in conscientia, imponendo poenam transgressoribus, ut in superioribus ostensum est, et potest obligare in conscientia sine adiectione poenae; ergo etiam obligare in conscientia solum ad debitum poenae . . .' (*De Legibus, Opera* vol.V p.424). Pink, 'Action, Will and Law', p.49 n.30.
52. DM §39.
53. Ibid. at L:322.
54. L:136
55. L:137.

Five
Ars Combinatoria *as* Urdoxa

1. Introduction: jurisprudence as *Urdoxa*

Up to now we have explored Leibniz's *Trinitas. Mens* fragment and attempted to show how it can be understood
according to what I have termed the square of power – a
conceptual device inherited from Aristotle via the Scholastics.
As part of that analysis I argued that Leibniz avails himself
of the theory of the supposit, which develops the Stagirite's
notion of *energeia* via Aquinas as substantial activity. At a
general metaphysical level, I claim that this substantial activity stands, for Leibniz, as the rational activity that is being
itself, and that there is an equivalence between the acts of
knowing of finite rational substances, who produce images in
thought, and the acts of rational being in God which produce
the ideas of the intellect. In this I claim that the similarity
relates Leibniz back to the Scholastic notion of *ens commune* –
a community of rational being guaranteed by an infinite One.
As Leibniz puts it in a middle period letter to the Landgrave
of Hesse-Rheinfels:

> As the arithmetic and geometry of God is the same as that
> of men, excepted that God's is infinitely more extended, so
> also natural jurisprudence, in so far as demonstrative, and
> every other truth is the same in heaven and on earth.[1]

Now in previous chapters we also had occasion to consider
volition, power and the hierarchy of the real, but I wish to
set this aspect of the square of power to one side for the
time being. The reason for this is motivated by the material
Leibniz gives us. During the Leipzig and Altdorf years a key
focus for our thinker is the community of intellectual activity

which his use of the supposit and the *Trinitas. Mens* fragment subsequently identifies. The principal claim of this chapter is this: that Leibniz will assume that there is one correct and common way to think about legal cases in general, and that legal disputes arise because one or more parties (specifically their lawyers) think about real legal issues in a manner that is incorrect, that is, divergent from that one common way of thinking. It is well known that this manner of thinking is the *ars combinatoria.* Here I seek to establish that Leibniz's use of the combinatorial art is linked to what will become his theory of the supposit and so the activity of being, and that, as the foregoing hypothesis indicates, Leibniz seeks to solve legal problems by reference to a common way of thinking about the real – an *Urdoxa,* to use a Husserlian phrase. In the wider scheme of this work this serves two additional functions: to establish the ingenuity and depth of Leibniz's understanding of activity as rational and juridical, and to support our later interpretation of the *Nova Methodus* in which the commonality of jurisprudential activity stands at the centre of Leibniz's doctrine about teaching and learning the law.

It is well worth emphasising that Leibniz brackets off the real content of legal decision making from our way of thinking about it. In doing this, Leibniz does nothing particularly novel for his time. Aristotle divides the construction of arguments in themselves (topics) from the forms of reasoning with their content (analytics). Later scholars will add the art of memory to the wider logical programme, and develop the topics into an art of invention which reaches its summit in the *ars combnatoria.* Leibniz, discussing the structure of the legal curriculum in the *Nova Methodus* of 1667, confirms the traditional distinction:

> §22. Habits proper to men are either of memory, of invention, or of judgment. Hence there is a threefold doctrine of these habits – mnemonics, topics, and analytics. For propositions, which are of course distinctive of men only, can be memorized, made, or judged.[2]

And as if to dispel any doubts that the 'making of' legal propositions from the raw matter of cases is nothing other than the combinatorial art, Leibniz adds two paragraphs later:

§24. The basis of the topics, or the art of invention, is the loci, that is, transcendent relations such as whole, cause, matter, similarity, etc. As we have shown in our *Dissertation on the Art of Combinations*, propositions are made from things connected by any such relation through the combinatorial art.[3]

When it comes to the correct activity of legal thinking, Leibniz is not interested in the raw material of legal cases – real or, one might say after Pufendorf, moral entities. Leibniz's primary focus is on the mind's constructive activity of thinking about these objects once given in the court or in the classroom. In a sense the legal results are somewhat secondary; his focus is jurisprudence as the activity itself of legal thinking.

Indeed, what we have here is not the claim that correct reasoning is also validly applicable in the subfield of jurisprudence, but quite the inverse, that (natural) jurisprudence *is* correct reasoning and that consequently all kinds of knowledge are developed according to a jurisprudential activity. In this way juridical thinking becomes a kind of *Urdoxa*: a collection of intellectual operations which are equivalent *qua* operations in every intelligent substance. Hence when Leibniz writes:

> The point is that jurisprudence, when dealing with matters which are not explicitly treated by laws or customs, is completely founded in reasons; for one can always draw forth [*tirer*] some law or natural right, in the absence of [positive] law, by means of reason.[4]

He makes very clear that jurisprudence is prior to any positive legal content and is grounded in reasons itself; that jurisprudence is the activity of reasoning as such, inclined by the end appropriate to it.

By reorienting the discussion of natural law away from the material of cases towards the very conditions of jurisprudence Leibniz is able to attain an overview of the legal process which permits comprehension of the diversity of perceptions of all the human agents involved. The perspectives of judge, lawyer, party, jury, all these will differ, and all these perspectives will be more and less distinct insofar as each

Mind applies the rules of jurisprudential reasoning to the case. Accordingly, Leibniz believes himself able to explain why we have legal cases at all; why it is that parties should differ in the first place as to their respective rights. It is a matter of points of view which maintain a certain structural distance from each other according to their integration of legal reasoning. The purpose of legal process then is the elaboration, from within each point of view, of the perceptions that are the demonstrative productions of a jurisprudential activity carried out according to the natural jurisprudential laws found operating also in the One.[5] The success of the process resolves in the coalescence of each point of view, not around a uniform perception (this is neither desirable nor strictly possible) but around a global vision of jurisprudence, a jurisprudence which publicly expresses the many relations of the constituent activities (private minds).[6] As Leibniz would phrase it at the very end of our period of examination: 'The just is what is useful to perfect rational society – the universal perfection of divine and human society.'[7] Leibniz's jurisprudence provides the 'rational society' which is to be perfected in the World.

Due to the technicality of Leibniz's thought, the examination of this topic will be quite involved, though I will do my best to explain matters intuitively. In sections 2 to 4 I seek to explain Leibniz's combinatorial theory on its own terms, and the focus here is the *Dissertatio de Arte Combinatoria*. Already in that text Leibniz gives examples derived from legal problems, but it is in *De Casibus Perplexis* that he sets out with the primary mission not only to solve perplexing cases in the law, but to show that his combinatorial art is an appropriate methodology. I examine the *De Casibus Perplexis* in section 4. The overarching aim will be to link combinatorial theory to Leibniz's mature philosophy and so the combinatorial treatment of jurisprudence in his dissertation to the later views on universal jurisprudence.

The argument of this proceeds as follows: first, I adopt the common ground that Leibniz inherits a rhetorical view of legal thinking which places great store in understanding problems by means of enumeration of all possible legal cases. Second, I explain Leibniz's development of the method for this enumeration, principally in his *Ars Combinatoria*, and spend some time explicating the key findings of his investigations. Third, I discuss Leibniz's early application of combinatorial methods to the investigation and solution of certain legal problems, thus establishing the clear linkage between combinatorial and legal method. Lastly, I consider the significance of Leibniz's claim that thinking about legal problems has a common structure, and how this foreshadows both his own arguments in the *Nova Methodus*, and wider criticisms of those philosophies which claim to find a common sense, or *Urdoxa*, at the heart of all thought.

2. The *ars combinatoria*

It is by no means perverse that Leibniz should seek to solve juridical problems by combinatorial methods. Leipzig, still bearing the influence of Renaissance thought but also, with Jakob Thomasius (1622–84), seeking to return to Aristotelean sources under the influence of Neo-Scholasticism, saw nothing particularly unusual in Leibniz's elaborate attempts at synthesis in the work he submitted to the university between 1661 and 1666, and indeed in the *Disputatio* he presented at Altdorf in late 1666. That the combinations of *discrete* things might indeed be the key to understanding the order but also the generation of the variety of the universe from the simplest elements was in any event an ancient idea, as Leibniz was fully aware.

In his *Disputatio*, Leibniz applies a theory permutation in quite a traditional manner in Problem IV, dealing with various classical poems and determining the permutations of letters of monosyllabic key words in a manner resonant of mystical practices. Yet our philosopher proceeds to justify his focus on such word games with recourse to Epicurean atomism, which he traces via Democritus to Aristotle's *De Generatione*. Significantly, quoting a verse from Lucretius *De Natura Rerum II* (hereafter the *Poem*), Leibniz glosses into the text his own combinatorial interpretation. It is a significance missed by English translators (to my knowledge), and so I quote a translation which takes in Leibniz's 'improvements':

As even in these very verses of mine
it is of great consequence with what letters [*combinations*],

and in what order [*permutations*], other letters are severally placed;
for the same letters,
signify heaven, sea, earth, rivers, sun; the same signify
corn, groves, animals;
if the words are not all, yet by far the greater part
are, alike, at least so far as to have some letters in
common; but truly they are distinguished by the positions
of the letters.
So likewise even in things materially,
when the [*intervals, passages, connexions, weights, impulses*],
collisions, movements, order, and figural position of the
atoms of matter are permuted, the things which are
formed from them must also be changed.
(Lucretius *De Rerum Natura*, II, lines 1013–22,
Leibniz's alterations are in square brackets[8])

The *Poem*, as Pierre Vesperini has argued,[9] is concerned first
and foremost with the way that thinghood is to be understood
as the activity of *naturing*, and that the 'nature of things' is just
this movement of combination and permutation described
in the text. But moreover, the *Poem* itself is this action of
combining and permuting its atomic elements – letters – and
the dynamism of the *Poem* in its unfolding of variety is to be
experienced by the listener as Nature naturing. For Leibniz,
the emendations of the poetic text suggest, however, a greater
focus on the logical mechanism of combination and permutation than the restrictions of poetic form or analogy. Lucretius
proposes the principle; it would be for others to explicate the
art of combinatorial *naturing*.

While the co-lineage between jurisprudence and early
combinatorics can be sketched through the forensic rhetorical
practices of invention outlined by Aristotle and expanded on
by the Roman orators, a technical great leap forward occurs
in European thinking with the Majorcan Ramon Llull's (1232–
1316) synthesis of Jewish mysticism and Moorish thought into
a proto-combinatorial method that aims at revealing to any
devotee of the Abrahamic religions that their doctrines are
but variations of the same underlying intensional logic. Thus
at one level this combinatorics of a fashion clearly fulfils its
rhetorical purpose of convincing differing sides of the overall

justice the case of each. Yet at a second level the combinatorial art offers now an algorithm which the legal orator can use to invent all the possible variations of cases that could exist and so both make reference also to these in argument, but also judge these possible cases even before they had occurred as exercises for the learning of law.[10]

The influence was great, with Llullism spreading across Europe and undergoing a second bloom in the seventeenth century. Borrowing heavily from the combinatorial investigations of Marin Mersenne, the German Athanasius Kircher established himself as the most famous Llullist of his time, holding as he did a professorship in Rome. Yet the scope of Kircher's programme had become universal, and ceased to be a purely legal method in the restricted Aristotelean sense. The *ars combinatoria* breaks out of the confines of rhetoric and assumed the role of science of Epicurean generation of the cosmos. This trajectory can already be seen in the natural tendency of early combinatorial thinkers to combine and permute any discrete objects that come to mind: Mersenne permuted musical notes to investigate composition, while Christoph Clavius (1538–1612) developed a Llullist combinatorial wheel for the composition of elements which seems to have so impressed Leibniz that he reproduced in it his own *Dissertatio de arte combinatoria*. For Kircher the combinatorial art became a theory of everything but this by no means amounts to a casting off of its jurisprudential function, for, on the contrary, it is precisely because God is the universal judge of what is good in the cosmos that the combinatorial art of invention provides such an excellent approximation of his choices of creation. As Eberhard Knobloch reports,[11] according to Kircher's *Wisdom*[12] this 'universal knowledge (*scientia*)' was an imitation of God's creative force which had arranged the world according to measure number and weight – a logic of creation which echoes Lucretius' poem. In a similar vein, Leibniz would hold theology to be a special case of natural jurisprudence concerning the very reasons of things.[13] In the years that followed there were published combinatorial works whose results and imagery would find themselves explicitly or implicitly deployed in Leibniz's university dissertations. Athanasius Kircher's pupil Kasper Schott published his *Magia Universalis* (1657–9) whence it seems Leibniz found the source of his terminology for what we call variations: 'variations as much as to combination or matter as to permutation or form'. Another possible source for this wording is the *Lighthouse of Sciences* (1659) by Spanish Llullist Sebastián Izquierdo. Finally, many results Leibniz obtained from Daniel Schwenter's *Hours of Mathematical and Philosophical Refreshment* (1636).

When examined against this historical light it should be no surprise then that Leibniz should regard the mathematics of counting and jurisprudence as natural, indeed canonical, bedfellows. One simply cannot engage in forensic rhetoric without an art of combinations, and no judge should decide a case without an appreciation of the whole scope of possible arrangements of argumentation from which counsel has chosen her case. But what exactly is this art for Leibniz, and how does it inform and continue to inform his legal theory through his life? A general comprehension can be gleaned from Leibniz's subsequent identification of the *ars combinatoria* with the Aristotelean topics in his *Nova Methodus*.

Now, as Otto Bird has noted,[14] Aristotle famously omits to define 'topic' in his *Topics*, and people are referred instead to a comment in the *Rhetorics* that a topic is an 'element of an enthymeme'. Reading this with the substance of the *Topics* one realises that Aristotle is effectively interested in the common kinds of ways that the matter of propositions and problems can be related to each other. For example, he analyses genus and species not in terms of what a genus or species is, but rather in the specific relation – of implication – that holds between them. For example, if an animal (genus) can sleep, then a human (species) can sleep. Hence Theophrastus provides a more helpful definition of topic:

> A Topic is a principle (*arché*) and element (*stoicheon*) from which we draw propositions that serve as a basis for reasonings on a proposed question; it is determinate as to circumscription (*perigraphe . . . horismenos*) and un-determined as to particular applications (*kath' hekasta aoristos*).[15]

Whether a human does stand as the species of the genus animal is irrelevant; the principle and element of the proposition 'if animals sleep then humans sleep' is the implication 'if

... then', and this implication can be extracted and applied to numerous other cases. Leibniz rephrases this in late Scholastic language in his *Nova Methodus* discussion: these are 'transcendent relations [*Relationes transcendentes*] such as Whole, Cause, Matter, Sameness etc'.[16] In other words, the study of topics through the combinatorial art is a study of the real insofar as we consider the very relatedness of reality itself. And this is no simple matter of aggregates, as the above example of sleeping suggests and our work in the previous chapter confirms. The hierarchy of the real, with its subordination and co-relation of reals within ever more complicated entities, is not just the proper domain of the topics, but an instantiation of the combinatorial structure of the world. That moral entities, such as obligations and rights form a specific subset of the real only underlines why Leibniz should regard juridical problems as tractable by his art. As we work through the specifics of the *Dissertatio*, bear in mind this parallel between the transcendent relations Leibniz investigates and the real relations he believes pertain in the existing world.

These observations remain general only. As with the natural physicist Spinoza, so with the logician Leibniz: there is no methodological substitute here for a hands-on engagement with the technicalities of the subject matter. We must ourselves re-learn how to count, and so engage closely with the *Dissertatio de arte combinatoria* that Leibniz, aged twenty, wrote as an expansion of the theses he submitted to the Faculty of Philosophy at Leipzig in order to qualify for a position there. That he still very much adhered to the Llullism of Kircher is perhaps manifest even in this title, for it was Kircher who just three years before had coined the term '*ars combinatoria*' in his *Polygraphia Nova et Universalis ex Combinatoria Arte Detecta* (1663).[17]

3. What legally counts?

Let us now take the plunge and attempt to understand Leibniz's combinatorial art, at least to a degree sufficient to engage with its application to legal problems.

Leibniz deploys a number of central operations and related definitions in his *Ars Combinatoria*, which I set out here before explicating them in some detail. However, as one might

Ars Combinatoria *as* Urdoxa

Table 5.1 Leibniz's combinatorial terminology

Leibniz's term	Modern equivalent
Variatio ordine/situs	Permutation
Complexions • Union • Com2nation • Con3nation • Com(*k*)nation	Combination • Singleton • Combination of two terms • Combination of three terms • Combination of *k* terms
Variations as much combinatorial or of matter as they are of situs or form[a]	Variation
Caput (pl. capita)	Subsets containing predetermined elements
Discerptiones or Zerfällungen	Partition
Complexiones simpliciter	Power sets
Exponent	Choice, i.e. number of elements to be combined/permuted

Note
[a] 'Variationes tam complexiones seu materiae quam situs seu formae.' This phrasing, so suggestive of Leibniz's train of thought, is highlighted by Eberhard Knobloch in 'The Mathematical Studies of G.W. Leibniz on Combinatorics' (1974) 1 *Historia Mathematica* 409–30, at p.412.

expect in the organic phase of modern mathematics, Leibniz's terminology is his own and so I set out both Leibniz's terms and what are accepted to be their modern equivalents (A:VI, i, 172–3; Table 5.1).

Knobloch notes[18] that by Paris, Leibniz had deferred to the practice of his contemporaries and deployed 'combination' as a catchall for any of permutation, combination or variation, and that from this point on (for reasons which will become apparent in due course) classifies the size of combinations as 'exponents'.

I now consider each of these concepts in turn, but in so doing a little anachronism will help. The modern language of set theory provides a concise rendition of these concepts and so I have determined to use just enough of naïve (i.e. non-symbolic) set theory as is necessary to convey what is mathematical intuition – I hope you will be able to see 'with the eyes of the mind' what Leibniz is driving at with his

157

combinatorial jurisprudence. For those not familiar with sets, here is an example: an ice-cube tray. We are not interested in the ice. What matters is that our ice-cube tray is partitioned into ten cube-shaped compartments of unit volume. If I give you a range of polyhedrons of equal unit volume you will find that only the cubes fit in the compartments. The tray sorts and filters the polyhedrons; the polyhedrons are entirely subordinated to the information contained in the tray (its partitions). Naturally we will also put water in the tray and freeze it; the water will only freeze, admittedly with some expansion, into the cube shapes. Again, the water is dominated by the information contained in this particular tray and indeed any water could be used, just as any cubes be they of water or gelatine could be used. We call this tray a set, and we see that for a set what is relevant is the information the set gives us about what it 'holds', not the specific things that it is holding at any given moment. Now because the 'presence' of the contents of a set is secondary to the 'what kind?', this image can be enriched by considering a special tray which only holds trays. Evidently this tray is entirely specified by it holding only trays; it could be but has not been specified what kind of trays are held. The point is to suggest generalisation: if a tray can hold trays, then these trays may also be tray-holders, and so on to infinity. Likewise, the set may break free of its contents and so generate a theory purely about sets holding sets, with all the paradoxes that may follow. The core for our purposes is this: the set is entirely specified by the information that determines its potential contents, whether they exist or not, and this is a much easier object to handle than detailing the aggregate of items one intends. Now, because the only identifier of a set is the information about what it potentially holds we need a rule to determine what happens when we have two sets which both specify the same information, for example two trays that both could hold ten ice cubes. In this case traditional forms of set theory specify an axiom – in this case an assumed rule – that basically states that if two sets could hold exactly the same contents then they *are* the same set. More correctly the informational code which determines what a set can hold is the only thing to compare when determining identity. As a matter of logic this informational code is called a set's *extension*, and the axiom that claims it holds for a logical system is called the *axiom of extensionality*.

I have given this brief introduction to set language because it will make our discussion of Leibniz's combinatorial art more tractable, but it comes with an interpretative disadvantage: sets and their logic of extensionality are, as Husserl would argue, fundamentally different in character from the logic of intensionality that prevails with Leibniz. If, however, we bear in mind the priority for Leibniz of intensionality and in a rough and ready fashion accept that we may speak of sets as something that may be intended by the Leibnizian mind then I do not think we stray too far in speaking about sets as objects of a Leibnizian world. The sets we will deal with are capable of combinatorial generation and that suffices. Leibniz's point is, it is not the informational marker of the set that determines its identity with some second set, but whether the combinatorial operations that produced both sets were equivalent.

With this little sketch made out, let us turn to Leibniz's combinatorial operations.

3.1 Permutations

Leibniz begins his *De Arte Combinatoria* with combinations, only then turning to permutations though these are simpler in the order of construction – we will discover that in Leibniz's theory combinations are built from permutations. I propose to begin with the simpler object of enquiry. Permutations he divides into those with and those without repetition. To determine the number of permutations with repetition let us consider two identical sets A_1, A_2 of five natural numbers $= \{1, 2, 3, 4, 5\}$ and ask how many ways we can take one element from A_1 and another from A_2 to create permutations of two elements $\{a_1, a_2\}$. Extend a straight line and array along it the five elements of A_1; now extend from your starting point a second line perpendicular to the first and array along this the elements of A_2. You should have what looks like a Cartesian 'graph' or plane. Now draw lines perpendicular up from the 'A_1' axis and across from the 'A_2' axis so that you obtain a grid. Name each point of intersection of the gridlines according to corresponding two numbers that are the sources of these gridlines for example from the first gridline arising from A_1 you will have the following permutations = {{1, 1}, {1, 2}, {1, 3}, {1, 4}, {1, 5}}. The repetition occurs in the first permutation; you see that 1 appears twice because our starting sets are really the same set A_i used twice. Evidently if you obtain five permutations with repetition from the first element of A_1 when it is extended or produced along A_2 then you have 1 *element of* A_1 × 5 *elements of* A_2 = 5, so if you do this for each of the five elements of A_1 you must produce 5 *elements of* A_1 × 5 *elements of* A_2 = 25 permutations with repetition.

It is thus not surprising that this simple idea is now called the 'multiplication principle'. Indeed, it is so simple Leibniz leaps straight into consideration of much more complicated questions concerning permutations with repetitions and fixed points (more later). Now I should be clear that the above explanation is anachronistic, but the nature of the permutations discovered is as Leibniz intended. The choice of a Cartesian plane as a possible mechanism of demonstration only seems to occur to Leibniz later in his treatment of matrices, where the discrete components are labelled by coordinates to permit further permutation. I deploy it here because it best permits intuition to the non-specialist. We can 'see' the permutations as a two-dimensional spatial array. It also permits immediate generalisation as follows. If we want the number of permutations with repetition of five elements from our set A_i then we need an axis for each of the five times we use A_i. That means we create a five-dimensional spatial array with A_1 × A_2 × A_3 × A_4 × A_5 = 5 × 5 × 5 × 5 × 5 = 3,125 permutations with repetition. The conceptual insight here is not to try and roughly imagine a five-dimensional object, but rather to experience producing each set of five elements by a new *intension,* such as we might imagine a rose cyclically unfurling its leaves, one for each new subset of permutations. It is this intensional activity which attracts Leibniz. With this image of the unfolding flower we can better grasp the most general idea that a set of size n may be multiplied by itself n times (n^n) to discover all its permutations with repetition.

So what of permutations without repetition, with which Leibniz begins his treatment of the subject in Problem IV of the *De Arte Combinatoria*? We count these permutations as follows: we start as before with our set of five elements and choose one element, say '1', but when it comes to choosing the next number we are not allowed to choose what we have already chosen namely '1'; only from {2, 3, 4, 5}. Thus we must choose from A_i reduced by −1 element and so on until there are no elements left to choose and the resulting permutation (if we so wish) contains one of each element of A_i only. Hence our calculation is $A_1 \times (A_1 - 1) \times (A_1 - 2) \times (A_1 - 3) \times (A_1 - 4) = 5 \times 4 \times 3 \times 2 \times 1 = 120$ permutations without repetition. We still use the image of the flower with a petal for each spatial grid constructed by producing an additional axis, but each axis or stalk, if you will, grows shorter as the flower unfurls, somewhat like an Arum lily. This method of counting in which we multiply a number n by that n less 1 each time is called a factorial and written $n!$. Leibniz correctly establishes[19] that this is the correct way of counting permutations without repetition and indeed that the factorial is defined by decreasing recursion until $1! = 1$ is obtained. Leibniz proves this with a counting argument (the long-winded way) which he also displays in Table 7 and which relies on what we now call the notion of a fixed point.

Through Problems IV–XII of *De Arte Combinatoria* Leibniz engages with two special kinds of problem which appear to have piqued his interest greatly, namely these fixed points and what Leibniz terms capitals. Let us examine these to obtain a further flavour of the intensional dynamism at the heart of Leibniz's theory.

Fixed points and derangements

In our discussion of factorials above we introduced the intensional image of an unfurling rose. Fixed points allow us to refine the use of such 'images' somewhat and Leibniz's deployment of such fixed points suggests a way of characterising his view of mathematical objects during his early period. Again, to 'see' what a fixed point is, imagine that you arrange a loop of string into a square shape on a table. You hold this square by one vertex (or corner). With the other hand you take a pen and mark on the vertex you are holding the letter A. On the three other vertices you mark each of b, c, d and make a mental note of the starting position, for example the top-left vertex is A and, having noted the vertex you hold, you then 'read' off the other letters from the top-left vertex. Doing so in this initial position gives you the follow-ing reading: $S = \{A, b, c, d\}$. Now you flip the square along the line of symmetry Ac always holding onto A thus exchanging corners b and d; you read $\{A, d, c, b\}$. You flip back $= \{A, b, c, d\}$. You now hold the top corners still while you exchange the bottom two c,d which twists the square and gives you $\{A, b, d, c\}$. You twist again to return you to the original position. In each case the A remains in situ with respect to the vertices b, c, d, and these three circulate in subgroups of two. Although S is permuted, A does not change position and so is called a relative fixed point. Any permutation in which no element retains its position is called a *derangement*. Leibniz has no spe-cific term for fixed points, but when he discusses the matter in Problem V he speaks of elements that remain in the same *situs* or locus, and of the moving elements as 'circulating' in a 'vicinity'. He appears only indirectly concerned with derangements, which are merely a consequence of discovery of all possible permutations.

That the free elements circulate is suggested by the arrange-ment of Table 7 in Problem IV to which Leibniz refers. Here Leibniz distributes the twenty-four permutations of $\{a, b, c, d\}$ by choosing one letter to hold fixed (which he capitalises), then holding a second letter relatively fixed while he cycles the remaining two, which two permutations he places in a square, for example Ab_{dc}^{cd}. Leibniz clarifies that this is intended to be written 'in circulo scripta'. The notion of circulation is apparently Llullist in inspiration, derived via the *Physico-Mathematical Delights* of Daniel Schwenter who Leibniz cites in Problem V. The quotidian image drawn is of a room with a door at each corner and a table in the centre, with four guests, one of which is fixed as Schwenter himself. How can we permute the most honoured guests in terms of seating priority?

Leibniz wants us to notice that these manipulations of four elements proceed as follows: we have four possible choices for the first position in the permutation (for example A), which once made reduces the possible choices for the second posi-tion to three, which choice once made reduces the choices of the third position to just two, determining the final position absolutely. Thus, Leibniz declares, 'the exponent of a given variation is to be made from the product of the variation of

the exponent of the antecedent'.[20] This theorem he underlines by adding both that (a) whatever order you choose for
subsequent elements, prior permutations have power over
them all; and (b) whichever thing holds its point fixed, the
remainder vary between themselves. Table 7 makes this clear
– the fixed point in a permutation of four elements reaches
across six different subsequent permutations. The fixed point
thus simultaneously determines, one might even say, emanates or *commands* the subsequent points *and* extends their
variety by a factor equal to its *power*. A little thought suggests
that we might represent this action by arranging each discrete element in descending order of power, and in this way
we obtain a sequence of permutations, each anchored in the
determinations of the prior powers.

Capitals

Although the traditional discussion of permutations in
Problems IV–VI seems to lack any connection to the discursive explorations of Problems VII–XII the two groups are
intertwined by Leibniz's fascination with invariant mathematical structures.[21] Capitals may be considered as 'fixed
complexes' which is to say that as with fixed points two or
more points remain unchanged during the permutation of
the remaining elements of a given structure. The task here is
to investigate the variations of this given structure. Indeed,
Leibniz clarifies that fixed points are capitals of size one, and
he calls them *monads*.[22]

The mathematics here is quite involved but again we can
'see' what Leibniz has in mind in his somewhat cursory exposition by expanding on the ideas discussed above. Take for
example a tetrahedron – a Platonic solid with four equilateral
triangles as surfaces. Label each vertex *a, b, c, d* respectively,
note which position you will count first, and hold the tetrahedron by vertex *a* (which again we capitalise). Rotate the
remaining vertices to achieve the following cycle: {A}{b, c, d},
{A}{d, b, c}, {A}{c, d, b} and back to {A}{b, c, d}. The focus now is
on the three-element cycle and the idea that each time a rotation occurs the three-cycle is mapped onto itself in a new way.
This is what Leibniz would call a non-homogenous capital.
Now observe that if we fix A then fix a second element by
the above rotation of the three-cycle, we can now determine

which direction to move around the upper triangle. So for example, from the fixing of {A}{b} we can move clockwise first to c then d or vice versa, giving either {A}{b}{c, d} or {A}{b} {d, c}. We thus have a two-cycle derived from a dominating three cycle. In so doing it is quite evident that we recreate Leibniz's Table 7 according to particular manipulations of a Platonic solid, which we may call the form or scheme of the variation in question. What has changed is indeed the focus on the vicinity or circulation of the capitals investigated. Leibniz considers both this scenario and those of homogeneity, which is to say that a cycle contains elements which are indistinguishable when exchanged, but I do not propose to examine this closely.

Our examination of the tetrahedron also brings out two different aspects of Leibniz's investigation which are worth stressing. We have considered the arrangements of the vertices of this form and noted how some can be held fixed while others vary, and that these can vary as if they are themselves 'sub-forms'. The logical structure of the form was in a certain sense the effect of our investigation. But the tetrahedron also revealed that to discover these arrangements we must *act* (vary) and that to vary the tetrahedron two types of action are in play. One action was the rotation of the form – the permutation proper; the other was the passage from one vertex to another. It is this latter act of passing along an edge of the tetrahedron and so combining the vertex of departure (say A) with the vertex of arrival (namely b such that {Ab}) and so fixing these in the result to which we now turn. We thus come to the operation Leibniz calls 'complexion'.

3.2 Complexions

Leibniz defines a complexion as the union of a smaller whole within a greater.[23] Hofmann[24] has shown that, inspired by Hobbes, Leibniz had difficulties with Euclid's axiom that the whole is greater than the part and so seeks a new basis. 'Wholeness' he explains as a certain act of the intellect in grasping together various parts, and operation which he claims is derived from encountering one being and abstracting unity from it. Whether or not Leibniz has in mind the second book of the *Parmenides*, or perhaps the work of Proclus, he clearly rejects the Scholastic derivation of numeric wholeness from the continuum (3 is a point on a line) in favour of a theory of wholeness as a function of an operation on discrete entities. As such complexion is a relation, and so with quality and quantity one of three modes or affections of being.[25] Note that the relation of union which complexion instantiates with respect to number is complemented by harmony (*convenientia*).

So we might regard complexion as the affection of the being in act of entities to generate new wholes, but if we can generate new wholes then does not Leibniz open himself up to arguments that all non-simple entities are created by intellectual acts, and perhaps even that ultimately all entities are but relations in a Scotist infinity? Whether or not Leibniz has sympathy for such a line of thought, he is very clear that we cannot complicate just anything; rather complexion is defined as taking place within a 'greater entity'. We must choose parts from a given entity, and so complexions will be lesser wholes derived from the greater. This makes sense within the confines of the monad (in the metaphysical sense): the complexion adds nothing to what already potentially has being within the monad.

By way of example, given the greater whole {*a, b, c, d*} we can complicate the following lesser wholes, which are termed by Leibniz according to their 'exponent' (Table 5.2).

Leibniz does not pick out the possibility of a zero-complexion but he does include this explicitly for each exponent in his Table ℵ of complexions. Notice that unlike permutations, order (*situs*) is not important for complexions, and that {ab} is an equivalent complexion to {ba}.

Why does Leibniz deploy the term 'exponent' for what we might call choice of elements or the cardinality of the resulting choice? Leibniz refers us to the usage of exponents in the

Table 5.2 Exponents and complexions

Exponent	Complexions
Unions	{a}, {b}, {c}, {d}
Com2nations	{ab}, {ac}, {ad}, {bc}, {bd}, {cd}
Con3nations	{abc}, {abd}, {acd}, {bcd}
Con4nations	{abcd}

geometric progression.[26] A geometric progression is a series which increases by a fixed ratio r, such that we might write the generic geometric progression as $S_n = ar^0 + ar^1 + ar^2 + ar^3 + \ldots + ar^{n-1}$. The exponents then are the numbers n. The series is called geometric precisely because of these powers; the series progresses because each new power indicates a change of spatial dimension. So, for example r is a line, while r^2 is a square, and so on. While two lines may be added to create a bigger line in the same direction, we must cross-multiply orthogonal lines, that is, lines of absolutely different dimensions. What does this have to do with the calculations of complexions in Table א? How can powers of a number relate to the choices that can be made from a greater whole of numbers? If we are to take Leibniz at his word – that he uses 'exponents' to mean combinatorial choices because this is suggested by the use in geometric progressions – then there must be some way in which powers of a number r are related to combinatorial choices. The answer we find suggests a profound geometric interpretation of combinatorial matters by Leibniz, one which he chose to extract from his *Dissertatio* and publish separately:[27] that the sum of the possible complexions for a given row of the triangle 'coincides with the sum of the geometric progression base-2'.[28] Thus Leibniz is interested in the following geometric progression: $S_n = 2^0 + 2^1 + 2^2 + 2^3 + \ldots + 2^{n-1}$. Each term of the series is the sum of the complexions for the elements of the greater whole, indicated by n. For example, the number of possible combinations, ignoring order, of three, four and five elements is respectively $2^3 = 8$, $2^4 = 16$, $2^5 = 32$. Thus in general the number of possible combinations for n elements is 2^n, and, most generally, the sum of all possible combinations of a series of increasing elements coincides with the sum of the geometric progression.

I claim that in this 'theorem' Leibniz has already made the core discovery of his dyadic[29] – the foundation of his system on combinations of 1 and 0 – for the combinatorial interpretation that Leibniz provides makes explicit that base 2 is chosen because it permits the characterisation of each lesser whole (or choice) from each greater whole via the exponent. This is perhaps easier explained by an example. Let us posit an operation which we will call the characteristic. The characteristic takes a given greater whole and it maps the parts of that

Ars Combinatoria *as* Urdoxa

Table 5.3 Example of con4nation

Exponent	Complexions	a	b	c	d
0	1	0	0	0	0
1	4	1	0	0	0
1		0	1	0	0
1		0	0	1	0
1		0	0	0	1
2	6	1	1	0	0
2		1	0	1	0
2		1	0	0	1
2		0	1	1	0
2		0	1	0	1
2		0	0	1	1
3	4	1	1	1	0
3		1	1	0	1
3		1	0	1	1
3		0	1	1	1
4	1	1	1	1	1

greater whole to a resulting lesser whole as follows: if given element i of the greater whole is to appear in the lesser whole, then we write '1'; and if the element i will not appear, then we write 0. Then if a greater whole $T = \{a, b, c, d\}$ is subjected to the characteristic, we generate the possible combinations of parts of T shown in Table 5.3.

Let us think about what is happening here as a movement of thought. You will remember that we described permutations as grids with an axis for each string of elements to be permuted. Well we have this also here, but the elements to be permuted are the dyadic set $2 = \{0,1\}$. There is one such dyad for each element of the object set being considered, so in Table 5.3 we have four dyads. Now each element is considered serially, such that in a way the combinations unfurl like a rose, each petal appearing as we consider each new exponent, that is open out a new dyad and so a new 'petal' or dimension. This image is quite different from the familiar tabular arrangement shown in Table 5.3; for example combinations of zero, one and two elements already appear with two dimensions, whereas in Table 5.3 we consider appearances of each element altogether. That Leibniz appreciates this image of unfurling permutations will be apparent from what follows. All in all, the total number of permutations of 2 then gives us the total number of choices that may be made (e.g. 2^4). From here, if we wish to extract individual choices of a required exponent then we must somehow factor out the complexions we are not interested in from this general sum. Here, and in Problem II, Leibniz struggles to find a convincing means for breaking up (*zerfällen* – literally tearing apart the cases) the total number of complexions into the correct proportions. It is evident from Table 5.3 that the exponents do not directly relate to the number of possible choices of a given exponent made; for example, there are not 2^4 different ways of choosing four different things from four things if order is ignored. Yet this reading allows us to note that even at this early stage we find in Leibniz's investigations a deep relationship between series (here, the geometric progression) and combinatorics (the exponents of the geometric series inform the determination of possible choices from a greater whole). In due course Leibniz will learn that another more complicated series is required to explain the distribution of the subsets of total choices, but in his investigation of series he is on the right track.

In the absence of a 'law' for the series of specific choices, Leibniz develops what he believes to be an original recurrence relation for establishing the numbers of possible complexions of a given exponent. His solution is correct, and while not original his method of explaining it may well be. As with permutations he deploys antecedent exponents to 'illuminate' us with Table ב (Table 5.4). Here Leibniz gives us a major whole of five letters and chooses complexions of exponent 3. He then partitions the results according to whether the result could already be chosen from (i) a major whole of only three letters, namely {a, b, c} only; (ii) a major whole of only four letters, for example {a, b, d}; or (iii) from all five letters only, for example {a, b, e}. In this way the partitions mirror the addition of each new element {c}, {d}, and {d}, which he partitions from the

Table 5.4 Leibniz's Table 2

	1	ab	c	3		
	2	ab	d			
	3	ac	d			
Number of Con3nations	4	bc	d	4	No. of things	
	5	ab	e			
	6	ac	e			
	7	ad	e			
	8	bc	e			
	9	bd	e			
	10	cd	e	5		

existing com2nations by a vertical line. This reveals that the total number of con3nations is the sum of the previous total number of com2nations and of unions, the latter being the simple total of elements to be combined. Accordingly, we find Leibniz again using exponents to determine the increase of possible choices.

Observe as promised that Leibniz seeks to synthesise the elements one by one in a series of unfurlings. The result, which Leibniz expands in a verbal exposition of various cases, is essentially the rule that the number of choices k one can make from n elements is equal to the sum of (i) the number of choices k one can make from n-1 elements *and* (ii) the number of choices k-1 one can make from n-1 elements. So for example, if I have ten roses, one of which is red, the remainder white roses of various quality, and I wish to choose four, I can either do so at random = 210 possible choices, or I can (i) refuse to choose the red rose and so discard it, thus limiting my choice of four to nine roses = 126 possible choices *and* (ii) deliberately choose the red rose, thus requiring me to choose only three more roses from the remaining nine white roses = 84 possible choices. Now 84 + 126 = 210, but evidently I cannot both deliberately choose and discard the red rose simultaneously – they are logically incompossible. What Leibniz has noticed again is that an increase of the power of the series renders what was incompossible now possible.

Table 5.5 Rearranged version of Leibniz's Table ℵ

				1						
			1		1					
		1		2		1				
	1		3		3		1			
1		4		6		4		1		
1		5	10		10		5		1	
1	6	15		20		15		6		1

⋮

This insight about the summation of incompossibles permits Leibniz to construct his Table ℵ of complexions, which I set out partially in the modern style in Table 5.5.

This is likely to be known to the reader as Pascal's triangle, but the name is not mathematically instructive. Far better to understand that Leibniz arrives at this structure through an appreciation of the interaction of cases and that more complicated combinations are directly constructible as combinations of immediately precedent, 'smaller' combinations in a rigorous hierarchy.

4. Intermediate conclusion on the *Dissertatio*

Why is understanding all this important? Remember that the *ars combinatoria* is the technique to be deployed in topics, which is to say it is the enumerative art of inventing all possible relationships between any given material. The topics are the principles and elements that bind together the real. And now Leibniz has developed a rigorous hierarchy of combinations and permutations which exhausts every possible case of what could be constructed and shows how any more complicated real entity can be constructed by combining less complicated real entities, and so on. On a narrow reading all Leibniz is doing is implicitly claiming that his *ars combinatoria* provides the correct way for students to understand how arguments can be generated by their transcendental relations, but he will go much further than this. By the *Nova Methodus* he will be arguing that thinking as he conceives it, including along these combinatorial lines, is teachable because it reflects an intensionality or way of thinking that is common to all. His intermediate step, in *De Casibus Perplexis*, is to advance on the assumption that combinatorial thinking is common to all rational substances and to argue that perplexity arising from legal cases can flow from a failure to appreciate this.

To summarise Leibniz's key findings on combinations:

(a) The sum of possible combinations of all sizes from a given set of size n is the base 2 raised to the power n, the two in question being the characteristic dyad $\{0, 1\}$, and the result being the power of the set.

(b) The sum of all such *powers* progresses as a geometric series of base 2.

(c) The number of combinations of exponent k from n elements is the sum of incompossible choices from n-1 elements, these choices being of exponent k and k-1 respectively.

(d) Alternatively, an increase in exponent increases the power of a set and renders the incompossible possible.

We will find applications of these results, and their intuitive bases, in what follows.

5. Early deployment of the *ars combinatoria* in jurisprudence

Leibniz scatters his juridical examples through the *Dissertatio de arte combinatoria*, and only explicitly engages combinatorics in his legal disputations at key points in the text. Nevertheless, we shall already see general and specific features of his natural legal philosophy. The general feature is teased out by Gaston Grua, who notes that in later texts Leibniz will clarify his tendency to hold that his juridical method must in a certain sense simultaneously be cut away from the practical application of laws, and then in its freedom be reapplied to the field of actuality without diminishing its internal coherence. Grua writes that:

It is a question here . . . of a natural jurisprudence that is not subordinated to legal interpretation, not conjectural as with the doctrines of fact. Natural law is independent of opinion, and the science of the true law will be much easier than the arts learned through practice. This perpetual law offers its field to received jurisprudence, for this scientific or rational method enunciates propositions to which the *ius gentium* and civil law bear witness.[30]

The reference to 'doctrines of fact' is to the method the judge uses in weighing evidence. A number of features of legal practice – evidence, judgement, forensic rhetoric, determination of obligations and property between various parties – form for Leibniz subsets of a universal natural juridical structure and indeed express this natural legal field. With reference to both Plato's *Laws* and Aristotle's *Rhetoric* Leibniz writes that 'at its core jurisprudence resembles geometry because it forms cases by means of the combination of elements'.[31] This is no metaphor: Leibniz immediately proceeds to sketch out an *Elements of Law* modelled on the geometrical masterwork of Euclid. Elements, Leibniz informs us, are simples – in geometry figures such as triangles and circles; in law acts, promises, transfers. Cases are complexions of these, and the variations of both are infinite. Both Euclid's *Elements* and the elements of law that can be found in the juridical 'corpus' are both notable for their inclusion of significant (*insigniores*) or special cases for consideration, and here Leibniz refers us to Llull's *Ars magna* as one source for consideration of these cases. Now the elements must be correctly established, and this Leibniz does, detailing four terms which are the origin of the diverse cases in law: persons, things, acts and rights.[32]

The function of these definitions is to act as simples. Simples are those which are not composed from others and so we must be careful as lawyers to decompose cases before us into their constituent simple terms. Leibniz concludes his sketch for an *Elementa Iure*:

Who does not see that he will produce infinitely many cases from these simple terms, when he repeats their parts enough times, and then with combinations, conternations etc. and complexions of these, and permutations?[33]

Now Leibniz's overreliance on existing legal categories is manifestly problematic for any such science of law, but one has the strong feeling that his view about the cut (*coupure*) between his natural legal combinatorics and civil legal practice has already been made. From the perspective of judge and legal scholar a given case for decision can be found to be a complexion and permutation of predetermined categories, but this combinatorial analysis is akin to the approximation of creation that Athanasius Kircher declares divides his work from that of God. In the case of law, however, the object of study are those legal complexions that are brought about by humans in society. So what is being approximated by the combinatorial art is the aggregate of human legal activity, namely the combinations and permutations of their self-perceived relationships with each other.

This is not to say that Leibniz is proposing to reduce legal matters to combinatorics or algebra.[34] A good portion of *De Casibus Perplexis* is spent narrowing down the scope of application of Leibniz's proposed methodology to 'perplexing cases'. Thus matters which can be resolved by simply applying the positive law – 'ON GROUNDS OF MERE LAW' – are of no interest to him.[35] Rather, Leibniz is concerned with those cases where according to the positive law claimants appear to have equal right. Perplexity has arisen because of a contingent, that is, incorrect relating of the claims, or elements of those claims, which results in 'antinomy'.[36] By this I understand Leibniz to be making a claim from topics: that perplexing cases are just those cases which have been generated by a false application of transcendent (here moral) relations to given objects. By way of illustration, if A sells a vase to B, and then sells the same vase to C, both B and C may feel they have a right over the vase, though each right necessarily excludes the other. How can this be resolved? The case is only perplexing because we believe that both B and C can own the vase. This is false; the property here is exclusive. A must choose from either B or C to whom he transfers property title, and the party that misses out has a personal claim in contract against A, not a property claim.

Leibniz then is concerned with the transcendent relations between moral entities, which is to say that he is attempting to write a 'Legal Topics' whose methodology is the *ars combinatoria*. Although we can easily find in Leibniz's wider legal discussions normative assumptions about the constituents of the legal field, we should not lose sight of the fact that this discussion of topics sets to one side the question of justice in favour of an analysis of human, juridical intension. The focus then is on the generation of the legal world by the activity of combination and permutations. We can see this in other parts of Leibniz's early work, for there is a clear mapping between the two foundational combinatorial activities: combination and permutation, and the two fundamental legislative activities which he introduces in the 1666 *Dissertation on Perplexing Cases* as *disposition* and *concourse* (*concursus*). To be clear Leibniz introduces both disposition and concourse within the context of perplexing cases, such that he gives us definitions of *dispositio perplexa* and *concursus perplexus*, but as these terms are clearly composites we are able validly to extract the relevant elements from them.

5.1 Disposition

In Article XII of the *Dissertation on Perplexing Cases*[37] Leibniz defines a disposition as an act by A that:

(a) is voluntary; and
(b) determines that something be done with the property of a disposing party B.

Leibniz is trying to cover off a number of private law acts here which we can recover by combinatorial means. Most simply, where $A = B$, then one and the same person is unilaterally willing a disposal of their own property, for example in the case of the gift or will. Where $A \neq B$ then we a dealing with some obligation on B to dispose of her property as A directs. This is most likely to occur in consideration of a second inverse disposition in which A agrees to dispose of his property as B directs. Leibniz characteristically calls this mutuality a 'circular disposition' but clearly he means primarily to cover contractual arrangements.[38] A third case is available which Leibniz could have mentioned: where neither A nor B are identifiable – the null case – in which circumstances the property is vacated and reverts to the supreme authority. We thus have arrived at one null case, two bilateral cases which combine as a contract, and one unilateral case, as would be expected with a juridical element with exponent two. Leibniz adds that we may quite naturally combine the disposition in a number of ways, allowing for further disposing parties – the multilateral contract – and stipulating a variety of conditions for each disposition. Somewhat presaging the engineer's dictum that the more parts a machine has the more that can go wrong, Leibniz identifies that each additional complexion poses new possibilities for legal perplexity.

The critical role of contracting had already been considered in the *Dissertatio de arte combinatoria*. In the discussion of the applications of Problems I and II, Leibniz draws[39] on the *Digests* of Gaius to consider the contract of agency (mandate) and explicitly applies the combinatorial method to enumerate the possible complexions generated by what he will term a disposition with three parties: the principal/mandator; the agent/mandatory; and the third party with who the agent deals on behalf of the principal. Leibniz specifies that he will focus on *for whom* the given mandate grants benefit, so some contracts may actually be gifts. Our author should expect that given three things there will be $2^3 = 8$ possible dispositions to be enumerated. He sets them out as shown in Table 5.6 (I tabulate for ease).

The result, if the null case is ignored, is that we have seven possible dispositions from which we then subtract the 'useless' contract in favour of the agent alone, leaving a total of six. Leibniz concludes with a dose of disappointment in Roman practicality: 'why [the jurisconsults] kept only five, omitting the con3ternation, I do not know'.[40]

In keeping with the visual style of the followers of Llull and indeed with Leibniz's pretensions to juridical topology, it is instructive to consider the example in Table 5.6 of the mandate as distributed on a triangle, each of the vertices labelled with the names principal, agent and third party. With this combinatorial object we can then trace off the solutions with our finger by picking out the form's structural elements. So, the points or vertices are one solution, the three representing the isolated individuals. The edges connect two points at a time, and there are three of these representing the solutions with two parties benefiting. The surface of the triangle connects all three at once, and there is one of these.

Table 5.6 Disposition as combination

Combinatorial choice	Legal application
1 possible way of choosing no one	None – Leibniz pre-emptively discounts this case and so only speaks of seven outcomes, though his method clearly accounts for the null case.
3 possible ways of choosing 1 person	Under this contract the sole beneficiary of the arrangement is either the principal, the agent or the third party.
	A contract in favour of the agent alone is deemed useless by the jurisconsults, for as such it is an advice not a mandate, so Leibniz discounts it.
3 possible ways of choosing 2 persons	Under this contract two parties are beneficiaries of the third's disposition, for example the principal gifts property to the agent with a mandate to share the property with a third person.
1 possible way of choosing 3 persons	This is the most common case, for here the principal seeks to contract with the third person but uses her agent because, for example, the agent and third person are geographically close (shipping for example).

No structural element of the triangle connects none of the elements, thus providing the null case.

It would be wrong to draw the conclusion from these examples that legal dispositions are simply elements to be combined – *the dispositions are the combinations*. What Leibniz is doing when he enumerates the possible dispositions is expanding on the investigations of Kircher, which is that the combinatorial method approximates the principle of generation in various fields of analysis. Combinatorics here is recreating the combinatorial dispositions which could happen and which have happened since the recognition of such contracts. There are evidently philosophical questions here about the relationship between combinatorial mathematics and the social facts of law, but such matters do not restrain Leibniz from proposing a reading of civilian law as a 'witness' to a deeper natural law. The purported relationship also indicates that Leibniz's understanding of this natural law is not so much of a system of eternal precepts, but ultimately as we have come to expect of a legislative activity. I claim that the act of disposing stands for Leibniz as one such fundamental operation which is to be comprehended combinatorially. This operation may then be defined as the act of choice: given a set of n elements the disposition chooses and so 'complicates' k elements. For example, if we have A, B, C then the disposition operation picks out various implicit combinations which it marks by binding them $\{AB\}$, $\{BC\}$ and so forth.

There is a further subtle aspect to Leibniz's analysis which should also be examined. It is difficult not to think of a disposition as a rule – a condition or obligation in Leibniz's terminology – between parties, o, one or many. The conclusion of Article XII makes clear that such conditions are the further source of perplexity, suggesting quite correctly that the conditions of disposition are analytically separate from the *dispositio* proper, which is the combining operation discussed above. Nevertheless, if we wish to consider the proper application of the disposition operation then at root three terms must be considered, the two parties to be combined (though the two may be identical) and the rule for transfer that operates on the resultant combination (rather than, in the absence of the combination, merely one of the parties). By adding further parties and iterating the disposition operation we are able to combine a desired number of parties, thus indicating that the *dispositio* is indeed a fundamental operation in this regard: it constitutes social relations which are then to be considered in a concourse according to the various points of view that constitute them.

5.2 Concourse

The definition Leibniz gives of *concursus* is decidedly legal, but this belies the combinatorial richness of its field of application. Concourse refers to the legal situation where various claimants have equal right to the same thing, but this right is subject to a (possibly conflicting) order of priorities. It is the notion of order here that is likely to have sparked Leibniz's interest, for as we have come to expect the question of concourse is to be comprehended by means of the theory of permutations. I give the definition before expanding on both these aspects:

(a) A *concourse* arises where A, B, C . . . have equal right to some property x which falls to them such that what is to be determined is not their right but the irreflexive *order of priority* in which x should be distributed to each of A, B, C . . . to meet their respective claims.

(b) A concourse is called *perplexing* where the order of priority leads to contradiction.[41]

Irreflexivity means that while A can be prior to B, which we will note $A > B$, A cannot be prior to itself such that $A \not> B$. Thus a perplexing case would be such as the example Leibniz gives, where we are told that $A > B$ and $B > C$, which by transitivity implies $A > C$, but some rule or condition tells us that $A < C$ which is itself a contradiction and implies by transitivity $A > A$ rendering the matter 'uncertain and circular'.

A modern illustration of a concourse is the determination of the respective right of creditors. A bankrupt is declared to have assets of 100 while it is proved that the bankrupt owes to debts of 75 to A, 50 to B, and 25 to C. Now if there is no order of priority between the creditors then English law applies the rule of *pari passu* such that the bankrupt's assets are divided proportionally between the creditors according to the debt each is owed. Thus there are total debts of 150, and A is owed half this, so A receives half the assets (= 50); B is owed a third, so receives just over 33; C receives the remainder representing his sixth interest as creditor. One can see that each creditor receives 0.66 for every 1 owed. But by disposition or special rule of law, one or more parties may have priority, for example if they have taken security over the bankrupt's assets or are favoured by state intervention. If A has security over the 100, then by priority A can use this 100 to repay the debt in its entirety provided that the excess goes back to the bankrupt for use in settling the remaining debts. If we assume B has a 'second-ranking' security in addition, the distribution of assets in the concourse proceeds as follows: A receives full satisfaction of 75 and returns 25; B then takes this 25 to part-pay the 50 owed and is forced to write off the outstanding 25; this leaves nothing for C. Creditor priority thus produces significant economic effects depending on the system preferred by a given legal system and this question of preferences goes to classical questions of justice also in Leibniz's day.

That is the legal conception at work, but what of the discrete mathematics? Combinatorially speaking *concursus* expresses the activity of permutation which as we have seen is the consideration of all possible orders of a given set of elements. Artosi suggests[42] the language of partial orderings is relevant here to understand Leibniz, but while relevant and notationally useful, Leibniz is clearly thinking in terms of permutations, not just because he speaks of order (*ordine*) but because he goes so far as to affix a Llullist mobile to the front of the dissertation, to which he expressly refers in his introduction of perplexing concourses. As the name suggests the mobile is designed to be moved, or, if one prefers, one can trace the movements with one's fingers. Leibniz's mobile is embellished after the baroque fashion but its essential combinatorial elements are reproduced in Figure 5.1.

As Leibniz clarifies, the triangle is a mobile form, which is indicated by setting it within the circle. The three persons are

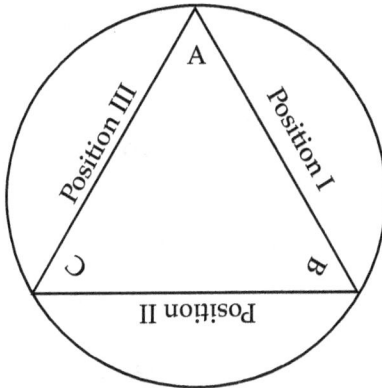

Figure 5.1 Leibniz's 'mobile' used for explaining *concursus*

Source: Leibniz's 'mobile' affixed to his *Dissertation on Perplexing Cases in the Law*.

Table 5.7 Leibnizian group of actions

	e	r	r^2
e	A	B	C
r	B	C	A
r^2	C	A	B

thus 'cycled' around as the triangle is moved always so that it is congruent with the starting position (in other words we cut out the triangle and can only set it back in the hole if its fits). I indicate in Table 5.7 the operations of doing nothing = e, and of rotating once r. Rotating twice is then $rr = r^2$:

You will observe that if you put your figure at any point of the triangle and then follow one of the above operations from that particular point you will end up at the point indicated in the table. Thus, starting at A and rotating twice goes to C, while if you begin then at that C and rotate once you obtain A. Doing this for all elements and noting the respective positions as in the table, we arrive at three of the desired permutations of three persons. Yet what of the missing three permutations which Leibniz should have expected, such as A > C > B? The manner in which Leibniz comes to this issue is indirect, which is to say his initial construction of definitions and indeed the mobile does not openly envisage this possibility. I suggest therefore that Leibniz struggled with a correct intuition for what the mathematics was telling him. He goes someway to achieving it as follows.

We are told that the mobile triangle is set against an immobile background, which are the relative positions I, II and III. So as the triangle and persons cycle so the positions permute relative to them. Within the context of the concourse Leibniz specifies the rule that while as between positions I and II and between II and III the 'UNDER' relation always holds (that is, I > II > III), III is always 'CONTRARY TO' I such that the relation III > I never holds.[43] This pre-ordering allows us to recover three priorities as indicated in the combinatorial table (Table 5.7), but having considered these cases Leibniz is moved to consider the manner in which legal doctors who uphold the doctrine of priorities use their quick-wittedness to subvert it when it suits their client. He writes in Article XXII:

I have quite admired the sharp-wittedness of those Doctors who extol that axiom expressed by them using the formula: If I defeat him who defeated you [then I will defeat you] but who do so when it is favourable to them only to rail against the same axiom whenever it puts them at a disadvantage. . . . In fact their reasoning begins from a starting point of their own choosing . . . as if there were no difference, but that is exactly what is relevant in such circles. Indeed, in children's circular counting, where we go around the circle to determine the last one to survive . . . it is very important which hand is outstretched first. And in such games it is possible to predict the outcome by computation.[44]

This is the required breakthrough that permits access to the 'missing' three permutations. It is a question of choosing to start in the direction of your left hand or right hand, of reading the mobile backwards, or, which is easier in the case of the mobile, flipping the triangle over and reading it forwards – the result is equivalent and grants this 'flipping' permutation the same tangible status as the rotation operation in a way which 'reading backwards' lacks. If we call this new permutation f, then our table can be expanded to the desired six permutations of three ordered persons (Table 5.8).

Note that flipping (or reading backwards) need only occur once, and that combining flipping with the existing rotation operation efficiently produces the result. The table could of

Table 5.8 Expanded Leibnizian group of actions

	e	r	r^2
e	A	B	C
r	B	C	A
r^2	C	A	B
f	A	C	B
rf	C	B	A
r^2f	B	A	C

course be extended rightwards to reveal a certain inner symmetry, but this is trivial for Leibniz's purposes.

The secret of the perplexity is thus laid bare: the doctors of law play on a hidden ambiguity with the principle of ordering which arises from the choice of direction in which one reads a given order. Here Artosi's ingenious interpretation of the text in terms of partial orderings is perhaps less elucidating than justified, but it does aid us some of the way. Leibniz will argue that in certain cases the choice of ordering direction (flipping) is itself in question and one must consider this higher order issue rather than presume that contradictions between orders have presented us with a perplexing case. The example given in Article XXIII is that of security (*hypotheca*) rights on the death of the grantor, and its permutations are also embellished on the mobile attached to his dissertation (but I have not replicated this very small text). Our grantor dies and there are three creditors of his estate: A has an earlier tacit or implied security right; B an immediate express security right; C is the dowry of the widow arising last in time, on the man's death. What is the priority? Well it could be argued that C's dowry has legal priority over the earliest security of A, but because A is prior in time A is as a matter of the law of security prior to B, so it follows (fallaciously) that C is prior to A – we have $C > B > A$. Leibniz considers other permutations, such as $B > C > A$. We can see that these two examples are in a sense incommensurate because they only arise depending on the direction in which we agree to read the relevant order, or whether we have flipped our mobile triangle. Our 'preferences' – our perspective – as to the direction of the order chosen 'must intervene only when a decision cannot be arrived at in any other way'.[45] In other words, the judge moves from the ontic perspective of present disposition to its mirror image: the deontic perspective of the future.

From the foregoing it is hopefully clear that it is the second combinatorial operation f which explains the incommensurability of the permutations of legal priority. Thus I cannot agree with Artosi that Leibniz's solution to the issue is indicated by recent developments in defeasible logic at the 'meta-level'.[46] Combinatorial methods of manipulating invariant structures – or capitals – are strong candidates for explicating Leibniz's reasoning, and I take particular support from the utility of the triangular mobile in illustrating just how this is achieved.

Finally, note the significance of Leibniz's move. As we saw in the introduction to this section, Leibniz heralds his approach to perplexing cases as geometric, and now he has made good on his claim that legal problems are so tractable. Following the topical method originating in Aristotle, Leibniz abstracts from a specific problem the elements of transcendent relations that bind together cases as moral entities. He then analyses these relations as if they were a geometric figure, rotating the structure in what might be called a moral or state space. From this he is able to generate all possible viewpoints on the problem and indeed both possible and impossible solutions.

Given the history of the *ars combinatoria* since Llull, who introduced his 'wheel' as a geometric device for investigating possible combinations in language, Leibniz's spatial approach to perplexing cases would not appear particularly novel. While we might praise him for first distilling the topical structure from the problem of debtors and then examining it, rather using a predetermined combinatorial structure as a Procrustean bed, such a method would just be a correct application of Aristotle's counsels on the matter. Nevertheless, Leibniz's conception of moral entities and their transcendent relations – the real as such – is significant, though we must look outside *De Casibus Perplexis* for the first indications of why.

Two years prior to the completion of *De Casibus Perplexis*, on 3 December 1664, Leibniz defended his *Specimen of Philosophical Questions Collected from the Law* (the *Specimen Quaestionum Philosophicarum* or SQP) before Johan Menzel.[47] Several common issues are discussed after the Scholastic fashion, before Leibniz turns to Question XVI: '. . . whether moral entities, such as *ius*, ownership, servitude, etc., are relations' and whether they are 'real entities or entities of reason'. In tackling the issue, Leibniz makes recourse to Erhard Weigel, his former Professor of Mathematics at Jena, who established three highest genera of entities: natural, moral and notional, each genus having its own qualities, quantities, estimations and actions, Leibniz continues: '[Weigel] thus reduces rights to moral qualities, and just as space is the substrate of natural action or motion, so the state is in a way a moral space, in which something like a moral motion is effected.'[48] Consider what this means in respect of concourse. We saw that the concourse presupposes confirmed rights of the parties, rights confirmed by the state. Before we even sit down to judge a particular case of distribution we are presented with a 'space' in which all the possible permutations of the parties are distributed in a certain and determinate manner. All possible rights stand to be chosen by virtual reorientation of the space. Impossible rights, such as rights under a contract which has ceased to bind are *atopon* – they are absurd, or literally have no place in the *topos* that is the moral space. Further elaboration is not provided, but it would seem that Leibniz's spatial approach to legal problems is neither simply a nod to combinatorial tradition nor an ad hoc solution limited to *De Casibus Perplexis*. Rather, Leibniz bears in mind a Weigelian conception of a moral or state space of real juridical relations. Could it be, therefore, that Leibniz's own methodology in *De Casibus Perplexis* expresses a wider commitment to a 'state space' theory of topics? Leibniz's trajectory to the *Elementa* suggests so.

We saw in section 3 that Leibniz had discovered relationships between the rules of disposition (combination) and concourse (permutation) and certain direct rules of generation for these, notably the result that the sum of complexions of n things was two raised to the nth power. Leibniz is thus discovering interlinkages between the *ars combinatoria* and law, but also between various of the structures he has investigated. In his November 1671 letter to Antoine Arnauld[49] he still envisages various planned works of jurisprudence, including an *Elements of Roman Law* which will state a 'few clear rules the combination of which can solve all cases'. It remains the case, therefore, that within shifting facets of the juridical prism Leibniz seeks to reunite all perspectives according not to a vision but a juridical common sense.

We will return to this revealing passage when considering the *Elementa Juris*, for I believe this indicator of Leibniz's belief in a moral or state *spatium* reflects a key component of his jurisprudential thought. For the purposes of this chapter, let us simply note that Leibniz's combinatorial approach to law locates the generation of legal relations within a *topos* 'or moral space', permitting a spatial consideration of juridical problems.

6. Jurisprudence as *Urdoxa*? – Initial considerations

The foregoing account of Leibniz's approach has drawn out two trends. First, Leibniz believes that the 'topics' of legal reasoning – the transcendent relations of the raw material of cases – are both (a) combinatorial in structure; and (b) common to all rational substances. Second, Leibniz seeks to characterise the transcendent relations between moral entities as if these relations are separate from their practical legal content and are capable of occupying a kind of 'moral space'.

To begin with the second point, which frames the whole discussion, we can note that Leibniz abstracts jurisprudential topics from the matter of legal disputes with inevitable results: 'universal reason, the laws of the universe, of universal nature, *subordinate* the individual to the species, the species to the universe'.[50] In taking up the key component of the *Topics* – the *element* (*stoicheion*) – and submitting jurisprudence to a formalisation, has Leibniz cut the cord between the data of legal practice and this new, highly abstract theory of jurisprudence?

One can usefully draw a parallel with Edmund Husserl's account of Euclid's *Elements*, and the way in which formalisation of what had begun as a series of rules of thumb used in practical fields such as surveying led to a separation of a discipline of geometry from its content. As Husserl puts it in *The Crisis of European Sciences and Transcendental Philosophy*, the axiomatisation of geometry, as method of the natural sciences:

> ... (or any science of the world) ... can master the infinity [*Unendlichkeit*] of its subject matter only through an infinity of method and can master the latter indeterminate [domain] only by means of a technical thought and activities which are empty of meaning [*sinnentleertes*] ...[51]

This is a meaning found in the materiality of the actual historical development of the science. What results is not a mathematisation of nature, but a naturalisation of mathematics[52] whereby an objective and universal nature is constructed as an objective form abstracted from its material conditions.[53] In similar vein, natural law as Leibniz understands it risks instantiating a naturalisation of a normative order applicable to infinitely many cases, but having no place any singular set of circumstances. What results historically is that the mathematical sciences now take as their object not nature but this very mathematical abstraction; a trajectory marked in its later stages by formalisation. Husserl's response to what he deems this crisis of naturalisation in the mathematical sciences is to supplement mathematical analysis of the 'real' not with a return to the material, which would be not only undesirable but 'countersensical'.[54] Rather Husserl engages with an examination of the a priori conditions of our encounter with the material. This science of the synthetic a priori forms is a central plank of phenomenology.[55]

Yet again we see parallels with Leibniz's own moves; perhaps even tentative steps where Leibniz has gone further. For Husserl makes this pact: to save mathematical sciences from their abstraction from the material without, however, collapsing into a naturalist mysticism he proposes to examine the conditions of materiality as such and names this the manifold (*Mannigfaltigkeit*).[56] In this way Husserl appears to have recovered the external world as opposed to the internal realm of mathematical formalism, but while he has not brought nature inside the mind, he has located the capacity to be in the world in the mind. It is the multiplicitous structuring of this world by mind which has been recovered. As he writes in *Crisis*:

> Every interpretation of . . . every opinion about 'the world' has its ground in the pre-given world. It is from this very ground that I have freed myself through the *epoché*; I stand *above* the world, which has now become for me, in quite a peculiar sense, a *phenomenon*. (*Crisis*, p.152, emphasis in original)[57]

Now, I claim that already in *De Casibus Perplexis* Leibniz is on the verge of an albeit pre-Kantian forerunner of Husserl's move: he will subsequently seek to construct a state space which universally determines the juridical real and which, being a human construct, can only reside in the minds of legal actors. I stress that this move has not taken place just yet, for it takes place through the *Nova Methodus* and the *Elements*. The construction of such a state space becomes thinkable just because of the topical abstraction of legal intensions which *De Arte Combinatoria* and *De Casibus Perplexis* effects, for the state space defines just what combinations and permutations are necessary or impossible (*atopon*), much as the manifold is not the neutral place of geometry but is, as Bernhard Riemann established, determinative of the kinds of possible geometries. Put another way, one can posit a synthetic a priori state space which actors consider the combinations and permutations of legal cases only because it is assumed that there is only one way of thinking jurisprudence. Juridical actors only belong to the same state space because they already (should) participate in the *ens commune* of abstract juridical thought. By placing certain highlights of Husserl's concerns against a Leibnizian background, and by showing certain parallels with Leibniz's juridical problematic, we also see just what is at stake is erecting this edifice. By assuming a single way of intending the law, capable of forming an abstract state space as normative community, Leibniz privileges the discipline of jurisprudence as such and raises it, here in its combinatorial form, to the status of universal rational *activity*. Universal jurisprudence is the activity of practical reasoning as such and is prior to all other legal doctrines, laws and opinions of the jurisconsults.

This permits us to focus on our first point: that Leibniz seeks to find in early modern combinatorics a common and formally correct jurisprudential activity. We should not be surprised that Gilles Deleuze saw a genetic link between the Leibnizian doctrine of a community of legal reasoning and the *Urdoxa* of Edmund Husserl and the phenomenologists. According to Deleuze the isolation of the various 'rational' *doxai* as *Urdoxai* – Deleuze terms this 'common sense'[58] – requires a corresponding transcendental critique of these relations deemed prior to sense data. What Leibniz and Husserl share, he feels, is too great a focus on the act of thought and not on what thinks or is really thought (as opposed to posited as manifold). In this we might say that both thinkers agree on the nature of equivalence. As noted in the introduction, extensional equivalence may be described as the axiom that if two classes have the same contents then they are the same class (it looks inside objects). It is this notion of equivalence which one finds in classical set theory and was particularly resurgent among Husserl's contemporaries. An alternative axiom of equivalence is intensionality, which looks at how a given object relates to any other given object (it looks at relations between objects). More specifically in our current context, we might consider two thoughts as equivalent if they relate to objects in the same way. For example, the act which places three balls in three boxes is intensionally equivalent to the act which places three cubes in three bowls. One can hopefully see that the equivalence is between the formal activity of thinking and ignores the contents of any given perception. The question becomes: did two or more given relations arise according to the same laws? An *Urdoxa* then can be understood, according to its own terms, as a set of intensional acts which are common to a group of persons, indeed common to all rational substances or minds because they stand 'above' a common phenomenon. There seems to be a duality to this commons: on the one hand the 'external world' has certain structural laws which are present to every subject; on the other every subject is capable of apprehending those laws in the same way. The *Urdoxa* acts as a kind of interface, a kind of inner world for every subject. The result is a double bind: the belief in a common sense is doxatic because in fact people do not always think the same way but must be taught to so think. However, it is also *Ur-doxatic* because a common way of thinking is presumed inherent, and a failure to think just this way is a defect of the thinker not the presumption.

We have seen that Leibniz's focus in the *De Casibus Perplexis* and *De Arte Combinatoria* has been on what we have called the topics of law – on the relationships between moral entities which, Leibniz argues, are tractable through the combinatorial methodology. Subtending these works is a view that the *ars combinatoria* is the correct route to reasoning about cases. The impossible problems of algebra are to be treated by just the same means as the perplexing cases of the jurists.[59] In both works Leibniz is keen to stress that he is speaking of a discipline which reaches beyond the particular. Thus, in his fourth corollary to the *De Casibus Perplexis* he writes:

All recognize that theory and practice differ in the law, but no one teaches the difference. A real and practical question, in brief, is: What should be decided today in the case at hand. The other questions are theoretical and doctrinal, such as the explication of the laws, the antinomies ... Thus Bachov ... says: In this question (whether certain actions pertain to the law of nations) I will not tolerate to be dismissed by the authority of some jurist, or indeed by Justinian himself, for the Emperor can establish the laws, but he cannot remove the truth and the reason of the things.[60]

In doctrinal considerations Leibniz finds that matters turn not to fact but theoretical questions such as the antinomies and the unfolding of the law, and for this he is prepared to cite with approval a claim that the truth and reason of things supersedes positive law. In similar vein, in the *Dissertatio de Arte Combinatoria*, Leibniz argues that number is something 'of great universality', pertaining as it does to 'union', which is none other than 'what we think in one intellectual act'.[61] Thus mathematics is not one discipline, but made up of small parts spread across many, though 'far be it for [him] ... to destroy the social distribution of the disciplines'.[62] For Leibniz: 'The art of forming [legal] cases is founded in our doctrine of complexions. For as jurisprudence is similar to geometry in other things, it is also similar in that both have [topical] elements and both have cases' (L:82). And indeed Leibniz goes on to argue that the doctrine applies in such fields as theology, music, the classification of things, and medicine.[63] Once we appreciate that Leibniz's combinatorial laws of thought (and so jurisprudence) are just these common intensional acts we are immediately led to understand why he finds a community amongst all rational substances, but also why he is bound to institute an *Urdoxa* for human beings. Husserl cites Leibniz as a notable figure in the 'incessant forward movement' from Galileo to his time towards a 'completely universal formalisation' of analytic thought. 'Leibniz, though far ahead of his time, first caught sight of the universal, self-enclosed idea of a highest form of algebraic thinking, a *mathesis universalis*, as he called it, and recognised it as a task for the future.'[64]

It is because Leibniz assumes that each rational being is capable of *intending* in the same way though each perceives the world from a different perspective, and that this activity can be considered as taking place separated from its material conditions, that the way is opened up towards a universal science of law, a science which is relocated to a formal state structure common to all.

We will return to the Deleuzian critique of *Urdoxatic* thinking as we approach Leibniz's *Elementa*. That development continues its course, perhaps inevitably, via Leibniz's concern regarding the distance between his doctrine of complexions as right reasoning and the irrational legal thought of his contemporaries. If moral entities are generated combinatorially within a state space – and we must now regard Leibniz as making the assumption that this is the unique and correct way of thinking about law – how can those who fail to appreciate this be brought to understanding?

7. Conclusion: towards the *Nova Methodus*

In this chapter we have shown how Leibniz's earliest approaches to legal problems are grounded in assumption about what I regard as an *Urdoxa*: a set of acts of thinking about the world, or intensions, which are common to and equivalent between rational substances. This doctrine has its source in the combinatorial approach to the *Topics* which Leibniz inherits from Ramon Llull via German combinatorialists such as Kircher and Schwenter. Importantly, the topics are the principles or elements which relate cases being considered, cases being understood in a rich, cross-disciplinary sense. Leibniz is not concerned here with either facts or the positive law and its application; he is concerned with the moral or transcendent relations between these entities, and keen to discover the figures they describe in abstraction He is concerned with the way in which our suppositive activity thinks jurisprudentially about a world of abstract dispositions, complexes, concourses, and so a kind of moral topology or state space within which they can be manipulated in order to generate all possible cases.

Leibniz holds that perplexing cases arise not because of a disagreement over facts or positive law, but because jurists have misapplied the juridical 'elements' to the case, and constructed absurd (*atopon*) scenarios. He has shown that often disputes are a matter of perspective, and that generation of all possible cases may establish that these perspectives are all observations of the same legal-topological structure. And all this assumes that just this way of thinking abstractly about legal problems is the correct and only manner of so doing, grounded in an intellectual community guaranteed by God. The question, now, however, is how to convince jurists that they all should think in this way, and that alternative approaches to law are defective. Leibniz's next legal project, the *Nova Methodus*, amounts to a programme for teaching and learning the law which, I will argue, is grounded in his belief in the commonality of an abstract, intensional realm of legal topics that is ready to be activated in every rational substance.

Notes

1. Letter to the Landgrave Ernst of Hesse-Rheinfels (September 1690), Gr:238–9, quoted by Patrick Riley in 'Leibniz and Natural Law in the *Nouveaux Essais*' in Marcelo Dascal (ed.), *Leibniz: What Kind of Rationalist?* (Tel Aviv: Springer, 2008), pp.279–92. Cf. the later Letter to Burnett (May 1706) Ger:III, 307.
2. A:VI, i, 277. Note that in a subsequent draft 'D' from the 1680s, Leibniz reformulates this paragraph, renaming 'topics' as 'heuristic', but he continues to define this as 'the art of invention', and defers a reference to the Aristotelean nomenclature to a redraft of para.24. See the *Akademie* notes to the text cited.
3. A:VI, i, 279. Again, in draft 'D' of the *Nova Methodus* 'topics' becomes 'heuristic' but again is defined as the art of invention. Leibniz also includes further combinatorial works, such as that of Athanasius Kircher who will feature in our discussion presently.
4. A:VI, vi, 427.
5. See the *Nova Methodus* (A:VI, i, 300).
6. 'Justum est quod publice interest.' *Initium Institutionem Juris perpetui* (1695?) Mollat 1–7.
7. 'Justem esse quod societatem ratione utentium perficit . . .,' (1700) Du:IV, iii, 273.
8. A:VI, i, 216. 'quin etiam refert nostris in versibus ipsis / cum quibus [*complexiones*] et quali sint ordine [*variatio situs*]

quaeque locata; / namque eadem caelum mare terras flumina solem / significant, eadem fruges arbusta animantis; / Si non omnia sunt, at multo maxima pars est / consimilis; verum positura discrepitant res. sic ipsis in rebus item iam materiai / [*intervalla vias conexus pondera plagas*] / concursus motus ordo positura figurae / cum permutantur, mutari res quoque debent.'

9. Pierre Vesperini, *Lucrèce: Archéologie d'un Classique européen* (Paris: Fayard, 2017).
10. See Eberhard Knobloch, 'Renaissance Combinatorics' in Robin Wilson and John J. Watkins (eds), *Combinatorics: Ancient & Modern* (Oxford: Oxford University Press, 2013) pp.123–5.
11. Ibid. p.135.
12. XI, 20, as quoted in Wilson and Watkins, *Combinatorics*, p.135.
13. GM: VI, 37.
14. Otto Bird, 'The Tradition of the Logical Topics: Aristotle to Ockham' (1962) 23(3) *Journal of the History of Ideas* 307–23 at p.310.
15. Theophrastus' definition quoted by Alexander Aphrodisias, *In Aristotelis Topicorum Libros octo Commentaria*, (Berlin: M. Wallies, 1891), II *proem*, 126, quoted by Bird, 'The Tradition', p.310.
16. A:VI, i, 279.
17. Knobloch, 'Renaissance Combinatorics', p.149.
18. Ibid. This chapter draws strongly on Knobloch's classification of Leibniz's combinatorial operations, but the explication and interpretation are my own.
19. Problem 4, *De Arte Combinatoria* (GM: VI, 61).
20. GM:VI, 61.
21. See further Knobloch, 'Mathematical Studies', p.415.
22. Ger:V, 71.
23. L:78, Def.9.
24. Joseph E. Hofmann, *Leibniz in Paris 1672–1676* (Cambridge: Cambridge University Press, 1974) pp.12–13.
25. L:76; Ger:IV, 35–75.
26. Ger:V, 14, Def.10.
27. The opening discussion and Problem I of *De Arte Combinatoria* were published as *Disputatio arithmetica de complexionibus, quam in illustri Academia Lipsiensi indultu amplissimae facultatis philosophicae pro loco in ea obtinendo prima vice habebit Mr GG Leibniz of Leipzig Lipsiensis*, JU Baccal. D.7 March 1666 HLQC (Ger: V, 18, n.).

28. Leibniz states 'coincides' because he seems unsure whether to count the choice of o elements as a complexion. He thus provides both the sum of choices without the one choice of nothing (2n-1, marked *) and, to his credit, the sum including the null-complexion (marked +). If the latter is used, then the correct result is indeed equal to the geometric progression base 2.
29. Maria Rosa Antognazza, *Leibniz: An Intellectual Biography* (Cambridge: Cambridge University Press, 2009), pp.357–9. See also Antognazza, 'Metaphysical Evil Revisited' in Larry M. Jorgensen and Samuel Newlands (eds), *New Essays on Leibniz's Theodicy* (Oxford: Oxford University Press, 2014), p.131.
30. Gaston Grua, *Jurisprudence universelle et théodicée selon Leibniz* (Paris: PUF, 1953) p.63.
31. *De Arte Combinatoria*, GM:V, 36.
32. The lists are quite long and legally specialised, importing jargon from civilian law.
33. *De Arte Combinatoria*, GM:V, 37.
34. Alberto Artosi, Bernardo Pieri and Giovanni Sartor (eds), *Leibniz: Logico-Philosophical Puzzles in the Law* (Dordrecht: Springer, 2013) p.73. Hereafter my references to the *Dissertation on Perplexing Cases in the Law* can be found in this work or in the original in the *Akademie* edition.
35. Art.IV *Perplexing Cases*, p.76.
36. Art.III *Perplexing Cases*, p.76.
37. Art.XII *Perplexing Cases*, p.84.
38. For perplexing cases of circular dispositions see Art.XVIII *Perplexing Cases*.
39. GM:VI, 22.
40. Ibid.
41. This is not the sense in which Frémont interprets 'perplexing' (Christiane Frémont, *Singularités – Individus et rélations dans le système de Leibniz* (Paris: VRIN, 2003)).
42. Artosi et al., *Leibniz: Logico-Philosophical Puzzles in the Law*, p.xxv.
43. Leibniz calls each such ordering a 'mode': Art.XIX *Perplexing Cases*. In his subsequent writings modality would always continue to be defined to include position ('status').
44. Cf. Daniel Schwenter, *Deliciae mathematicae* (Nuremberg: GP Harsdörffer, 1636) I, prop.47.
45. *Perplexing Cases*, p.97.
46. Artosi et al., *Leibniz: Logico-Philosophical Puzzles in the Law*, p.97.

47. A:VI, i, 73- 95. Translated in Artosi et al., *Leibniz: Logico-Philosophical Puzzles in the Law.*
48. A:VI, i, 94. *SQP*, Question XVI, in Artosi et al., *Leibniz: Logico-Philosophical Puzzles in the Law*, p.34.
49. L:149–50.
50. Notes on Wachter (Gr:669–72), my emphasis.
51. '... [eine] Naturwissenschaft (und Weltwissenschaft überhaupt), welche die Unendlichkeit ihrer Thematik nur durch Unendlichkeiten der Methode beherrschen and diese Unendlichkeiten auch nur durch ein sinnentleertes technisches Denken und Tun beherrschen kann ...' Edmund Husserl, *Die Krisis der europäischen Wissenschaften und die transzendentale Phänomenologie* (Hamburg: Meiner, 2012) p.57.
52. Ibid. pp.56–8.
53. Ibid. p.57.
54. Edmund Husserl, 'Philosophy as Rigorous Science' in *Phenomenology and the Crisis of Philosophy* (Quentin Lauer trans.) (New York: Harper Torchbooks, 1965), p.78.
55. See further Jairo da Silva, 'Mathematics and the Crisis of Science' in *The Road Not Taken: On Husserl's Philosophy of Logic and Mathematics* (London: College Publications, 2013), p.347.
56. For the importance of this term in the wider history of ideas, the reader is referred to Bernhard Riemann, 'On the Hypothesis which lie at the Bases of Geometry' (William Kingdom Clifford trans.) in Jürgen Jost (ed.) *On the Hypothesis which lie at the Bases of Geometry* (Switzerland: Birkhäuser, 2016).
57. Quoted by Barry Smith, 'Common Sense' in Barry Smith and David Woodruff Smith (eds), *The Cambridge Companion to Husserl* (Cambridge: Cambridge University Press, 1995) pp.394–437 at p.429.
58. See for example Ch.III of Gilles Deleuze, *Difference and Repetition* (London: Athlone Press, 1994).
59. Art.IV *Perplexing Cases*, p.73.
60. *Perplexing Cases*, p.118.
61. L:76.
62. L:77.
63. L:80–2.
64. Husserl, *Krisis*, p.44.

Six

A New Method of Teaching Law

1. Introduction

This chapter argues that it is wrong to interpret Leibniz's *Nova Methodus* as a 'strongly empirical' text that understands teaching as entirely sensory habituation. On the contrary, I claim, Leibniz's use of sensation assumes the intensional equivalence of human minds, that is, *that the activity of thought is the same, even if what is thought differs.* Indeed, the basic lesson of the *Nova Methodus* is that teaching law means revealing intellectual activity to itself. I situate the *Nova Methodus* in the context of Scholastic tradition, indicating parallels between Leibniz's *New Method* and Aquinas' *New Law*, before once more drawing links with Husserl's later concept of *Urdoxa*. At the heart of the analysis is an application of the interpretative framework offered by the square of power, for we see how Leibniz engages both the activity of the mind and its finitude with respect to the objective world of power in his account of learning what he terms 'institutions'.

2. Habit and moral formation in the tradition

In this short section I prepare the ground a little for the reading of the *Nova Methodus* by examining certain key terms which appear in Leibniz's text: namely *habit* and *state* (*status*), and one which I will argue is implicit: *divine* or *New Law*. On investigating the Scholastic tradition, it will be seen that the divine or New Law arises out of Aquinas' distinction between habit and state, and I will argue that our awareness of this tradition throws the ostensible lack of law in the General Part of the *Nova Methodus* into a new light.

Leibniz: A Contribution to the Archaeology of Power

I begin with habit. As is well known, for Aristotle, habits are a determinate and stable species of disposition or arrangement (*diathesis*), which is itself a species of quality (*Meta.* V [1022b1ff]; *De Anima* IX, 11 [1152a 30–3]). Habits become human nature, and as such qualify an individual by means of a determinate arrangement of natural qualities addressed to ends.

Habit then is an acquired disposition that can serve to perfect the individual. It is no surprise then that habit should be situated by Aristotle and the Schoolmen within the wider structure of activity, power and actuality which is used to analyse the metaphysical nature of individuals (and which we have examined in detail in Chapters 1 to 4). To summarise, we find the activity (*energeia*) of a finite rational substance attempting to actualise itself in the world, but each such action is determined by the acts of other substances. These determined acts – these differential relations of action and passion – are the qualities of that being from time to time. As we shall presently see, a habit is just that quality which endures such that a series of acts bear the same determination, even if the original determining passion ceases to be present. Now, one may feel that any restraint of a substance's activity can only mitigate its own self-actualisation, but this is not so. By definition our substance is finite, which is to say also that it is finite in its nature or essence. The trick here is to observe that this finitude is not a simple limitation, but serves a critical purpose: the originary lack places the individual substance in a world full of other substances that the first requires if it will be able to perfect itself. Certain determinations of a substance's action, therefore, are not solely limiting, but rather serve to complete what the substance lacks, and it is only by acquiring these determinations, or habits, that the substance is able to perfect itself. Thus the essence of a chair need not specify whether it be made of wood or metal, only that it be rigid in its matter; it is the essence of wood or matter which is acquired by the chair (or the artisan) in order to perfect it as chair. In this gap between the substance's initial activity, and the perfected substance which requires many other substances, is a basis for the distinction Aristotle makes in substantial activity between *energeia* (the setting to work) and *entelecheia* (the actuality towards which work is aimed).

Alberto Ferrarin has shown[1] that givenness is central to Aristotle's theory of habit formation, and this is particularly explicit in the givenness of intellectual habit, which Aristotle names memory. Ferrarin draws out this contrast with both Plato and later Hegel: habit and memory are constructed of contingencies, and their presence after the given is one of replication of an image or sound. The habit or sign amounts to a presence of absence of the original contingency. Evidently a person is involved in the contingency of habit forming, for passions must affect some prior nature, and the result is this habituated person. Thus the habit is also the presence of a contingently determined human nature, as is captured by Aristotle's definition. The difference from Plato and Hegel though runs deeper: for Plato and in quite a different way for Hegel, something else is also present in the acquired habit, image or memory. This something else is variously the idea, concept or spirit. By way of example, for Hegel the human finds in the painting not simply the representation of the signified, and so its absence, but also the presence of human technical creativity in being able to paint this representation as such – the human finds spirit manifested. This is not to say that the Aristotelean theory of habit bears no relation to the Hegelian doctrine; the Stagirite does provide certain inspiration particularly in the role played by the habit-acquiring human. Indeed, it is Aristotle who cites the plasticity of the mind, its capacity to fulfil many functions, as a strength and not a weakness of mind. But Hegel raises capacity to potency in the post-Thomist sense,[2] and sees habituation as a stage along a path to mind's awareness of this potency.

We see this duplex nature of habituation in Scholasticism – unsurprising given the twofold teleology of ends and the End. Aquinas achieves this distinction in two discrete steps. Habits are first discussed in *Summa* II-I, where Aquinas considers whether habits are properly to be considered qualities, and if so, what rank of quality. The doctrine is roughly this:[3] first, qualities are modes of being of a substance, and these modes are either natural or accidental determinations of that substance which allow us to measure how perfect the actuality of that substance is. Second, habits are considered qualities because they go to the nature of the substance in question;

more particularly, the acquired dispositions are together what actually forms this presently existing substance. Third, the modality of habituation then discloses a spectrum with respect to substance whereby we can say a substance is more or less perfect at a given moment by reference to the degree of dispositions or habits it has acquired.

It is worth stressing that the Thomist sense of habit has a strong flavour of teleological subordination, a flavour which is most apparent when we consider general Scholastic debates about quality. For Aquinas, Umberto Eco tells us in his discussion of aesthetic qualities such as beauty,[4] the quality of a thing considered goes to its gathering of various disposed properties which together serve the substantial form of that thing. One can say then that the composite dispositions are subordinated to and united by the substantial form. This model hinges on the unifying power of the substantial form, yet is also in a sense rather flat. But for the transcendent unity of the substantial form, the various dispositions are simply bundled together – the colour, texture, shape and magnitude of the artwork all serve the whole, and are perceived as the beauteous quality of the work. Compare this, as Jeremiah Hackett does,[5] with the realism of Duns Scotus. Remember that the Subtle Doctor proposes a subordinated order of the real in which various simpler quiddities interlock to support quiddities of greater complexity, all terminating in a *haecceitas* which is a concrete individual. Scotus's model is more strongly hierarchical and, after a fashion, 'dense', because the quality of a thing may be constituted by the qualities of various subordinated quiddities, and so on to the simplest things. I raise it here principally to throw a certain relief on the Scholastic notion of habit as quality: a habit is not simply some randomly acquired disposition, but is a disposition which more or less serves to perfect just this substantial form. Hence the derivative sense of quality which still stands in legal discourse: a thing is of satisfactory quality if it is fit for purpose.

If we can already apply a measure to quality by assessing how habits serve to perfect the nature of this individual, it would seem that individuation is the end for which habits are acquired. Unsurprisingly the Scholastics will introduce a higher end of habit, and to do this new terminology is introduced. In the moral part of the *Summa Theologiae*,[6] Aquinas makes a further distinction between habit and state (*status*). If habit recalls aspects of the Aristotelean notion of an acquired readiness to act for some end, Aquinas now reserves a negative sense for this word: the vicious have individuating habits, but some of these habits are now regarded as 'bad habits' with respect to a higher end. This appears to be inconsistent with the earlier discussion of habit. There, habit pertained to the nature of an individual, and it would seem strange that a nature be intrinsically bad if only because acquisition of a habit increases a thing's perfection. And Aquinas states as much: a habit is neither good nor bad; rather it is the potency that is deployed to act according to a nature or habit that is good or evil.[7] The confusion will be seen to be resolved once we appreciate two factors.

First, by indicating that it is potency and not nature that renders an act vicious or virtuous, Aquinas is relying on the metaphysical difference between the acts due to a finite substance and the acts due to that substance which require the acquisition of other bodies (growth, building of tools etc.) to accomplish. In part at least, we are being referred to 'bad habits' or acquisitions of improper potencies by an individual.

Second, however, all individual habits are also referred to an end which is not that individual, but some higher End which the individual should also pursue: the Good. For Aquinas human individuals are not the ultimate end for habitual qualities. In a small step towards the Scotist hierarchy of the real, we find that human dispositions of various kinds are directed to greater composite unities such as state, church and so the *Civitas Dei*. In this respect the perspective on vicious potencies is flipped: the reason for a republic behaving wrongly is not the nature of the republic but derives from its deployment of improper potencies, which are nothing other than the citizens which constitute that republic. We thus come to the notion of office, or official function, which already in Cicero grounds notions of duty to serve the higher entity.

Status fulfils the function of naming those dispositions which perfect that higher 'social' end: '"Status," properly speaking, denotes a kind of position, whereby a thing is disposed with a certain immobility in a manner according with its nature' (ST II, ii, q.183, a.1).[8] Aquinas is keen to stress that state is more than a mere standing, but that it is a kind of 'stillness' which goes to the nature of freedom or servitude of a person. That alone seemingly pertains to a man's state, which regards an *obligation binding his person*, insofar as a man is his own master or subject to another, not indeed from any slight or unstable cause, but from one that is firmly established.[9] On the one hand then, a person's state is their self-determination according to permanently established rules of acting; on the other it is permanency of governance by self or another. This notion of permanence raises an interesting question: what is the requisite immutability? Aquinas has no problem referring us to the eternal law of God, but he also extends the notion to civil law. Can civil law be considered permanent? Aquinas leads the horse to the water, so to speak: he argues that the loss of position as a senator (dismissal) is not a loss of status as it does not go to the nature of freedom and servitude. Then, in the next article he moves swiftly on to the role of status in the Church. Given the church doctrine that all offices and states are universal and eternal, one can clearly see the intention on Aquinas' part: there is a divine governance that is manifested in the actuality of the glory: the *status gloriae*[10] which parallels the state of grace (*beatitudino*). From this we distil the following: that servitude and freedom, in their spiritual sense, are statuses just because of the eternity of their cause. Whereas acquired dispositions or habits derive their potencies from the actions of other finite substances, statuses derive their potencies from the absolute and immutable potency of God.

So much for Aquinas' primary sense of *status*; but the term plays a second and derivative role in the *Summa*: a person's state can vary according to the law which governs him.[11] Such a proposition may seem a surprising contradiction with the foregoing; the reason for it is the orthodox need to explain the distinction between the Old Law and New Law that underpins Pauline teaching. The person governed by the Old Law is said to be in a different state from the one governed by the New. This difference though is not simply one of substantive legal content; rather, Aquinas makes a distinction between the communicative efficacy of the two laws as follows:

(a) The Old Law compels by inducing fear (*timor*) of punishment, which is to say that it engages the passions to
determine a person's effective action.
(b) The New Law compels by pouring love (*amor*) by grace
into persons, not so that the person will be affected to
act, but because the New Law directs what is perfect and
imperfect (ST II, i, q.91, a.5).

In the third response to this Article Aquinas indicates the
underlying framework which explains the distinction he has
made: a distinction between natural law and divine law.[12] The
natural law is shown to be a product of darkness in the sense
(i) that it is applied via general precepts (elsewhere called the
eternal law[13]) to all contingent things, rational or otherwise;
and (ii) it operates through these things to determine us via
the passions. Hence a subdivision: the natural law can operate
through fear or pleasure, and in the former case we have the
Old Law at least as experienced in the Old Testament. The
divine law operates in a completely different fashion: (i) it can
only be apprehended by rational minds because it ordains
the intelligible good; (ii) rational minds respond to it insofar
as it directs the (im)perfect; (iii) the divine law thus acts at
the level of subjectivity, at the level of activity and of end
(actuality).[14] It is for this reason that Aquinas stresses the link
between the state of freedom and the state of the New Law,
which link is expressed in the state of self-determination ('the
boy under a teacher has now become a man no longer under
a teacher').[15] The principle mechanism for communication
of the New Law was baptism, and for immediate contextual
purposes I will focus on this, but I should note for our later
discussion of Leibniz's treatment of change at the level of the
subject (the supposit) that Aquinas and the other Schoolmen
will seek to explain various theological events, such as the
apostles' gift of tongues and transubstantiation,[16] by reference to just such a substance-modifying change or *infusion*.

Christoph Haar's research[17] establishes the centrality of
this distinction between a bodily and subjective law to the
question of grace and original sin, a question which was
heavily debated at the Council of Trent (1545–63) especially
in sessions 5 and 6 (1546–7). To put the matter briefly, the
Council finds that before the Fall the body of Adam has

submitted to God, such that both body and intellect 'origi-
nally' and with a certain necessity seek God. The Fall is
explained as a breach between body and mind; body no
longer automatically submits but rather pursues its own
volitions, leading mind astray. The path to salvation was a
new submission to God by mind through body: 'not only a
remission of sins but also the sanctification and renewal of
the inward man through the voluntary reception of grace and
gifts whereby an unjust man becomes just.'[18] Accordingly,
while baptism conferred grace on the mind this was not
enough for the theologians of Leibniz's time – both Lutheran
and Catholic.[19] The reception of grace cannot be simply
passive, but must both be voluntary and engage the inward
renewal of man. Thus, on the one hand the reference to volition indicates that the body must work for the just, that it
must be yoked to just ends provided that these just ends are
in the nature of the mind. On the other hand, but also consequent on the duplex structure of the will, the nature that
determines the voluntariness of action must itself express
the activity or supposit of the individual, a supposit infused
with grace. Baptism then confers grace, but operates as it
were to plant a seed of subjective activity which must still be
expressed in works.

It would seem then that 'state' implies a certain moral
perfection referred to a normative order, where perfection is
understood as the actuality of the individual substance being
considered, an actuality which is twofold in its expression of
the grace of intellectual activity through the works of a justified bodily nature. Whereas the natural law operates from
the depths, engaging the passions to promulgate and enforce
itself, the divine law, as New Law, is a rational normative
order which operates at the level of the spiritual subject itself
by ordaining the perfections that lead to the End. I will claim
that Leibniz's New Method of teaching the law engages a
version of this duplex notion of status renewal.

3. The *Nova Methodus*

3.1 Background to and revisions of the *Nova Methodus*

The text

The *Nova Methodus Discendae Docendaeque Jurisprudentiae*[20] was written in 1667 during Leibniz's journey from Nuremberg to Frankfurt am Main. It thus forms part of Leibniz's jurisprudential canon which also comprises the *De Conditionibus, De Casibus Perplexis*, the legal applications of *De Arte combinatoria*, and the *Elements of Law* from the years 1666 to 1671. While the *Nova Methodus* was published, like the *Elements* remained after a certain fashion a working draft for Leibniz's jurisprudential thinking, from which later texts draw. Of particular interpretative importance is Leibniz's decision in the 1690s, when his thinking on volition was crystallising in the drafts for the *Nouveaux Essais*, to revise the earlier work. Interestingly we find not wholesale theoretical change but rather recalibration of terminology: for example 'imagination' becomes 'perception'; 'activity' is linked to force; to 'will' is added a definition derived from 'conatus'. As Leroy Loemker has noted,[21] the effect of the revisions is to manifest the structural similarity of many of Leibniz's views from his early to middle periods. Maria Rosa Antognazza reports that even in the year of his death, Leibniz was still seeking comments on the *Nova Methodus* from the Hanoverian jurist C.U. Grupen.[22]

I am going to read the *Nova Methodus* in light of my interpretation of Leibniz's theory of Mind, but it is worth emphasising that the key texts used for understanding that theory derive from the period immediately following the writing of the *Nova Methodus*. The key documents for understanding the intensional nature of the supposit – *Trinitas. Mens*, the *Catholic Demonstrations*, and various sketches on action in physics, are all drafted in some form from 1668. On the other hand the *Nova Methodus* contains no clear statement of these notions. Does this mean that the *Nova Methodus* is a juvenile work whose treatment of teaching and learning the law is unrepresentative? My response to this is twofold in character:

(a) I would say that the work is informative, and this not least because of Leibniz's continued support for the text up to his death and his lack of material alterations to its basic tenets (if anything, he makes clarifications of terminology). Key elements of Leibniz's thinking on substantial activity are already present in earlier work, as Antognazza has shown in detail. First, the *Dissertation on the Principle of Individuation* already holds that internal nominal-conceptual completeness individuates an entity, citing Suárez as authority for the view. Second, Leibniz had developed two axioms for his further study: find clarity in signs (*ars judicandi*) and seek 'usefulness in things' (*inventio*). These complemented each other because well-ordered signs reflected reality itself, and under the initial influence of Athanasius Kircher and Ramus, he began his search for a well-ordered 'alphabet' of human ideas that was so reflective. Third, the *Dissertatio de Arte Combinatoria* (1666) was the most original contribution during this early period, manifesting as it did the foundation of possibility in the iteration of combinatorial activity ('by *one* [as a whole] we mean whatever we think in one *intellectual act* ... we often grasp a number'[23]). Fourth, *De Conditionibus* of 1665 grounds its definition of conditional rights in contracts by reference both to will (understood here as action) and the weight of the utility of that condition to the person who wills (acts).[24] Clearly there are also differences in language between these texts, but especially the theoretical results evoke Leibniz's subsequent work and are owned by him as of continued relevance, notably in his jurisprudential work.

(b) The second aspect of my response to the claim that the work is mere juvenilia is connected to the above regarding Leibniz's long-term support for the work. I propose to read the *Nova Methodus* subject to the manuscript revisions made in the late 1690s, and will indicate when I do so. At this time Leibniz produced three new sets of amendments straight onto the first printing of the 1667 edition: the first resulted in comments throughout the text; the second amounted to a 'clean' handwritten version of the first reducing the number of changes; the third further small notes onto the second, again reducing the changes.[25] There is no fully rewritten version of the *Nova Methodus*. As we shall see, these amendments expand on and clarify many of Leibniz's articles, giving greater density to several terms and linking them explicitly to the middle period doctrines.

The primary function of the *Nova Methodus* itself was as a job application: Leibniz, Loemker tells us, was attempting to catch the attention of Johann Philip von Schönborn, the catholic Archbishop-Elector of Mainz so that he might secure a position at his court. Von Schönborn was relatively open-minded and a conciliator who had proved a successful mediator during the Thirty Years' War, and it is perhaps this reputation which drives Leibniz to be quite explicit about (even showy with) his reference points in the opening part of the text, for we find almost immediately discussions of alchemy, Thomas Hobbes, the Christianising neo-stoic Justus Lipsius and the classics, all leading into a more Scholastic framework of actions, influxes and habituations.

The *Nova Methodus* is structured into a general and specific part. The general part covers matters 'common to all the faculties' and amounts to a theory of pedagogy very much led by Leibniz's thinking on psychology. The specific part covers the more traditional content of a treatise on law, such as the kinds of law and right. Both parts adopt Leibniz's style of establishing a conceptual framework before constructing chains of definition and categorisation that flow from the framework and encompass the field in question. For our immediate purposes we focus on the *Prima Pars* – the general part common to all faculties – as it is here that we may draw out the implications of Leibniz's construct: *Trinitas. Mens*, for his thinking on law. It might therefore be helpful, before proceeding, to summarise where we stand in our understanding of the Leibnizian mind.

Our understanding of the Leibnizian mind reviewed
In earlier chapters we have spent a considerable amount of time attempting to understand the Trinitarian structure of Mind according to Leibniz. At the heart of our interpretation is the *suppositum* as the intensional activity of the mind, and using this idea we were able to interpret the final column of Leibniz's tabular sketch for his theory of mind as a series of intensions: *esse–scire–agere seu conari*. These intensions

produced in Mind, be it divine or creatural, are the respective extensional components: intellect, imagination, will or
potentia. We observed that Leibniz, perhaps following Duns
Scotus, held that being was in common between all minds,
and not simply by analogy. Indeed, Leibniz goes further in at
least two key ways: first, he makes the intensional activity of
esse itself intellectual, and second, he avoids the Spinozist trap
of substance monism implied by Scotism's pure differentiation of God and creature by power, by imposing an absolute
metaphysical individuality on substances – a separateness
which is nevertheless intellectually communal by virtue of
a principle of intensional equivalence. In this way God and
creature are, and as being they are active, this activity being
immediately intellectual in the same way. The result, Leibniz
hopes, is that each Mind thinks, and that this activity of thinking programmatically should produce the same formal ideas,
the same possibilities. Only God, being unconstrained activity, is capable of thinking all formal possibilities; every other
finite creature thinks these same possibilities to the extent of
the power it contingently has.

Each mind, as substantial form, takes up the products of
its thinking activity and endeavours to raise them to actuality
(entelechy). In God this movement is immediate; finite creatures must combine the particular actions deriving from their
activity with some external potency. Indeed, the logical structure of finite creatures contains an inbuilt lack (the pretensional
Nothing) that differentiates creature from creator. Combining
the volitional structure of Suárez with the mechanical philosophies of Hobbes and Spinoza, Leibniz defines finite will as the
combination of action and the aggregate affective inclinations
that determine it. These inclinations are derivative of primary
passive power, and are imbued by God with pretensions, or
demands to exist. It is these pretensions – understood as real
possibilities or contingencies – which the finite creature must
yoke if it is to achieve both kinds of actuality: individuality
and the glory (the *Civitas Dei*). In nature the derivative action
and potencies are entirely determinative of the resulting
effect, which due to a divine distribution of pretensions to the
final cause results in maximal reality (the greatest effect). But
in the case of intelligent creatures – those who are as actively
thinking – an additional volitional spontaneity is involved

which permits choice. The Mind is so constituted that it continuously thinks possibility, but in the simplest case even Mind thinks two foundational formal ideas: Being and Nothing. The Mind immediately grasps Being as the incontrovertible truth of itself, for Being is the activity of thinking, and by grasping Being, Mind acts, that is, it chooses itself and cannot be prevented from so choosing. At the same time, Mind has not chosen Nothing, and this negating act of choice – the choice of Mind to the exclusion of what it is not – defines also the World 'out-there' from a particular point of view. Hence via Suárez's doctrine of the combined will, Leibniz returns to the Aristotelean roots of the theory by adding in a notion of spontaneous choice whereby the subject chooses and so determines itself: the ground of freedom. A different, but equally revealing approach to this distinction, is that while will pertains to the extent that an individual's *action* (or nature) is reflected in the potency of 'matter', spontaneous choice pertains to the extent that the *activity* of Mind is reflected in the volition: and this reflection is the actuality (or entelechy) of the good will. In this way the final cause of pretensions in physical matter has its thinking parallel in the self-determining final causes of individual and divine entelechy, where thought is reflected and magnified by intelligent beings.

Leibniz's *Nova Methodus* will place particular store in the intensional equivalence of intellectual activity, and will accordingly focus not just on increasing the power of lawyers' minds, but on engaging their defining actuality as self-determining minds, as we shall now see.

3.2 A New Method for a New Law?

The duplex nature of the Rational State

Leroy Loemker argues that the *Nova Methodus* has 'a strongly empirical emphasis',[26] and that it is only by 1679 when Leibniz has developed his logic that this supplements his thinking across all fields. This claim is surprising, not least because we have already alluded to several significant works Leibniz had produced which focus on the *intellectual act* and its combinatorial order. It would be surprising if a certain combinatorial logic did *not* feature in the *Nova Methodus*, or at least an 'alphabet' of human thought.

This is not to say that the 'empirical emphasis' is absent. Leibniz's method of teaching clearly involves the use of affections, and we will have occasion to investigate this in the next section. One reason for delaying that treatment is highly relevant to our concern with logic: Leibniz does not begin the First Part with the 'empirical' discussion; he grounds his general treatment in reason and the 'order of reasons of studies, in general'. The opening articles of the General Part read:

§1. A reason of studies is a species of some form of Rational State [*Status*], that is, a mode of arriving at a state of perfected actions.[27]

§2. This state is called Habit, which I define as: a permanent but acquired readiness to act.[28]

§3. A subject of Habit is whatever is capable of action. . . .[29]

The historical, theological and theoretical background to this text strongly implies that we should find a duality in Leibniz's approach: the duality between intellectual or free, subjective activity, deriving from grace, and the determinate bodily affections deriving from nature. That we do so *pace* Loemker, is readily seen from these opening definitions, for:

(a) Leibniz initially deploys the term 'modus' as an alternative descriptor for Rational State. In draft D of the *Nova Methodus* 'modus' is promoted to *the* defining term in a reordered statement of §1: 'Studiorum Ratio est modus . . .' The 1667 usage of 'mode' appears to be relatively traditional: Suárez for example will define mode as an affection of the Subject whereby there is granted something from outside the subject's complete individual and existing essence.[30] Suárez will give illustrations of his meaning, such as inherent qualities, and the union of substantial form and matter. The point here is 'mode' is broadly understood in the Schools as a particular affection of a substantial form explicable also by some external thing. By draft D Leibniz is questioning the mode's utility as a concept, because his own complete concept theory of individuality denies an 'outside', but he is still using the term in this sense: a mode is as to a substantial form as a derivative active force is as to a primary active force insofar as determined by particular passive force.[31] Hence the mixed nature of mode as used in draft D, and confirmed in drafts E and F. We can conclude that Leibniz understands Rational State as a mode, that is, as mixed.

(b) Now from our discussion of the political theology of *status* we understand this to imply a normative order, and at least two of these: the kingdoms of grace and of nature. Following the Council of Trent view, we can regard nature, and so the body, as being one such order capable of mutation form unjust to just. In §2 Leibniz inflects this basic duality by defining state not in a directly Scholastic manner, but by employing what appears to be the Aristotelean notion of habit. That this was his intention is confirmed by draft E, retained in F, where the Stagirite is explicitly cited and the definition only slightly modified: 'habit, in the sense generally defined by Aristotle ... is a durable acquired facility to act'.[32] Leibniz appears with this move to combine opposing classical and theological doctrines, inserting the contingency and dare I say mechanism of bodily habituation into the theory of grace. It must be remembered, however, that Leibniz regards nature, and thus affections, as subject to a normative order characterised primarily by repugnance and derivatively by pretension, an infinitesimal order that only God can maintain. Hence the bodily status is itself a normative order: Nature. The key difference from the Schoolmen is that the bodily order is not a moral status specific to the human (to have fallen), but a physical state universally governed by the laws of nature.

(c) We are dealing though with not the natural state alone, but one termed a 'Rational State', which is to be understood as a mode. By substitution, if a mode is mixed then what it defines – Rational State – is also mixed. Given that state alone is referred to the habituation, the question arises whether the qualifier 'Rational' identifies a subset of the state of nature or is rather some extra thing acting on nature? As we might expect, Leibniz will adopt the second position: that Rational State combines the primary force of subjective activity with the determinate actions of physical cause. This is made explicit in draft F's version of §2:

> Whence if the mind is impressed towards good action, it is called Virtue, which is twofold [*duplex*]: intellect and will. . . . The general doctrine [of which we speak here] concerns Subject and Cause; the special [doctrine of the Second Part] concerns Actions themselves and the Object.[33]

(d) Finally, Leibniz makes a critical clarification to §3, by extending the definition of a 'subject of Habit' as follows: such a subject is 'whatever is capable of acquiring a facility to act, especially if it acquires the action and insofar as it is habituated to act.' In so doing I understand Leibniz as wishing to emphasise that a subject of action is indeed acting according to its nature, and is not merely replicating an impressed action of some other (a passion). In drafts E and F Leibniz will replace his alchemical examples of this process with new scientific ones, including here an interesting reference to his thinking on elasticity. The point of immediate relevance is that the primary/derivative distinction once again plays a role, here with Leibniz identifying a subject of action which is the reference point for particular habituations and actions. By way of example, wood could be said to be habituated to table-ness, or the drunk to alcohol, but I suggest that Leibniz would hold that here the wood and the drunk are passive – table-ness and drunkenness are affected by them. Leibniz does not want his sense of habit to cover these cases; rather, he wishes habit to be referred to the acquisition of a facility to *act*, and, because actions derive from a primary force of subjective activity, only that facility to express this subjective activity qualifies as the kind of habit Leibniz is concerned with. In short then, habituation is habituation with respect to and in accordance with a subject.

From this it can be seen that Leibniz's thinking on habituation is not as empirical as Loemker suggests. Through the mode of Rational State, habituation is not habituation of just anything, determined only by the contingencies of nature, but is habituation referred to a subject, and thus subjective activity. The Rational State then qualifies the status of nature, whereby habituation can occur, by presupposing[34] a principle of action: the subject as inherently rational in its activity. Habituation is to be understood by reference to the subject, and habituation is only habituation in Leibniz's sense if the *subject* is habituated to act, that is, learns to express its own inherent activity. And this is the key point: that Leibnizian habituation rests on the assumption that what is being taught will impress on the pupil a habit which expresses that pupil's inherently rational subjectivity. We will return to this point in due course.

The types of habituation

From influxion Leibniz proceeds to 'assuefaction'. The choice of this word over any variant of habituation (*habituari*),[35] with its inherent passivity, appears to be quite deliberate though it must also be admitted that contemporary authors would use assuefaction in the sense of 'accustoming'.[36] *Assuefaction* literally means 'to make something a part of oneself', that is, to act in such a way as to include something within the circle of one's own customs or *assuetudines*.[37] It would be strange if Leibniz were not to have either spotted this sense or not linked it to his understanding of learning as reflective of the activity of a subject. It would seem that assuefaction is to be a subset of habituation, if the complement of assuefaction in habituation is to be understood as just those habits which are suffered to be taken on by the inanimate (think of the wearing down of a pebble). Yet the initial, physicalist discussion of assuefaction appears to promise a determinist, even physicalist theory of learning in which we are all pebbles in the sea. Leibniz's account of assuefaction bears the hallmarks of Hobbesian materialism and Cartesian mechanics, in which bodies are trained through impact of forces. One can certainly understand why Loemker would find the doctrine 'empiricist' in approach. I claim that Leibniz does construct a more subtle theory, and that to see this we must trace the specifications Leibniz makes as he refines assuefaction to the point at which he can introduce his own theory of teaching.

The initial account of assuefaction in §10, if anything underscored by additions in D and E, defines this term as that 'which is done through quantum of impressions'. Quantum is then divided into extension, caused by the number of actions, and intensive quantum, caused by the strength (*fortitudo*) of impressions required to impress the habit. Leibniz treats of the two separately, but his set up of intensive strength and extensive repetition echoes so readily the corporeal mechanics of 'force of motion', or momentum, known from Hobbes and Descartes, that it is all but inevitable that he should combine them into a single mode: 'it is most advisable to refine frequency with magnitude'.[38] It appears that Leibniz was sufficiently impressed by this theory that in drafts E and F he determined to promote the physicalist analogy to §3 of Part 1 of the *Nova Methodus*, replacing the earlier alchemical example with a more wide-ranging discussion of contemporary science:

> But this is shown by Mechanics in the assuefaction of inanimate [things], being nowhere more manifest than as appears in elastic bodies. For in the branches of trees, and in sheets of metal tempered by flame, just as in the contortion of bows, experience teaches us the use of bending in the acquisition, admission, mutation into, a determinate force of acting [*vim agendi*].[39]

This all sounds as if Leibniz has reduced learning to blacksmithing, but already there is a subtle current that some additional aspect is required. Implicit in the discussion of metals and bows is the idea that even these materials are assuefacted only because they are apt to the acquisition of just these habits. The yew branch possesses the *potentia* of becoming a bow, whereas the green wood of the hazel is simply too soft and would not suffer a drawstring. In the range of possible states of the yew, one finds that subset of states: 'being a bow'. Yet we also appreciate the being a bow is the potency of the yew *for* the bowyer, and in this the yew serves as a constituent within a greater composite 'the bow' envisaged by the bowyer. Leibniz does not explore this aspect of habituation – substantial aptitude – because he wishes to move quickly to focus on 'sentient' beings, but we might venture to bridge the gap. In the case of animate beings, as we have seen, the purposiveness of will determines a putting to use of a potency for self, whereas in the traditional division of inanimate objects these are put to the use of another rational being. Leibniz's focus on 'sentient' beings is explicitly a focus on the 'sense or sensation' of putting a potency to one's own use in the act of self-making. This indicates a subset of modes of assuefaction – of instances of frequency tempered by magnitude – which are not simply passively undergone as the metal undergoes smithing, but which are sensed by the animate being as reflective of that substance's own activity.

Hence to the mechanist explanation of assuefaction Leibniz adds a third term applicable to the 'sentient': *pleasure* (*jucundus*). It is pleasure which marks the difference between assuefaction of an inanimate object in which is potency is brought out for another, and sentient beings capable of that very sensation that arises with respect to what is learnt. This pleasurable assuefaction is teaching. It is important here that pleasure is applicable to a wider range of assuefaction than just teaching the law, as it grants us additional interpretative material. Training animals, medical care and academic teaching combine frequency, magnitude and pleasure. The former two components of assuefaction, now refined as speed and carefulness/soundness, are confirmed as the means of introducing habits themselves, whereas pleasure pertains to the agreeableness of the mode of acquisition.[40]

Now, as §19 confirms, pleasure remains too generic a term to completely define the kind of assuefaction Leibniz seeks to link to his method of teaching and learning, though the hints and asides multiply. Animals take pleasure also, and what they learn through feeding treats and petting, the human can learn through usefulness of what is taught and through being honoured. This suggests that at the level of teaching the pleasure engaged is broad enough to cover affections. It would be surprising, given the antiquity of the doctrines of the passions and of teaching (particularly dogs!), which come down from such as Plato and the Stoa into the works of Hobbes, Descartes and Spinoza, that Leibniz should not include in assuefaction a pleasure which we might describe as 'bought' by passing joys such as food. It would also be surprising, given the Scholastic heritage, that Leibniz should not seek to refine further the range of pleasure. And indeed, having briefly introduced pleasure as the third component of assuefaction, Leibniz will now move to the heart of his theory and specify a subset of teaching – by *Institutions*. In this, many of the subtle hints as to spontaneity and reflection will be gathered together, for this refinement is not due to teaching as a movement from tutor to pupil, but will engage just those kinds of knowledge which procure movement from pupil to knowledge of self.

What is teaching by institutions?
Having defined the Rational State and assuefaction, Leibniz is now in a position to present his theory of teaching. In §16 he declares:

> ... We must now come to Teaching [*Doctrinam*]. To teach [*docere*] is to effect a habit in a perceiving thing [*sentiente*], insofar as it is, or through sense. Hence this art is called *Didactic*, for even those who learn spontaneously [*spontè*] teach themselves, hence the name 'autodidact'.[41]

Now this definition is wide enough even to cover the teaching of animals. As we shall see shortly, this notion is only a part of the way towards the teaching that is the object of Leibniz's *Nova Methodus*. Thus what follows in the text covers the methods of teaching which are also effective with respect to animals, but as we move through the remaining articles it is necessary to piece together the sense of teaching most applicable to humans and particularly lawyers, and to ignore much of the branching structure of the text as it categorises various aspects of the general curriculum. There is something else going on and in what follows I highlight this central thread of argument.

As we saw, the efficacy of teaching comes from three mechanisms: that teaching be firmly implanted by frequency of action; that it be quickly implanted by magnitude of action; and that the teaching be pleasant. Learning is pleasant not only if the *ends* are pleasant, due to their utility, but also if the means are pleasant. Yet here the text apparently breaks, avoiding the opportunity to investigate the link between pleasure and the teaching of sentient beings further. Leibniz says: '§21 ... we have spoken of the cause of habit common only to beasts and men, namely *teaching*. It remains to discuss the cause of habit proper to men: *Institutions [Instiutione]*.'[42] This term 'institutions' is new and unexpected, and suggests nothing of pleasure. Nevertheless, once we have unpacked this term *Institutions* we will find that it is intimately linked to pleasure of mind. As a starting point, I claim that it needs to be read in conjunction with two further articles which nestle between a categorisation of various academic topics and logical divisions. These are:

> §31. Now follow the *habits of the mind*. Every action of the mind is thought, for to will is nothing but to think the goodness of a thing. ... [T]he sense perception of man is never without some reflection.[43]
>
> §34. Sensible qualities are of two kinds: some perceived in the mind alone, others in fantasy or by means of mediating bodily organs. In the mind are perceived only two qualities: thought and causality. *Thought* is a sensible quality either of the human intellect or of something 'I know not what' within us which we observe to be thinking. ... [t]his quality is also in God and the angels.[44]

These statements, to which I return shortly, are bound together by this term: *Institutione*, which Loemker translates as 'principles'. This choice can be understood, but we do lose an overtly normative aspect of what *Institutione* is trying to convey which is worth dwelling on. In one contemporary sense, ascribed not incorrectly to Leibniz by Stahl,[45] institution means positive will, and divine institution means divine positive will. This indeed is the Thomist sense of institute: for an institutor is someone who gives the thing instituted its strength or power. Is this the sense that Leibniz intends? Two arguments confirm this. First, moving from the source, we find in Aquinas a well-known tying of the power of institution[46] to the spiritual effect of the sacraments.

> ... the sacraments are instrumental causes of spiritual effects. Now an instrument has its power from the principal agent. ... Now the power of a sacrament cannot be from him who makes use of the sacrament: because he

works but as a minister. Consequently, it follows that the power of the sacrament is from the institutor of the sacrament. Since, therefore, the power of the sacrament is from God alone, it follows that God [and by extension Christ] alone can institute the sacraments.[47]

This appears a decidedly orthodox statement of the position. Second, we can make the bridge to Leibniz's own thought via his contemporary treatment of the sacraments from *c*.1668. As we have seen earlier, Leibniz explains transubstantiation – the coming of the presence of Christ's body in the host – by means of Christ's concurrent mind understood as the action of a supposit (*actiones sunt suppositorum*). The efficacy of the host derives not from a corporeal change, because for all relevant purposes the bread remains bread; the sacramental difference is that the primary force or activity instantiated continuously through the host is Christ's body's organising principle: 'the substance of Christ's body being present in all places where the bread and wine exist'.[48]

My suggestion is that Leibniz's use of *Institutions* is made in the shadow of this conception of habituation by means that go only, ultimately, to substantial activity and not corporeal accidents. By 'in the shadow of', I mean that Leibniz will in fact offer a different account, but this account is to be discovered by moving through a discussion of substantial change. On this model the student of such institutions remains in terms of corporeal 'accidents' just the person they were, but the organising activity elaborating itself through those accidents is expressive of the institutions that have been taught. Now, if I am right about the tripartite relationship between Thomist sacramental theory, Leibniz's transubstantiation theory and his theory of the institutions, are we to conclude that teaching through institutions constitutes transubstantiation? Is the substantial activity of the pupil in some way altered?

First, I would negatively respond that both the *Nova Methodus* and the middle period theory of substantial forms work to deny such a reading. As we say above, the *Nova Methodus* already contains an account of substantial change cognate with transubstantiation: spiritual influx. It would seem highly irregular then that Leibniz remained committed,

even in the 1690s, to his allocation of teaching through institutions to a sub-branch of the causes of habits that are proper
to humans. This inconsistency becomes insupportable once
the complete concept theory of the individual is taken into
account, for that thesis renders substantial change entirely
miraculous and certainly outwith habituation in the senses
Leibniz intends.

Second, the thread of Leibniz's argument in the *Nova
Methodus* highlighted by the quotations from §31 and §34
above suggests a different mechanism is in play, providing a positive argument against a reading of teaching by
institutions as substance-altering. The key phrase, from §31
is: *hominis imaginatio nunquam est sine aliqua reflexione*. The
essence of this short article is that the differentiating feature
of the 'Habitus animi' as between beasts and minds is the role
of reflection in thought. Draft D (from the 1690s) confirms
and expands on this conception:

> The action of the mind is thought, for to will is nothing other
> than endeavour from thought, or to endeavour toward
> something on account of the goodness of his remarkable
> [*cogitam*] thought. Furthermore, all thoughts are proposed
> in Enunciations or Propositions or affirmations and nega-
> tions, for even the simplest use of terms involves the
> affirmation of possibility, and reflective actions recognise
> [*agnoscit*] something actual [*actuale*] in ourselves.[49]

Deploying the structure of primary and derivative active
forces, I read this text as follows: the primary activity of
mind produces various derivative actions, or perceptions. A
given perception also contains something which expresses
its primary activity, and the greater this expression – or
reflection – the greater its goodness before the mind, for
the mind remarks something of itself in it. There is a consequent movement of actualisation, an affirmative movement
however constrained by negation (finitude), such that there
is produced a striving for the good. There is then a reflection
proper – the mind finds in the actuality of what is willed
something of itself made manifest.

Now, interpreting this revision from the 1690s, one is
struck by Leibniz's consistency of thought because the

expanded imagery of reflection leads us straight back to the
Elements of Law of 1670–1,[50] suggesting that the amendment
to the text is largely one expressive of the ideas that drove the
original submission to the Elector of Mainz. In the *Elements*
Leibniz defines honour (*honestas*) as pleasure of the mind, in
like manner to his deployment of honour and pleasure in the
Nova Methodus. He then completes the knot by linking pleasure of mind to reflection, thus leading us to the mechanism
by which the *Institutions* educate us. Pleasure, Leibniz tells
us, is duplicated by reflection (*Duplicatur autem jucunditas
reflexione*), and it is just this folding which occurs when 'we
contemplate the beauty within ourselves that is the case of
the virtue of our unexpressed conscience'.

Bringing all of this together suggests that education
through *Institutions* is both generically an education of mind
which activates pleasure, and also specifically that education
of mind which activates reflective pleasure. Now, in the case
of self-contemplation this pleasure derives from grasping in
thought the unexpressed *nescio cujus rei* (*I know not what*)[51] of
the self, and thereby actualising this primary activity. I would
suggest that education through institutions attempts to do
something similar: the mind of the pupil is presented with
principles which reflect the activity of the mind. The institutions thus go to intensionality itself – the way of thinking
– in order to develop in the pupil a recognition of what was
always unexpressed: the *esse commune* of intellect identified in *Trinitas. Mens*. Hence the concluding element of our
thread (*Nova Methodus* §34) which announces a treatment of
the Logic that will form part of the general curriculum: the
quality of thought which grasps that the something that is
thinking is also in God and the angels.

So far as the first, general part of the *Nova Methodus* proceeds, Leibniz's account of education through institutions
assumes a kind of intensional equivalence (perhaps even
an eidetic equivalence) between mental activity of the pupil
and of God. That Leibniz should think this is quite apparent
from his acceptance of a version of the *esse commune* thesis
which he supplements by a rigorous identification of being
and rational activity. To teach a lawyer jurisprudence, one
must approach the matter at the level of the very activity
of thought itself. The young lawyer is engaged in a training

that deploys a subtle method of habituation combining force, frequency and a pleasure instilled through procuring rec- ognition of self *qua* self and *qua* rational. Yet even assuming this universal guarantee of an intensional equivalence, why should education through institutions be of particular rel- evance to lawyers? Even if logic is deemed relevant to aspects of jurisprudence (rhetoric and dialectic), why does Leibniz lead us to this form of teaching above all others?

The social dimension of teaching law

The answer, I venture, is to be found back in the discussion of reflection in the *Elements of Law*. In the first draft (Concept A, c.1670), just after binding pleasure to reflection, Leibniz introduces a social dimension to his thinking:

> But as a double refraction can occur in vision, once in the lens of the eye and once in the lens of a tube, the latter increasing the vision of the former, so there is a twofold reflection in thinking. For every mind is like a mirror [*speculum*] and one mirror is in our mind, another in the mind of someone else. So if there are many mirrors, that is, many minds, recognising our goodnesses, there will be a greater light, the mirrors mixing the light not only in the eye but also among each other, the gathered splendour constituting the glory. There is an equal reason for deform- ity [*deformitas*] in the mind, otherwise there would be no shadows to be increased by the mirrors' reflection.[52]

This eloquent passage fully shifts our focus from the com- munity of being as intellective activity to the *Civitas Dei* as the actuality or being made manifest of finite minds. A certain inversion has incurred: whereas with the teaching of law the teacher can activate the *esse*–intellect of each pupil just because that *activity* has its root (*radix*) in the divine principle, now with what will become a doctrine of justice, Leibniz seeks to rely on the hope that communal actuality (the 'glory') will indeed be that actuality which best expresses the divine activity with respect to the world. Now the notion of justice is discussed elsewhere; I wish to focus on just that aspect which informs our understanding of the *Nova Methodus*: the notion of deformity.

The whole of the first and general part of the *Nova Methodus* is predicated on the unicity of thinking as such and thus the capacity of humans to learn through institutions. Yet as any teacher knows, every pupil is different, and capacities vary. In the above-quoted passage from the *Elements* we find now a brief reference to just these differences: there is an 'equal reason for deformity [*deformitas*] in the mind'. In my view this notion goes to the finitude of the creature. 'De-*form*-ity' is chosen as term precisely because Leibniz is not identifying contingent factors which may prevent this or that person from self-recognition; he is identifying necessary determinations of the creature which constitute its finitude. In the language of *On the True Theologica Mystica* every creature is a combination of Being and Nothing.[53] Translated into a discourse of light and reflection, the substantial form of any mind always bears the mark of shadow – there is ever a blemish which distinguishes creature from the divine light. After this fashion Leibniz continues a Neoplatonic and Scholastic tradition of originary limitation and lack, now using this to ground a social claim: that no single creature can fully actualise God in the world; rather, only a diverse plurality – a social body – can do so through a mutual reflection of the divine activity. This is the 'glorious' city towards which Leibniz's *Nova Methodus* travels, but in its account of teaching and learning the law, the theory of pedagogic institutionalisation is indicative of how the wider social process of attaining universal justice can be conceived, at least during Leibniz's early and middle years.

The student of law is presented with a double bind: the intellectual structure of jurisprudence is said to express the divine activity within the student's conscience itself, but any defect in that expression, any failure to recognise the truth in its luminescence, is ascribed to an originary, necessary deformity in the student's substantial form. Implicitly Leibniz directs our student to her teachers and colleagues, indeed to the living actuality of the principles which each individual student cannot fully recognise in their own learning, an actuality which is expressed through their learning in common and so reflecting that commonality of intellectual activity Thus we might say that through the institutions as active principles, the student approaches the active principles in the actuality of *the* institution.

4. Institution and *Urdoxa*

In this section I propose to draw some connections between
the richness of the *Nova Methodus'* theory of legal education
and the work of Husserl, particularly Husserl's notion of the
noemata and his foundation of sense in an *Urdoxa* discussed in
the last chapter. These connections will assist in the framing
of the remaining chapters. Now, the relationship between
the thinkers is well-established, and Deleuze's critique of
Husserl's engagement with Leibnizian thought well known
– Sjoerd van Tuinen for example providing a penetrating
account that centres on Deleuze's *Le Pli*.[54]

Drawing on the work of Krzysztof Michalski, the Husserl
of the *Ideen I* recognises that philosophy has for too long
obfuscated a distinction between sense and object; a proper
understanding of this distinction is inseparable from any
effort to clarify the structure of consciousness and intentionality. Sense itself is now understood to stand between
subject and object, being neither mental or of nature, so to
speak, and in his grappling with the structure present in this
sense, Husserl posits the *noema* as a structure of sense linked
to the doxic modalities of consciousness: characteristics of
probability, questionability and so forth. This modal realm
is precisely that in which the teaching of law operates, for
the general part of the *Nova Methodus* is preparatory to a
treatment in the specific part of just such (ultimately deontic)
modalities.

Husserl stresses that the *noema* is autonomous from the
object of perception and that it is independent even from
various points of view. What Husserl will not give way to
though is an anarchy of sense (Deleuzian non-sense). As
Barry Smith has noted,[55] while the Husserlian *epoché* commits
to a rational break of the I from the World, which the former
stands above, Husserl preferred to withhold publication of
his work (*Ideen II*) because of the problems he faced in trying
to account for intersubjectivity. One unsatisfactory solution,
according to van Tuinen,[56] is Husserl's positing within sense
itself a rational modality of common sense (the *Ur-doxa*). Each
'I' is part of a world of common meaning ascribable to possible objects, and each Other is likewise in that same world. As
van Tuinen puts it: 'others are then . . . intersubjective others

or alter egos in the same world (the phenomenological *Welt* or *Urdoxa . . .)'.*[57]

Applying this crudely sketched lens to the Leibnizian structure of a world, we can see as Merleau-Ponty did[58] that whatever advantages derive from the Leibnizian model of the substantial form and later monad – particularly the interiorisation of world within the monad and so the denial of an exterior or public 'nature' – these advantages are betrayed by the assumption of a common system of rational sense-giving which is guaranteed by God. Whatever I perceive as Other, for Leibniz, I always endeavour to make sense of by reducing it to a real constituent of the single objective world demanded by God. Does this not foreshadow Husserl's own concern that an idea of true being, which a rational account of the world strives to approach asymptotically, is the correlate of the idea of a subject which would sustain itself into the infinite, either as an indefinite community of persons or an infinite God?[59] With our examination of the *Nova Methodus* we have discovered that this anchoring in God rests not simply on the *esse commune* of the Scholastics, but attains a certain novelty from the notion of education through institutions. The very possibility of this mechanism of teaching rests on the presupposition that the manifestation of a way of thinking legally will have, through reflection of rational activity, a meaning which is then capable of abstraction (eidetic reduction) from the classroom and reapplication in the court. This assures a common state space which makes sense for every supposit by means of institutional reflection. The juridical consequence: the facts of cases are made sense of according to the law. Leibniz's applied legal works of the period – the *De Arte Combinatoria, De Conditionibus, De Casibus Perplexis* and the drafts for the *Elementa* – all in greater or lesser measure can be understood as premised on the following model: that the law student should learn to reflect the institutional common sense of a state space, not by simply synthesising contingent legal data, but by apprehending the combinatorial elements of any possible juridical thinking.

5. Conclusion

Leibniz's *Nova Methodus* is not a purely empiricist work, and in particular it does not ape the mechanistic accounts of learning which characterise the philosophies of Hobbes, Descartes and Spinoza. By viewing learning and teaching from the perspective of the Scholastic, and particularly Thomist, accounts of status and the New Law, we find in Leibniz a critical discussion between mere learning such as would train an animal, and learning through institutions, which is appropriate to rational substances. This latter form of learning employs a key feature of the Leibnizian Trinitarian mind: the distinction between the action of thought (the image as determined by passions) and the supposit as primary activity of being. Specifically, the institution is learnt just by its reflecting the activity of Mind, for on presentation of the institution there is a spontaneous movement of the supposit itself to grasp the institution. The theory is of general application, but its application to legal learning is not accidental. First, it appears that Leibniz draws inspiration from the Thomist account of the New Law to argue that there is something in jurisprudence itself – something both rational and actual – which attracts Mind because it reflects a commonality redolent of the Scholastic *ens commune* or community of intellectual being.

Second, learning by institutions also engages the real side of the mental equation, which is to say that learning is not merely a return to being through intellection. Rather, learning is constructive of institutions, and it must be so because of the manner in which finite minds are defined – as lacking in some way a full representation of the world. Each finite Mind, to the extent that it has developed itself, reflects some small portion of all the activity of the World. Leibniz appears strongly to believe that the force of institutions is grounded in their reality; grounded in the great variety of reflections at many levels which can be brought together and experienced by tutees of the law. We might therefore speak of an institutional speculum, or institutionalism through the spectacle, whereby those who will be taught law experience law as the affective force of its reflection by a great number of individuals. A powerful theory, but one which is open to the criticisms raised by Deleuze: that absent a unifying God the common sense of the law works because it presumes a commonality, a single institution shared by all, which the pupil must learn if she is to 'fit in' with the learned jurisconsults.[60] For Deleuze such an apparatus of capture employs the affective force of numbers who believe in the institutional common sense, and it is the experience of this spectacle of 'what is obvious' which frames our very thought.[61] Indeed, Deleuze notes in *Difference and Representation*, the law of large numbers grounds Leibniz's whole account of sense: '*infinite representation does not free itself from the principle of identity as a presupposition of representation*'.[62] In other words, the infinite does not escape the One, but is captured by it, and in this way 'diversity is compensated by identity'.[63]

Our analysis of the *Nova Methodus* has been effective because we have applied our understanding of the Scholastic framework as recalibrated through Leibniz's doctrine of *Trinitas. Mens*. In particular the interaction between the activity of the supposit and its derivative formal actions on the one hand, and the passive force (or in-potency) of the real on the other – indeed the whole apparatus of the square of power – has permitted a refinement of previous academic analysis of this work. Yet one feels that on such a narrow subject as teaching and learning law we have not been able to fully explore the consequences of this framework. A similar issue has already been faced in our review of *De Casibus Perplexis*. The issue is this: Leibniz seems to be very good at explaining how lawyers (should) think about the law, but he always takes the raw material of cases as given data, as reals to be combined and permuted, as conceptual institutions to be recognised. Yet surely a lawyer is most interested in legal relationships and the contents of norms, of obligations and rights. Both Hobbes and Spinoza may provide a brutal, force-based account of how one learns, but the account is entailed by a theory of real social relations based on power which is decidedly convincing. Even Spinoza, who offers with the *Scientia intuitiva*[64] a route to a higher knowledge, accepts its attainment is rare and relegates the majority to a law founded on the dynamic between violence and security. Is Leibniz's theorising about jurisprudence a strictly academic exercise, to be studied in the schools? By treating real cases as simply given, does he regard legal disputes as contingent data of relevance only when coming before the court, and does he go as far as regarding such matters as governed by 'laws' reducible to the mechanics of *conatus* and *potentia*? It would seem that Leibniz is just so inclined to follow Hobbes's views on real legal relations in part, at least in the earliest drafts of his next work, the *Elementa Iuris*. We will see, however, that this initial acceptance of the Hobbist programme is quickly qualified, and Leibniz reintegrates its material account of reality, and particularly human volition, within Leibniz's own Trinitarian framework. This move, designed to preserve free will against determinism, leads to a remarkable innovation on Leibniz's part.

Notes

1. Alberto Ferrarin, *Hegel and Aristotle* (Cambridge: Cambridge University Press, 2009) pp.300–1.
2. See for example Gwenaëlle Aubry, *Genèse du Dieu souverain* (Paris: Vrin, 2018).
3. ST II-I, q.49, a.1. For detailed commentary see Nicholas Kahm, 'Aquinas on Quality' (2016) 24(1) *Brit. J. Hist. Phil.* 23–44.
4. Umberto Eco, *The Aesthetics of Aquinas* (Cambridge, MA: Harvard University Press, 1988) p.206.
5. Jeremiah Hackett, 'Duns Scotus: A Brief Introduction to his Life and Thought' (1991) 26(1) *Studies in Scottish Literature* 438–47.
6. Specifically ST II-II, q.1183ff.
7. ST II-I, q.49, a4.
8. 'Status, proprie loquendo, significat quandam positionis differentiam secundum quam aliquis disponitur secundum modum suae naturae.'
9. ST II, ii, q.183, a.1.
10. Adam Tanner (1572–1632) traced the origins of status theology back to Hugh of St Victor (c.1096–1141) and Peter Lombard (c.1096–1160). On this and the pre-Thomist and later Jesuit conceptions of status, see Christoph Haar, *Natural and Political Conceptions of Community – The Role of the Household Society in Early Modern Jesuit Thought, c.1590–1650* (Leiden: Brill, 2019), ch.1.
11. ST II, i, q.91, a.5.
12. ST II, i, q.91, a.5, r.3.
13. ST II, i, q.93, a.5.

14. ST II, i, q.91, a.5, r.3.
15. ST II, i, q.91, a.5.
16. E.g. ST III, q.64, a.2.
17. Haar, *Natural and Political Conceptions*, pp.32–4.
18. *Canons and Decrees of the Council of Trent*, session 6, ch.7, 33 quoted in Haar, *Natural and Political Conceptions*, p.34.
19. Particularly Jesuits such as de Soto and Suárez.
20. A:VI, i, 260–364; L:85–92 (First Part (trans.)); Johns, *Science of Right*, Appendix (Second Part (trans.)). Here I focus on the general discussion of teaching law of the First Part only.
21. L:85.
22. Maria Rosa Antognazza, *Leibniz: An Intellectual Biography* (Cambridge: Cambridge University Press, 2009) p.84.
23. L:76, my emphasis.
24. A:VI, i, 140.
25. A:VI, i, XVIII. These manuscript amendments are known as D, E and F respectively, and are given in the footnotes to the *Akademie* edition.
26. L:91 n.13. The allegation is repeated in n.6 and n.20.
27. A:VI, i, 266.
28. A:VI, i, 266.
29. A:VI, i, 267: 'Subjectum Habitûs est, quicquid actionis capax est.'
30. Suárez, *Metaphysics* 7.1.18.
31. L:502.
32. A:VI, i, 266.
33. A:VI, i, 266, draft F.
34. My thanks to Ed Thornton for suggesting this point.
35. Cf. for Scholastic usage, Werner Dettloff, *Die Entwicklung der Akzeptations- und Verdienstlehre von Duns Scotus bis Luther mit besonderer Berücksichtigung der Franziskanertheologen* (Münster: Aschendorff Verlag, 1963), pp.37ff.
36. Thomas Browne, writing in his decidedly Hermetic *Christian Morals* of 1716, uses the term as follows: 'Forget not how assuefaction unto any thing minorates the passion from it, how constant Objects loose their hints, and steal an inadvertisement upon us' (Part iii, line 153).
37. I thank Anton Schütz for this interpretation.
38. §15 A:VI, 273. 'Refine' translating 'temperare' meaning to temper and sharpen metal, *contra* Loemker who uses 'mix' (L:87).
39. Draft F, A:VI, i, 267.
40. A:VI, i, 274–5.
41. A:VI, i, 274.

42. A:VI, i, 277.
43. A:VI, i, 284.
44. A:VI, i, 286.
45. François Duchesneau and Justin E.H. Smith (trans.), *The Leibniz-Stahl Controversy* (New Haven: Yale University Press, 2016) p.342.
46. Compare with Aquinas' account of how the eternal law is communicated: ST II, i, q.91, a5, r1.
47. ST III, q.64, a.2.
48. L:115.
49. A:VI, i, 284.
50. A:VI, i, 459–65; L:131ff.
51. A:VI, i, 286; L:89.
52. A:VI, i, 486; L:137.
53. L:364.
54. Sjoerd van Tuinen, 'A Transcendental Philosophy of the Event: Deleuze's Non-Phenomenological Reading of Leibniz' in Sjoerd van Tuinen and Niamh McDonnell (eds), *Deleuze and the Fold: A Critical Reader* (London: Palgrave Macmillan, 2010) ch.7.
55. Barry Smith, 'Common Sense' in Barry Smith and David Woodruff Smith (eds), *The Cambridge Companion to Husserl* (Cambridge: Cambridge University Press, 1995) pp.394–437 at p.429.
56. van Tuinen, 'A Transcendental Philosophy of the Event', p.174.
57. Ibid.
58. Maurice Merleau-Ponty, *The Visible and the Invisible* (Noyes St Evanston, IL: Northwestern University Press, 1969) pp.222–3.
59. Max Scheler, *Formalism in Ethics and the Non-Formal Ethics of Values* (Evanston, IL: Northwestern University Press, 1973) pp.396ff., quoted by Smith, 'Common Sense', p.437.
60. Gilles Deleuze, *Difference and Repetition* (London: Athlone Press, 1994) pp.131–7. van Tuinen, 'A Transcendental Philosophy of the Event', ch.7.
61. Deleuze, *Difference and Repetition*, pp.134–5. See also Gilles Deleuze, *The Fold: Leibniz and the Baroque* (London: Athlone Press, 1986) p.78.
62. Deleuze, *Difference and Repetition*, p.49, emphasis in original.
63. Leibniz, *Elementa Iuris Naturalis*, A:VI, 484.
64. See e.g. *Ethics* II, prop.40 sch.2.

Seven

Power and Obligation in the 1660s

1. Introduction

The drafts of the *Elementa Iuris Naturalis* have been the subject of detailed study by several authors, both from the legal and the logical angles. Christopher Johns in particular has provided an almost line by line account of the internal structure of the texts of 1669–71 and so it might not be apparent that a further such analysis is required. I claim, however, that by tracing the philosophy of activity and power from texts such as the *Nova Methodus* into the *Elementa*, we can reveal much of interest which one might pass over if the text is interpreted on its own terms and with reference to the traditional Leibnizian 'interlocutors' such as Hobbes, Grotius and Pufendorf. At the heart of this chapter is the argument that the well-known deontic modal square of the *Elementa* is not simply an ad hoc methodological import inspired by Aristotle but an explicit repetition of a framework of questions involving activity and power which characterise Leibniz's early and middle period thinking (at least). Support for this argument is drawn from the Scholastic tradition, in which we see a tendency towards uniting theological natural law and Roman *ius* in a coherent metaphysical framework. I will argue that Leibniz will attempt to complete this synthesis by identifying obligation with primary activity towards an end, and right with derivative action (or possibility) to an end. To do this I focus, in this chapter, on discussing texts precedent to the *Elementa*, to demonstrate how they are already informed by the square of power. More particularly, I claim that the central problem of the relationship between physical determinism and free will can already be understood and is understood by both Hobbes

228

and Grotius through a version of the square of power. It is because of Leibniz's familiarity with the square of power that the challenge of Hobbesianism is immediately comprehended, and it is because of the utility of this methodological framework for Leibniz and his contemporaries that our philosopher seeks to solve what he regards as the problems posed by natural right theory by reworking and reconceiving that square of power. This reworking takes place over a number of texts and drafts, notably the *Nova Methodus*, the *Specimen Quaestionum Philosophicarum* and the *Elementa Iuris*. As this chapter establishes the presence of the square of power in the works proper to the *Elementa*, it will identify early forms of Leibniz's key defences of natural law. The broad outline of his move will become quickly apparent. Leibniz integrates Grotian right into a metaphysical theory of rational obligation, with a view not to re-establishing a Thomist priority of reason over both command and appetition, but rather to situate right as the moral motor which aids reason to pursue the end. A typically Leibnizian move to attempt reconciliation of natural law and natural right. Yet as we advance into the *Elementa* we will begin to discern a more fundamental metaphysical shift taking place. Right is a product of *potentia*, but strictly speaking the square tells us that *potentia* determines the individual from without, in this context in the form of the state and of God. If Leibniz is to synthesise the external *potentia* of state and God with the rational legal activity of the individual, what does this entail for the division between activity and power; for the foundational metaphysical division between interior and exterior? These latter questions subtend this and the next chapter.

2. Synthesising right and obligation – key Scholastic debates

A consideration of the *Elementa* requires an assessment of several definitions and distinctions which are brought together in the drafts with little hint of their significance. One such distinction, which opens Concept B of the *Elementa* and which merits contextualisation is:[1]

$$\left.\begin{array}{l} \textit{right (ius)} \\ \textit{obligation} \end{array}\right\} \textit{is} \left\{\begin{array}{c} \textit{the power (potentia)} \\ \textit{the necessity} \end{array}\right. \left\{\begin{array}{l} \textit{of the good person, for what Grotius} \\ \textit{called Moral Qualities are} \\ \textit{nothing other than the qualities} \\ \textit{of the good person} \end{array}\right.$$

Christopher Johns, for example, focuses on the immediate interpretative threads offered by the reference to Grotius, a later one to Aristotle, and the use of 'Moral Qualities' which I agree sends us immediately to the discussion of qualities of the *Nova Methodus*. These are all critically important, but it is Gaston Grua who picks up on the significance of the distinction, though he only sketches what this might be. Here Leibniz conjoins two traditions in legal theory which had already been converging in the baroque period. The one – that of obligation – is characterised by the Thomist heritage in that obligation is linked to the rational governance of the world as part of theology. The other – that of right – is a practical construct of Roman law which, however, by the baroque had begun to take on theoretical significance as part of the natural rights tradition, with Grotius and others, but also within Scholasticism. The late Scholastic approach to right (*ius*) is not simply a response to this new natural rights trend; we might say, rather, that the Schools' engagement with the Roman law and the need to explain the practical deployment of *ius*, *dominium* and so on by lawyers, already provides an account of right inflected by the metaphysics of Catholic theology. Whether this inflection is determinative of the meaning of *ius* is, however, up for debate. One might say, for example, that Domingo de Soto's treatment of these concepts, though structured according to Scholastic conceptions such as volition, is simply a functional legal account not designed to import theological significance. This might explain certain inconsistencies in these doctrines, leading Grua to remark that Francisco Suárez's own explanation of the relationship between obligation and right is 'imperfect'. In what follows I will provide a brief survey of these traditions insofar as they bear on Leibniz's *Elementa*. This will help us to establish what Leibniz is attempting to do in effectively defining right as a particular instance of obligation.

Power and Obligation in the 1660s

2.1 Right and obligation – the context of the 1660s

We have seen in our discussion of volition that Leibniz combines the entelechies or final causes of Aristotle and Aquinas with the 'a-parte-rei' theory of Duns Scotus. In terms of providing for a rich ontological structure of the natural and the moral it would seem that such a combination is quite productive for Leibniz. Yet when the Thomist and Scotist traditions are considered with respect to the notion of obligation, the difference of the Scotist theory of will comes to the fore.

Aquinas divides the reactions of the will into sensual appetite and rational appetite. Rational appetite chooses the means presented by reason in order to pursue the end of self and End. This leads to happiness. In this way a certain determinism holds such that the virtuous will follow rational appetite to happiness. This acting according to reason is virtue. As such the obligatoriness of natural law is inbuilt into the rational nature of things. Now, according to the account of Thomas Williams,[2] Scotus in effect rejects this view, but he does so by distinguishing two kinds of willing: (i) a willing which amounts to rational appetite, named the *affectio commodi* and (ii) willing undetermined by happiness, called the *affectio iustitiae*. Scotus takes issue with the introduction of determinism that is implied by making the will subject to a single rational order and a kingdom of final causes. Instead the will of the *affectio iustitiae* is rendered free to will or not will what is presented to it, instituting a strict freedom of practical action. This argument also serves a second critical function, in that Scotus is brilliantly aware that the rational order of essences does not completely determine the real, that is, that the existence of two alternative possibilities may both be logically possible to reason, with nothing more to tip the balance. In the field of natural law this balance is tipped by the *command* of God, exercised absolutely freely, and our wills mirror this freedom in being able to choose *contingently* between the possibles presented by reason. Thus, in place of Thomist virtue Scotus sets a *praxis* of right reasoning (or prudence) in which the choices of the will do not slavishly follow reason's road to the end, but rather are in conformity with reason's suggestions as to what is commanded within its logical parameters. The result is to open up a greater field for practical action, which we see particularly in Scotus's treatment of the divine law. Here, the Decalogue is interrogated and understood to provide an extremely broad framework of obligations from which human reason must deduce, and necessarily add, its judgements about what the positive and natural law is in a given circumstance.[3]

A commandment, which Duns Scotus links to obligatoriness of an act,[4] has two key characteristics in Duns Scotus's thought: (i) they are ordered according to a hierarchy at the pinnacle of which is that commandment towards the ultimate End (love God); and (ii) the content of derivative commandments reflects the contingency of real relations. Möhle provides the following useful example, namely a commandment to help the community, for example through charity, combined with an injunction for failure to do so. Now, the core commandment derives from the Decalogue (love thy neighbour) and is thus part of the foundational commandments of this world. What though of the injunction, backed by punishment, against omission? Why is it part of this derived commandment? The point here is that Duns Scotus does not wish to deduce specifications and determinations of the natural law from their primary definition, as Leibniz might. These additional calibrations are justified by the contingency of the sphere of the primary commandment's application. Thus, in the example given by Möhle, the real relations of community and of the human are such that humans are apt to will protection of their personal property rather than the community good, and so an additional injunction is required to render the primary commandment effective. As if to emphasise this point, Duns Scotus will then distinguish natural law from positive law again according to a realist account: a primary commandment to worship may be effected according to different possible liturgical orders depending on the contingency of the community in question; the decree could promote one liturgy or the other, and as such is not a commandment of natural but positive law.

All this wraps up within an understanding of the primary commandments as themselves subject to an infinite contingency in the will of God. God has provided for an order, and it is from and within the constraints of this order that every subordinate decree can be found, inflected according to the real field of its application. Yet God, absolutely powerful, has the freedom to change the commandments, and to substitute a new order. It remains, though, that this exercise of absolute power is not arbitrary – the ordered power is to be replaced in its entirety so that an order prevails; there is no suspension of order. This insight flows down the chain of commandments so that we must understand that each decree specific to a real relation reflects the divine *potentia ordinata* – not in the sense, I emphasise, that each commandment is derivable logically from the first, but in the sense that this contingent world, possible according to certain basic laws such as non-contradiction, permits reason to ascertain within real contextual parameters a number of possible juridical solutions to a specific problem and to judge which is the most appropriate to realise. In this way obligation only appears to be a matter of blind obedience to a sovereign command, for Duns Scotus has attempted to open up, in the field of the real, a huge space for free practical choice tempered by right reasoning. The juridical centre of gravity is thus shifted to the Franciscan brother 'on the ground' prudently making rules befitting of circumstance, giving rise to a great diversity in positive and natural law. The subtlety of Duns Scotus's position though should not reduce the challenge posed for successors such as Francisco Suárez by an iteration of the basic principle of voluntarism to all levels of the actually existing legal real – that obligation is imposed by command, divine or temporal, and that it is enough that the command is willed that it be binding.

If we jump forward to the sixteenth century, Suárez then must account for Thomist and Scotist theories of obligation. As with the theory of elicitation, it is Suárez's work on obligation which – via the Scholastic curriculum of continental universities – appears to offer most interpretative assistance for us. Following the reading of Terence H. Irwin,[5] in some respects refining and correcting those of John Finnis and Thomas Pink,[6] and eschewing the all too brief comments of Gaston Grua,[7] we might summarise Suárez's thinking on obligation as follows. At its heart there appears to be a voluntarism – that what turns a good or bad action into an action that is obligatory (to do or avoid) is not right reason alone but, critically, a superior will. Hence: '. . . the dictate of intellect without will cannot by itself have the character of a command in relation to another, nor can it bring about in the other a special obligation . . .'[8] Irwin shows how Suárez is keen to draw a distinction between what is owed (*debet*) naturally and what is obligatory.[9] Nature has a way of indicating that certain actions or omissions are bad, and the punishment so to speak is swift. For example, eating poisonous fruit is bad; acting violently may well elicit a harmful response.[10] These 'bads' (and the respective goods) lack the character of obligation, however, without also a 'special' added something:

> For if this law forbids something because it is bad, it brings about its own special necessity of avoiding it, because this is intrinsic to forbidding. At the same time, however, it proves that this law assumes something which pertains to an intrinsic natural debt [*debitum*], because everything in a particular way ought not do anything inconsistent with its own nature. But in addition to this owing, the law imposes a special *moral obligation*, and we say that this obligation is the effect of this law. The jurists customarily call this a natural obligation, not because it is not moral, but in order to distinguish it from a civil obligation.[11]

In this Suárez is not so far from Aquinas, for the latter also makes a distinction between the inclinations that arise from the body suggesting the good and the bad, and the ends that are determined by reason without bodily influence, that is, rational appetite.[12]

This division between good/bad arising naturally and a prescription applicable to the free will as such opens up a debate regarding whether obligations require *debita* as pre-conditions of existence, but this is not relevant for our purposes because Leibniz will run obligatoriness and owing-ness[13] together under the name of necessity. The more pertinent issue is the character of obligation itself, if indeed it is not manifest indicatively in nature. Irwin picks out the following definitions which follow the discussion of 'special obligation' quoted above: '. . . because obligation is a certain kind of moral moving [of someone] towards acting. Now, moving another to operation is a work of will. (*Obligatio est*

motio quaedam moralis ad agendum. Movere autem alium ad oper-
andum opus voluntatis est).'[14]

It is here that I deviate slightly from Pink's cautious analysis. There are two reasons for this. First, I do so because
Pink implies 'causation' into the 'moral movement'. Second,
because Pink's intermediate conclusion on Suárez's view of
obligation – that '[w]e introduce an act of obliging when an
obligation is laid on us or imposed on us' – serves only the
limited aim of rebutting Finnis' reading. This intermediate
interpretation does not help us grasp the nature of obligation.
Picking up on our work of the previous chapters, the reference to moral movement here is surely a reference not to an
(efficient) cause by the ultimate End on the moral agent, but
rather an elicitation of the will of the moral agent towards
the ultimate end as principle. Once again several difficulties are clarified if due distinction is made between the supposit of the agent, the agent's intellection of formal ideas,
the movement of the agent's will with respect to those ideas,
and the role of the ideas of ends in this process. We can see
how moral movement links the elicitation of the will with the
(idea of the) End, and that after a manner of speaking it is
the agent's will which is the free cause of its own choice, but
that no choice can be made without elicitation with respect
to the (idea of the) end.

Pink is on the right track here in his appreciation that
obligating need not imply perfect determination, that is, that
the command of a superior is only an obligation if obedience immediately follows. Obligating is not force; rather it is
elicitation to moral movement – an inclining to will as such
which the free will may refuse. Pink structures this analytically as an argument that obligation by A of B does not imply
success, and that B is not so 'impressed' by the obligation
that he satisfy it, but that we may still say A exerted pressure
on B. The problem again though is the language of impression and pressure is all too naturalistic for the period, and
whether Pink intends this or not, it is a further instance of
physicalism in the sphere of ends. My passing suggestion is
that elicitation is once again at work, but now at the level of
the free will (that is, spontaneously). Remembering that each
particular volition is derived from activity and refers to the
end, but that it is bound up with the particularity of ideas, we

must distinguish the primary or free will as such, as Suárez, de Soto and, as we have seen, Scotus do. In each particular case the volition's elicitation is with respect to a particular object, and we can conceive of mind as full of various such objects and so particular volitions from which the individual chooses, acting via its 'primary' free will. What though moves this free will to action, given that it ranges across numerous diverse and conflicting volitions? My argument is that this free will has as its objects the individual and the ultimate end. On this reading then the obligation in question morally moves the free will, eliciting a volition to pursue its 'higher' ends, a volition which may be nulled.

One qualification, though, does intervene: it could just be that Suárez's account of obligation shares something of the implicit aim of de Soto's account of free will as the condition of dominion (and so the capacity to impose obligation with respect to a good). This aim could be that both de Soto and Suárez wish to say nothing of import about will or ends; rather they are providing a functional legal definition of certain terms of art, structured according to the Scholastic tradition but allowing a certain greyness of definition that permits the necessary flexibility that a practical juridical term requires. This though is a separate debate about the nature and function of Spanish baroque legal theory; our concern is Leibniz's attempt, inspired initially by Thomasius, Weigel and Hobbes, to rationalise law starting from first principles.

So much for Suárez's theory of obligation; what is his theory of right? As we noted earlier, *ius* has its origins in Roman legal practice, and indeed no theoretical definition of right as such seems to have been deployed by the jurisconsults. It is perhaps unsurprising then that Aquinas' account of *ius* almost completely assimilates the term within the rational theory of obligation: a right is equivalent to what is a just particular, that is, right is a particular instance of what reason (as prudence) determines to be obligated with respect to the end. As such right is defined as the object of justice. It may appear surprising then that in *De Legibus* (1612) Suárez defines *ius* as the moral quality of a competent person to have or do something just.[15] This formulation apparently suggests that the source of right is the habituated moral quality of the individual, not an obligation imposed by reason or a superior. Suárez's treatment of the topic is not helped by his drawing together of various strands, with even the central definition of *ius* he offers being comprised of two separate derivations, but the broad thrust appears to be in line with the Thomist account. Following the one central derivation, *ius* is a moral power or faculty that arises in the context of a relationship with person or goods, and here Suárez refers us to *ius suum*. We might then read this definition as not locating the source of *ius* in the individual but in the system of relationships that exist in a legal order. That this is indeed Suárez's intent is supported by the second central derivation: that *ius* and *lex* are as genus to species, for both derive from a sense of '*iubendum* (ordering)' that derives from a '*iussio* (command)'.[16] One might conclude for our purposes then that while Suárez refers *ius* to the will as moral power, as with obligation the rightfulness of the right requires an order that is commanded. Volitions are merely volitions; they only gain juridical significance within an ordering of right. The top-down vertical ordering of right is thus preserved, even as *ius* is granted a more nuanced status.

The double derivation offered by Suárez is to a degree reflected by Hugo Grotius. Grotius' first definition of right in *De Iure Belli ac Pacis* (1625), Christoph Stumpf argues,[17] is very much in line with the tradition of the Schoolmen: right is nothing other than what is just, and what is just is what is not unjust. The sense of this definition is to refer the just, as Suárez does, to an overarching order of justice. Furthermore, Stumpf tells us that Grotius even adopts the view that this sense of right is only applicable to those virtues that fall under the regime of justice, which is to confirm that individual practical action is not 'rightful' unless an order of justice pertains. Grotius' second definition also appears to follow the tradition, but here there is greater innovation, variously noted by Grua and Stumpf:[18] (a) right is extended to all virtues, not just those gathered under 'justice'; (b) lacking this anchoring in an order of justice, rights are now characterised according to a subjective, somewhat Aristotelean, notion of perfection, whereby: (i) rights are faculties of the person insofar as they are perfected moral qualities; (ii) rights are aptitudes or functions of the person to the extent, we might say, granted by another. As Stumpf argues, the discussion roughly corresponds to the metaphysical distinction between *actus* and *potentia* which we too have encountered, though Stumpf does not follow up on the significance of this. After all, an act in Aristotelean terms is just that which expresses a thing's essence, and we may assess its perfection by reference to its determination by another nature. It seems that the perfections of right are those which are incapable of being determined – and so each a *ius suum* – in the sense that they can have no degree. The classic example given is a property right (*dominium*) where this right is taken as the *absolute* ability to alter, use and destroy the thing in question.[19] This we might contrast with a usufruct, which being limited and subordinate to the title owner would be an 'imperfect' right in Grotius' sense. An even more illustrative example, given by Stumpf, is the right of an officeholder, for here Grotius displays his debt to Stoic philosophy in understanding the clothing of a person with an *officium* as imposing additional, transitory 'proper functions' (*aptitudo*) on the person over and above those due to human nature.

This disjunction of the senses of right enables a partial severing of the link between a regime of obligation ordered by reason or command, and right. Now at least, the perfected sense of right is no longer but an instance of obligation. We might think of this move according to the logic of the time as follows: the Schoolman orders obligations in such a way as to constitute a totality or jurisdiction, if you will; right (*ius*) names moral acts which are particular instances of justice. In short, the rational or commanded necessity of obligation implies the right as possible. Grotius now suggests that it is the actually existing particular right which subsists even if the total ordering is lacking. This is indeed the logically correct position, for necessity cannot imply existence. It is a move Grotius makes because, like Hobbes, he effectively posits the lowest tier of the theologico-juridical hierarchy – natural law – as subject to determinable norms *even if* (*etiamsi*) God were not to rule.

Hobbes,[20] if we take *Leviathan* as the reference point, likewise adopts the division of right into what Eleanor Curran calls[21] unprotected, original or natural rights and (socially) protected or claim rights. Right, insofar as it is the liberty to choose to do or to forbear, is possessed in the State of Nature, whereas rights in the sense of claims to something as against another can only result from a social relation founded on the mutual obligations of the contract. Unlike Grotius, however, and against the Schoolmen, right is explicitly defined as 'inconsistent' with law – it is as opposed as liberty is to obligation, and for the same reasons, Hobbes claims.[22] It is a claim though which is a little misleading, for I would say that the division returns to Hobbes material treatment of power.

Liberty is grounded in *power*, which in *Leviathan*[23] and in *De Cive*[24] is either original to the body and mind of the individual, or such as is acquired by original power by skill or luck. If we move further back to the material foundations of Hobbes's thought, as we must, we see as others have done that power refers to some event produced, and this plenary power which explains the event is divisible into its efficient cause (or active power) and material cause (or passive power). Ignoring the difficulties of this division, and even the benefits of the explicit denial of distinct essential/formal and final causes as explanations, I wish to draw our attention to the concept of passive power in a patient. Having introduced the agent as having power insofar as it is the cause of some effect, Hobbes now speaks of the patient:

> In like manner whensoever a patient has all the accidents it is requisite it should have, for the production of some effect in it, we say it is in the power of the patient to produce that effect, if it be a fitting agent. (*De Corpore*, II, 10)

The physics of a lawyer, no doubt, for the introduction of aptitude reminds us immediately of Grotius and the Stoa once again. Our patient receives some degree of motion, and this motion is transferred by an agent body, but what our patient does with this motion depends on the patient's fittingness, for depending on whether the patient is a soft or hard body it will absorb or 'reflect' the motion in a certain degree. The patient has power, but it is a power to which it is fitting or apt with respect to its determination by the agent. Only both these aspects of power – efficient and material cause – grant us the plenary sense of power which will be used in general discussions in *De Cive* and *Leviathan*. To speak, with Hobbes, of civil rights as claims over some person or thing is to speak of a power (*potestas*) deriving from a transfer, and thus of the fitness of the recipient assessed by its requisite accidents. Powers as acts of an agent are primary, corresponding to rights in the 'pure' sense; powers as effects in a patient are secondary, derive from transfer, and ground a social order in which fittingness (and so the Stoic language of duties) is constructed. The system of obligations – deprived of its ground in formal and final causes – is but the consequence of the system of rights, divided according to the problematic logic of agent and patient. It is this model, though, which renders explicit the capacity of the human to vary power and increase rights, for whereas the rights of the rational human are deemed relatively stable, power like fame increases as it proceeds,[25] which is to say that as bodies become the patients of the human agent, whether by skill or luck, so according to their aptitude the rights of the human increases. The result: the end of the human is shown to be this extension of right – dominion over the world – an end which flows from the nature of power; not from a final cause.

Initially under the influence of Weigel, who might be regarded as a leading voice for a rationalisation of law, Leibniz was primed to see that the debate over the structural relationship between obligation and right (and so the field of justice) had at its core a methodological dispute: was the logic of the Schoolmen to govern in an explication of the justice, or would Hobbesian materialism be granted the right to amend logic to reflect the new physics? In effect Hobbes takes the square of power and collapses the upper level, into the lower. This has been achieved by (i) regarding formal causes produced by an active mind as unnecessary for explanation, for efficient causes of any *given* event can be determined from that event (and nothing more); and (ii) regarding the moral motion imputed from without by final causes or ends to lack distinct basis, because ultimately 'moral' activity can be traced back to the conative desire of natural individuals in the State of Nature. Consequently, the Scholastic debate between the Thomists, who situate obligation in the correct comprehension of the rational order of formal essences (I see how a given thing should be perfected), and the Scotists and Jesuits, who broadly posit the motives for compliance with the rational order in sovereign command (understood as end), is suspended. It is the role of the interaction of efficient

and material causes in the individual, which together constitute power and natural right, to constitute a civil order contingently so that a system of reason and command is brought
about in the guise of the Leviathan.

2.2 Leibniz on right and obligation

This section builds up to the *Elementa Iuris* and takes issue
with one aspect of Christopher Johns's reading of that text.
The reason that this particular criticism is so prominent is
because the issue must be addressed head on for the following reason. The argument up to now has proceeded using
the intensional nature of activity and the square of power,
in the guise of *Trinitas. Mens*, as the conceptual framework
appropriate to reading Leibniz during the period under consideration. As we shall see, this interpretative framework
continues to aid us in analysing Leibniz's account of the key
categories of law of the seventeenth century – namely right,
obligation and their relationship to justice. This conceptual
structure will be deployed with success as we engage in texts
prior to the *Elementa Juris*, namely the *Specimen Quaestionum
Philosophicarum* and the *Nova Methodus* once again. A key
result of that analysis will be that the legal 'world' as it were
is populated by real relations known as moral qualities, and
that these are duplexes of two opposed terms: right and obligation. However, as we take up a reading of the *Elementa*, I
will highlight Johns's interpretation that right *qua* possibility
is not opposed to obligation (necessity) but is like to it in
quality and indeed implied by it. And this is not an idle claim;
Johns provides a strong argument for it from modal logic. My
approach will be first to contextualise the obligation/right
debate before interpreting Leibniz's earlier texts using the
square of power framework. By establishing how Leibniz can
be said to map obligation and right onto the square of power,
and showing the utility of this reading of the texts, I hope to
argue positively that this reading of the *Elementa Iuris* is also
to be preferred. I then analyse the *Elementa* itself, providing
also a negative argument against Johns, which I hope can be
understood as a point of clarification. Overall I will argue
that obligation and right continue to be in opposition through
the *Elementa* period and into the 1690s revisions of the *Nova*

Methodus, as part of the general argument of this work for Leibniz's legal conceptualism.

Preliminary systematisation in the early period: Specimen Quaestionum Philosophicarum

Gaston Grua argues that as early as 1664 Leibniz has taken up this convergence of the traditions of right and obligation and tried to systematise their relationship. Leibniz begins by orienting his thinking on 'power'. In the Scholastically organised *Specimen Quaestionum Philosophicarum* (SQP), Questions XVI and XVII consider relations and specifically 'moral entities e.g. rights, dominium, and servitude', entities which are *real*. Leibniz claims that the categorisation of relations as real cannot be doubted. The discussion is dense with the treatments of others, including Grotius, Weigel and Giphanius on the status of moral quantities, but following the work of Artosi et al. we might extract the following theses apparently adopted by Leibniz:

(a) Relations are duplex: they have a reason and a foundation. The foundation of a relation is either substantial, in which case it inheres immediately, or it is qualitative. The reason of a relation is that through which it is induced or becomes actual (Q.XVII, 1).

(b) Moral entities such as rights are relations and as such are real in the technical sense that they can exist and belong to a specific state. Given Scotist and Jesuit theses in this regard, the positing of a kingdom of morality or will is not particularly unusual (QXVI, 4).

(c) Relations, however, are weak (*debile*) entities, but they are not nothing at all (QXVI, 5).

(d) Such relations are incorporeal states of affairs, as the Stoa argued,[26] and as such are perceived by reason, not the senses.

(e) Right is anterior to action, for one must have the right to do before one does, and this is said 'in a similar way to a *potentia*, for which reason it is also called a *potestas*' (QXVI, 5).

If we are to approach the *Nova Methodus* and *Elementa* treatments of right correctly, I claim that we must appreciate

the significance of this text, for it contains the core structure underpinning Leibniz's subsequent account of the
right–obligation relationship. I propose to elaborate on these
theses, drawing out aspects relevant to the legal arguments
of the *Elementa*.

The duplex nature of moral qualities (thesis a)
At the heart of the SQP's treatment of relations such as moral
qualities is the Scholastic notion that relations are duplex
– that they enfold two terms. I think that there is a strong
argument that this adoption by Leibniz can be read consistently with the later *Nova Methodus*, where, as we have seen,
an impression of a mind towards good action is described
as duplex: intellect and will.[27] In the later text the twofold
nature in question is the combination of suppositive activity
of mind and the acquired facility to act, or habit. On its face
the *Nova Methodus* conception seems to conflict with that of
the SQP, because the latter divides relations into those with
a substantial foundation (*quod inest subjecto*) and those which
are qualities, as opposed to combinations of intellect and
will. This conflict is only apparent, however, for the division
simply replicates the Aristotelean argument concerning the
pure act. If a substantial relation can be actualised without
determination, then we have a pure or inherent relation, such
as the reflexivity of the mind we explored earlier. But where
the activity of the finite substance is determined, the resultant effect – a quality – is not only due to the substance but to
some other thing. Furthermore, the *reason* for the actuality of
an induced quality is its principle, that is, the *for what* of the
actualisation. In this combination of substantial activity and
movement towards a principle leading to actualisation, the
one effect or moral quality combines intellection and volition,
as the *Nova Methodus* makes explicit.

What is to be noticed here is that Leibniz has already
inherited a quadripartite structure of inherent and relative
moral qualities which operates vertically and horizontally
as follows: (i) vertical because we have a division of 'higher'
reasons for a particular quality into substantial activity and
principle or end (actuality); and (ii) horizontal because the
particular relation either is entirely explained by the substantial foundation (inherent) or substantial activity is

determined by other particulars, themselves moved towards a principle. We therefore have a fourfold structure which informs Leibniz's encounter with the Grotian and Hobbesian account of faculties, powers and obligations.

Moral entities: the moral spatium *(theses (b–d))*
Moral entities are weak entities, and are constituted not as discrete, complete beings, but within a kind of moral 'field of presence', to use Foucault's archaeological term.[28] Perhaps the single most intriguing comment[29] in Leibniz's discussion of moral entities is 'reply 4':

> And the Illustrious Weigel ... my preceptor and revered patron, established three highest genera of entities: natural, moral, and notional. And in each of them he looks again for quantity or estimation, quality and action. He thus reduces *jura* to moral qualities, and just as space is the substrate of natural action or motion, so the state is in a way a moral space, in which something like a moral motion is effected.[30]

My suggestion *pace* Artosi et al. is that 'jura' should be translated here as laws rather than rights, for this would accord with the sense of Weigel's philosophy of moral entities. This said, Weigel's conception of obligations marries aspects of law and right as Wolfgang Röd has shown,[31] for Weigel deploys the term 'obligation' in two senses, both critical to Leibniz. One is mathematical: society can be accounted for by analogy with the laws or 'obligations' that exist between numbers. An illustration: the integers 1,2,3 ... are particular, discrete numbers in an order between themselves, but one can also find further orders, for example with their powers 1,4,9 ... The powers offer a substrate which both evaluates the integers and discloses a rule for the generation of those integers (roots). In the social sphere the analogous structure, according to Weigel, is the order of relations between particular individuals and the substrate of social or state relations. The second sense of obligation, which as Röd states[32] forms a bridge between the mathematical and social realms, is referred to the analogous physical obligations he finds in 'cohesiveness, adhesion or affinity between material parts', which are accounted *tendencies* explicable by teleological means. It should be noted though that Weigel is careful to retain a distinction between the value-free realms of mathematics and physics, which do have some influence on natural law, and the value-laden realm of society, where that value is referred to a principal, or *'Vorsteher des gemeinen Wesens'*.[33]

In light of Röd's interpretation, I claim that we should regard the *jura* to which Leibniz refers as those obligations in the second sense, that is, tendencies to moral motion explained by the end. Yet whereas Weigel, on Röd's account, points to the superior 'Vorsteher' as the relevant end, Leibniz is keen to place the emphasis on an incorporeal state space as the root of all value-laden obligations. This suggests a primary moral *spatium* of the end which has as its derivative particularities the tendencies of certain things to act, tendencies which are mutually determinative because of the finitude of the particulars. From this it is seen why the sense of 'jura' is difficult to translate: it can be understood as 'laws' because a certain obligatoriness derives from an end: the state space as superior; but when viewed in each particular case as a tendency referred either to nature, society or God as end, as part of a real space of mutually determining tendencies, one could also regard the 'jura' as the respective rights of the particulars. On this reading, rights are relations, they are moral qualities, and thus are duplex: they speak to a relation between a rational substance and the obligations determined by a principle.

Potentia *as anterior principle, that is,* potestas *(thesis e)*
The previous conclusion suggests a way of approaching the apparent equivocation Leibniz posits between *potentia* and *potestas*. The relevant text is: '... action is subsequent; right [*ius*] is anterior and in a way similar to *potentia,* for which reason it is also called *potestas*.' Artosi et al. translate the last thesis's *potentia* as faculty, the *potestas* as power, and this is perhaps understandable given the categories deployed by Giphanius, whose contrary claim that right proceeds from habituated action (and so faculty) Leibniz explicitly denies.[34] However, we have seen that Grotius opposes *potentia* to *facultas*, while Hobbes has power underpinning both facultative and transferred right. Furthermore, Grua claims that the text

itself wishes expressly to equate *potentia* and the moral category *potestas*; it would seem strange if Leibniz had proposed to equate faculty and power, but not then used the readily available term for the former to go against the teachings of Grotius and others. Further, if faculty is intended, and if it is understood in the sense of inherent potentiality (intellect or will), such an equivocation would sit uneasily with Leibniz's own distinction of relational foundations, that is, between inherent substantial relations and qualitative relations. Finally, in the *Nova Methodus* Leibniz defines *facultas* as a right over things (property), while defining *potestas* as the power to force an action – quite separate senses.[35] What is going on here?

I suspect that in the apparent equivocation of *potentia* and *potestas* we are seeing a consequence of the relational interpretation of *jura* discussed above. We have two nodes of the relation to consider. On the one hand we have the moral space constituted by the end. Where the end is the superior, we have the Ciceronian sense of *potestas* as the capacity of the superior to issue commands; where the end is the self, we have the self-preserving sense that Hobbes calls natural right and which Grotius calls *facultas*, because the act perfects the agent. It could be argued that Leibniz is using *potestas* here as a catchall for *potestas* and *facultas* in the sense just discussed, but when we consider *potentia* the weight of interpretation could be said to fall on the side of regarding only the 'superior' or 'Vorsteher' sense as being considered. To see this, note that Leibniz focuses at this point on moral actions 'issuing from habit'. These habituations, as we have seen, amount to organisations of the potencies of lower real entities into an actually existing human, potencies which aid the human in perfecting its work, but which bear with themselves their own tendencies *per* Weigel. Accordingly, habit is distinguished from the inherent activity of the substance here, and only action issuing from habit is referred to as *potentia*. The result is a bipolar relation: the *potentia* issuing from acquired habit is a potency to act by reason of the tendencies elicited from all real components by a *potestas*. With Weigel we can suspect that the levels of the real are subjected to different ends – natural, notional, moral – and only the moral entities are moved to a *potestas* in the moral and legal sense. Yet to the extent that they are, we can speak of right as a claim set in motion by a *potentia* elicited by a *potestas*, leading us to conclude that, as with *jura*, power is duplex in the moral sphere: a *potentia–potestas* so to speak, and to ascribe *potentia* to an existing thing is not to speak of that thing having a power to do *simpliciter*, but always simultaneously to refer to some *potestas* which is the very condition of that *potentia*.

Preliminary systematisation in the early period: the Nova Methodus *view*

As I have hinted at above, the *Nova Methodus* offers a clarification of Leibniz's thinking leading into the Mainz period, and combines the treatment of right as power with obligation. Given this fuller treatment, I propose to set out the analysis in full, taking it as Leibniz's intended systemisation of the received wisdom.

The central statement appears as paragraph §14a of the 1667 edition, the 'a' apparently having been inserted because of a rushed miscounting of previous paragraphs rather than an addition to a middle period draft. The paragraph reads:

> *The Morality* however, or Justice or Injustice of the act of a person originates from the quality of the person in view of the order of action, arising from preceding actions,[36] and is called: *Moral quality*. Since, however, the Real quality in the order of action is duplex – power of acting [*potentia agendi*] and necessity of acting – this moral power [*potentia*] is called *Right* and moral necessity is called *Obligation*.[37]

Given our consideration of SQP's treatment of moral relations, this paragraph offers both clarification and innovation. A real quality is a relation and so duplex, and a subset of these relations are the moral qualities. The moral qualities originate in the person, deriving from the self-relation that maps back to the SQP notion of an inherent or substantial reason for the quality. These moral qualities, being duplex, are also determined by the power and necessity of acting, which on the face of the text refers to an external or objective pole which renders a merely moral quality a just one. This text though must be read in light of the *Nova Methodus'* treatment of habituation, for it can be seen that Leibniz does not deal with whether right and obligation are subjective or objective; he seems to be considering both cases.

Essentially what Leibniz is doing is re-partitioning inherent and habitual relations, because he wishes to justify the importance of learning the law as an internalisation and remembrance of inherent relations that produces virtue. Christopher Johns puts it well when he writes: 'For Leibniz, it means that the morality of any action is grounded not in some external law, but in the freedom of rational substances.'[38] We can see with Johns, following Brian Tierney,[39] that Leibniz takes up the subjective sense of right as a self-determined morality – a giving-law-to-self – and makes this what Hegel would describe as the 'ungrounded ground' of moral action. To use the square of power as a guide, we may posit moral quality as that relation in which the activity of mind posits rational acts, rational acts which are elicited by the self-as-end to volition. Teaching the law presents reasons to the mind, aiding its return to self. This 'closing of the circle', so redolent of the *actus purus essendi* – the very movement of self-relation – is the moral quality in question. Yet we should be careful not to impute to Leibniz an absolutely free ground of moral quality. First, the being and knowing of every substance is intensionally grounded in God; the acting of substance is pretensionally oriented to the self as image of God. Leibniz accepts the Hobbesian characterisation of subjective right as free on condition that that freedom is equivalent in a strong logical sense to God's freedom, differing only in the ability to achieve the fruits of that freedom. It is very much a case of that tradition of thought, perhaps exemplified by Husserl and critiqued by Gilles Châtelet and Deleuze, that the subject is not a single point of view, but rather always shares within it a transcendental perspective or 'Total Space' which allows it to unify the world which it perceives.[40]

It must be emphasised that Leibnizian subjective right is hardly simple or absolute, but rather is remembered constructively through the process of assuefaction. It is more correct to say that subjective right is acquired through training in the *Urdoxa* of jurisprudence, and forms part of self-actualisation and acts as the basis for a gradation of moral quality. In this Leibniz is closer to Aristotle's notion of the self as work (*ergon*) and end (*telos*), and the view is reflected in Christian Wolff's doctrine that the inherent law of nature is that we seek our self-perfection. What we do not have is either a radically free conatus to motion, or a determinate conatus to motion which, however, is at its core infinitely productive; the Leibnizian inherent activity demands a complicated process of training premised on the assumption that what is being learned inheres in the Godhead, and so denying the critical truth that subjective rights are only 'common sense' trained into students so that they may be socialised in a very specific, constructed social space.

Be this as it may, the effect of §14a is to erode the sharp SQP distinction between inherent and qualitative relations by (a) internalising habituation as a training of the legal subject; (b) permitting the legal categories of right and obligation to range over all moral qualities, thereby also internalising the law as objective 'state space'. In the two following paragraphs Leibniz will address both subjective and objective perspectives. The discussion of the subject of moral quality appears as an uninteresting juridical statement about persons and things and the kinds of rights and obligations (such as services) that can be predicated of them. It is not without theoretical interest, however. The 1667 draft C appears to account for the acquisition and transmission of rights according to the logic of accidents (habituation). The idea is that the subject of moral qualities may be modified by the acquisition of a right to a service, and that on death this right may transfer to the successors (the same reasoning being applicable to obligations). Leibniz here is setting up the left-hand side of the square with the subject as primary activity, and its particular rights being determined, in the examples, by contingent acts of obligation with respect to some other person. Two examples given are illustrative:

(a) In draft C Leibniz argues that where a horse, gifted a military medal, is sold to another, the purchaser takes the horse and the medal follows the horse. The draft C account essentially argues that *things* are capable of habituation (acquisition) of right, presumably because a horse is a substance and the categorical logic suggests such a thesis. In the middle period draft D Leibniz abandons this view: if the horse has a right to the medal it is a right derivative of its owner: the right or obligation of a thing can be 'reduced' to persons.

(b) Tellingly Leibniz also deals with the maximal subjective case of God, following the *actus purus* logic: God is of the highest right but not of any true obligation – a simple statement that God acts without determination, or specifically coercion, that could be called obligation. The square collapses into a self-reflective structure of divine subject and infinitely many rights oriented towards self as highest End.

If §15 provides some further indications on the theoretical framework Leibniz deploys with respect to the subjects of right and obligation, §§16–17 tackle the objects of right and obligation in a way that reveals Leibniz's thinking about Grotian and Hobbesian categories. Here we find a treatment of faculty and *potestas*, which may be understood according to the following structure:

(a) Right
    (i)   over my body:= freedom;
    (ii)   over things:= *facultas*;
    (iii) over persons:= *potestas* (the right to coercion).
(b) Obligation
    (iv) binding the person to do or not do something:= absolute obligation;
    (v)   not to interfere with another's freedom, things or *potestas*:= private law of obligations (*magis privativae*);
    (vi) not to obstruct the *potestas* of another over me:= positive obligation.

Observe how Leibniz at this stage in his thinking has reduced the scope of the Grotian moral category of *facultas* and likewise reconfigured *potestas*, a moral quality per se identified by Grotius and Pufendorf, as an aspect of right (and so of *potentia*). This decision has several consequences:

(a) Following Hobbes, Leibniz begins with the freedom that flows from (natural) right, and defines obligation either as a corresponding 'natural' aspect of a freedom or faculty, or as the coercion of my freedom through the *potestas* of another (*Nova Methodus* §17).

(b) The rearrangement calls into question Grua's claim that *potestas* and *potentia* are always equivalent for Leibniz, for it seems here that he appears to make *potestas* a special case of the latter. Yet once the duplex nature of the real relation is accounted for, we see that the duplex *potentia–potestas* here finds its home in the framework as that specific relation between persons such that person *A* has the right to coerce or obligate person *B*.

(c) The Grotian priority of faculty over *potentia* has been inverted. *Potentia* in its moral frame is now right enfolded with obligation, while faculty is not even perfected right insofar as that relates to a person's substantial being; rather it only relates to property: namely *dominium*, usufruct and servitude.

(d) Obligation does not imply right, but nor does right logically imply obligation, which is to say that the one is not a derivative of the other alone. Rather, obligation is understood as opposed to right, and both are implied by the duplex nature of moral qualities.

This latter point takes us back to the precise relationship between obligation and right in the *Nova Methodus*. As with Hobbes, obligation is seen as a determination of freedom, but the categorical framework is very much more expressive of the Aristotelean tradition:

> §20. The causes of right in one person are a kind of loss of right in another; that is, the second person has an obligation to the first. Conversely, acquiring an obligation from another is the cause of a recuperation of right i.e. liberation.

Once we understand the duplex nature of moral qualities, we are able to allocate right and obligation according to the Stagirite's logic. It is interesting that Christopher Johns picks up on this language, even finding confirmation for its meaning as late as 1696, but does not pick up on the apparent contradiction with his subsequent interpretation of the modes of right in the *Elementa*. I will deal with that in the next section, but I propose here to set out the results of our interpretation. Given both the mechanistic account of Hobbes, the Aristotelean heritage concerning power and our own reading of Leibniz, our philosopher's meaning at this pre-*Elementa* stage in his thinking appears to be quite clearly grounded in the square of power structure as follows:

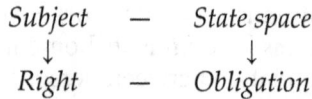

$$\begin{array}{ccc} Subject & - & State\ space \\ \downarrow & & \downarrow \\ Right & - & Obligation \end{array}$$

In the case of God only the left-hand side is relevant; in the case of a rational substance the subject is also, if you will, the state space for what will become the body, where the lower real entities are obligated to motion towards the self as end. Each rational substance then is first also a self-obligating substance, a whole square if you will, and if we speak of a person's right as deriving from 'their' *potentia*, this attribution of power is only correct on the understanding that the power implies a *potestas* of the self as end, and that the right is always duplex. One might observe that if obligation derives from the subject and its state space, why isn't obligation already at least implicit in them? Leibniz will come to see this, and make appropriate refinements of the square. As the square stands though, this is nothing other than a juridical refinement of the idea of the real and creatable: that the potency of marble is a potency with respect to the mason. Now each rational substance exists together with others, and so, as with physical bodies, encounters are explained according to the mutual coercion of rights within a total space named the state. Appreciate though that this space, unlike the hard physico-intellectual world of Spinoza, is strictly moral and that the entities in question are weak relations, and that the economy of right and obligation cannot be accounted for by a deterministic reckoning. The motors of all the tendencies or *potentiae* that support the moral structure are not the infinitesimal forces of efficient causes, but rather the inclinations to moral motion deriving from ends which the subject is taught to recognise by the *Nova Methodus*.

The square of power and the three degrees of right

From the square it is easy to derive Leibniz's account at §§73ff. of the 'three degrees of right': strict right; equity; piety, which have been discussed at length by Christopher Johns, Riley and others. *Strict right* means to harm no one in order not to give the right of war, and 'to this belongs commutative justice, and the right which Grotius calls faculty'. Having established that *facultas* amounts to perfected power or inherent relation, we can say that the 1667 view is that strict right is grounded in the core (left-hand) relation between substantial activity as primary force and its derivative actions, which actions in finite creatures are determined by a constant struggle with nature. Here Leibniz is initially prepared to define the right over unthinking things as the successful outcome of this struggle, where the human is not destroyed in the act of exerting *dominium*, echoing somewhat the Hobbesian State of Nature. In the middle period draft D, however, Leibniz moves away from a purely subjectivist account of natural right, best seen if we compare the amendment:

> [Draft C] §73 . . . If therefore one harms another, either in his person or his things, this gives him the right in things, that is, the right of war.

> [Draft D] §73 . . . If therefore one harms another, either in his person or his things, this gives him the right *not only to defend himself, but to be offended by the aggression, in order to halt the harm.*

This change marks a significant reintroduction of objectivity into the theory of right, just where Hobbes and Grotius have isolated subjective right. To see this, note the language of offence and consider why Leibniz should consider this an improvement on the language of war and a factor additional to self-defence. You will remember the Scholastic theory of the real continuum, taken up readily by Leibniz, in which the qualitative distance between two points is explained by a mutual repugnance to occupying the same locus simultaneously. This moralising space requires governance by a sovereign capable of exacting a tendency to compliance in infinitely many cases. The requisite candidate for this role is God, and the product of his moralisation of all formal points is called Nature. By inserting a notion of 'offence' Leibniz in effect inflects the right to self-defence with an additional moral repugnancy that implies the *potestas* of an infinite state (the *Civitas Dei*). Yet by referring what was subjective right to infinite objective power, has Leibniz reduced strict right to what he will call piety which is referred to the will of a superior God? I would say not, for in this instance of offence against violence to self, the mathematical form of justice applicable to strict right – commutative justice – remains distinct. As Johns notes, the essence of commutative justice is that it applies equally to all, though we might more correctly say that commutative justice requires that there be equality of differences between people. This equality is what we have here: each subject of right, person and thing, is capable of equal offence *with respect to* the violence of another. The subjectivity of this degree of right is retained, provided that we accept that the condition precedent of being a member of the moral space is repugnance. There can be no right, for Leibniz, without at least the constitution of a moral space by a superior. This form of right is then merely constitutive of the moral order *qua* moral, much as the imposition of unity is the basis for the sequence of integers according to the Neoplatonist doctrine.

Equity or equality concerns the 'ratio or proportion between two or more [rights claims],[41] and consists in harmony or congruence'. According to the Aristotelean tradition as explicated by Keyt and recently Ambrosi, this amounts to saying that equity holds where the ratio of A to B (that is A:B or A/B) is as the ratio of C to D (that is C:D or C/D). A proportion is just a ratio of ratios: A:B :: C:D, which can be written $\frac{A}{B} = \frac{C}{D}$, and this geometric device can also be found contemporaneously in Spinoza.[42] Notice that the structure of the square of power maps perfectly well onto the algebraic account, which is hardly surprising since they have the same source. Notice that (i) the upper vertices of the square are universals or wholes, while the lower vertices account for particulars, or parts of the wholes, and (ii) we are dealing with subjects of right, that is, active substances, their acts and the moral tendency of those acts. We are thus invited to consider a scheme in which the ratio of rights due to one legal subject is compared to the ratio of rights to another, or:

$$\frac{Subject\ A}{Right} = \frac{Subject\ B}{Right}$$

provided always that the sign of equality is a norm, and that what is owed in equity is the difference between the congruent norm and the actual rights A and B have respectively. Variation, through compact, is accounted for by observing that Subject B and her right stand in contradiction and contrariety respectively to the right of A, and as such behave much as primary and derivative determinations of A's acts by what will become a kind of juridical force – coercions as obligations. Leibniz's assumption here[43] is that an equitable distribution of rights is bound to occur provided each subject is aware of all facts when making a compact; inequity is limited to cases of deception and wickedness, for here the result is disproportion in the distribution of rights. Hence Leibniz underlines the precept that each is to be given what is due, but this again is just a consequence of the weakness of moral relations and the structure of the square of power in which 'owingness' is a disproportion or variation from the normal.

The third degree of right according to draft C of the *Nova Methodus* is the will of the superior, an all too Pufendorfian formulation that is replaced in draft D by 'the general Good which is rendered by the guardianship of God',[44] a formulation which better reflects the following discussion of the draft C text. Here the full content of the square of power is brought to bear, for the structure of strict right (the self-determining left side of the square) and equity (the relationship between strict rights in an order of mutually determining moral proportion), are shown to be instances of a world divided into infinite and finite subjects of right. The result is that each finite subject of right is to be considered over against the right-hand side of the square, that is as determined 'by nature' as in God, whose will is in part either:

(a) 'natural, to which piety is owed . . .', and which accords to the particular obligations or moral tendencies we encounter in the world;
(b) 'or lawful, which belongs to divine positive right' and which commands move directly from the superior or highest End.

Leibniz clarifies that nature in the sense used here is not necessarily a matter of physical bonds, but is rather a bonding aided by God. This reminds us that that *real* qualities are not only duplexes of *potentia–potestas*, but are part of a general hierarchy of the real in which creation is constituted from substantial forms which require other forms to be actualised. The pious order of the republic, or *Civitas Dei* as it will become in the middle period, is differentiated from the world of strict right understood simply, because the latter merely has as its condition a generalised tendency to moral offence when faced with violence. The republic on the other hand is not a flat equality of repugnance, but an ordered functional hierarchy of the real towards which pious rational substances *ought* to move.

Observe then that after a manner of speaking two spaces are in play between which moral agents carry out their activity of compacts and collegial endeavour: the infinite space of moral agents grounded on strict right, and the 'final' or 'total' space of the state towards which moral agents move and which is ordered according to the hierarchy of the real. From the perspective of practical action it is this volitional movement from the possible (or contingent) to what is realised as ordered, which now becomes the focus of Leibniz's endeavours. Should it surprise us then that we recover once again *Trinitas. Mens*, with its tripartite structure of activity, formal mind and real world, now considered from the juridical perspective. To function in its world as a moral agent we might say three things are required: (i) a supposit or intensional activity; (ii) the formal manifold of infinite intellect, which the creature seeks to comprehend (imagine) as an order of subjective rights; (iii) a totalised state space, into which the intensional activity of the creature endeavours to 'glue together' its pious image of justice, and which as it is constructed provides a canvas for that activity.

To my mind then, the conceptual framework of intensions and particulars, of rights opposed to obligations according to the square of power and its Trinitarian manifestation, provide a most useful way of reading Leibniz's pre-*Elementa* attempts at systematisation of natural right. I also hold the stronger view that these conceptual objects are in fact at work behind the scenes of Leibniz's thought, being almost explicit at times and permitting engagement with others, such as Hobbes, Grotius and Weigel, who deploy versions of the same ultimately Aristotelean ideational structure. Yet, now, as we read the *Elementa*, we must address what I regard as an only apparent structural reorientation which appears to make right a particular case of obligation. Let us see why this interpretation could have been advanced, and why I feel it should be approached very carefully.

3. Conclusion

As Leibniz arrives at Mainz to begin his work rationalising jurisprudence, his work circles around key questions raised by natural rights theorists for any natural law framework. Leibniz seeks to reconcile the theories of Grotius and Hobbes with those of the Schools, and perhaps initially this appears a tractable research programme just because the arguments of the natural rights theorists continue to reflect the square of power, and so the Aristotelean methodology built upon by the Scholastic and indeed Reformed theologians. In particular, Leibniz observes that 'ius' can be severally mapped onto the perfected *facultas* of substantial activity and the imperfect *qualitates* that are acquired by the substance in the world. He can therefore see that a route to synthesis is to unite in the individual a natural law grounded in rational activity, and so the *ens commune*, and a natural right that modally combines instances of rational action and determination of that action by a justified external power. In other words, Leibniz moves towards a position, as with his account of volition, in which rational act is combined with the potency of the real to elicit spontaneous choice. The risk, however, is that an individual becomes determined by brute power, by either historical contingency or the chain of physical causes. Notably, in initially following Grotius and Hobbes in regarding obligation as externally imposed and a restraint on liberty, Leibniz risks undermining a key discovery of his own legal theory: that juridical *Institutiones* have normative force because they reflect something internal to Mind. The kinds of obligations Leibniz is interested in ought not to be external impositions but should flow from the individual's own reflection even as they are common to all in the kingdom of ends. I understand Leibniz's development of the Weigelian state space as an initial attempt to win conceptual coherence through aligning internal and external obligations. Yet as we shall see, Leibniz becomes aware that the link and similitude between the subjectively determined obligations of natural law (or indeed by any theoretical social contract) and the obligations imposed by a given state is tenuous at best – a point he will make to no less than Hobbes.[45]

The Leibniz of the Mainz period thus faces a number of apparent contradictions: (a) between the *Institutiones* of rational Mind and the contingency of actual, imposed obligations; (b) between the spontaneity of individual equity and piety and the power of any state, spiritual or temporal; (c) between a conception of the individual as internally determined by its own eternal rational laws and a conception which grounds natural right in the temporal appropriation of nature's external power. Concerns about the theory of will and its relation to *potentia* are translated into the juridical domain as a conflict between the private realm of rational jurisprudence and the public sphere of power, right and contingency. By deploying the square of power to interpret Leibniz's response to these challenges, we see how Leibniz both perceives the possibility of reconciliation but also what, theoretically, is at stake as he manipulates his framework of activity, power and end to solve legal-theoretic problems. The drafts of the *Elementa Iuris* constitute a sustained attempt to achieve reconciliation in a manner that preserves both reason and, let us be clear, piety as Leibniz comes to conceive it. Faced with the contradictions highlighted above, and so an apparently irresolvable struggle in theory and in practice between private and public, Leibniz pursues an aleatory route to a reconception of the divide which is of considerable significance in the history of power.

Notes

1. A:VI, i, 465.
2. Thomas Williams, 'How Scotus Separates Morality from Happiness' (1995) 65 *American Catholic Philosophical Quarterly*, 425–45.
3. Hannes Möhle, 'Scotus's Theory of Natural Law' in Thomas Williams (ed.), *The Cambridge Companion to Duns Scotus* (Cambridge: Cambridge University Press, 2003) pp.312–31.
4. *Ordinatio* III, 27, q.un, in which Duns Scotus considers the

relationship between the theological virtues and command: 'in what way is a rational creature obligated to love God above all else?'

5. Terence H. Irwin, 'Obligation, Rightness, and Natural Law: Suárez and Some Critics' in Daniel Schwartz (ed.), *Interpreting Suárez: Critical Essays* (Cambridge: Cambridge University Press, 2012) pp.142–62.
6. Cf. John Finnis, *Natural Law and Natural Rights* (Oxford: Oxford University Press, 1980). Thomas Pink, 'Reason and Obligation in Suárez' in Benjamin Hill and Henrik Lagerlund (eds), *The Philosophy of Francisco Suárez* (Oxford: Oxford University Press, 2012).
7. Gaston Grua, *Jurisprudence universelle et théodicée selon Leibniz* (Paris: PUF, 1953) p.223.
8. *De Legibus,* ii.6.22, quoted by Irwin, 'Obligation, Rightness, and Natural Law', p.151.
9. Irwin, 'Obligation, Rightness, and Natural Law', p.150.
10. *De Legibus* ii.6.13, quoted by Irwin, 'Obligation, Rightness, and Natural Law', p.152.
11. *De Legibus,* ii.9.4, in Pink, 'Reason and Obligation in Suárez', p.154.
12. ST II-I, q.43, a3.
13. I will avoid translating *'debitum'* as 'duty' because this imports a great deal of Stoic and Kantian baggage.
14. *De Legibus* II, 6, 22.
15. *De Legibus* I, 2, 5, quoted by Grua, *Jurisprudence universelle,* p.222.
16. *De Legibus* I, 2, 6.
17. Christoph A. Stumpf, *The Grotian Theology of International Law* (Berlin: De Gruyter, 2006), pp.19–20.
18. Grua, *Jurisprudence universelle,* p.223; Stumpf, *Grotian Theology,* p.20.
19. Echoing Domingo de Soto's treatment, discussed above.
20. See generally David Gauthier, *The Logic of Leviathan* (Oxford: Clarendon Press, 1969); Gregory Kavka, *Hobbesian Moral and Political Theory* (Princeton: Princeton University Press, 1986); Jean Hampton, *Hobbes and the Social Contract Tradition* (Cambridge: Cambridge University Press, 1986). Also, Howard Warrender, *The Political Philosophy of Hobbes, His Theory of Obligation* (Oxford: Clarendon Press, 1957).
21. Eleanor Curran, 'Hobbes' Theory of Rights – A Modern Interest Theory' (2002) 6(1) *Journal of Ethics* 63–86.
22. Thomas Hobbes, C.B. Macpherson (ed.) *Leviathan* (London: Penguin Books, 1968), II, xiv, p.189.

23. Hobbes, *Leviathan*, I, x.
24. Thomas Hobbes, Howard Warrender (ed.) *De Cive* (Oxford: Clarendon Press, 1984) VI, xvii, where Hobbes defines *potentia* as natural and original, and distinguishes this from (moral) *potestas* which arises in the civil state.
25. Hobbes, *Leviathan*, I, x.
26. Émile Bréhier, *La théorie des incorporels dans l'ancien stoïcisme*, 9th edn (Paris: Vrin, 1997).
27. See Chapter 4.
28. Michel Foucault, *The Archaeology of Knowledge* (Bristol: Tavistock Publications, 1972) p.57.
29. Highlighted by Christopher Johns, *The Science of Right in Leibniz's Moral and Political Philosophy* (London: Bloomsbury, 2013) p.139.
30. A:VI, i, 94.
31. Wolfgang Röd, 'Erhard Weigels Metaphysik der Gesellschaft und des Staates' (1971) 3(1) *Studia Leibnitiana* 5–28.
32. Ibid. pp.10–11.
33. Roughly, the principal or head of the common being.
34. Alberto Artosi, Bernardo Pieri and Giovanni Sartor (eds), *Leibniz: Logico-Philosophical Puzzles in the Law* (Dordrecht: Springer, 2013) p.37.
35. A VI, i, 304, §16.
36. Struck through in the middle period draft D.
37. A VI, i, 301. 'Moralitas autem, seu Justitia, vel Injustitia actionis oritur, ex qualitate personae agentis in ordine ad actionem, ex actionibus praecedentibus ortâ, quae dicitur: Qualitas moralis. Ut autem Qualitas realis in ordine ad actionem duplex est: Potentia agenda, et necessitas agenda: ita potentia moralis dicitur Jus,necessitas moralis dicitur Obligatio.'
38. Johns, *Science of Right*, p.139.
39. Brian Tierney, *The Idea of Natural Rights* (Grand Rapids, MI: Emory University, 1997) p.51.
40. See Gilles Châtelet, *Sur une petite phrase de Riemann* (1979) *Analytiques* 3.
41. Inserted by Johns, *Science of Right*, p.16.
42. Stephen Connelly, *Spinoza, Right and Absolute Freedom* (Abingdon: Routledge, Birkbeck Law Press, 2015) pp.103–4.
43. A:VI, i, 344.
44. Ibid.
45. L:105–6.

Eight

Power and Obligation in the Elementa Iuris Naturalis: *The State Space*

1. Introduction

1.1 Towards the Leibnizian state space

The drafts of the *Elementa Iuris Naturalis* have been the subject of detailed study by several authors, both from the legal and the logical angles. Christopher Johns in particular has provided an almost line by line account of its various exploratory definitions and amendments. Gábor Gángó notes[1] that there is a general academic consensus that it was during the Mainz period that Leibniz made a decisive breakthrough in his ethical thought and paved the way for his definition of justice as the 'charity of the wise' (a concept which has been extensively explored by others, and on whose work I rely).[2] These authors rightly focus on the so-called 'three degrees of right', which Leibniz derives, probably via Hobbes as much as the Schools, from Aristotle, and how these are reinterpreted in various creative ways. Certain of these accounts also consider Leibniz's deployment of modal and deontic logic, and there is common agreement that usefulness, if not utility proper, is a feature of Leibniz's thinking already in *De Conditionibus*.

What though of *power*? The purpose of this final chapter is to use our understanding of the relationship between power, real entities, substantial activity and the intellect to reread the *Elementa Iuris Naturalis* from the perspective of power. Our central hypothesis is this: that Leibniz, perhaps inspired by Weigel, uses his *iuris modalia* to construct a notion of a 'state space' that plays the role of primary power (*dunamis*), a role which determines the temporal activity of a character Leibniz constructs: the Good Man. The thus determined practical actions of the Good Man are named *obligation* and *right*.

To do this the chapter proceeds as follows: having set out Leibniz's development of the terms obligation and right in his drafts of the *Elementa*, I situate his linking of these to necessity and possibility in the debates of period concerning predestination. I argue that we can only fully understand obligation and right in light of the distinction between two kinds of necessity well known to Leibniz's contemporaries. This reading is allied to Rescher's account[3] of Leibnizian justice as reality maximising which already takes form in the *Elementa* as the acts of the 'Good Man.' I then locate this distinction within the wider framework of the *Iuris Modalia* to show that the type of necessity in which Leibniz is interested is the necessity that links condition and consequence, and that he envisages a Weigelian inspired 'state *spatium*' of these consequential relationships. This space of consequences is created according to certain rules prescribed by a legislator (God, prince etc.), and so defines what is morally necessary/ prohibited, permissible in the space, with multiple spaces being nested in each other. On the one hand the Good Man is prohibited from willing any consequential relationship that is morally repugnant in that space, that is, impossibly reality maximising; on the other, that the Good Man ought to do what is necessarily reality maximising in that space. This permits a like treatment of right in relation to possibility and contingency, but we note that Leibniz gathers these two modal terms under the name of *potentia* and in so doing, we claim, takes a decisive step on the road from Duns Scotus to Hegel in identifying contingency as a ground of human power.

1.2 The context and drafts of the *Elementa*

The drafts of the *Elementa Iuris Naturalis* were drawn up and reworked in two distinct periods. The first period (1669–72) is very much linked to Leibniz's time at Mainz, where numerous letters show how Leibniz was employed by von Schönborn to work closely with court jurist and counsellor Hermann Andreas Lasser on a rationalisation of the law: the *Ratio Corporis Iuris Reconncinandi*.[4] Lasser was very much of von Schönborn's camp,[5] and so as with the *Nova Methodus* we might well expect an expression of the latter's policies of religious and political reconciliation. The drafts thus follow the *Nova Methodus* and a presumed revised edition of the *De Conditionibus* under the title '*Specimina Iuris*'.[6]

We are led to understand that Lasser divided the workload with Leibniz, and while the rational organisation of the current civil law as the *Ratio Corporis Iuris Reconncinandi* was very much a product of Lasser, Leibniz chose to undertake the foundational work on the elements of natural law and of civil law. Leibniz's initial enthusiasm, however, led to an underestimation of the task's difficulties, and it is for this reason that we are left with partial manuscripts which the Akademie editors have collected into six drafts of the *Elementa Iuris Naturalis*. It is worth emphasising this point, to which we will return: that the *Elementa* only deals with natural law; it does not cover the promised foundations of positive civil law, and only implicitly deals with the divine law (in the sense that divine command institutes the natural law via creation of this world).

It is worth noting that the *Elementa* was prepared in the wake of Leibniz's applied political advocacy. Gabor Gángó argues[7] that it was in his argumentation in favour of his employer's choice for succession to the Polish crown (the *Specimen Polonorum*) that critical work was done to develop Leibniz's sense of right and justice. Gángó notes, however, that his interpretation is contradicted quite strongly by Hubertus Busche[8] and recently Gerd van den Heuvel,[9] which latter see in these Mainz-period political texts little of value theoretically. While I would agree with Gángó that the arguments of the *Specimen Polonorum* do echo Leibniz's theoretical architecture, on issues such as the applicability of his third degree of right (*honestas/pietas*) Leibniz appears to deviate from his own doctrine – discrepancies in fairness Gángó highlights. In becomes a question of interpretation whether the deviations affirm Leibniz's ethical development or indicate that his existing theoretical structures are being boot-strapped onto a political problem. For the purposes of what follows I assume, with the majority, that these political texts are largely ad hoc aand evidentially unreliable for our investigation of *potentia*.[10]

The second period in the life of the *Elementa*, as Christopher Johns identifies, is the post-Paris late 1670s beginning with what the Akademie has titled the *Modalia et Elementa Iuris Naturalis* of 1678 (hereafter, the *Modalia*). The editors of the Akademie edition surmise[11] that it was shortly after taking up his post at Hanover that Leibniz learned of the death of Lasser, and that he subsequently requested Lasser's executors that his own notes from Mainz be sent on to him. Receipt of these earlier notes appears to have stimulated a new attempt at progress towards a science of right. The first draft of the *Modalia* picks up the deontic logical structure of the *Elementa* and attacks once more the foundational issues of right and obligation, only again to be strangled by the limitations of the Aristotelean formalism deployed. A second draft, and then various ancillary definitions and methodological forays, lead Leibniz to adopt a new approach in the *De Iustitia et Iure* (1678–9)[12] which, with its emphasis on right reason, still very much bears the hallmarks of Scholastic jurisprudence. This approach will lead to the well-known summit of Leibniz's middle period legal thought: the definition of justice as charity of the wise.

2. Right and obligation: the *Elementa*

2.1 Concept A (1669–70)

The preliminary notes we have for the *Elementa* (known collectively as Concept A) indicate a surprising change of direction, perhaps under the influence of Lasser. From a wealth of interesting material I wish to draw two relevant, significant trends in the drafts: (i) an initial absence of treatment of right and obligation; and (ii) an attempt to treat of moral acts according to a Trinitarian structure which foreshadows the *Trinitas*. *Mens* sketched out just a year later. Resolution of both these points will assist our reading of Concept B, which Johns regards as the central conception of the whole exercise. The editors of the Akademie text have identified four subdrafts, N121–4, and I use this numbering here to situate these two points in flow of the exploration.

The Concept A notes focus unsurprisingly on a discussion of the merits of Grotius and Hobbes, but it is striking that right and obligation receive limited consideration until the very last sentences of the papers. N121 amounts to a series of notes taken directly from Grotius, focusing largely on God and the *officium*. Just at the end of these notes Hobbes is brought in by way of contrast, and here briefly Leibniz points out that whereas for Grotius right flows from wisdom (i.e. it flows from a perfected faculty), Hobbes denies this, presuming right in any case. Leibniz then breaks off mid-sentence, and starts afresh with research note N122, which begins in far more Leibnizian style with a series of catenary definitions. Yet he starts by defining the just and unjust, and according to definitions which will ultimately disappear by Concept B; right and obligation do not feature, and we might suppose that the reason for breaking off N121 was not linked to some revelation on how to deal with right; Leibniz just starts a completely new route through the problem. The road, however, appears unfruitful, for the definitions quickly degenerate into expansive discussions and justifications, weaving through various classical and juridical sources, before collapsing again into tables and lists of definitions (including the Trinitarian concept to be discussed in due course). Now, at the very end of N122 Leibniz's penultimate definition introduces obligation in Hobbesian vein: 'obligation is the performance of something to the happiness of another and the reduction of our own. It is Just.'[13] So we see here the idea elaborated in the *Nova Methodus* that obligation is a determination of some subjective aspect, but the aspect here is *felicitas*, and right is not to be found in the series of definitions. Rather, the final definition treats of equity in a manner somewhat removed from what we found in the *Nova Methodus*, for there is no direct reference to ratios, proportions or harmony; instead equity is defined by reference to equality of goodness amongst the plurality of people *subject to* maximal goodness universally. I mention this because N123 amounts to a reworking of the final chain of definitions which now prioritises equity with respect to justice but excludes all mention to both obligation and right.[14] The reasons for this subtle stepping back from an explicitly geometric approach to the general good will be explained shortly.

I hope to have conveyed something of the aleatory route to N124 which abandons the catenary definitions in favour of prose once more, although the final paragraph could be read as a definitional series. The text begins with an examination of *felicitas* and spends some time exploring how increasing this is a foundation of justice, and closes on defining *iustitia*. It is at this moment that the whole of Concept A suddenly closes on our terms of interest: obligation and right:

> ... the true and perfect definition of *Justice* is the habit of loving others, or the conscious [*capiendi*][15] willing, from one's opinion, of the good of another in any event.
> *Equity* is to love all others in any event.
> We are *Obligated* to do (we owe) what is equitable.
> The *Unjust* is to not desire the good of others in every case.
> The *Just* (permitted) is whatever is not unjust. The just therefore is not only what is equitable ... but what is not unjust in any event.
> Right [*ius*] is the power of doing [*potentia agendi*] what is just.[16]

There are two key moments here, which are best explained by reference to the juridical square of power discussed in our treatment of the *Nova Methodus*. The first concerns the relationship between the unjust and the just, and the equitable and the obligatory. The set of what is just is defined negatively – what is just is anything that is not unjust in any event, and this is a wider set of things than what is 'only' equitable, it would seem. Now the square of power, on our interpretation, would confirm that the forbidden in any case is a universal negative not only opposed to what one could otherwise do, but in contradiction to it. In terms of the SQP and *Nova Methodus* this is the state *spatium* (or total space) which evaluates all particular rights as a whole with reference to an end. It declares, in effect, that there is a range of possible harmonious distributions of rights and obligations in that whole which ought to pertain, and anything outside this range is morally impossible. On that model, though, an obligation is integrated as a particular instance of the whole which opposes and determines a subject of right's power of acting. Now obligation is removed from a prohibitive role and replaced by the unjust which, and here I agree with Johns, is that which ought not to be done.

This change in Concept A from (i) a fixed state space which coerces the subject and so determines their right to (ii) a space defined by the unjust in every case can be explained, I think, by a desire on Leibniz's part to free up the space of moral action from the aegis of a predetermined total moral space as end. This move is most easily identified from the perspective of the modal logical distinction between metaphysical and hypothetical truths which we have already had occasion to discuss in the context of the Scotist real and its Leibnizian manifestation in the principles of non-contradiction and repugnance. The unjust, now defining a set of acts which are forbidden in every case by the moral law, plays a role analogous to metaphysical necessity in that it defines a set of possible acts in this world which ought not to be undertaken. These acts are impossible in the weak moral sense; the possible worlds attainable by unjust acts ought not to be attained from this world. This leaves the just a degree of hypothetical freedom, which is to say that there are a range of just acts which could be undertaken in this world, and while the commission of one act necessarily excludes the possibility of the commission of another, it is not necessary that I ought to have undertaken the one act and not the other. So, by way of example, I cannot gift the same thing absolutely to two different persons, but I can choose which person to gift it to and this choice could, morally, have been otherwise. I stress the morality of this because we are speaking of weak relations – of course I can try to gift the same object to two different people, but then I am at fault. What Leibniz has set in place is a moral space, but this moral space is not a predetermined order of what should be done in every case; rather, it is a predetermined order excluding only what is morally repugnant, and otherwise allowing the route to Justice to be pursued according to hypothetical modality. This in its turn explains the shift in the definition of equity away from an explicit geometric proportion towards an implicit maximisation of the good which needs to be discovered by moral agents.

The second, highly significant point concerns what is occurring at the level of particularity, that is, at the level of the just and so of right. By withdrawing the unjust into universal prohibition – that which ought to be done in no case – and then defining the just as that which is not unjust, Leibniz has widened the scope of the just beyond the subaltern of the obligated so that it ranges across (a) the subaltern of the obligatory; *and* (b) the subaltern of the prohibited. The significance of this move is not yet clear within the terms of Concept A; this is one reason why I brought forward the discussion of modal logic from Concept B to the previous chapter. With that modal apparatus in the forefront of our minds, we see immediately that Leibniz has brought under the term '*iustus*' both the formally possible and the really contingent.

Now at this stage, with Concept A in front of us, it is not altogether clear why Leibniz has done this. Why has he placed a duty on the subjects of law to do not only what they reason to be possible but also what might be contingent? Surely what is contingent is only so relative to the finitude of the individual, and, being a product of the World as a whole, is characterised as beyond the limits of the individual's reasoning about possibility? How, for example, can we accept that someone be responsible for that which can only be 'caused' by them accidentally?

I think it is telling that it is at just this point that Leibniz's Concept A breaks off. It is perhaps not as dramatic as Spinoza's theoretical about-turn on social contract theory mid-paragraph in his *Tractatus Theologico-politicus* (TTP),[17] but given the way in which the binding of possibility and contingency is formalised in Concepts B and C, I would venture that Leibniz effects a similarly striking reappraisal of his own theoretical trajectory at just this point. As with Spinoza, Leibniz has begun with certain Hobbesian premises (as we saw above) although unlike Chapter XVI of the TTP they do not constitute the focus of discussion. The premises that Leibniz has in mind as Concept A closes, are, I claim, the Hobbesian account of individual action as determined by both will and *potentia*; by the agent's volition and the *potentia* of some external cause, helpful or constraining. We have already seen the importance of that doctrine for Leibniz in Chapter 4, but as if to drive home its prominence in Leibniz's mind we find our philosopher writing one of his more self-absorbed letters, to Hobbes himself, just as he was preparing the *Elementa* with Lasser. The letter[18] is dated 22 July 1670[19] and so is sent just as Concept A drafts N123–4 are in preparation. In this letter we find Leibniz opening with a nod to Hobbes own doctrines and their movement from the physical to the political, before a more detailed consideration of rational jurisprudence, followed by an interesting discussion of motion and certain concerns Leibniz has about the unity of aggregate bodies. Leibniz offers the interpretation of Hobbes's work that Leibniz deploys to 'enlighten' his own research on 'rational jurisprudence' and highlights the way in which transfer of will constitutes the supreme power in the state.[20] Leibniz notes, however, that this does not happen in every actual case, but that the advantage of this theoretical deficiency is that it highlights the need for an underlying community. Leibniz locates this in the kingdom of God. In other words, 'there is no purely natural state' in which only human wills strive against each other, because man always finds himself willing within the natural legal community and thus always subject to the supreme power 'of God as common monarch of all'. Like Spinoza, Leibniz takes Hobbes's own theory to its conclusions, but unlike Spinoza he has the temerity to inform the Sage of Malmesbury of this by letter. Not just the well-known interaction of physical and legal, but also the inflection of individual volition by its situation in a community defined by *potentia*, confirm Leibniz's own trajectory beyond Hobbesianism just as he is preparing Concept A.

A natural legal theory of just actions is grounded in and cannot contradict a theory of physical action, and so Leibniz takes on board the notion that the range of physical actions which an agent could undertake will involve both what the agent actively determines to be possible and the contingencies of the World to which any finite agent is subject. It would seem that the Hobbesian approach of combining will and *potentia* leads Leibniz to the consideration that defining just acts as just what is possible for the agent (in the narrow sense of the modal logic of his time) would overly restrict his theory of the just act. Hobbes is pushing him to widen his scope, and his other principle interlocutor in Concept A – Grotius – eases the passage through his theory of aptitudes as imperfect powers of the individual, but powers nonetheless to be exercised appropriately. Hence, I believe, Leibniz makes his move, but he appears immediately to appreciate that it has a greater significance for his own thinking. The contingent captures all that is encountered by the individual *in Nature*, but the unjust is defined *as if* what is in Nature falls within the modal domain of the individual. Furthermore, the negative definition of the just does not merely append contingency to itself; *iustus* is defined by reference to the universal prohibition of the unjust, that is, what is prohibited in the World as a whole. Thus if the individual is to remain responsible for her just actions, she must aim to take into account the prohibitions of the whole World, and this universal perspective too is imported into the deontic frame of the individual. In terms of power, the contingent is the subaltern of a negative universal (the unjust), but if the subaltern is sutured to the acts of a subject, then surely the negative universal must too be appropriated within its subject, if that subject is to be able to reflect on institutions? Is all this intended? Is it desirable? I would say that Leibniz breaks off Concept A and begins Concept B just as one would expect: by a ground-up reworking of modal and deontic logic to investigate just what is going on here. As we shall see, after a quite involved analysis of Leibniz's thinking and influences, our philosopher will embrace the striking consequences of internalising the World because he sees, in the appropriation of contingency, a route to saving free will even while physical determinism is confirmed.

2.2 Concept B (second half of 1671)

Concept B eschews the prose analysis of its predecessor in favour of a structured presentation of a modal and deontic logic, combined with catenary definitions of key terms. As mentioned above, it appears to be a concerted effort to model a rational jurisprudence using the kind of modal logic inherited from Aristotle's *Prior Analytics* via the Schools and even their Reformed counterparts. If Concept A begins with the lawyers Hobbes and Grotius, Concept B resituates Leibniz's thinking within theological debates about possibility, contingency and predestination. The common thread is the subaltern just and the world that defines the conditions of possibility of the just. It is for this reason that our reading of Leibniz's thinking on natural law must now appear to leap to an apparently different frame of reference. Our questions will be juridical – responses to the challenge of Hobbes – but I argue that the responses Leibniz constructs, *pace* previous readers of the *Elementa*, must be understood according to a quite advanced modal logic developed by theologians to tackle their own specific problems. It is the complexity of this modal doctrine, and what it entails for reading Concept B, which occupies the remainder of this section 2. Only once it is understood may we return to the wider legal theoretic significance of the text.

Looking at the *Elementa*'s Concept B we run into only apparent confusions inherited from Concept A, which are highlighted through Christopher Johns's analysis of this text. The core of the problem is the role of necessity and power of the Good Man with respect to possibility, a problem which might be condensed into the observation that there seems to be a contradiction in Leibniz – a defender of rational freedom – advancing a doctrine that privileges necessity. The strength of some of Leibniz's contemporaries, both lawyers like Hobbes and Grotius, and theologians such as Voetius (drawing to an extent on Suárez), is that they explain obligation by coercive necessity, thus implying that the patient of the coercion could have willed otherwise and so is inherently free. As we will presently see, Leibniz places necessity on the side of the patient, so to speak, apparently negating spontaneous volition. Christopher Johns summarises the Leibnizian position:

> How did Leibniz discover this relationship? Very likely, he saw that since *right* designates moral *power*, and power means *possibility*, that possibility means 'able to be done' or permitted – and that's what a just action is: possible for some good person to do. Similarly, *obligation* designates moral necessity and necessity means 'must be done or owed,' which is an equitable action.[21]

The difficulty with Johns's approach, I would suggest, is that he takes Leibniz's reasoning a step too far and is too quick to combine the idea that obligation is a form of necessity with the proposition that the equitable or owed is necessary. In terms of modal logic, as Leibniz shows with respect to *potere*, it is quite valid to define necessity and possibility (and indeed contingency and impossibility) in terms of any one of others. Johns reconstructs the square as follows:

A. Necessary		E. Impossible
Equitable	—	Unjust/forbidden
↓		↓
I. Possible		O. Possible not
Just	—	Omissible

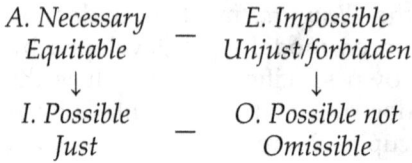

But it is well known[22] that any of the following constructions are interchangeable:

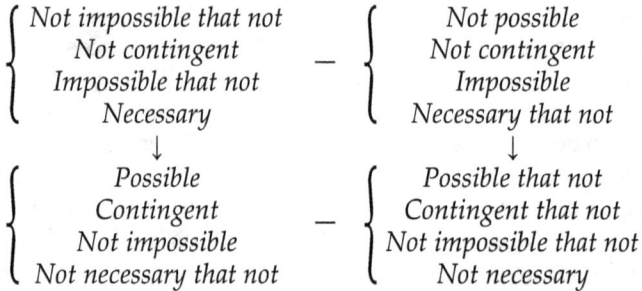

{ Not impossible that not Not contingent Impossible that not Necessary	—	{ Not possible Not contingent Impossible Necessary that not
↓		↓
{ Possible Contingent Not impossible Not necessary that not	—	{ Possible that not Contingent that not Not impossible that not Not necessary

So when Leibniz defines obligation as the necessity of the Good Man, which is nothing other than the qualities of the Good Man, I am not sure it is altogether desirable to restrict necessity to one vertex of the modal square; necessity ranges across all modalities. It so ranges because when we consider modal propositions it is important to account for the dictum and the mode separately. Necessity is just such a mode, and as can be seen from the above, we must consider the quality of a proposition (affirmative/negative) in terms of a negation of the mode – (not) necessary – and a negation of the dictum – necessary that (not) *x*. If necessity so ranges, as logically it must, then this puts in question any claim to identify necessity and the equitable, not least because so doing produces strange results. If necessity for the Good Man is restricted to what cannot not be done by him, then there is nothing morally stopping the Good Man doing what is forbidden. Yes, such an act may be unjust because it is morally impossible for the Good Man to do it, but *he is not obligated not to do it* – a result which undercuts an entire exercise in rationalist natural law. However, if we admit that logically the entire mode of necessity is engaged by Leibniz, then we see that the Good Man will not do what is unjust because *it is necessary*

that he not do x, and that prohibition is accounted an obligation because moral necessity is engaged if permitted to range
across all four modes of possibility.

One might further observe the case of the just, which is
now identified with what is licit or permitted, and defined
as what is possible for the Good Man to do. The full modal
account would allow us to render 'it is possible for the Good
Man to do *x*' as 'it is not necessary that the Good Man not do
x'. The point here is that negation occurs both with respect
to the mode and the dictum, and insofar as we consider the
mode – necessity – this is cancelled. In other words necessity
ceases to be relevant to the permissible, and the same argument can be made with respect to the omissible (not necessary that *x*).

Leibniz carries out an alternative procedure, for he seeks
to define everything in terms of possibility, but my point
is rather that each of the four modes provides a complete
account of modality with respect to dicta. Furthermore, as
we just saw, modal negation 'cancels' a universal mode with
respect to particularity, and a particular mode (such as possibility) with respect to universality. Hence Leibniz's other
reduction of the four modes to just two deontic modalities
(obligation and power) of the moral qualities of a person. In
this Leibniz has made quite a traditional move – Aristotle
does a very similar thing in the difficult discussion of modality in the *Prior Analytics* A,[23] reducing the four modes to
necessity and contingency.

Further support for this reading flows from another aspect
of modality and its distinction from the dictum. I suggest
that the very modality of necessity and power to do derives
from the linkage Leibniz constructs between them and the
moral qualities of the Good Man. Qualities are a mode of
a substance, and Leibniz appears to be seeking to deploy
the mode/dictum distinction in the *Elementa* by attributing
modality to the agent, and the propositional content to the
act to be considered. What is necessary is necessary for a
person with the requisite qualities, and the order of definitions clearly separates that necessity from the necessity of the
equitable act, for otherwise Leibniz would have interposed
the mediate term between obligation and necessity, namely
equity, given that necessity is a constituent of equity.[24]

To this I might add that the consideration of the qualitative negation or affirmation of a mode is but one half of the matter, and that Johns's square does not consider the quantitative relationship between mode and dictum, for example the difference between what is necessary in every case and what is necessary in some cases. To represent these would require a logical octagon, but I see no reason to elaborate on that here. It is enough to note again that obligation as necessity for the Good Man ranges much further than we might expect.

Now you may ask why am I labouring this point? I do so because the effect of Johns's interpretation, I respectfully suggest, is to posit moral necessity as that which implies possibility for the Good Man, which amounts to stating that what is possible for the Good Man is a subset of what is necessary. I counsel against this consequence because:

(a) As noted above, it would seem strange that a philosopher so keen to stress human freedom would make moral possibility illusory for the Good Man. While it is correct to make the proposition 'it is possible that Peter do x' a subaltern of 'it is necessary that Peter do x', the two cases cannot simultaneously subsist in the same individual – they are alternatives. Yes, the moral necessity of Peter's act implies that it is possible for Peter to act, but it is still necessary that Peter act. Moral choice is between doing or not doing what is obligatory; on this reading it no longer bears on hypothetical choices between dicta.

(b) The exclusion, mentioned earlier, of impossibility from the realm of necessity even as Leibniz retains impossibility under the name 'unjust' goes too far in attributing to Leibniz a purely subjectivist theory of right. It suggests that the Good Man is entirely morally characterised by the left-hand side of the modal square, becoming in effect a god. The function of the universal negative (impossibility as primary passive power), according to the earlier texts, is to stand as a moral pole in a *potentia–potestas* real relation. Accepting that Leibniz's tendency will be to collapse the world into a monad, we should not go so far as to deny a continued persistence of this negative universal within the finite individual by reducing it to necessity in the narrow sense advanced by Johns. It is simply that the state space has ceased to be a static distribution willed by God, drawing towards it the moral tendencies of creatures. Rather, impossibility names basic norms which *ought not* to be broken by the Good Man in any moral world. As already stated, this amounts to an analogy with metaphysical necessity.

(c) Necessity also suffers from this limitation, because if necessity pertains only to what the Good Man must do in every case, this necessity simply replicates the ossified 'state space' of Weigel and denies choice. As Hintikka argues, Leibniz is far to subtle for that despite allegations from Lovejoy and others that this necessity doctrine means that the Good Man is not free – that he always wills the best like an automaton.[25] If we understand that impossibility fulfils the function of excluding what is repugnant in any world, necessity (as affirmative universal) is freed to play a slightly different role. That role flows from the shift, already seen in the *Nova Methodus* and through Concept A, from defining obligation purely as a contradictory coercion (by a superior) to now grounding it in a moral necessity linked to the love of others. I wish to treat of this evolution in the penultimate section of this chapter, but I indicate here that love of others is the moral expression of the physical doctrine of maximal reality. If this is so, then necessity for the Good Man now reflects not restraint but the moral relationship between *agere seu conari* and the pretensions of the possibles to reality.

All these confusions arise because Johns does not account for the dual sense of necessity operating in the seventeenth-century field of modal logics that Leibniz is investigating. By failing to do this, moral necessity is reduced to a metaphysical necessity: it is what cannot not be done in every case, and the ought is reduced to the will be. The mistake is common enough – Hintikka berates Lovejoy specifically for advancing a similar reading with respect to Leibniz's God, with the consequence, Hintikka argues, that God becomes an *akrates* (or person incapable of regulating their acts) who cannot but produce the best world. Such a thesis is Spinozist, and surely cannot be due to Leibniz with his belief in divine and human spontaneous freedom. We could adduce numerous statements supporting this view, but it is far more instructive to see how Leibniz distinguishes two forms of necessity and why this is a common practice of the seventeenth century. By so doing, we will be able to draw a line between Leibniz's treatment of divine choice of worlds and the account of obligation in the *Elementa Juris*, permitting a richer interpretation of the latter.

I draw on two sources here, Vos and Decker's account[26] of the contemporaneous treatment of necessity as duplex, and Nicholas Rescher's succinct treatment[27] of the role of duplex necessity in Leibniz's possible worlds argumentation.

2.3 Francis Turrettin, necessity and hypothetical universalism

As to context then, we return once again to Duns Scotus who builds on Boethius to provide the Schoolmen with a critical modal distinction between the necessity of the consequence (*necessitas consequentiae*) and the necessity of the consequent (*necessitas consequentis*).[28] The basic idea is this: given a conditional statement of the form 'if p then q', we can apply the mode of necessity in two ways. We can either say that the whole condition is necessary, that is, we say that: '"if p then q" is necessary', or say that the consequent of the condition, q, is necessary, such that 'if p then necessarily q'. Scotus for his part calls the former structure, in which necessity ranges across the whole condition, the 'composite sense'; the latter, where only the consequent q is necessary, the 'divided sense'. Formally the distinction is obvious, but what is the interpretation of the formalism? The key, I think, is to observe the axiomatic equivalence between the following two statements: (i) it is necessary that (if p then q); and (ii) if necessarily p then necessarily q. In other words the mode of necessity applicable to the consequence is distributive. In the form of (ii) we can then clearly see that the *necessitas consequentiae* sets a higher standard on the condition p, than the *necessitas consequentis*. With *necessitas consequentis* it need only be the case that p is possible that, if in fact p is posited, we necessarily obtain q; with *necessitas consequentiae* the necessity of the consequence only obtains if p itself is necessary (this relation today being called the **K**-axiom). It is this insight,

Vos and Dekker argue,[29] which will be heavily used both by
the Schoolmen and by Reformed and Lutheran theologians
of the seventeenth century – notably Voetius – to explain
freedom of divine choice against a background of predestination. Richard Muller refers us to diverse theologians such as
Heinrich Bullinger, Wolfgang Musculus, Zacharias Ursinus
and Girolamo Zanchi, and notes that several members of the
Synod of Dort wrestled with these doctrines.[30]

A case in point is Francis Turrettin (1623–87), a Geneva-
based Reformed theologian, author of the *Instituto Theologiae
Elencticae* (three parts, 1679–85), and indirect correspondent
of Leibniz. Indeed, Leibniz refers approvingly Turrettin's
account of divine freedom in his *Theodicy*. Note that there is
no evidence that either thinker directly influenced the other's
views on necessity, especially Leibniz's treatment in the early
and middle period, but we only require the weaker contextual claim to proceed, established by Vos and Dekker (on
whom I draw closely), namely that the Scotist distinction is
well known and much used across theological divides and, I
would estimate as Rescher does, very much part of Leibniz's
conceptual inheritance. It is important for us to clarify that
Turrettin's Calvinism fell under that specific variant known
as Amyraldism,[31] and which for our purposes shall be treated
as a form of Reformed hypothetical universalism. Calvinists
hold to a form of predestination which might be simplified
as the doctrine that God chooses *ab initio* for all eternity who
is elected to be saved and who not, denying therefore both
that human acts in this life could change this outcome and
that God would change his mind and save who was previously damned. The hypothetical universalists were in part
interested in explaining how God could be so bound, even
by himself, thus denying an absolute power to do otherwise. Turrettin's thinking on necessity is aimed at this and
related questions of necessity, absolute power and predestination, and he uses the Scholastic toolkit with some skill.
The kernel of Turrettin's argumentation seems to be this: that
a distinction is to be made between absolute, non-relational
necessity ('metaphysical' necessity) and implicative necessity (hypothetical necessity). The former is essential, in that
the consequence necessarily follows because the condition
necessarily is the case, flowing as it does from the nature of

the thing. He gives the examples of: God is good and God is just, where it would be metaphysically 'absurd' to derive the opposite conclusion given the way in which God is defined. This maps onto necessity of the consequence, which as we saw demands that condition and consequent both be necessary. Hypothetical necessity, however, only requires that the condition be possible and that it may not be posited, or, as Turrettin puts it, that the entity in question behave differently (depending on the condition).

An initial result of this is that Turrettin can speak of real entities necessarily existing *if* God so wills it, but God's will need not be posited and so the necessity of the real entity's existence is not absolute, but simply hypothetical – it would be so if God willed it. The point here is the Turrettin has seized on hypothetical necessity to explain something critical about the nature of predestination: it is not metaphysically necessary that God create this world or save these elect and not others; it is only hypothetically necessary, in the sense that if God willed it, and he could have willed otherwise, then these things follow necessarily. Now, however, we have simply removed the question of predestination one step to God's will. Is Turrettin trying to trick us? Is he committing a sleight of hand by giving the name 'necessity' to what is really a contingent volition of God, or does he accept predestination with full force such that a hypothetical necessity combined with God's will is in the last analysis just as necessary for all time as metaphysical necessity? We have not advanced much. Well, Turrettin's next move is to capitalise on having removed necessity from the sphere of the intellect to that of the will, and so from the formal to the real. He does this by bringing in the Scotist notion of repugnance to develop a new distinction, one which prevents hypothetical necessity from collapsing into either pure contingency of will or metaphysical necessity. The key passages cited by Vos and Dekker are:[32] 'What matters is God's *potentia absoluta* by which He can do those things that are not repugnant to his most perfect nature and do not imply any contradiction.'[33] The innovation comes by distinguishing logical from a new kind of contradiction:

Something is an impossible of nature [*impossibile naturae*], with respect to secondary causes. Another concept is that of what is *impossible by nature* [*impossibile naturâ*], that is, what is repugnant to the nature of reality with respect to all kinds of causes. (Modified translation)[34]

Vos and Dekker translate *impossibile naturâ* as 'structurally impossible' and this conveys something which is opaque in my 'impossible by nature'. Vos and Dekker underline that it is important to understand that *impossibile naturâ* is explicitly an impossibility by reference to 'logical *incompatibility*', and this is a matter of contradictory predicates: 'The *contradictory* is called what is *logically impossible*, what is *repugnant* and what includes *contradictory* predicates.'[35] Here, Vos and Dekker inform us,[36] Turrettin makes a didactically useful distinction between explicit and implicit contradiction which illustrates his meaning. In the proposition 'man is not man' we have an explicit contradiction of the modern type '*P* & not-*P*', which, if 'man' means the same thing, cannot hold. Yet we might also take 'Socrates is walking' and 'Socrates is not walking'. While Socrates could be in either state at any time, he cannot be in both states simultaneously. This is the key point: they two predicates of Socrates are not *possible together*; they are *incompossible*.[37]

From this the implicit contradiction follows. For example, 'God is corporeal and mortal' is a contradiction because deductively unpacking the term 'God' reveals that the subject is indeed inconsistent with the predicates (they are *termini repugnantes*).[38] From here it is a question of observing that what is impossible by nature describes that situation in which the agent is supposed to undertake some act which is repugnant to her nature. Hence God's not willing the best is impossible by nature just because in a world in which God is defined as he who wills the supreme good, the proposition 'God wills the not-best' contains repugnant terms. The subject and the object simply cannot be and not-be simultaneously.

It is this impossibility of existing within the same 'realm'[39] which is the necessity Turrettin identifies with hypothetical necessity. It is not metaphysical necessity because the realm of the possible is wider than reality (at noon tomorrow Socrates could walk or not walk, but not both), and while in its nature a possible may be in logical accord with the other ideas in God's intellect, the realisation of that possible may still be incompatible with the realisation of certain subsets of the possible as a world (God cannot choose that P and not-P obtain simultaneously in a given realm). On the other hand, this necessity is not merely a rebranding of the utterly contingent, for it is not open to will the realisation of just any possible; every possible's realisation is to be gauged according to its 'real' compatibility with existing nature as conceived by a God who by nature wills the best. Thus, the function necessity of the consequent plays is this: the condition p is on its own a simple possibility, but within this hypothetical universalist theology, that condition is subject to a universal assessment of compatibility or repugnance with respect to the nature of the agent in this realm.

It is that universal assessment which is central to the hypothetical universalist position on predestination. It flows as necessary consequence from the goodness of God that God wills to save everyone, but God also engages in a universal assessment of the created world and knows that some will reject him. Accordingly, God chooses to will to save just those who are faithful and to damn the rest. He could have done otherwise in each individual case, but the weight of repugnance is such that this grants, in the shadow of impossibility by nature, a certain mediate necessity between metaphysical necessity and arbitrary possibility. Turrettin's move then is to take the Scotist notion of logical repugnance, used by the Subtle Doctor to explain God's absolute power to choose this or that metaphysically coherent world, and to replicate it in the explicitly moral sphere of grace. Whether Turrettin has succeeded in explaining the coherence of divine rationality, predestination and free will, must be left to others. From this analysis I wish us to draw this central idea: moral necessity is distinguished from moral possibility by a hypothetical universal assessment of a proposed real's repugnance or otherwise to the nature of a God that is creator of nature as a whole.

2.4 Leibniz on possible worlds and duplex necessity

From what point in time Leibniz is aware of the precise logical mechanics of the *necessitas consequentiae/consequentis* is a matter of debate. Loemker takes the view[40] that Leibniz begins with the philosophical interpretation – that necessities in God are either intellectual or volitional – and is seeking for a logical substructure that explicates it through the 1670s. At the time of Concept B's development, we find Leibniz writing to Hamburg jurist Magnus Wedderkopf:

> 'what is the reason for the harmony of things? Nothing', and to argue that God makes the possibility and existence of things in different ways. Why then are existent things necessary? Because God, having a perfect mind, cannot but be 'affected by the most perfect harmony, and thus to do the best by the very ideality of things'.[41]

Now Nicholas Rescher, in his *'Contingentia Mundi*. Leibniz on the World's Contingency',[42] establishes the relevance of the *necessitas consequentiae/consequentis* distinction for Leibniz's treatment of divine creation and possible worlds theory. The essence of Rescher's argument on this can be gleaned from his gloss on Leibniz's response to Samuel Clarke.[43] This gloss is interwoven with the French text and involves formal symbolism, so I paraphrase it here. It is true that this proposition: 'if this work is the most worth *then* God wills it' is necessary. But it is not true that he wills it necessarily, that is, the statement 'if, as is necessary, this work is most worthy, then necessarily God wills it' is not true. This is because the condition 'this work is the most worthy' is not a (metaphysically) necessary truth, but an indemonstrable (i.e. contingent) truth of fact. Leibniz does believe that one can generally say that this proposition is necessary: that His will acts according to the greatest inclination. But it doesn't follow at all that he will act necessarily – that this following is necessary (*necessitas consequentiae*). It is like when it is necessary that future contingents be determined, but it is not true that they are necessarily determined, for otherwise they would not be contingent. It is a necessary proposition that 'God wants the best' (for) God is necessarily (essentially) he who wills the best, but it is not the case that he necessarily wills the best. He wills it freely, that is, *if* (contingently) this work is the worthiest, *then* necessarily God wills it. The Leibnizian doctrine, as Rescher notes,[44] could not have been expressed more clearly provided one observes the distinction of roles in practical action of intellect and will: the divine intellect determines all the possibilities of action and presents these to the will; the will evaluates the reality of each such possibility (for the will's field of application is the real or creatable) and is inclined towards that act which maximises reality; it is a necessary property of God that he wills the best, and so he necessarily wills that which is most worthy. On this account we can see that whereas intellect and willing the good are both moved by necessity, the will's evaluation of the real (the middle step) is not so moved. Why this should be will be considered in section 3 below. In liberating the middle step Leibniz hopes to protect the freedom of a will which can then be adjudged virtuous or vicious not so much by its final choice, but by *how* it arrives at that choice: (im)prudently. It is open to God's free will to evaluate the real poorly, and still necessarily choose the best from a diminished subset of choices. In prioritising a sense of prudential negligence over inherent goodness, this is the morality not of the saint but the functionary. But it is the price Leibniz will pay in order to break the determinism that would otherwise hold between the intellective presentation of all that is possible and the metaphysically necessary, that is, definitional goodness of God.

I have taken up Rescher's analysis of this point because it provides clarity, using Leibniz's own doctrine, in an area of modal logic in which Leibniz himself struggled. Yet this comes with a difficulty for our interpretation of the *Elementa Iuris*. Rescher's arguments tend to draw on Leibniz's late period, and our reliance upon Rescher's results requires some qualification. The main sources deployed by Rescher are the Samuel Clarke correspondence[45] and the *Theodicy*[46] providing quite a late temporal marker for our purposes, though he does reach back to 1680.[47]

Does this mean that we cannot ascribe to Leibniz knowledge during the *Elementa Iuris* period of the *necessitas consequentiae/consequentis* distinction? Where does this distinction become sufficiently formalised in Leibniz's mind, and how relevant is that moment to our juridical discussions? A range of scholars are prepared to locate sufficient logical precision of the distinction in the first half of the 1670s on logical and interpretative grounds, which, when combined with our knowledge of the post-Scotist heritage in both the Schools and Reformed thought, would seem to be a justified position on their part. Jean-Pascal Alcantara provides a useful summary of the thinking in his 2012 piece,[48] which uses modern terminology to name the distributive axiom which produces the *necessitas consequentiae*, the so-called **K**-axiom.

> Some commentators such as Adams, Sleigh and Griffin have agreed to identify an equivalent of the K-axiom in an extract dated of December 1675, *De mente, de universo, de Deo*, written between *Confessio philosophi* dated 1673 and some noticeable rectifications brought in in 1677, following a series of discussions that Leibniz had in Hanover with the Danish geologist Stenon . . . rectifications whose result was, in the margins of [the] *Confessio*, the explication 'per se' linked to 'necessary', read in the final writing, so that the bearing of a modality is divided in two.[49]

Certainly, we might add, by the time of his 1675 letter to Simon Foucher,[50] which draws on Paris notes of 1672, Leibniz has developed a specific if naïve terminology to describe the necessity denoted by *necessitas consequentis*, and which will be retained by modal logicians: hypothetical possibility, impossibility and necessity. By this letter Leibniz seeks to complement the metaphysical truth of the Cartesian *cogito* by arguing that there are two absolute truths: 'that we think; the other, that there is a great variety[51] amongst our thoughts [*une grande varieté dans nos pensées*]'.[52] His focus is this second axiom which indicates that there is something other than us which is the cause of the variety of our experiences. What follows is a causal version of his argument for divine governance, interesting not least because it does not fall back on a single ultimate cause directly, as Aristotle does, but rather relies on the complete ordering of appearances we find at every level, no matter how microscopic. It is the order of every variety *as* variety which is the 'proof' of the second axiom – that every individual body and matter should act as the order of the whole variety demands.[53]

This deep discussion provides the framing for our understanding of hypothetical necessity, and explains why Leibniz should explain it not by reference to an easy example – something intuitive contingent such as the roll of a die

– but remarkably by justifying geometric postulates. Leibniz writes:

> [T]hus you will grant us hypothetical truths . . . So we at once save arithmetic, geometry, and a large number of propositions in metaphysics, physics, and morals, whose convenient expression depends on arbitrarily chosen definitions, and whose truth depends on those axioms which I am wont to call identical [such as non-contradiction] . . . (L:151)

The key here is once again to understand that the contingency of the postulates attains hypothetical necessity insofar as they can be instantiated in the global or universal completeness of the form. Hence the circle might be considered a certain justification of the axioms, postulates and definitions of Euclidean geometry because we find in every 'point' of the circle a 'necessary' relationship to each and all which expresses these norms of space as a whole. The norms could have been otherwise, and with the development of mathematics we see that other systems of geometry are available to us. But this possibility, impossibility or necessity (as not possibly not) is no chimera which we create, for they all consist in our recognising them as regularities in the variety of our sensations. The priority thereby moves from the variety of sensations backwards to the laws which are expressed globally by them. We might then say that Leibniz's treatment of the ideal and moral laws does not begin by asking 'What are the laws of nature?' but rather with the methodologically charged question: 'What is it for a nature to have laws?', for it is only in normatively expressive nature that we can begin to discover the laws of *this* world.

Thus, there are the two general truths already cited that confirm the existence of actual things, a metaphysically necessary truth as to the actuality of our thought as act, and a hypothetically necessary truth which, following the geometric example, is experienced in the global coherence of the great variety of our thoughts.[54] The letter to Simon Foucher provides a rich bridge between Leibniz's thinking on contingent systems of global norms in geometry, physics and morals, but we must accept that the formalisation of the logical difference it implies in its treatment of two kinds of necessity is not yet in this text.

In summary, the primary and secondary sources do not confirm that the precise logical distinction is known to Leibniz at the time of the Wedderkopf letter and so at the time when Concept B is being prepared. Observe, however, that we do not need to go so far as to discover a specific axiom that accounts for the distribution of necessity in the *necessitas consequentiae*. For our purposes it is enough that Leibniz is aware that (i) he needs to explain a difference of necessity operating in intellect and will; (ii) that a key feature of the distinction is that the former requires a higher standard of the condition, that is, metaphysical necessity; and (iii) that the latter's condition is hypothetical only, in the literal sense that one assumes the condition to obtain the consequent. Furthermore, it is important to note that the basic tenets of the *Iuris modalia* are resurrected in the 1680s, though ultimately abandoned, and that this resurrection discloses no specific emendation of the logical structure, particularly the relationship of the kinds of necessity. Compare this with the changes annotated to the *Confessio* identified by Alcantara. We thus have a period ending with this final attempt at the *Elementa Iuris* in which to identify Leibniz as a thinker of the necessity distinction, at least naïvely, in line with thinkers of his time.

With these qualified assumptions in mind, we can now turn to the function necessity plays in the *Elementa Iuris*. In outline I will argue, by means of a restatement of the central logical structure, that the two senses of necessity are implicitly at work in the *Iuris modalia*, by which I mean that hypothetical necessity is not named as such but is present. I claim that this distinction which foreshadows Leibniz's treatments of universal hypothetical truths in the letter to Foucher, permits him to speak of a necessity of the Good Man which is conditional on the giving of a universally owed obligation – an obligation which is identified as applicable in every case by the Good Man. To do this I proceed to outline the role of the two necessities in the *Elementa* according to an interpretation that explicitly deploys the terminology of consequence identified by Rescher *as if* Leibniz had adopted these descriptors in 1671. Second, in the next section I reconstruct the wider argument of Concept B (and indeed Concept C) to give the full sense which I believe Leibniz intended for the necessity of the Good Man. This contextualisation will support the reading of obligation as at once hypothetical but determined to be applicable in every case, and thus necessary in the sense of universal.

2.5 Preliminary interpretation of necessity in the *Elementa*

So, let us interpret the *Elementa* in light of the distinctions of necessity. In outline we might say that the necessity of the Good Man can be read as a finite parallel of the necessity of God: it is a moral or hypothetical necessity, that is, it is false to say that it is necessary that 'the Good Man does a deed that is obligatory' (*necessitas consequentiae*); rather, Leibniz means to say that *if* a deed is obligatory, *then* 'it is necessary that the Good Man do the deed' (*necessitas consequentis*). It is necessary that 'God wants the best', because by definition God is a being that wants the best, but it is false to say that God necessarily wants the best, because he is free to will imprudently and, whatever the best is, it is contingent on the whole world in which it is to be realised.

To make this fully explicit, I set out the core analysis. Necessity of consequence distributes necessity across the terms of the condition,[55] whereas necessity of the consequent is just that: only the consequent is necessary. Whence we have seen that Rescher has:

(1A) If w is the best possible world *then* God chooses w, is necessary; which can be restated via a distribution axiom as:

(1B) If necessarily w is the best possible world *then* necessarily God chooses w;
   or

(2) If w is the best possible world *then* God necessarily chooses w.

We might observe an equally suggestive application of this moral logic in the realm of the possibles themselves. You will remember that each possible strives to exist, and following Leibniz's language I have named this movement a pretension to exist. We can now attack this Leibnizian problematic from the angle of his moral theory by observing the following distinction at work:

(1) if x exists then x is possible, is necessary (*necessitas consequentiae*).
(2) if x exists then x is necessary (necessarily possible) (*necessitas consequentis*).

These formulations best clarify the nature of pretension, for statement (1) above is not a statement that x necessarily exists, but *only* a statement that the relationship between possibility and existence is necessary, that the latter implies the former. And this more limited pretensional relation is indeed necessary, for (a) if something is possible then hypothetically it could exist and moreover it is impossible that it could not exist, and (b) if something exists it must be hypothetically possible and moreover it is a contradiction that it be impossible. One can see that statement (2) is only true if x's existence is itself necessary, for if otherwise we can suppose x not exist, and then even if x did exist it could have been otherwise, and so x's necessity is contradicted: x is not necessary but contingent. This argument throws light on Leibniz's ontological proofs, where God does benefit from the necessity of the consequent, for being defined as necessarily existing, it follows by absolute and not implicative necessity that God exist and we recover statement (1) in distributed form.

One can now hopefully see then that Johns's treatment of the *Elementa Iuris* must be read in light of this distinction of necessities. Returning to the basic definitions of Concept B, we see that Leibniz's construction of the Good Man as a man acquiring a qualitative status indicates the following: it is not metaphysically necessary that any man do what is obligated, because a man is not good by definition, unlike God. It may seem obvious, but it is worth confirming that the necessity in question only relates to the Good Man. Then we have the question of the kind of necessity in play – metaphysical or moral – when it is said that what is obligatory is that which is necessary for the Good Man to do. We have the following interpretations in the form attributable to Duns Scotus and Turrettin:

(1) 'The man does the obligatory act if he is a Good Man' is necessary (*necessitas consequentiae* or the composite sense).
    a. Again, in modern framing: it is necessary that, for any act (if the act is obligated *then* the Good Man will do the act).

(2) 'The man does the obligatory act' is necessary, if he is a Good Man (*necessitas consequentis* or the divided sense).
    a. Or in a more modern form: for any act (if the act is obligated *then* it is necessary that the Good Man do the act).

It can be seen that statement (1) claims that the doing of the obligatory act is necessary, but this is false, for the doing of a truly moral act is hypothetical or contingent and not necessary in a strict sense; the agent could have done otherwise. If we are to take our lead from Leibniz's account of divine choice and the distinction between metaphysical and moral necessity, the necessity deployed in the *Elementa Iuris* ought to be understood as a moral necessity of the consequent, that is, a necessity of the form stated in (2) above. We might then imagine Leibniz claiming that while 'the Good Man does what is obligated' is necessary, it is not true that he does it necessarily. For the proposition 'this act is obligated' is not a metaphysically necessary truth, but a contingent one of fact. In the order of practical action, the Good Man first has to determine whether the act is obligated at all, and he may either find that it is not, or err in believing that it is not. With this in mind, we can now account for the other terms that are placed in relation of necessity of consequent.

3. Widening the interpretation: consequence in Concepts B and C

3.1 Two kinds of juridical necessity

I now turn to Concepts B and C of the *Elementa Iuris* and will attempt to show that Leibniz will use both *necessitas consequentis* and *necessitas consequentiae* in this legal text, and in this way he is able to deploy two levels of necessity, explaining in particular why he speaks both of the owed as what it is necessary for the Good Man to do, and obligation as the necessity of the Good Man. To establish this, I claim to significantly deepen the analysis of Johns, whose account misses the doubling of necessity precisely because it misses the relationship between the *Iuris modalia* and the Reformed Church's theology of predestination and necessity.

Note that for this purpose I will treat Concepts B and C together, for they are grounded on the same conceptual plan and Concept C differs largely in the details and emphases on certain points. These differences of detail and emphasis will be highlighted where relevant in what follows.

Let us first deal with the role of *necessitas consequentis* in Concepts B and indeed C. The earlier discussion of the modal square of possibility and necessity feeds into Leibniz's definition of the following natural legal terms:[56]

(a) Just, licit is whatever is possible for the Good Man to do.
(b) Unjust, illicit is whatever is impossible for the Good Man to do.
(c) Equitable, owed is whatever is necessary for the Good Man to do.
(d) Indifferent is whatever is contingent for the Good Man to do.

I claim that these definitions *assume* the condition p as their hypothesis, and iterate the possible consequences, one of which has the form of *necessitas consequentis*. To do this we must first observe that the 'whatever (*quicquid*)' of the above definitions is a dummy variable. Leibniz has not introduced reality maximisation just yet in the analysis; that *quicquid* is just what is intended: a placeholder, to be filled in in due course. I shall therefore speak of x formally subsisting, which is to say that x, whatever it is, is logically (not necessarily morally) possible. Then we have:

(a) Just, licit = if x formally subsists then it is possible that the Good Man do the act x ($x \rightarrow possibly\ q$).
(b) Unjust, illicit = if x formally subsists then it is not possible that the Good Man do the act x (*not p → not possibly q*).
(c) Equitable, owed = if x formally subsists then it is not possible that the Good Man not do the act x ($x \rightarrow not\ possibly\ not\ q$, that is, *necessarily q*).

(d) Indifferent = if *x* formally subsists then it is possible that the Good Man not do the act *x* (not *p* → *possibly not q*).

It is worth emphasising that the condition *x* is entirely hypothetical; the modal operators only range over the consequent. Accordingly, on inspection we find the classic instance of hypothetical action: case (c) has the form of *necessitas consequentis*. We can thus remark that Leibniz ties the definition of what is equitable or owed to that form of argument he also reserves to God's creation of the world. From this observation it is hardly surprising that the content of *x* should be interpreted along of the lines of Rescher's reality maximisation, though this step in Leibniz's thinking is only implicit in Concept B and only indirectly dealt with in Concept C (as we shall presently see). What we are looking for is a discussion of the above modalities which hypothetically posit *x* defined in a manner akin to a reality maximising act. Certainly Concepts B and C advance with the idea of 'loving all' along lines whereby the Good Man maximises the contingent accidents that accrue to the perfection of all (the 'multiplication of cases').[57] However, Leibniz proceeds too quickly to consideration of the Good Man as a special case, and misses a step which may have aided exposition, specifically a step which I now propose to insert as a bridge to the discussion of right and obligation.

This bridge asks whether the condition '*x* is reality maximising' is to be inserted, following Rescher, into the *Iuris Modalia*. It should be possible to write, for example: if *x* is a reality maximising act then it is necessary for the Good Man to do *x*. This would certainly accord with Rescher's account of necessity of the consequent with respect to world creation. The problem, which Leibniz appears to have noticed, is that this hypothesis produces logical and moral difficulty. The logical aspect of the problem is simply this: that negation of *x* produces strange results for the interpretation. For example, we could write: if *x* is *not* a reality maximising act then it is impossible for the Good Man to do *x*.[58] This is far too strong an outcome for such a model, for the contradictory of reality maximising is also what is merely indifferent as to reality maximisation, and why should we wish to restrict the freedom of the Good Man to choose to do what is omissible? Alternatively, we could restrict ourselves to negating the condition x alone, but the outcome of this for the interpretation is even worse: if x is not reality maximising, then the Good Man should do x.

From an interpretative point of view the negation itself appears insufficient; surely the true contrary of reality maximising is reality minimisation or even reality destruction. Yet Leibniz makes no effort in either Concept B or C to entertain this possibility. And this is largely due to his own moral commitment to the goodness of reality. Here we need to read an indirect reference to this issue in Concept C, found in the definition of '*omnes*'.[59] Here the definition degenerates into a nevertheless helpful discussion of what loving and, importantly, its opposite act are. In characteristic fashion, Leibniz is prepared to argue that there is goodness in every possibility and it is all a matter of degree. It suffices, he writes, that we love even the worst, but that in case of a competition between choices the inferior option – the least reality maximising – should give way.[60] Accordingly Leibniz appears not to be prepared to countenance any form of reality destruction on account of the inherent goodness of this world.

The difficulty for the interpretation might thus be viewed as deriving from the hypothetical nature of the statement posited, for the problem the Good Man faces is determining just when x is the reality maximising act sought. Simply assuming that x is such an act tells us observers what the Good Man will do, but it reduces the Good Man to the subject of an external command, namely the hypothesis that we observers impose on him. Leibniz's natural legal concern, however, is to determine what the subject is to do when faced with the very contingency of x. The result: a statement that x is a reality maximising act cannot simply be appended to the definitions of just, unjust, owed and indifferent. Leibniz needs to reflect modality not just in the consequent, but also in the condition.

We are now left with a lacuna: the condition x remains undetermined. It is into this placeholder that Leibniz adds his second limb of necessity and related modalities. He now[61] writes that:

(1) Right (ius) is the *potentia*[62] of the Good Man;
(2) Obligation is the necessity of the Good Man.

Let us assume for the moment that we know what *potentia* means in the context, and that we can temporarily translate it, to distinguish it from mere possibility, as *potentiality* or *potentially* as sense requires. We will hold off investigation while we examine what these new statements are aiming structurally to achieve.

Now these definitions, I claim, are designed to determine the condition x of the terms just, unjust, owed and indifferent, and they do so exactly by replicating the difference, identified by Scotus, Turrettin and by Rescher, between *necessitas consequentis* and *necessitas consequentiae*. By importing the notion that the Good Man loves all and so seeks to maximise reality, into the conditions defined above, the desired conditional statements are constructed as:

(a) If 'potentially' x is a reality maximising act then it is possible for the Good Man to do x.
(b) If necessarily x is a reality maximising act then it is necessary for the Good Man to do x,

which latter can be rewritten:

(c) Necessarily (if x is a reality maximising act then the Good Man does x) (*necessitas consequentiae*).

In other words Leibniz has structurally defined obligation through necessity of the consequence *not* necessity of the consequent. The latter was completely appropriate with respect to a necessarily free God, for God is free to determine the rational conditions of any reality maximising act, but for a finite creature, embedded in a rationally ordered world, it would be plausible to speak of a determination of freedom by the conditions of that world. And as if to confirm this reading, immediately following these definitions in Concept C Leibniz adds a third statement in the prose discussion which being not ten lines from his initial definition of the unjust clearly is to be considered an innovation and to be collected with the definitions of obligation and right:

(d) Unjust (or prohibited) is what is absurd, because it implies a contradiction for the Good Man.

This we simply rewrite as Leibniz suggests: we contradict what is potentially for the Good Man:

(e) If impossibly x is a reality maximising act then it is impossible for the Good Man to do x (if you will, *impossibilitas consequentiae*).

Which confirms our view that the necessity of the condition is a moral necessity derived from the Scotist notion of repugnance and absurdity. By treating of the two limbs of necessity in the conditional statements, and regarding the condition itself as subject to a hypothetically universal analysis of what would be repugnant to the whole of reality, we see quite clearly why Leibniz should speak of contradiction. It is not contradictory to the Good Man because he is in two minds, or because it would be against his essence so to do, but *because the act is deemed to contradict reality*. It is, so to speak, 'moral nonsense' in a way which reminds one of phenomenological approaches to the experience of law breaking as the disappointment of a certain expectation as to order.[63]

Up to now I have argued that we need to account twice for necessity in the *Iuris Modalia*, and I think by doing so we have a better explanation of necessity's appearance in both the definitions of owed and obligation, and of the relationship between theological considerations of world creation and predestination, and Leibniz's own thought. But I wish to take one further step before preceding to evaluate these results: I wish to integrate the terms back into the square of power which has informed this interpretation and which sits behind the *Elementa* even into its middle period drafts.

3.2 The Leibnizian state space and its significance for any archaeology of power

In this section I relate Leibniz's account of juridical conditions back to his doctrine of activity, and thus place it within the genealogy of power. To do this I briefly demonstrate how the conditional relationships (the arrows if you will) of the *Elementa Iuris* are locatable within an augmented square of power. This allows a visual comparison with the square of power, clearly indicating the moves Leibniz has made. My principal argument will be that for all Leibniz's explicit focus on obligation and right, we can only fully appreciate the early and middle theory of natural law by accounting for moral absurdity as a determinant of the 'world' in which a person's obligation and right operate.

First, we notice that the distributive axiom which we applied to obligation, and which allows us to extract the modal operator from the terms of the consequence, is likewise applicable to the case of *ius* and absurdity, and by implication the case of contingency. By doing this we obtain:

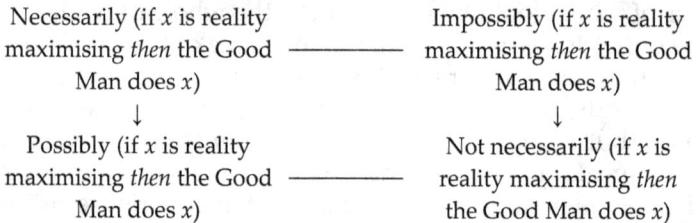

Necessarily (if *x* is reality maximising *then* the Good Man does *x*)	Impossibly (if *x* is reality maximising *then* the Good Man does *x*)
↓	↓
Possibly (if *x* is reality maximising *then* the Good Man does *x*)	Not necessarily (if *x* is reality maximising *then* the Good Man does *x*)

With this we see that Leibniz's aim has been to augment the square of power with an account of conditional relationships, building on his focus in *De Conditionibus*. In setting out the terms of obligation, right and moral absurdity in this way, we can orient their role within the wider genealogy of activity, power and entelechy. We can see, for example, that the *potentia* of the Good Man is determined by the contingency of the world, a contingency which derives its force from what is morally repugnant: that which is impossibly reality maximising in this world.

What has Leibniz done here then? How do we situate this move within a genealogy of power? Two shifts may be observed. First, by gathering both possibility and contingency under the sign of *potentia* Leibniz extends the Thomist notion of power to incorporate Scotist contingency. Whereas the Thomist God has absolute power precisely because He knows Himself and needs only Himself to achieve what He wills, the finite creature as practical agent is defined by the differential between a power proper to the essence of the individual and the determinations of the world beyond. Leibniz at once confirms that finite creatures' intellects can

only extend so far in their combinatorial iteration of the possible, and so can only truly will what is known, but nevertheless extends power so that it also makes use of what cannot
be known: the infinite depth of Nature. This indicates the
second shift: that *potentia* no longer refers directly to what
was once *dunamis*, but in binding contingency to the existing
individual, *potentia* derives its 'pretensionality', so to speak,
from a new conception of moral spatiality. In this Leibniz
goes further than Spinoza, for whom an infinite *potentia* subtends every individual. For Spinoza Nature – the 'out-there'
– is but God's absolute power under a different aspect, and
suffers from the homogeneity of infinitude if only through
a kind of overdetermination or superfluity of reality. The
spontaneity of the Spinozan individual is an indistinguishable enthusiasm for life. With Leibniz, the out-there of the
state *spatium* subtending contingency is as defined and conceptually complete as the individual concept, for it is precisely what the individual is not; it is as it were, the reflection
of the *suppositum*, constituting each individual as a kind of
dipole of subject and objective world. But if the out-there
is constituted by the determinations of the internal life of
the supposit, then can one see in this extension of *potentia* to
cover both the necessary determinations of the possible *and*
the contingent derivatives of space, a first step towards the
full integration of the outside within the monad? And if this
is so, can we say that Leibniz has decisively advanced that
philosophical development of grounding right (as *potentia
viri bono*) on contingency itself; a development the beginnings
of which Aubry finds in Duns Scotus, and which culminates
in Hegel's own account of contingency as groundless ground
of freedom in the *Science of Logic*?

We should be under no misapprehension as to why Leibniz
should make this move of internalisation of the contingent. I
find his motivations most clearly expressed in the *Discourse on
Metaphysics*, a middle period work prepared even as Leibniz
confirmed and edited these earlier jurisprudential works:

Every substance is like a whole world. (DM:§9: L:308).

But it seems that [essentialism][64] will destroy the distinction between contingent and necessary truths, that it will

leave no place for human liberty, and that an absolute fatalism will rule over all our actions as well as over the other events of the world. (DM:§13: L:310).

Leibniz must bring contingency under the right and *potentia* of the subject because only this can liberate the Good Man from Spinozistic determinism and make space for free will. But so doing comes at this price: contingency is finally caused by a primary passive force of (moral) impossibility imposed on the real, and for the Good Man to claim *power* over in-potency itself rather than be mechanically determined by it, this (moral) impossibility must be brought within the substance also and made its own. As noted in section 2 above, Leibniz managed to insert a middle step between intellection of the possible and willing the real which instituted a certain freedom. We now see that that middle step is the integration of contingency with volition under the name of *potentia*.

The consequence is dramatic, for importing impossibility as universal condition amounts to importing a global perspective, that is, internalising a whole world.

The significance of this grafting of the outside onto a substance's 'inside' extends far beyond jurisprudence, though one might say that legislative judgements are the conditions of any philosophy. Gilles Deleuze, for example, engages in critique of the phenomenological view that commonality of sense and intensionality guarantee participation in the same World, without reference either to transcendental essences or noumena. Part of his argument against Husserl and Merleau-Ponty, whereby Deleuze shows that this commonality internalises a single, fixed manner of thinking as if natural to the subject, relies on showing how Leibniz has already undertaken just such an internalisation of a common world. Of particular resonance for our purposes are the following claims, already highlighted by Sjoerd van Tuinen[65] in the context of the phenomenological debate:

(a) 'The world must be placed in the subject in order for the subject to be for the world.'[66] Being for the world here is understood as the consequence of internalising the contingent. Remember that the contingent, as determinant of will, is experienced as passion or affect of the individual. What is the force of the contingent? The pretensions are demanded by primary passive force, that is, by the morality of universal repugnance. Each substance then internalises a 'derivative force' from the outside as if it is its own, and in this way, Deleuze argues, is captured by external power.

(b) Deleuze, quoting Gabriel Tarde: 'The true opposite of the self is not the non-self, it is the mine; the true opposite of being, that is, the having, is not non-being, but the had.'[67] Deleuze in part aims here at just that appropriation of power which is at the heart of Leibniz's move: the world is laid claim to, even as it continues to determine the contingent. Specifically, Tarde identifies the in-potency that is the contrary of the supposit not with non-being (the null), but at least in the moral sphere with possession if not also property.

(c) Phenomenological common sense has its origins in the Leibnizian interaction between what is presented by contingency as perceived by the individual and the 'spontaneous' choice of that individual motivated by reflection. This reflection, Deleuze claims, is of the whole world – the global primary passive force brought within the substance – for how else could every substance increase this reflection together in a community, as we have seen in Chapter 6? Hence there follows: 'the transformation of the currently perceived world into an objectively real world, into an objective Nature'.[68]

One might question whether Deleuze has fully accounted for Leibniz's internalisation of the world. It seems contradictory to suggest that a subject be captured by a world when metaphysically that world is internal to each substance already. Yet of course the contradiction only arises if the premise of a priori internalisation is accepted. Deleuze's critique of Leibniz and of phenomenology is that no such unitary, ordered World pre-exists, and that the doctrine of common sense inherits from Leibniz the imposition of a single World (*Welt*) whose rational coherence is anchored in God. Common sense is as much a denial of the truly new, the chaotic World-breaking event, as it is its programmatic guise as property claim, a permission for the subject to submit the environment (the *Umwelt*[69]) to common sense and therefore bring it into line with the rationally ordered World.

We see then that jurisprudential significance of Leibniz's surgical grafting of a world into substance itself extends to foundational philosophical debates, but our purpose is not to wander so far; rather we can already draw specific conclusions for Leibniz's conception of the Good Man.

Observe then that on this world-internalising interpretation, the necessity of the Good Man extends to the absolute power of creation – it refers not to an isolated act but situates a proposed act within the reality of a world, and is thus universal for that world. In this way obligation rightfully stands in place of a universal quantifier which implies the particularity of *ius* as its subaltern. The obligated act is itself twofold. In its choice it is evaluated according to its reality maximising capacity, and as such it is immediately referred to its variety in this world. But also in its actualisation it is an objective act constituting the future conditions of a world (like a choice of axiom schema) within which further just acts are possible. This universality is founded on a kind of intellectual repugnance which derives from the second axiom which Leibniz wishes to set beside the *cogito*: that there is a multiplicity amongst our thoughts. Variety and its expansion is desired by us subject to our affectation by its order and coherence. If we understand 'density' in its topological sense, as infinitely intersecting constituent parts or neighbourhoods, then Leibniz constructs his Good Man as someone obligated by the hypothetical necessity of not a Weigelian legal *spatium*, but rather a dense reality of cohering and well-ordered reals. The Good Man is endowed with an evaluative perspicacity (*pernoscere*) for just this purpose.

Hence Leibniz's universalism is not discrete and iterative. We earlier observed that the work of the substance is its own perfection, and the work of the human substance is the human as rational animal. The choice to self-determine as *the* work could so easily have been translated as a universal duty to complete all humans *as* work and so to replicate the inner life in the outer. Leibniz's second truth sees the affective movement of love as coming from the posited 'outside', from a nature or multiplicity which is, however, the dual of the act of thought. The division marks out *potentia* and so right as a separate sphere which is not bound deterministically to the intensionality of intellect, and accordingly it demands attribution of an obligation which reflects this converse direction of travel (nature to end) and the character of the source: not subjective intension but the objective relations of an ordered manifold – the World.

3.3 What is it that a Good Man wills?

We now introduce into the formal discussion the following construction that is the lodestar of the *Elementa Iuris*: *vir bonus amat omnes* (the Good Man loves all), which I argue turns out to be a universalist obligation in the truly Leibnizian sense of that term: the Good Man does not love each discrete person, but rather loves maximal reality.

First let us briefly reprise our understanding of will and reality from Chapter 4. Both God and human share intensional and pretensional equivalence: on the one hand the mind intends a great variety of possibles as it reconstructs the divine intellect; on the other the contingent real entities pretend to existence, and there is equipollence of these pretensions for God and human world. The order of the real is a hierarchy in which lower real entities compose higher real entities, and the *motus primo primi* of this composition is the pretension towards perfection or entelechy whereby the lower reals *demand* to compose and so be realised in higher reals. Finite real entities cannot perfect themselves save with the assistance of other real entities, but they need not compose reality at every level; it is enough that a constituent real entity serve its purpose for the higher without the higher engaging in an infinite analysis of the real. In this way finite entities must engage the *potentia* of matter in order to attain perfection

The human is situated within this hierarchy and the human will is set before the affections which are nothing other than the demands of infinitely many real entities striving for realisation at the human level. These pretensions at the human level are primarily directed towards the human entelechy in such a fashion that while each composed real entity strives for further composition of some kind, it is for the human to superadd its spontaneous choice as to which compossible to realise *for* attainment of this individual human's perfection. This capacity to range across not just individual actions, but also these passions, to range across the subaltern active potencies and the contradictory passive potencies, raises will to an in-potency in just the sense Aristotle ascribes to the crafts or practical sciences,[70] and in the sense Leibniz would ascribe, if Stahl is to be believed, to a positive institution.[71] This free choice, however, remains determined by the rationality of the institution, for as with God each realisation at a given level must neither contradict the laws of reason that hold at that level nor be internally inconsistent. This is most easily seen in the physical example of mass which refuses any composition that endeavours to compose two masses in a new entity that would occupy the same position – the composing masses would find this composition repugnant and would repel each other by virtue of the derivative force they derive from primary matter (subsequently primary passive force).

This hierarchy of the real is emphasised in the definition of love elaborated in Concepts B and C the *Elementa Iuris*, which amounts to seeking the optimum status of a person, this status being not their individuating principle as such but rather the aggregate of qualitative accidents, that is, their contingent real constituents.[72] In light of middle period developments of this doctrine, exemplified by the *Discourse on Metaphysics*, optimum status can be understood as that aggregation of real entities which is maximal, or *maximal reality*. Accordingly, Leibniz's Good Man does not will for every person what he wills for himself; rather he wills the greatest ordered variety at every level of a world: *amat omnes* all the way down. And given that the choice of a real entity is nothing but the choice of rules that maximise reality by permitting the greatest range of possibilities that constitute that real entity, we might say that the Good Man wills a world, and a world of worlds, to infinity. We might say, following Nicholas Rescher, that the Good Man seeks the maximal reality of some person, both downwards as a real entity subordinating real, constituent entities, and upwards within a collegium or other reals or moral entities whose pinnacles are the state and the *Civitas Dei*. The state *spatium* becomes a nested structure of real interdependence.

3.4 State spaces and obligation

What are the natural legal consequences of Leibniz's integration of power *qua* state space within the concept of the finite rational individual? Compare Leibniz's position with his most immediate starting point in the new legal thinking: Grotius. Leibniz's three degrees of right take on a new aspect, and now stand in marked difference from the Dutchman. For Grotius the second degree of right – equity – is an *aptitude* of the individual, that is, an imperfect *potestas* of a person to make judgements according to conscience when a strict application of the law is found wanting. Leibniz, as Grua notes,[73] raises this mere aptitude to an obligation. But we can say more than this, provided we understand that the Good Man is constructed as having internalised what we have called the state space, that is, the well-ordered field of consequences. The Leibnizian perspective, already nascent in Part II of the *Nova Methodus*,[74] proceeds in two stages. The first pertains to equity, which now is to be conceived as the mind of the Good Man being inclined by the reflective pretensions of what is possible *and* what is contingent. In this way equity operates just because the contingent exceeds the rational ordering of the law which the finite mind has endeavoured to produce.

The second stage, which marks the clear break, is the designation of the third degree of justice – piety – as formally 'universal' insofar as it reflects the whole world of the individual in which and for which it makes its judgements.[75] Here the differences between Concepts B and C of the *Elementa* indicate that Leibniz has developed the conceptual apparatus underpinning piety before he designates this apparatus as the third degree of right. Particularly, Concept B speaks of the universal intellection (*pernoscere*) which is at the root of the love of the Good Man, but in what follows he appears to designate the acts consequent on love as a moral power. In Concept C we find the bridging sentence to a formal definition of the third degree of right: that 'the wise . . . can neither do nor believe possible . . . deeds which harm piety or which are against good morals'.[76]

By 1693 Leibniz would phrase his thinking on piety as follows: strict right and equity 'are perfected through piety, that is, by what one owes [*debet*] to God'.[77] Does this perfectibility not speak directly to Grotius, who relegates considerations of equity to imperfect aptitudes,[78] so denying justice the status of perfected faculty? In the Good Man Leibniz raises justice to perfection, and he does so by referring the Good Man to God through means of what is owed. What is owed is the exigence placed in all matter by God's *potentia*, but Leibniz has sited this *potentia* within the individual, permitting the identification of a global ordering through moral repugnance with an individual's universal obligations. 'What is truly just is that which is not against conscience', that is, that which has 'been impressed under a Universal aspect'.[79] A mere Grotian *potestas* to do now becomes a *potentia*, thereby replicating at the finite level the move first made by Aquinas and Duns Scotus in granting absolute power to God and sovereign. In this way Leibniz completes his movement away from the mechanistic accounts of Hobbes and others, for whom external power is a determinant and restraint of individual liberty, and internalises this state power, indeed this power of nature, as an absolutely effective *potentia* and *obligation* of the Good Man.

We can be under no doubt that this new conception moves Leibniz beyond mere amelioration of the strict law, as equity requires. The obligations and *potentia* of piety are moved by the realm of the real, and so of the pretensions to exist of an infinity of real entities. Leibniz makes constant reference in his *Elementa* definitions of the Good Man to *pernoscere* – the knowing a thing's actions to the least degree, that is, through all its combinations and so 'universally'.[80] In the great hierarchy of the Leibnizian real the Good Man is inclined not just by defects within the strict application of rules at a given level, but by the *potentia* of a great many realities striving to exist. Through requiring the Good Man to compensate identity through diversity, Leibniz speaks to a power of, if not creation, then realisation of difference. Yet though this power be manifested in contingency as much as possibility, it remains anchored in the rationality of a world, and every real subset of that world. The universal power of the Good Man is therefore neither a homogeneous superfluity such as we find in Spinoza, nor a power of equality which must apply the same principle equally across all coexistent cases. The universality of Leibniz's power is a universality of depth, extending into the infinitesimal and applying the obligation to realise maximally at every level.

4. Conclusion: the internalisation of power

By redefining *potentia* as constituted both of action and contingency, Leibniz heralds the internalisation of objective Nature, that is, the World. Hobbes's mechanism, and the stronger rational determinism of Spinoza threaten free will precisely because of the scientific force of their doctrines. Leibniz's gambit is to preserve the physical laws of nature, and the rationality of intellect, by grafting onto each subject the contingency that derives from the world around. The conceptual move is perhaps not wholly original. Simo Knuutilla argues[81] that Duns Scotus does something not dissimilar by placing contingency within the power of God. Specifically, Duns Scotus observes a strict modal difference between what is logically necessary in a given world and what could exist in a number of different states. Contingency indeed, in a narrow sense, but observe that for an infinitely powerful God the global appreciation of the best arrangement of contingent states converges on necessity after a fashion. Indeed, so powerful is God in this respect that He can choose whole frameworks of necessity and contingency – the reality of a World *in toto* – so demonstrating his *potentia absoluta*. Leibniz's move is truly striking, for he places contingency under the power of human beings, affirming as he does the finitude of the individual.

Leibniz achieves this reconceptualisation of power in a series of ruptures. He moves from the consequentialist heritage to determine a difference between necessity of the consequence and necessity of the consequent, and he holds that the Good Man be obligated to know that certain consequences in a given reality are obligated or prohibited, that is, that certain acts are morally necessary/absurd in every case or universally. It seems then that Leibniz imports into the practical activity of finite creatures the kinds of universalist considerations heretofore reserved to the divinity. And as if to underscore the demand Leibniz makes on individual conscience, Leibniz understands universality not simply as every case understood as a simple aggregate, but invests each case with subsidiary cases, mirroring the Scotist nested hierarchy of the reals. To maximise reality the Good Man must 'see thoroughly' the great variety of reals that can be brought together in greater and greater communities.

To bring both necessity and impossibility, what is owed and what is prohibited, together in the same individual, Leibniz unites the two terms, previously markers of subjective and objective perspectives, together under his redefinition of obligation. The logical result? That which was sought all along: that if the primary passive cause of contingency is now built into the subject as its World, then contingency also follows. Now the right of the Good Man ranges over not just what is permitted and derivative of the supposit's activity, thereby reflecting rational will, but also over what is omissible and contingent, and which has its roots in the internalised World. Here is a finite *potentia* that has laid moral claim to the World even as it fails truly to grasp it intellectually.

The trick of such an internalisation is what would become known as common sense. If we assume that the World is rationally ordered, guaranteed by God, then much of the radical potential of Leibniz's move is lost, for there remains an echo of Scotism in that anchoring of Nature in the infinitely powerful One's choices. Thanks to such a God we can be assured that the *ens commune* of rational being is mirrored by a single order of the real – a City of God – and that the spontaneous action of the creature reflects on the universal coherence and density of that order. Yet what if no such order subsists, and what if the out-there of Nature (the environment) is an as yet unordered or variously ordered manifold? What if *the* World is something individuals actualise because contingency, in the guise of affects, rewards the appropriation of the environment within a purely ideological framework named common sense? Leibnizian contingency remains bound to a certain universality, and in this way remains still all too 'safe'. At least two routes freeing up contingency as power would seem to be immediately open, however. One is to free such power from universal conditions altogether, regarding them as pure signs of simple concatenations of contingent events. This could be an interpretation of the challenge of Hume, for whom a right, for example to govern, can indeed be the contingent product, and no more, of the imaginative association by a populace. The other is locate in individual contingency a groundless ground, that is, creative power of willing which constructs its own universality in time as right. These though are matters for further investigation.

Notes

1. Gábor Gángó, 'The Formation of Leibniz's Mature Ethics and his *Specimen Polonorum*', working paper given on 31 October 2018 at Mainz, <https://www.db-thueringen.de/servlets/MCRFileNodeServlet/dbt_derivate_00040557/leibniz_mature_ethics_gango.pdf> (last accessed 2 November 2019), pp.1–2.

2. See for example Donald Rutherford, *Leibniz and the Rational Order of Nature* (Cambridge: Cambridge University Press, 1995) pp.46–7; Gregory Brown, 'Happiness and Justice' in Maria Rosa Antognazza (ed.) *The Oxford Handbook of Leibniz* (Oxford: Oxford University Press, 2018) pp.623–40; Gregory Brown, 'Disinterested Love: Understanding Leibniz's Reconciliation of Self- and Other-regarding Motives' (2011) 19 *British J. Hist. Phil.* 265–303; Christopher Johns, *The Science of Right in Leibniz's Moral and Political Philosophy* (London: Bloomsbury, 2013) ch.1; Robert J. Mulvaney, 'The Early Development of Leibniz's Concept of Justice' (1968) 29 *J. Hist. Ideas* 53–72.

3. Nicholas Rescher, '*Contingentia Mundi*. Leibniz on the World's Contingency' (2001) 33(2) *Studia Leibnitiana* 145–62.

4. Maria Rosa Antognazza, *Leibniz: An Intellectual Biography* (Cambridge: Cambridge University Press, 2009) pp.81–5.

5. Antognazza, *Leibniz*, p.84.

6. A:VI, i, XIX.

7. Gángó, *Specimen Polonorum*, p.2.

8. Hubertus Busche, *Leibniz's Weg ins perspektivishe Universum: Eine Harmonie im Zeitalter der Berechnung* (Hamburg: Meiner, 1997) p.357, cited by Gángó, *Specimen Polonorum*, p.3.

9. Gerd van den Heuvel, 'Theorie und Praxis der Politik bei Leibniz im Kontext des Glorious Revolution under der hannoverchen Sukzession' in Friedrich Beiderbeck et al. (eds), *Umwelt und Weltgestaltung. Leibniz' politisches Denken in seiner Zeit* (Göttingen: Vanderhoek & Ruprecht, 2015) pp.511–26, cited by Gángó, *Specimen Polonorum*, p.2.

10. I thank Stuart Elden for this point.

11. A:VI, iv, 2758.

12. A:VI, iv, 2777.

13. A:VI, i, 454.
14. A:VI, i, 455–6. Technically speaking *ius strictum* does appear, but the term appears to be applied as if borrowed, and its narrow sense here is explained by reference to equity (contrary to the *Nova Methodus* which distinguishes the two); it is not a foundational term.
15. *'capiendi'* denotes a sense of apprehending the volition.
16. A:VI, i, 465. I have broken up the paragraph into a list for ease of comprehension.
17. Namely Chapter XIV TTP, Samuel Shirley (trans.), *Spinoza: Complete Works* (Indianapolis, IN: Hackett, 2002).
18. Ger:VII, 572–4; L:105–7.
19. 13 July 1670 according to the Julian calendar applicable in England until 1752.
20. The quotations here and in the remainder of the paragraph are from the letter of 13/22 July 1670, L:105–6.
21. Johns, *Science of Right*, p.50.
22. The point is rudimentary, see e.g. Johan van Bentham, *Modal Logic for Open Minds* (Stanford: CLSI, 2010) p.12.
23. Robin Smith (ed.) *Aristotle's Prior Analytics* (Minneapolis: Hackett, 1989) A13.
24. A:VI i, 465.
25. Jaakko Hintikka, 'Was Leibniz's Deity an *Akrates*?' in S. Knuutila (ed.) *Modern Modalities* (Dordrecht: Kluwer, 1988) pp.102–3.
26. Antonie Vos and Eef Dekker, 'Modalities in Francis Turrettin – an Essay in Reformed Theology' in Maarten Wisse et al. (ed.), *Scholasticism Reformed: Essays in Honour of Willem J. Van Asselt* (Leiden: Brill, 2010) pp.74–91.
27. Nicholas Rescher, '*Contingentia Mundi*. Leibniz on the World's Contingency' (2001) 33(2) *Studia Leibnitiana* 145–62.
28. On Duns Scotus see also Gwenaëlle Aubry, *Genèse du Dieu souverain* (Paris: Vrin, 2018), pp.241–6.
29. Vos and Dekker, 'Turrettin', p.88.
30. Richard A. Muller, 'Review of English Hypothetical Universalism: John Preston and the Softening of Reformed Theology by Jonathan Moore' (2008) 43 *Calvin Theological Journal*, pp.149–150.
31. After Moses Amyraut (1596–1664).
32. Vos and Dekker, 'Turrettin', p.76.
33. *Institutio*, I-3, 21, 3.
34. *Institutio*, I-3, 21, 8.
35. *Institutio*, I-3, 21,11: 'Contradictorium enim illud dicitur quod est impossibile *logice*, id quod habet *repugnantiam*, et

quod includit *praedicata contradictoria.'* (Trans. of *repugnantia* modified from Vos and Dekker, 'Turrettin', p.77).

36. Ibid.
37. *Institutio*, I-3, 21, 12: 'Contradictoria autem sunt impossibilia, quia sunt in*com*possibilia.' Quoted by Vos and Dekker, 'Turrettin', p.77.
38. *Institutio*, I-3, 21, 12: '*Alia* mediate et *implicita*, quando termini repugnantes virtualiter tantum et *implicite* contradictionem includunt ... Talia enim involvunt praedicata contradictoria, quae incurrunt in principium indubitatae veritatis: *impossibile est idem esse et non esse simul.'* Vos and Dekker, 'Turrettin', p.78.
39. To use Vos and Dekker's neutral synonym for 'world'.
40. L:147 n.1.
41. L:146.
42. Rescher, *'Contingentia Mundi'*.
43. Ibid. pp.155–6.
44. Ibid. p.156.
45. Rescher, *'Contingentia Mundi'*, pp.155–6, using Gr:493.
46. 'This great example of the laws of motion shows us in the clearest possible way how much difference there is among these three cases, first, *an absolute necessity*, metaphysical or geometric, which can be called blind and which depends only on efficient causes; in the second place, *a moral necessity*, which comes from the free choice of wisdom with respect to final causes; and finally in the third place, *something absolutely arbitrary*, depending on an indifference or equilibrium.' (*Theodicy*, quoted by Rescher, p.157.)
47. A:VI, iv, 2577, quoted by Rescher at p.147: 'From God's own essence and supreme perfection it certainly follows, and so to speak by consequential necessity (*necessitas consequentiae*), that God chooses the best. But he chooses the best freely, for in the best there is no absolute necessity' (some time between 1680 and 1684).
48. Jean-Pascal Alcantara, 'Leibniz, Modal Logic and Possible World Semantics: The Apulean Square as a Procrustean Bed for his Modal Metaphysics' in Jean-Yves Béziau and Dale Jacquette (eds), *Around and Beyond the Square of Opposition* (Basel: Springer, 2012) 53–71.
49. Ibid, pp.61–2.
50. A:II, i, 386–92; L:151–5.
51. Some consideration is to be given as to the translation here. The sense of *varieté* in French is of a number of discrete and different items, and I have cautiously adopted the English

'variety' and not the more suggestive 'multiplicity' accordingly (as does Loemker).

52. A:II, i, 388.
53. L:154.
54. We may observe that Deleuze will radicalise this second 'truth' by making it productive of the first (the subject) in his rereading of Hume: Gilles Deleuze, *Empiricism and Subjectivity* (New York: Columbia University Press, 1991).
55. We should note that this is an axiom of some modal logics, and was certainly taken as axiomatic by the Schoolmen after Scotus.
56. A:VI, i, 465 (Concept B); 480 (Concept C).
57. A:VI, I, 466–7 (Concept B); 481–5 (Concept C).
58. I.e. not $x \rightarrow$ not possible that the Good Man do x.
59. A:VI, i, 481–2.
60. '... Quisquis potest debet. Sufficit ergo ad amorem etiam pessimi capacitas boni. Sed in casu conscursus cedere deterior debet' (A:VI, I, 482).
61. In Concept C these definitions naturally follow the definitions of *iustum* etc., whereas in Concept B they precede them (A:VI, i, 480).
62. As we shall see in the next section, *potentia* here ranges across both possibility and contingency.
63. See for example Alan Norrie, *Justice and the Slaughter Bench: Essays on Law's Broken Dialectic* (New York: Routledge, 2016).
64. The context here is that Leibniz is considering what is elsewhere called a 'complete concept' definition of a substance, though he uses the terms 'essence' and 'definition' here in a manner redolent of Spinozist determinism.
65. Sjoerd van Tuinen, 'A Transcendental Philosophy of the Event: Deleuze's Non-Phenomenological Reading of Leibniz' in Sjoerd van Tuinen and Niamh McDonnell (eds), *Deleuze and the Fold: A Critical Reader* (London: Palgrave Macmillan, 2010) pp.155–83 at pp.174–5. The quotations from Deleuze that follow are also highlighted by van Tuinen in a different context.
66. Gilles Deleuze, *The Fold: Leibniz and the Baroque* (London: Athlone Press, 1986) p.26.
67. Deleuze, *The Fold*, p.110.
68. Deleuze, *The Fold*, p.105.
69. van Tuinen, 'A Transcendental Philosophy', p.173.
70. ... διὸ πᾶσαι αἱ τέχναι καὶ αἱ ποιητικαὶ ἐπιστῆμαι δυνάμεις εἰσίν. *Meta.* IX [1046b2–3].
71. See Chapter 6, 'A New Method for a New Law?' and also

François Duchesneau and Justin E.H. Smith (trans.), *The Leibniz-Stahl Controversy* (New Haven: Yale University Press, 2016) p.342.

72. A I, i, 466–7; 482–3.
73. Gaston Grua, *Jurisprudence universelle et théodicée selon Leibniz* (Paris: PUF, 1953) pp.229–30.
74. A:VI, i, 342–5; *Nova Methodus* §§71–5.
75. Ger:III, 386–7; L:422–33, *Preface to the Codex Iuris Gentium Diplomaticus* (1693).
76. A:VI, i, 480.
77. Ri:63, from the *Meditations on Common Concept of Justice*.
78. L:422, and Grotius, *De iure belli et pacis*, I, i, 5.
79. A:VI, i, 463, *Elementa* Concept A.
80. 'Pernoscere est, nosse quid res agere aut pati possit scil. tum per se, tum aliis combinata. . . . Hinc sequitur neminem esse ullius rei pernoscentem nisi idem sit sapiens seu pernoscens univeralis.' A:VI, i, 466.
81. Simo Knuuttila, 'Time and Modality in Scholasticism' in S. Knuuttila (ed.), *Reforming the Great Chain of Being* (Dordrecht: Reidel, 1981) pp.163–259, and the discussion by Gwenaëlle Aubry in *Genèse du Dieu souverain*, (Paris: Vrin, 2018) p.233.

Conclusion

In her *Genèse du Dieu souverain*, Gwenaëlle Aubry makes a methodological point particularly pertinent to the present study:

> Such an archaeology [of power] thus also goes against a necessitarian and continuist reading of the history of metaphysics, which inscribes at its source a principle thought of violence.[1] It renders visible the contingent rather than fated character of the familiar settlement [*dispositif*] which identifies both being with the first being and this with power [*puissance*], by recalling that Aristotelian metaphysics bears another settlement, radically distinct and thus also an alternative. In the end, decoupling the *arché* from the effects generally attributed to it must allow the manifestation, indeed the liberation, of others.[2]

While Aubry's particular concern here is Agamben's isolation of a notion of inefficacy or inoperativity (*argon*) in Aristotle, which he opposes to the traditionally developed link between power and *real* work, the archaeological animadversion against linear histories of power has wider application. Leibniz is a particular thinker of power who appears, if anything, to reverse trends but also innovates (or at least renovates) the linkage between power and spatial order.

Our survey of Leibniz's key legal texts from his early period, in the light of their revisions in the middle period reflecting his philosophical development, has focused on his rearticulation of *potentia* and its relationship to what Leibniz, following the Schoolmen, terms the supposit. At the beginning of this work I posed three questions to guide my enquiry, and we might record these answers to them.

Conclusion

First, Leibniz effects a reversal to the trends of the medieval thinkers by ostensibly decoupling *potentia* from God and reverting to an apparently more Aristotelean privileging of activity whereby *potentia* becomes but a mark of finitude. He does not avail himself of activity as such, however. He initially takes up the Scholastic notion of the supposit which is to be understood as a self-actualising activity. It is this line of thought which leads Leibniz, by the middle period, to prefer an explicitly Aristotelean term for just this kind of movement: entelechy. It should be stressed that Leibniz is thereby not abandoning all that the Schoolmen have to offer, for in a sense the power of the Thomist God also flows from the necessary movement of his self-actualisation: the *purus actus essendi*. According to this line of thought, this absolute divine power is very much experienced and suffered by finite creatures, either through its eminence or excess. What we have termed intensional equivalence permits Leibniz to put forward a theory in which the rational activity of being acts as self-sufficient principle which need not act on anything else. Rather, from the perspective of final causes the effects of this rational being are not *caused* by it, but have being as their principle. On the Leibnizian account this amounts not to a movement from cause to effect, but a movement from effect to principle, that is, from possible to existence to end: the pretension. This doctrine is manifested most elaborately in the notions of reflection and reality, in which that real which is constituted by the most subordinate reals is deemed best in the 'eyes' of God and Good Man because this effect reflects the multiplicity of the divine activity.

Observe a subsidiary metaphysical shift of emphasis here: for thinkers of absolute power, Scholastic as much as Spinozist, the inherently absolute, unthinkable and otherwise homogenous nature of absolute power entails a corresponding need that the very supremacy of this power can only ever be known to us through its effects. What exists, therefore, is naturally right because existence can be the only measure of this power. If the given can be said to lack, it always lacks with respect to an eminent power defined through its assumed excess of the finite. Leibniz makes a double identification of being and intelligibility, and this with God, and places this construct on a plane of intensional and indeed pretensional equivalence with rational creatures. The effects become the means to reflect intelligible being, but the reference point always is that rational activity itself (not its approximation) – hence Leibniz's consistent attempts to draw out the 'elements' of rational activity, be they the combinatorial structures of jurisprudence, the dispositions of any state space, or the innate or primary ideas.

We might usefully situate Leibniz's account of power and the rational activity of being against the reprise of absolute power in the work of Carl Schmitt, much as Aubry does with her own conclusions concerning the Schoolmen.[3] Noting that for Schmitt the modern correlate of the miracle – manifestation of God's absolute power – is the *state of exception*, Aubry following Agamben[4] makes explicit the relation between Schmitt's omnipotent, albeit marginal legislator who is capable of triggering the state of exception in the place of legislation, and respectively the *ordered power* and *absolute power* of medieval theologians.[5] Could it be said that Leibniz's God, retaining a residual infinite capacity to realise any world without determination, thereby also retains an absolute 'power' (though named activity)? Our discussions of hypothetical necessity suggest that even the absolute privilege of creation is bounded within laws. That God chooses the best is not necessary, but *if* he chooses, *then* the best is chosen, and the best is grounded in a global assessment of what is not contradictory (*atopon*) for this world. In holding to a bare minimum of order in the miraculous exercise of the absolute power of creation, I would say Leibniz is not so far from Duns Scotus properly understood. For even this leading thinker of *potentia absoluta* held that whatever world could be created, there were some creations *repugnant* to the mind of God and therefore impossible to be created.

Second, Leibniz's demotion of *potentia* operates on a second front, against the materialism of new philosophers such as Hobbes and Spinoza. On the one hand, by making *potentia* that which is not explicable by the finite will, Leibniz appears prepared to accept seventeenth century ideas that the action of a corpuscle is to be determined by the power of some other thing, but on the other, he also entertains the interpretation that *potentia* and passion are not equally deleterious. Rather, one can understand that a body has appropriated *potentia*, and that its own action is achieved or supplemented though not explicable entirely by its own reasons. In this way, we arrive again at a hierarchy of reals, or now substantial forms, which comprise an inbuilt need for a great many other reals, and so *potentia*, to achieve actualisation. This allows Leibniz to change perspective from the particularities of actions and passions, and thus from effects, to the perspective of their principles. By applying the interpretative square of power, we see how Leibniz could have come to the view that action and passion, volition and *potentia*, are but subalterns to their respective universals: activity and *materia prima*, which by the middle period Leibniz has renamed primary active force and primary passive force. The discursive framework of *potentia* then is capable of reappraisal through a new explanatory apparatus of universal primary forces. This 'universal' standpoint permits explanation from the perspective of the whole world or system in which events occur, and thus can speak to the degree of reality by which a specific event reflects that whole system. Again we may note that this shift of focus rearticulates a homogenous power–effect relation as a rationally ordered principle–reality relation. The violence of mechanism is situated within a universal appraisal of a kingdom of ends.

Third, while Leibniz initially appears to have relegated *potentia* as a concept, a conceptual node once variously filled by *dunamis, dunamei, potentia* and *materia prima* is not abandoned but is now filled with the principle of primary passive potency, a notion which, for our juridically focused purposes, is elaborated as a kind of principle of normative spatiality. In the context of Leibniz's *Elementa Iuris* we have argued that Leibniz develops such a normed space from Weigel's state *spatium* as a modality. This space, which seems cognate with Leibniz's notion of World, which may have its roots in Duns Scotus's modal theory. It is to be understood as the basic universal conditions or parameters of what ought (not) to exist in a given world as part of that whole. A given modality determines both what is necessary and so obligated, for it is universally the case for every real in a world, and what is impossible and so prohibited, for it is *atopon* and has no place in that world. From these universal conditions the possibilities and contingencies of what is just and omissible flow. Our reading of pretension has allowed us to observe that this modality is no static settlement of any space; rather, it is in the very nature of primary passive force that every derivative possibility is invested with a moral force, that is, with a juridical claim which is reflected by degrees in the activity of our being. Thus once again we find Leibniz opposing, with his conception of a space which is well-ordered because of its subjection to a norm, that conception of power which Aubry claims has its 'ultimate root in a determinate concept of power as immediate and *non-normed* efficiency'.[6]

Leibniz's theory of space, of which the state constitutes a special case, thereby comprises several remarkable innovations which are in stark opposition to the a-normativity of absolute power. These moves include: (a) the interiorisation of the world within the substantial form as that which the entity is not; (b) the conception of each such world as the logical contrary of the individual, such that it also is both rationally ordered and primary cause of its spatial effects; (c) the conception of a world not as an effect, that is, a distributed order but as a set of modal and indeed deontic principles capable of axiomatic application in every case, that is, universally; and (d) the consequent imbuement of every possible element of a space with a morality deriving from these universally applicable norms.

Already perhaps we can discern certain key features in Leibniz's legal thinking which manifest themselves via Christian Wolff in the universal duty of Kant, that is, in a norm which is applicable to every possible case irrespective of the presence of a given human. Yet in our text we have had occasion rather to refer to Husserl, and the suggestive lineage to the phenomenologist's theories concerning *Urdoxa*, common sense, and the very conditions of apprehending a spatialised, sensuous World. Taking up again Aubry's warning to the archaeologist that the branches and indeed possibilities of the metaphysics of power are irreducible to one history, might we observe that far from the traditional history of Schmittian absolute power, we find through Leibniz's thinking of a normed or state space, a different lineage of power? A lineage in which normed spatiality – be it physical, sensuous, economic, moral, juridical – and the 'elements' through which space is built, play out a parallel history.

Frankfurt am Main, 2020

Notes

1. Here Aubry references Jacques Derrida's 'Violence et méta-physique. Essai sur la pensée d'Emmanuel Levinas' collected in *L'Écriture et la différence* (Paris: Seuil, 1967).
2. Gwenaëlle Aubry, *Genèse du Dieu souverain* (Paris: Vrin, 2018), p.282.
3. Aubry, *Genèse*, p.274.
4. Giorgio Agamben, *État d'exception. Homo sacer II, 1* (Paris: Seuil, 2003), p.43.
5. I thank Anton Schütz for editorial assistance on this point.
6. Aubry, *Genèse*, p.281, my emphasis.

Bibliography

R.M. Adams, *Leibniz: Determinist, Theist, Idealist* (Oxford: Oxford University Press, 1994)

Giorgio Agamben, *Potentialities: Collected Essays in Philosophy* (Stanford: Stanford University Press, 1999)

Giorgio Agamben, *État d'exception. Homo sacer II, 1* (Paris: Seuil, 2003)

Giorgio Agamben, *The Kingdom and the Glory* (Lorenzo Chiesa trans.) (Stanford: Stanford University Press, 2011)

Georgio Agamben, *Creation and Anarchy: The Work of Art and the Religion of Capitalism* (Adam Kotsko trans.) (Stanford: Stanford University Press, 2019)

Lilli Alanen and Simon Knuuttila, 'Modality in Descartes and his Predecessors' in Simon Knuuttila (ed.) *Modern Modalities* (Amsterdam: Kluwer, 1988)

Jean-Pascal Alcantara, 'Leibniz, Modal Logic and Possible World Semantics: The Apulean Square as a Procrustean Bed for his Modal Metaphysics' in Jean-Yves Béziau and Dale Jacquette (eds), *Around and Beyond the Square of Opposition* (Basel: Springer, 2012) 53–71

Maria Rosa Antognazza, 'Inediti Leibniziani sulle polemiche trinitare' (1991) 83 *Revista di filosofia scolastica* 525–50

Maria Rosa Antognazza, 'Leibniz de Deo Trino: Philosophical Aspects of Leibniz's Conception of the Trinity' (2001) 37 *Religious Studies* 1–13.

Maria Rosa Antognazza, *Leibniz on the Trinity and the Incarnation* (Gerald Parks trans.) (New Haven: Yale, 2007)

Maria Rosa Antognazza, *Leibniz: An Intellectual Biography* (Cambridge: Cambridge University Press, 2009)

Maria Rosa Antognazza, 'Metaphysical Evil Revisited' in Larry M. Jorgensen and Samuel Newlands (eds), *New*

Bibliography

Essays on Leibniz's Theodicy (Oxford: Oxford University Press, 2014)

Thomas Aquinas, *Opera Omnia. Leonine Edition*, vols 4–12 (Vatican City: Typis Polyglottis Vaticanis, 1882–)

Thomas Aquinas, P. Marc, C. Pera and P. Caramello (eds), *Liber de veritate catholicae Fidei contra errores infidelium deu Summa contra Gentiles*, vols 1–4 (Turin and Rome: Marietti, 1961)

Roger Ariew and Marjorie Grene, *Descartes and His Contemporaries* (Chicago: University of Chicago Press, 1995)

Aristotle, J. Barnes (ed.), *Complete Works of Aristotle: Revised Oxford Translation*, 2 vols (Princeton: Princeton University Press, 1984)

Aristotle, Robin Smith (ed.) *Aristotle's Prior Analytics* (Minneapolis: Hackett, 1989)

Aristotle, C.D.C. Reeve (trans.), *Aristotle: Metaphysics* (Indianapolis: Hacket, 2016)

Alberto Artosi, Bernardo Pieri and Giovanni Sartor (eds), *Leibniz: Logico-Philosophical Puzzles in the Law* (Dordrecht: Springer, 2013)

Gwenaëlle Aubry, *Dieu sans la puissance: dunamis et energeia chez Aristote et chez Plotin* (Paris: Vrin, 2006)

Gwenaëlle Aubry, '*Ousia Energeia* and *actus purus essendi* – from Aristotle to Aquinas: Some Groundwork for an Archeology of Power' (2015) *Tijdschrift voor Philosophie* 827–54

Gwenaëlle Aubry, *Genèse du Dieu souverain* (Paris: Vrin, 2018)

Alain Badiou, *Being and Event* (London: Continuum, 2005)

Alain Badiou, *Logics of Worlds* (London: Continuum, 2009)

Alain Badiou, *Mathematics of the Transcendental* (London: Bloomsbury, 2014)

Pierre Bayle, *Recueil de quelques pieces curieuses concernant la philosophie de M. Descartes* (Amsterdam: H. Desbordes, 1684)

Jonathan Beere, *Doing and Being: An Interpretation of Aristotle's Metaphysics Theta* (Oxford: Oxford University Press, 2009)

Yvon Belaval, *Leibniz: Initiation à sa philosophie*, 6th edn (Paris: Vrin, 2005)

Stefano di Bella, 'Some Perspectives on Leibniz's Nominalism and its Sources' in Stefano di Bella and Ted M. Schmaltz (eds), *The Problem of Universals in Early Modern Philosophy* (Oxford: Oxford University Press, 2017)

Otto Bird, 'The Tradition of the Logical Topics: Aristotle to Ockham' (1962) 23(3) *Journal of the History of Ideas* 307–23

G.A. Blair, 'Aristotle on Ἐντέλεχεια: A Reply to Daniel Graham' (1993) 114 *American Journal of Philology* 91–7

G.A. Blair, 'Unfortunately, It Is a Bit More Complex: Reflections on Ἐνέργεια' (1995) 15 *Ancient Philosophy* 565–80

David Blumenfeld, 'Leibniz's Theory of the Striving Possibles' (1973) 5 *Studia Leibnitiana* 163–77

A. Boehm, *Le 'vinculum substantiale' chez Leibniz* (Paris: Vrin, 1962)

David Bostock, *Plato's Theaetetus* (Oxford: Clarendon Press, 1988)

Pol Boucher, *GW Leibniz: Des Conditions* (Paris: Vrin, 2002)

Olivier Boulnois, 'Contingence et alternatives' in O. Boulnois (ed.) *La Puissance et son ombre. De Pierre Lombard à Luther* (Paris: Aubier, 1994)

Olivier Boulnois, 'Un autre concept de Dieu est possible, ou la fin de la Théodicée' (2010) 761 *Critique* 803–14

Christophe Bouton, *Time and Freedom* (Christopher Macann trans.) (Evanston, IL: Northwestern University Press, 2014)

Émile Bréhier, *La théorie des incorporels dans l'ancien stoïcisme*, 9th edn (Paris: Vrin, 1997)

Franz Brentano, *On the Several Senses of Being in Aristotle* (Rolf George trans.) (Berkeley: University of California Press, 1975)

Angus Brook, 'Substance and the Primary Sense of Being in Aristotle' 68(3) *The Review of Metaphysics* (March 2015) 521–44

Gregory Brown, 'Disinterested Love: Understanding Leibniz's Reconciliation of Self- and Other-regarding Motives' (2011) 19 *British J. Hist. Phil.* 265–303

Gregory Brown, 'Happiness and Justice' in Maria Rosa Antognazza (ed.) *The Oxford Handbook of Leibniz* (Oxford: Oxford University Press, 2018) pp.623–40

Oscar J. Brown, *Natural Rectitude and Divine Law in Aquinas* (Toronto: Pontifical Inst. Medieval Studies, 1981)

Thomas Browne, *Christian Morals* (London: Cambridge University Press, 1716)

Bibliography

Jean Buridan, *Summulae de Dialectica* (Klima trans.) (New Haven: Yale University Press, 2001)

Myles Burnyeat, *The Theaetetus of Plato* (M.J. Levett trans.) (Indianapolis: Hackett, 1990)

Hubertus Busche, *Leibniz's Weg ins perspektivishe Universum: Eine Harmonie im Zeitalter der Berechnung* (Hamburg: Meiner, 1997)

Peter J. Cameron, *Combinatorics: Topics, Techniques, Algorithms* (Cambridge: Cambridge University Press, 1994)

Gilles Châtelet, *Sur une petite phrase de Riemann* (1979) *Analytiques* 3

H.F. Cherniss, *Aristotle's Criticism of Plato and the Academy* (Baltimore: Johns Hopkins University Press 1944)

Marcus Tullius Cicero, *On Duties* (Cambridge, MA: Harvard University Press, 1913)

Stephen Connelly, *Spinoza, Right and Absolute Freedom* (Abingdon: Routledge, Birkbeck Law Press, 2015)

Robert Manuel Cook, 'Speculations on the Origins of Coinage' (1958) 7 *Historia* 257–67

Louis Couturat, *De l'infini mathématique* (Paris: Alcan, 1896)

Richard Cumberland, *De Legibus Naturae*, 2nd edn (Lübeck and Frankfurt am Main: Samuel Otto, 1683)

Eleanor Curran, 'Hobbes' Theory of Rights – A Modern Interest Theory' (2002) 6(1) *Journal of Ethics* 63–86

Haskell Curry, Robert Feys and William Craig, *Combinatorial Logic* Vol. 1 (Dordrecht: N. Holland, 1958)

Marcelo Dascal, 'Leibniz's Early Views on Definition' (1980) Suppl. 21 *Studia Leibnitiana* 33–50

Gilles Deleuze, *The Fold: Leibniz and the Baroque* (London: Athlone Press, 1986)

Gilles Deleuze, *Empiricism and Subjectivity* (New York: Columbia University Press, 1991)

Gilles Deleuze, *Difference and Repetition* (London: Athlone Press, 1994)

Jacques Derrida, 'Violence et métaphysique. Essai sur la pensée d'Emmanuel Levinas' collected in *L'Écriture et la différence* (Paris: Seuil, 1967)

Werner Dettloff, *Die Entwicklung Der Akzeptations- und Verdienstlehre Von Duns Scotus Bis Luther Mit Besonderer Berücksichtigung Der Franziskanertheologen* (Münster: Aschendorff Verlag, 1963)

Marinos Diamantides and Anton Schütz, *Political Theology: Demystifying the Universal* (Edinburgh: Edinburgh University Press, 2017)

François Duchesneau and Justin E.H. Smith (trans.), *The Leibniz-Stahl Controversy* (New Haven: Yale University Press, 2016)

Simon Duffy, *The Logic of Expression* (Aldershot: Ashgate, 2006)

John Duns Scotus, *Opera Omnia* (Vatican City: Typis Polyglottis Vaticanis, 1950–)

John Duns Scotus, *Sur la connaissance de Dieu et l'univocité de l'étant*, in Olivier Boulnois (ed.) (Paris: PUF, 2011)

Umberto Eco, *The Aesthetics of Aquinas* (Cambridge, MA: Harvard University Press, 1988)

Alberto Ferrarin, *Hegel and Aristotle* (Cambridge: Cambridge University Press, 2009)

Michel Fichant 'Les concepts fondamentaux de la mécanique selon Leibniz en 1676' in CNRS (eds), *Leibniz à Paris: 1672–1676: Symposion* (Wiesbaden: Steiner Verlag, 1978) pp.219–32.

John Finnis, *Natural Law and Natural Rights* (Oxford: Oxford University Press, 1980).

John Finnis, *Aquinas* (Oxford: Oxford University Press, 1998)

Juan-Carlos Flores, *Henry of Ghent on Substance and Relation as Modes of Uncreated Being* (Leuven: Thesis, 1999)

Juan Carlos Flores, *Henry of Ghent: Metaphysics of the Trinity* (Leuven: Leuven University Press, 2006)

Henri Focillon, *La Vie des formes* (Paris: PUF, 1964)

Michel Foucault, *The Order of Things* (Bristol: Tavistock Publications, 1970)

Michel Foucault, *The Archaeology of Knowledge* (Bristol: Tavistock Publications, 1972)

Michael Frede, 'Aristotle's Notion of Potentiality in Metaphysics Θ', in T. Scaltsas, D. Charles and M.L. Gill (eds), *Unity, Identity, and Explanation in Aristotle's Metaphysics* (Oxford: Oxford University Press, 1994)

Christiane Frémont, *Singularités – Individus et rélations dans le système de Leibniz* (Paris: Vrin, 2003)

Henricus Gandavus (Henry of Ghent), Raymond Macken (ed.) *Opera omnia* (Leiden: Brill/ Leuven: Leuven University Press, 1991)

Bibliography

Gábor Gángó 'The Formation of Leibniz's Mature Ethics and his *Specimen Polonorum'*, working paper given on 31 October 2018 at Mainz, <https://www.db-thueringen.de/servlets/MCRFileNodeServlet/dbt_derivate_00040557/leibniz_mature_ethics_gango.pdf> (last accessed 2 November 2019)

Daniel Garber, *Descartes' Metaphysical Physics* (Chicago: University of Chicago Press, 1992)

Daniel Garber, *Leibniz: Body, Substance, Monad* (Oxford: Oxford University Press, 2009)

David Gauthier, *The Logic of Leviathan* (Oxford: Clarendon Press, 1969)

Lloyd Gerson, 'On the Greek Origins of the Actus Essendi' (draft paper not embargoed), <https://www.academia.edu/37305791/DRAFT_On_the_Greek_Origins_of_Actus_Essendi> (last accessed 31 December 2019).

Étienne Gilson, *Jean Duns Scot: Introduction à ses Positions Fondamentales* (Paris: Vrin, 1952)

Étienne Gilson, *L'Être et l'essence*, 3rd edn (Paris: Vrin, 2008)

Étienne Gilson, *Le Thomisme – Introduction à la philosophie de saint Thomas d'Aquin* (Paris: Vrin, 1989)

Jorge J.E. Gracia (ed.) *Individuation in Scholasticism* (Albany: SUNY, 2004)

David Graeber, *Debt: The First 5,000 Years* (Brooklyn, NY: Melville House, 2011)

Daniel Graham, 'The Etymology of Entelecheia' (1989) 110 *American Journal of Philology* 73–80

Gaston Grua, *Jurisprudence universelle et théodicée selon Leibniz* (Paris: PUF, 1953)

David Grumett, *Teilhard de Chardin: Theology, Humanity and Cosmos* (Leuven: Peeters, 2006)

Martial Gueroult, *Leibniz: Dynamique et Métaphysique* (Paris: Aubier Montagne, 1967)

Martial Gueroult, Montaigne (ed.) *Spinoza 1: Dieu* (Paris: Aubier, 1968)

Christoph Haar, *Natural and Political Conceptions of Community – The Role of the Household Society in Early Modern Jesuit Thought, c.1590–1650* (Leiden: Brill, 2019)

Jeremiah Hackett, 'Duns Scotus: A Brief Introduction to his Life and Thought' (1991) 26(1) *Studies in Scottish Literature* 438–47

Leibniz: A Contribution to the Archaeology of Power

Ian Hacking, *The Emergence of Probability* (Cambridge: Cambridge University Press, 1975)

Jean Hampton, *Hobbes and the Social Contract Tradition* (Cambridge: Cambridge University Press, 1986)

Hartmut Hecht, *Gottfried Wilhelm Leibniz: Mathemathik und Wissenschaften im Paradigma der Metaphysik* (Stuttgart: B.G. Teubner, 1992)

G.W.F. Hegel, *Wissenschaft der Logik*, Bd.V (Frankfurt am Main: Suhrkamp, 1969)

Mark M. Henninger, *Relations: Medieval Theories 1250–1325* (Oxford: Clarendon Press, 1989)

Gerd van den Heuvel, 'Theorie und Praxis der Politik bei Leibniz im Kontext des Glorious Revolution unter der hannoverchen Sukzession' in Friedrich Beiderbeck et al. (eds), *Umwelt und Weltgestaltung. Leibniz' politisches Denken in seiner Zeit* (Göttingen: Vanderhoek & Ruprecht, 2015) pp.511–26

Jaakko Hintikka, 'Was Leibniz's Deity an *Akrates?*' in S. Knuuttila (ed.) *Modern Modalities* (Dordrecht: Kluwer, 1988) pp.102–3

Thomas Hobbes, C.B. Macpherson (ed.) *Leviathan* (London: Penguin Books, 1968)

Thomas Hobbes, Howard Warrender (ed.) *De Cive* (Oxford: Clarendon Press, 1984)

T.J. Hochstrasser, *Natural Law Theories in the Early Enlightenment* (Cambridge: Cambridge University Press, 2000)

Joseph E. Hofmann, 'Über frühe mathematische Studien von G.W. Leibniz' (1970) 2(2) *Studia Leibnitiana* 81–114

Joseph E. Hofmann, *Leibniz in Paris 1672–1676* (Cambridge: Cambridge University Press, 1974)

George Edward Hughes, 'The Modal Logic of Jean Buridan' in *Atti del Congresso Internazionale di Storia della Logica: La teorie delle modalità* (Bologna: CLUEB, 1989) pp.93–111

Edmund Husserl, 'Philosophy as Rigorous Science' in *Phenomenology and the Crisis of Philosophy* (Quentin Lauer trans.) (New York: Harper Torchbooks, 1965)

Edmund Husserl, *Die Krisis der europäischen Wissenschaften und die transzendentale Phänomenologie* (Hamburg: Meiner, 2012)

Ruedi Imbach (ed.), *Traité du Premier Principe* (Paris: Vrin, 2001)

Bibliography

Terence H. Irwin, 'Obligation, Rightness, and Natural Law: Suárez and Some Critics' in Daniel Schwartz (ed.), *Interpreting Suárez: Critical Essays* (Cambridge: Cambridge University Press, 2012) pp.142–62

Christopher Johns, *The Science of Right in Leibniz's Moral and Political Philosophy* (London: Bloomsbury, 2013)

Nicholas Kahm, 'Aquinas on Quality' (2016) 24(1) *Brit. J. Hist. Phil.* 23–44

Georges Kalinowski, 'La logique juridique de Leibniz' (1977) *Studia Leibnitiana* 166–89

Gregory Kavka, *Hobbesian Moral and Political Theory* (Princeton: Princeton University Press, 1986)

Louis G. Kelley, *The Mirror of Grammar: Theology, Philosophy and the Modistae* (Amsterdam: Benjamins Publ. Co., 2002)

Anthony Kenny, *Aristotle's Theory of Will* (London: Duckworth, 1979)

Peter King 'Duns Scotus on Singular Essences' (2005) 30 *Medioevo* 111–37

Morris Kline, *Mathematical Thought from Ancient to Modern Times*, 3 vols (Oxford: Oxford University Press, 1972)

William and Martha Kneale, *The Development of Logic* (Oxford: Clarendon Press, 1968)

Eberhard Knobloch, 'The Mathematical Studies of G.W. Leibniz on Combinatorics' (1974) 1 *Historia Mathematica* 409–30

Eberhard Knobloch, *Der Beginn der Determinantentheorie* (Hildesheim: Gerstenberg Verlag, 1980)

Eberhard Knobloch, 'Renaissance Combinatorics' in Robin Wilson and John J. Watkins (eds), *Combinatorics: Ancient & Modern* (Oxford: Oxford University Press, 2013)

Eberhard Knobloch, 'Leibniz's Theory of Elimination and Determinants' in E. Knobloch et al. (eds), *Seki, Founder of Modern Mathematics in Japan: A Commemoration on His Tercentenary* (Tokyo: Springer, 2013) pp.229–44

Simo Knuuttila, 'Time and Modality in Scholasticism' in S. Knuuttila (ed.), *Reforming the Great Chain of Being* (Dordrecht: Reidel, 1981) pp.163–259

Simo Knuuttila, *Modalities in Medieval Philosophy* (Abingdon: Routledge, 1995)

Simo Knuuttila, 'Duns Scotus on the Foundations of Logical

Modalities' in L. Honnefelder, R. Wood and M. Dreyer (eds), *John Duns Scotus: Metaphysics and Ethics* (Leiden: E.J. Brill, 1996) pp.127–45

Simo Knuuttila and Lilli Alanen, 'The Foundations of Modality and Conceivability in Descartes and his Predecessors' in S. Knuutila (ed.), *Modern Modalities: Studies in the History of Modal Theories from Medieval Nominalism to Logical Positivism* (Dordrecht: Kluwer, 1988)

Aryeh Kosman, *The Activity of Being* (Cambridge, MA: Harvard University Press, 2013)

M. Kusch and J. Manninen, 'Hegel on Modalities and Monadology' in S. Knuuttila (ed.) *Modern Modalities: Studies in the History of Modal Theories from Medieval Nominalism to Logical Positivism* (Dordrecht: Kluwer, 1988) pp.109–77

Liddell and Scott's *Greek-English Lexicon*, 21st edn (Oxford: Clarendon Press, 1884)

Paul Lodge, 'Force and the Nature of Body in Discourse on Metaphysics §§17–18' (1997) 7 *Leibniz Review* 116–24

A.A. Long and D.N. Sedley, *The Hellenistic Philosophers Vol.1* (Cambridge: Cambridge University Press, 1984)

Brandon Look, 'Leibniz and the *"vinculum substantiale"*' (1991) 30 *Studia Leibnitiana: Sonderheft*

Brandon Look, 'On Monadic Domination in Leibniz's Metaphysics' (2002) 10(3) *British Journal for the History of Philosophy* 379–99

James McEvoy, 'The Sources and the Significance of Henry of Ghent's Disputed Question "Is Friendship a Virtue?"' in W. Vanhammel (ed.) *Proceedings of the International Colloquium on the Occasion of the 700th Anniversary of his Death (1293)* (Leuven: Leuven University Press, 1996)

Dietrich Mahnke, 'Leibniz auf der Suche nach einem allgemeinen Primzahlgesetz' (1912/13) 13(3) *Bibliographica mathematica* 29–61

Benson Mates, *The Philosophy of Language: Metaphysics and Language* (Oxford: Oxford University Press, 1986)

Stephen Menn, 'The Origins of Aristotle's Concept of Ἐνέργεια: Ἐνέργεια and Δύναμις' (1994) 14 *Ancient Philosophy* 73–114.

Stephen Menn, 'The Great Stumbling Block' in Roger Ariew and Marjorie Grene, *Descartes and His Contemporaries* (Chicago: University of Chicago Press, 1995)

Bibliography

Christia Mercer, *Leibniz's Metaphysics* (Cambridge: Cambridge University Press, 2001)

Maurice Merleau-Ponty, *The Visible and the Invisible* (Noyes St Evanston, IL: Northwestern University Press, 1969)

Hannes Möhle, 'Scotus's Theory of Natural Law' in Thomas Williams (ed.), *The Cambridge Companion to Duns Scotus* (Cambridge: Cambridge University Press, 2003) pp.312–31

Thomas Muir, *The Theory of Determinants in its Historical Order of Development* (London: Macmillan, 1906)

Richard A. Muller, 'Review of English Hypothetical Universalism: John Preston and the Softening of Reformed Theology by Jonathan Moore' (2008) 43 *Calvin Theological Journal* 149–50

Robert J. Mulvaney, 'The Early Development of Leibniz's Concept of Justice' (1968) 29 *J. Hist. Ideas* 53–72

Alan Norrie, *Justice and the Slaughter Bench: Essays on Law's Broken Dialectic* (New York: Routledge, 2016)

L. Pena, 'Essence and Existence in Leibniz's Ontology' (1997) 12(2) *Synthesis Philosophica* 415–31

Thomas Pink, 'Action, Will and Law in Late Scholasticism' in J. Kraye and R. Saarinen (eds), *Moral Philosophy on the Threshold of Modernity* (Netherlands: Springer, 2005) pp.31–50

Thomas Pink, 'Reason and Obligation in Suárez' in Benjamin Hill and Henrik Lagerlund (eds), *The Philosophy of Francisco Suárez* (Oxford: Oxford University Press, 2012).

Giorgio Pini, *Categories and Logic in Duns Scotus* (Amsterdam: Brill, 2002)

Proclus, *Elements of Theology* (E.R. Dodds trans.), 2nd edn (Oxford: Clarendon Press, 1963)

Samuel von Pufendorf, *On the Duty of Man and the Citizen* (Cambridge: Cambridge University Press, 1991)

Christof Rapp, 'Tackling Aristotle's Notion of the Will' (2017) 41(2–3) *International Philosofical Inquiry* 67–79

Paul Rateau, *Leibniz and the Problem of Evil* (Oxford: Oxford University Press, 2019)

Stephen Read, 'John Buridan's Theory of Consequence and his Octagons of Opposition' in Jean-Yves Béziau and Dale Jacquette (eds), *Around and beyond the Square of Opposition* (Basel: Springer, 2012) pp.93–110

Nicholas Rescher, *Leibniz: An Introduction to his Philosophy* (Oxford: Blackwell, 1979)

Nicholas Rescher, *GW Leibniz's Monadology: An Edition for Students* (London: Routledge, 1992)

Nicholas Rescher, '*Contingentia Mundi*. Leibniz on the World's Contingency' (2001) 33(2) *Studia Leibnitiana* 145–62

Bernhard Riemann, 'On the Hypotheses which lie at the Bases of Geometry' (William Kingdom Clifford trans.) in Jürgen Jost (ed.) *On the Hypothesis which lie at the Bases of Geometry* (Switzerland: Birkhäuser, 2016)

Patrick Riley, *Leibniz's Universal Jurisprudence* (Cambridge, MA: Harvard University Press, 1972)

Patrick Riley, 'Leibniz and Natural Law in the *Nouveaux Essais*' in Marcelo Dascal (ed.), *Leibniz: What Kind of Rationalist?* (Tel Aviv: Springer, 2008)

Wolfgang Röd, 'Erhard Weigels Metaphysik der Gesellschaft und des Staates' (1971) 3(1) *Studia Leibnitiana* 5–28

Bertrand Russell, *The Philosophy of Leibniz* (Oxford: Routledge, 1997)

Donald Rutherford, *Leibniz and the Rational Order of Nature* (Cambridge: Cambridge University Press, 1995)

Todd Ryan, *Pierre Bayle's Cartesian Metaphysics* (Abingdon: Routledge, 2009)

Herbert John Ryser, *Combinatorial Mathematics* (Rahway, NJ: Mathematical Association of America, 1965)

Max Scheler, *Formalism in Ethics and the Non-Formal Ethics of Values* (Evanston, IL: Northwestern University Press, 1973

Daniel Schwenter, *Deliciae mathematicae* (Nuremberg: GP Harsdörffer, 1636)

Seneca, *Letters to Lucilius* (Cambridge, MA: Harvard University Press, 1932)

Michel Serres, *Le système de Leibniz et ses modèles mathématiques* (Paris: PUF, 2001)

Réné Sève, *Leibniz et l'école moderne du droit naturel* (Paris: PUF, 1989)

Michael Sherwin, *By Knowledge and by Love* (Washington, DC: Catholic University Press of America, 2005)

Christopher Shields, 'Leibniz's Doctrine of the Striving Possibilities' (1986) 24 *Journal of the History of Philosophy* 343–57

Bibliography

Samuel Shirley (trans.), *Spinoza: Complete Works* (Indianapolis, IN: Hackett, 2002)

Jairo da Silva, 'Mathematics and the Crisis of Science' in *The Road Not Taken: On Husserl's Philosophy of Logic and Mathematics* (London: College Publications, 2013)

Barry Smith, 'Common Sense' in Barry Smith and David Woodruff Smith (eds), *The Cambridge Companion to Husserl* (Cambridge: Cambridge University Press, 1995) pp.394–437

Richard Sorabji, *Necessity, Cause, and Blame: Perspectives on Aristotle's Theory* (Chicago: University of Chicago Press, 1980)

Baruch Spinoza, *Complete Works* (Shirley ed. and trans.) (Indianapolis: Hackett, 2002)

Lloyd Strickland, *Leibniz's Monadology: A New Translation and Guide* (Edinburgh: Edinburgh University Press, 2014)

Christoph A. Stumpf, *The Grotian Theology of International Law* (Berlin: De Gruyter, 2006)

Francisco Suárez, *Opera Omnia*, 28 vols (Paris: Vivès, 1856–78)

Paul Thom, *Medieval Modal Systems* (Farnham: Ashgate, 2003)

Brian Tierney, *The Idea of Natural Rights* (Grand Rapids, MI: Emory University, 1997)

Richard Tuck, *Natural Rights Theories and their Development* (Cambridge: Cambridge University Press, 1979)

Johan van Bentham, *Modal Logic for Open Minds* (Stanford: CLSI, 2010)

Sjoerd van Tuinen, 'A Transcendental Philosophy of the Event: Deleuze's Non-Phenomenological Reading of Leibniz' in Sjoerd van Tuinen and Niamh McDonnell (eds), *Deleuze and the Fold: A Critical Reader* (London: Palgrave Macmillan, 2010

Sjoerd van Tuinen and Niamh McDonnell (eds), *Deleuze and the Fold: A Critical Reader* (London: Palgrave Macmillan, 2010)

Pierre Vesperini, *Lucrèce: Archéologie d'un Classique européen* (Paris: Fayard, 2017)

Antonie Vos and Eef Dekker, 'Modalities in Francis Turrettin – an Essay in Reformed Theology' in Maarten Wisse et al. (ed.), *Scholasticism Reformed: Essays in Honour of Willem J. Van Asselt* (Leiden: Brill, 2010) pp.74–91

Howard Warrender, *The Political Philosophy of Hobbes, His Theory of Obligation* (Oxford: Clarendon Press, 1957)

Michael V. Wedin, *Aristotle's Theory of Substance* (Oxford: Oxford University Press, 2000)

Daniel Westberg, *Right Practical Reason* (Oxford: Oxford University Press, 1995)

Thomas Williams, 'How Scotus Separates Morality from Happiness' (1995) 65 *American Catholic Philosophical Quarterly*, 425–45

G.A. Wilson (ed.), *Summa (Quaestiones Ordinariae), arts I–V* (2001), in *Henrici de Gandavo Opera Omnia* (Leuven: Leuven University Press, 1979 et seq.) (initially also Leiden: E.J. Brill)

Robin Wilson and John J. Watkins (eds), *Combinatorics: Ancient & Modern* (Oxford: Oxford University Press, 2013)

Christian Wolff, J. Ecole et al. (eds), *Gesammelte Werken* (Hildersheim and New York: Georg Olms Verlag, 1964–)

R.S. Woolhouse, 'The Nature of Individual Substance' in Micheal Hooker (ed.) *Leibniz: Critical and Interpretative Essays* (Minneapolis, MN: University of Minnesota Press, 1982)

Index

Index

Index